Twentieth Century Conceptions of Language

To my family

Twentieth Century Conceptions of Language

Mastering the Metaphysics Market

Rudolf P. Botha

First published 1992

Blackwell Publishers
108 Cowley Road
Oxford OX4 1JF
UK

238 Main Street, Suite 501
Cambridge, Massachusetts 02142
USA

British Library Cataloguing in Publication Data
A CIP catalogue record for this book is available from the British Library.

Library of Congress Cataloging-in-Publication Data
Botha, Rudolf P.
Twentieth century conceptions of language: mastering the metaphysics market / Rudolf P. Botha.
p. cm.
Includes bibliographical references and index.
ISBN 0–631–18198–9
1. Linguistics—History—20th century. I. Title.
P77.B67 1992
410'. 9'0904—dc20 92–7328
CIP

Typeset in 11/13pt Garamond by Graphicraft Typesetters Ltd., Hong Kong
Printed in Great Britain by T.J. Press Ltd, Padstow, Cornwall

Contents

Acknowledgements ix
Mapping out the Market xi

1 Merchandizing Language as Matter: 1
Bloomfield, Harris

1.0 Hankering after hardware 1
1.1 Mulling over a meta-matter 2
1.2 Selling sounds and scratches 4
1.3 Ripping up the roots 6
1.3.1 Spurning the spirit 6
1.3.2 Making much of matter 9
1.3.3 Ravaging reality 12

1.4 Sterilizing science 13
1.4.1 Mincing metaphysics 14
1.4.2 Knifing knowledge 17
1.4.3 Fixing it with fictions 21
1.4.4 Trampling on truth 23
1.4.5 Insulating it with instrumentalism 26
1.4.6 Spitting on speculation 28

1.5 Getting a fix on physicalism 32

2 Billing Language as Behavioural: 35
Hall, Hockett, Pike; Skinner, Zuriff; Wittgenstein, Quine

2.0 Messing on The Market 35
2.1 Brunching on post-Bloomfieldian burgers 36

2.1.1 Munching the metaphysical meat 36
2.1.2 Rummaging for the recipe 39

2.2 Supping on psychological stuff 43
2.2.1 Stoking up on stimuli and responses 43
2.2.2 Ripping into raw reinforcement and the rest 46
2.2.3 Diversifying the diet 53
2.2.4 Defending the dish 56

2.3 Feeding on philosophical fare 59
2.3.1 Biting into behavioural bangers 59
2.3.2 Weighing the Wittgensteinian wurst 64
2.3.3 Dishing up dispositions 68

2.4 Boiling it down to the basics 70
2.5 Washing it down with a word of warning 75

3 Selling Language as Soul 79
Chomsky, Fodor and Others

3.0 Magnifying mind 79
3.1 Generating the gospel 80
3.1.1 Crusading against commonsensicality 81
3.1.2 Exorcising externality 83
3.1.3 Invoking internality 86
3.1.4 Anointing an abstraction 90
3.1.5 Beatifying the body 94

3.2 Founding the faith 98
3.2.1 Hallowing humanity 98
3.2.2 Sanctifying science 103

3.3 Reforming the religion 107
3.4 Slumbering sectarianism 111
3.5 Waging war over the word 120
3.5.1 Misprising the module 122
3.5.2 Mocking Moses 132

3.6 Getting rid of the ghost 143
3.7 Saying 'selah' 145

4 Pushing Language as Platonic (not to Mention Popperian): 148
Katz, Postal, Langendoen; Popper, Carr

4.0 Levitating language 148
4.1 Performing Platonist passes 149
4.1.1 Concealing conceptual compartments 151
4.1.2 Motivating the magic 159
4.1.3 Siting the show in science 164
4.1.4 Appraising the abstractist act 168

4.2 Practising Popperian prestidigitation 183
4.2.1 Working World 3 wonders 183
4.2.2 Withdrawing into the world of wizardry 189

4.3 Bowing out to bouquets and boos 197

5 Stocking Language as Social Stuff 199
Saussure, Labov, Sapir; Dummett, Pateman, Itkonen

5.0 Offering *objets de couture* 199
5.1 Flocking after a fashion 200
5.2 Styling it à la Saussure 202
5.3 Lining it with Labovian lore 207
5.4 Slipping into something Sapirean 211
5.5 Getting dressed down like Dummett 220
5.6 Poring over Pateman's pattern 227
5.7 Being in with Itkonen 230
5.8 Veiling it verbally 237
5.9 Reviewing the rage 240

6 Balancing the Book(s) 243

6.0 Philosophizing faunally 243
6.1 Muddling through metaphysically 244
6.1.1 Having no need for niceties 244
6.1.2 Doing one's own thing 249
6.1.3 Pursuing a pluralist policy 254

6.2 Exercising eschatologically 258
6.2.1 Focusing on their fertility 259
6.2.2 Probing their 'perfectability' 261

Shutting up Shop 266
Notes 270
Bibliography 313
Index 332

Acknowledgements

I would like to thank various colleagues and friends for invaluable contributions to this study, chapters of which were informally distributed in preliminary versions as Botha 1989b, 1990a,b and 1991a,b.

Walter Winckler read all the versions of the manuscript, suggesting numerous improvements in the content and presentation. Without his detailed suggestions the straight sections would have been much less focused and the playful parts much more pedestrian.

Peter Mühlhäusler, helpfully, drew my attention to various interesting points bearing on limitations of (neo-)Bloomfieldian conceptions of language. And, once again, Riny Huybregts generously gave me access to his vast collection of unpublished papers, throwing in with characteristic perceptiveness, a variety of enlightening comments as well. I am very much indebted to Jerrold Katz and Paul Postal, too, for making available to me copies of two versions of their important paper on conceptualism and realism in linguistics. That the study was completed at all is in no small measure due to the late Dwight Bolinger. At a time when I was thinking seriously of abandoning it, his comments encouraged me to carry on with the project.

Hildegard van Zweel, Sonje Ottermann and Gerhard van Wyk rendered valuable editorial assistance. So did Sue Ashton on the publishing side. I am most grateful to them for the hours they spent on eliminating technical flaws in the manuscript. And also to Mrs L. Gildenhuys for doing another splendid typing job.

As always, Hanna, Elizabeth and Philip were a supportive and forgiving family. It is to them that I, gratefully, dedicate this book.

R.P.B.

Mapping out the Market

Suffering, Dear Reader, from a bad case of Ontological Angst? For this malady, the Metaphysics Market has just the medicine. No mistake – it's where you may yet find the right stuff against the distress brought on by agonizing over that classic question 'What is language in essence?'

Forming the heart of a town in which the trade in ideas is a time-honoured tradition, The Market knows no match when it comes to Merchandise of Mind. And, in a special section, in this cavern on a corner of Carfax, there is on sale a singular selection of a conceptual commodity called 'conceptions of language'. This is what one can buy as a cure for the condition caused by wearisome worrying about the nature and essence of language. Exploring The Market, I can assure you, will anyway be much more fun than getting into Thing Therapy for your Angst.

On The Market, you will find language on sale as something material, something behavioural, something mental, something biological, something abstract, something social or something cultural – to mention some of the stuffs language has been supposed to consist of. As for shapes, language is thrust down one's throat as a thing, pushed as a process, promoted as a procedure, auctioned as action, flogged as form, sold as system and marketed as means. Which brings us to diversity in design, conceptions of language being available in many a mode: nominalist, conceptualist, realist, obscurantist, eclecticist and so on. And each conception of language has its own finish. So you can purchase the Product with a folksy flavour, an ordinary (language) odour, a terminological tang, an a-theoretical aroma and a theoretical ring. As for origin:

conceptions of language come with all kinds of credentials, tagged as Aristotelian, Platonic, Cartesian, Humboldtian, Saussurian, Bloomfieldian, Sapirean, Wittgensteinian. Chomskyan, and so on and so forth.

Those I have mentioned represent but a small sample of the conceptions of language offered for sale on The Market. Some dimensions of diversity – ontogeny, function and so on – I have not even mentioned. And about the quaintest conceptions of all – the collector's items in the Curio Corner – I have told you nothing yet at all. Which is also true of the Delicatessen Department, where customers can consume conserved conceptions of language, including Processed Plato, Dehydrated Descartes, Marinated Malinowski and, a recent addition, Pickled Pike. Buyers who cannot bear being dry are looked after too. There is a Portly Publican who will pour them for a pound or two Vintage Wundt, V. O. Vossler and Fortified Firth in flasks functionally formed for a Hallidayan Hip.

The Market, however, derives its mercantile magnificence only in part from the Products it has on offer. It is the Manufacturing Masters, the Designing Deans, the Producing Professors, the Retailing Readers, the Leasing Lecturers and the Trading Tutors that form the pulse proper of this humming hive of scholarly enterprise. Here you will find Cambridge Captains of Conceptions Industry, Mercantile Metaphysicists from Manhattan, and Cool Customers from California, not to mention Chancers from Chicago, trading shoulder to shoulders with Boston Bears, Brooklyn Bulls and Berkeley Brokers who rate boldness and bellicosity as the best means of making it on The Market. A sentiment shared by the Yale Yuppies, Harvard Hustlers, Penn Pushers and assorted other Producers of the Product, including Continental Conceptioneers and Old World Ontologists. And how could one forget to mention the Meta-managers of The Market? Hailing from the Fords and the Fields, the Bridges and Burghs, this Blazered Breed has, through epistemic engineering, created a quaint kind of college kid: a Buying Blue (whom you will soon come to know better).

The paramount question, of course, is 'What to buy, and from whom?' The answer, Dear Reader, is anything but simple. But let me try. If you need a conception of language for no purpose other than to provoke people in the pub, to sound profound at a party, to discourse donnishly on and on at dinner or to name 'knowledgeably' in a note, there are dozens that will do. But if, driven by deep distress, you have to get to the bottom of the question 'What is language in essence?', not just any old (or new) conception will do.

And this is where I enter. For what you clearly will need is Conceptual Counselling: on the range of Products, their qualities and malformities; on the strategies for selecting something superior from the shelf and the recipes for recognizing rubbish on the rack; on the merchants and their multifarious modes of making money; on tricks and traps, snags and snares for buyers who fail to beware. In a nutshell: on how to buy and behave so as to stay solvent and sane in The Metaphysics Market. This is exactly the kind of advice that I will administer. As for Products, I will suggest what to inspect, and why to reject. As for Producers and Promoters, I will indicate how to debate, who to deflate and who not to underrate.

There is one thing, however, Dear Reader, which quite expressly I will not *deliver: complete coverage of the countless conceptions of language offered on The Market. Recycling being as rampant as it is on the Faculty Floor, you will come across many a reconditioned conception of language which is not worth a second look. So, we will have to be selective, focusing on leading twentieth-century conceptions that portray language(s) as essentially material (chapter 1), behavioural (chapter 2), mental/biological (chapter 3), abstract (chapter 4) or social (chapter 5). And, since we will be concerned with matters of a conceptual kind, I will not delve too deeply into the past of these conceptions either.*

Which brings me to a little extra that I do have to offer: e-mail access to the acuity and acumen of an assortment of outspoken Ontological Oracles. When puzzled or perturbed by peculiarities of a conception of language, we can call on them to act as outside advisers. Just listen to what one or two of these Metaphysical Magi have had to say on the intellectual enterprise called 'ontology': 'Ontology is alive and kicking. Its business is to stake out the main traits of the real world as known through science. Only bigots still believe this business to be balderdash' (cf. Bunge 1977: 5ff.; Bhaskar 1978: 36).

You appear ready, Dear Reader, to venture into the Hub of the

Humanities, also known as The Market. But could you control your Angst for just one moment more? There is still a matter of money to be mentioned. Strange as it may sound, the long history of The Market has always produced the odd trader who would not accept cash in any currency for his conception of language. Rather, they would insist on the buyer's surrender of his Scholarly Soul in payment for their Products. Trading in the tradition of the Terrible Tempter, these dealers have devilishly tried to possess purchasers by means of their Products – extracting, on oath, the buyers' linguistics loyalty for life (and thereafter). I urge you, Dear Reader, always to remember that by mortgaging your mind to a Merchant in the Mephistophelean Mould, you become conception-blind, unable to tell the good from the bad. This is a debilitating disease. Indeed, in the long run it is far more distressing than Ontological Angst.

For discussing the Products on the Market, we will adopt a type of Two-track Talk. I will outline core aspects of conceptions in the familiar, formal fashion, using a suitably straight – some would say 'stifled' – style. The warts and wrinkles of conceptions and the wondrous ways The Market works, by contrast, we will reflect on in the more relaxed but robust register that I have been using so far. Incidentally, straight sections will be printed in reassuring roman. Stretches containing stronger stuff will be in inciting italics and, accordingly, carry a health warning: they are bound to bring on a foaming at the mouth in the case of Serious Scholars who cannot take their metaphysics laced with a modicum of mirth.

1

Merchandizing Language as Matter

1.0 Hankering after hardware

Let me guess what is on your mind as we get ready to enter The Market. You are hoping that language will turn out to be something reassuringly real, something soothingly solid. Or, at least, something of a stuff that can be sensed: touched, seen or heard. No, Bewildered Buyer, I cannot really read your mind. It is simply that a craving for the concrete forms a predictable part of the metaphysical malady known as Ontological Angst. And it is only to be expected that you will be anxious to look first for a conception that pictures language as an essentially physical phenomenon.

Let us head, then, for the Ontological Outlet of the Empiricist Emporium – located on Leonard's Lane, opposite a pub, the Pighead and the Positivist – where the most classic conception portraying language as matter is on offer. But beware, Dear Buyer, this is a dangerous area of The Market, run, if not roamed, by the most Physical(ist) of Fellows. Set on stamping out everything they cannot sense, these Marauding Materialists have wielded, as you will shortly see, such vicious-looking weapons as Carnap's Cutlass, a Wiener Kris, Bloomfield's Blade and even a Positivist Pole-axe. For these Conceptual Cut-throats – as they have been called by some – language has to be part of what can survive their murderous onslaught on the nonmaterial.

All of this sounds pretty grim, I immediately agree. But cheer up, Beginner Buyer, there will be moments of light relief as well. Such as meeting, for example, a Gang of Engaging Gauls. Though fiercely physical too, they have shown themselves experts at putting some fun into philosophy. But inspecting the Bloomfieldian materialist conception of language – its fibres, roots, fruits and flaws – will remain our prime pursuit. As a run-up, however, we first have to consider a rather pressing meta-matter: What would count as a conception of language in the milieu of The Metaphysics Market?

1.1 Mulling over a meta-matter

To get a better idea of what a conception of language is, let us consider it from the points of view of function, content, genesis and epistemological status.

As for function, a conception of language has to answer the question: 'What is language in essence?' This question has been alternatively phrased as 'What are the essential properties of language?' and 'What is the general nature of language?' In this context, the expression 'language' has conventionally been used to mean 'language in general and individual languages'. A conventional conception of language, thus, has to answer the above-mentioned questions with respect to both language in general and individual languages. This study will keep to the conventional use of the expression 'conception of language', unless explicitly indicated otherwise. Concretely, the expression 'the Bloomfieldian conception of language', for example, will be used to mean 'the Bloomfieldian conception of language in general and individual languages'.

Which brings us to the meaning of 'in essence'. It may be clarified with reference to a distinction drawn by Jerrold Katz (1981: 224) between the essential and the accidental properties of something. In terms of this distinction, essential properties are such that 'their bearers would not be what they are without them'. Accidental properties, by contrast, 'reflect nothing of the nature of their bearers'. Katz (1981: 224) illustrates this distinction with reference to living hearts: 'it is a true regularity that living hearts make beat sounds but the property of making beat sounds is not an essential property of the heart: a heart would not be a heart if it weren't a pump, but it might be a silent pump.' This is to say: whereas being a pump is an essential property of living hearts, making beat sounds is an accidental property of such hearts.

In these terms, then, an essential property of language is a property without which language would not be what it is. Or, equivalently, such a property will reflect the nature of language. We will be primarily concerned with conceptions of language to the extent that they attempt to capture the essence, essential properties or general nature of language in terms of such ontological categories as 'material', 'behavioural', 'mental', 'biological', 'social', 'cultural', 'abstract' or 'autonomous'. (In this context, too, 'language' means both 'language in general' and 'individual languages'.) It has been contended that pursuing questions about the essence of language(s) and other entities is a 'misguided', 'senseless' etc. thing to do. To this contention we will return in chapter 2.

As for content, a conception of language is made up of basic beliefs about the essence of language: beliefs about what makes language what it is. Unlike, for example, theories of GB-syntax, lexicalist morphology, metrical phonology, cognitive semantics etc., a conception of language is not a theory of linguistic structure expressing technical claims about structural principles, parameters, levels, tiers, systems, properties, categories, units etc. of language(s). As we proceed, it will become clear how conceptions of language are interlinked with theories of linguistic structure.

A conception of language, moreover, is not a methodology or epistemology for linguistic inquiry. It is not its function to give an answer to the question: How may linguistic reality be known? A conception of language, accordingly, does not include epistemological principles, for example, inductivist, falsificationist, empiricist, intuitionist or scepticist principles, to be followed in investigating linguistic reality. As part of a linguistic ontology, a conception of language is a set of claims about this reality itself. Conceptions of language or linguistic ontologies, do, however, have close links with epistemologies. Again, as we proceed, the nature of these links will be made clear in a concrete way.

As for genesis, a conception of language is the product of systematic thinking about language(s), thinking informed by reliable observations, facts and insights established by the relevant sciences. This position is compatible with Bunge's (1977: 5) characterization of the 'business' of ontology: to stake out the main traits of the real world *as known through science*. A conception of language, however, is not the product of lexicographical investigation. Specifically, it is not a dictionary definition that defines – or stipulates – the meaning of the words *language* and *languages.*[1] To see this, consider the following dictionary definition of the word *language*: 'the system of human expression by means of words'.[2] If accurate, this definition captures (part of) the meaning of the word *language.* The definition is an outcome of lexicographical investigation of a word; it is not a product of systematic thinking about the thing(s) denoted by the word. Consequently, this definition does not directly incorporate any basic beliefs about the nature of the thing called 'language'. Hence it does not count as a conception of language.

As for epistemological status, the beliefs incorporated in a conception of language have to be justified. A conception of language is not capsulated dogma. The beliefs making up a conception of language have to be subjected to close critical appraisal, carried out systematically on the basis of appropriate standards. As we proceed, a variety of these standards will be identified and illustrated. In order to be amenable to critical appraisal, the beliefs included in a conception of language have to be formulated explicitly and precisely. Vague and woolly assumptions about language(s) cannot form part of a conception of language.

1.2 Selling sounds and scratches

Language is something material that can be observed. This is the core of the classic materialist conception of language. On this conception, language is primarily something audible and secondarily something visible. Spoken language, also called speech, exists as sound waves in the air. And written language, a secondary manifestation of language, exists as marks on solid surfaces.

This conception of language is often called 'Bloomfieldian' after the American linguist, Leonard Bloomfield, who is credited with assembling its core components in the late twenties and early thirties. Since followers of Bloomfield's, notably Zellig Harris, have contributed to the fleshing out of this conception, it is more accurate to consider it a 'Bloomfieldian conception' rather than 'Bloomfield's conception'.

An individual language, on this Bloomfieldian conception, is a collection or corpus of utterances. On this conception, 'utterances are the reality of a language', as Jerrold Katz (1981: 25) has aptly put it.[3] Spoken utterances are considered to be stretches of sound, sound waves or disturbances in the air. Sound waves were characterized by Bloomfield (1931: 219–21) as 'slight displacements of matter'. This makes spoken utterances physical events. Written utterances, by contrast, are inscriptions, scratches or ink marks on surfaces. This makes written utterances products of (writing) events.

On this materialist conception of language, then, language and languages have no aspect that is not ultimately physical. Every aspect of language(s) either is evidently physical or can be reduced to something that is physical. Specifically, this conception deliberately refrains from attributing to language(s) any property that is mental, as is clear from the following remarks by Bloomfield (1936: 93):

> Non-linguists (unless they happen to be physicalists) constantly forget that a speaker is making noise, and credit him, instead, with the possession of impalpable 'ideas'. It remains for linguists to show, in detail, that the speaker has no 'ideas' and that the noise is sufficient – for the speaker's words act with a trigger-effect upon the nervous system of his speech-fellows.

This quotation also indicates what, on the Bloomfieldian conception, language is *not*. It is not part of a speakers' nervous system. Viewed from a 'biosocial' point of view, language merely triggers nervous systems. Viewed from a 'biophysical' point of view, language merely forms a 'bridge' between nervous systems. Thus, Bloomfield (1931: 219–21) remarked: 'By virtue of this common attunement the members of a speech-community cooperate; the space between their nervous systems is bridged, from moment to moment, by the sound-waves which they utter and hear.' And the 'bridge' is a physical one. This follows from Bloomfield's (1931: 219–21) view that speech sounds are nothing but 'slight displacements of matter'.

In sum: on the Bloomfieldian conception, language is noise. And the 'objective' study of languages is the study of 'a set of events – sound waves or ink marks' in the words of Harris (1970: 438). The grammars written in terms of the Bloomfieldian conception of language are, as Katz (1981: 25) puts it, 'theories of disturbances in the air or deposits of substances on surfaces'.

You are more than moderately impressed with the 'sensible solidity' of this No-Nonsense-Nothing-but-Noise Notion of language? You even hope, Brightened-up Buyer, that it could be the cure for your worries about what language is?

But, hang on, we have barely scratched the surface of the materialist conception of language. We still have to inspect it and reflect on it before we can decide whether to accept or reject it. For there is a Market Maxim that matter-of-factly says:

> *Blind buying brings bankruptcy.*

So we will have to dig deeper, as we are joined by our Buying Blue, a Wordly-wise Window-shopper. Not yet fully weaned of Wittgenstein College, he, curiously, combines a kind of Cultivated Commonsensicality with pronouncedly Positivist Passions in what strikes me as a somewhat prickly personality.

1.3 Ripping up the roots

Let us proceed by considering the matter of motive: Why would a scholar such as Bloomfield wish to think of language as something material? What drove him to conceive of language as an essentially physical phenomenon? What are the roots of the sounds-and-scratches conception of language?

Two things lie at the basis of the Bloomfieldian conception of language as something material: a rejection of animistic mentalism and an adoption of an empiricist view of science. The first will be considered in this section (1.3); the second in section 1.4 below.

1.3.1 Spurning the spirit

Bloomfield rejected nineteenth-century mentalism because it appealed to mentalistic entities – for example, mind, spirit, soul and will – of a specific sort. These are mentalistic entities that were taken to lack a material basis. Moreover, these immaterial mentalistic entities were of an animistic kind in that they were held to 'animate' the body.[4] Bloomfield believed that to appeal to such 'pre-scientific' entities – entities described by Katz (1964) as 'occult' or 'theologized' – makes it impossible to explain or predict linguistic behaviour with reference to causal laws. On Bloomfield's view, such mentalistic entities, because they are nonmaterial, simply do not exist. And entities that do not exist cannot cause anything that does (materially) exist. Thus, Bloomfield (1933: 32) contended that:

> The *mentalistic* theory . . . supposes that the variability of human conduct is due to the interference of some nonphysical fact, a *spirit* or *will* or *mind* . . . that is present in every human being. This spirit, according to the mentalistic view, is entirely different from material things and accordingly follows some other kind of causation or perhaps none at all.

So Bloomfield (1931: 172–3) rejected terms such as 'mind', 'consciousness', 'will', 'perception', 'emotion' and so on as 'spectres of our tribal animism'. On his view, these animistic terms originated in 'pre-scientific times' and could at best form the basis for 'popular animistic pseudo-explanations' only. Along with such animistic terms, Bloomfield rejected nineteenth-century mentalism as a basis for a 'scientific' conception of language.

The first root of the Bloomfieldian materialistic conception of language, thus, is of a reactionary sort: Bloomfield's rejection of an animistic form of mentalism, a rejection whose reverse side is his acceptance of a particular form of materialism. A mentalistic conception of language could not be the basis for a causal explanation of linguistic conduct. Only a conception in which language is something material – such as sounds and scratches – could. This root of Bloomfield's conception of language, then, can be reduced ultimately to his view of what a 'scientific' explanation should be.

Bloomfield was not always an anti-mentalist. In an early phase of his development, he believed in the mentalistic psychology of Wilhelm Wundt.[5] Thus, Bloomfield (1914: vi) once declared that 'I depend for my psychology, general and linguistic, entirely on Wundt.' And, in the Wundtian mentalistic idiom, Bloomfield (1914) said such things as the following about language:

> Language is the form of expressive movement adequate to the mentality of man. (1914: 15)

> The word is . . . psychologically a complicative association of those perceptual and emotional elements which we call its meaning or experience content with the auditory and motor elements which constitute the linguistic symbol. . . . (1914: 66)

> [Linguistic phenomena] without consideration of their mental significance are unintelligible. . . . (1914: 71)

It was under the influence of his psychologist friend Albert Paul Weiss – and indirectly that of Weiss's teacher, Max Meyer – that Bloomfield resolved to cut out the Wundtian doctrine of ideas from his thinking; that he came to reject nineteenth-century mentalism as 'pre-scientific'; and that he came to accept materialism (or mechanism) as a basis for his conception of language.[6]

As noted by Erwin Esper (1968: 179), Meyer and Weiss opposed the sort of introspection and mentalism 'found in the pages of Wundt's *Psychologische Studien*'. And it was Weiss who, in Esper's (1968: 174) words, transmitted the objectivistic naturalism which had been developing, from the mid-nineteenth century, among biologically orientated psychologists in Germany. The postulates of this 'objectivist naturalism', as formulated by Weiss on the basis of the writings of Meyer and his teachers, stated that:

> the phenomena studied by psychology are complications of those studied by physics, chemistry, and biology; the principle of determinism applies in psychology as in the other natural sciences; the phenomena studied by psychology depend upon the properties of the human nervous system in its interactions with the environment; the principle of evolutionary development applies not only to biological phylogenesis but to the history of individuals and of social institutions; the data of psychological research are responses to sense-organ stimulation, or to the after-effects of such stimulation – responses which are observable, recordable, and – ideally – quantifiable. (Esper 1968: 176)

Against this background, Weiss characterized behaviourist psychology as that type of investigation and theory which assumes that human activities – educational, vocational and social – can be fully described or explained as the result of forces found in the natural sciences. No other forces entered into such descriptions and explanations. The central problem of psychology did not concern the nature of mental faculties. Rather, it concerned habit-formation or learning on a stimulus-and-response basis.[7]

Bloomfield took over this view of psychology, replacing the Wundtian doctrine of ideas by the Weissian stimulus-response doctrine. As noted by Esper (1968: 187), this 'obviated the obligation and temptation to interpret linguistic observations in terms of the introspections (or mentalistic speculations) of individual linguists'. Moreover, Bloomfield's adoption of Weissian naturalistic psychology 'facilitated the linking of a purely linguistic set of postulates with the postulates and definitions of psychology and other sciences. . . '.

In sum: Bloomfield's anti-mentalism (and materialism or mechanism) came from an old naturalistic intellectual doctrine. This doctrine was transmitted to him by Weiss and, indirectly, Meyer, scholars whom Bloomfield (1931) considered to be 'perhaps two of the greatest men of [his] time'. Weiss, in fact, was further elevated by Bloomfield; he saw in Weiss someone who 'will [probably] be counted as a heroic figure in the progress of science'.

I do tend to agree, Dear Buyer, that Bloomfieldian anti-mentalism may be regarded as more than a mere root of the materialist conception of language. It could, indeed, be thought of as a Conceptual Carrot for Pagan Patrons of The Market. Surely, Bloomfield's spurning of the spirit, his thumping of the theologized, his trouncing of the tribe may seduce Secular Shoppers who are revolted by anything that 'reeks of religion'. But on a Mobile Market, where metaphysicists are constantly on the move, one cannot afford to cling to outworn sentiments, surviving as Slick Slogans and nothing more. And, Dear Buyer, not everything that reeks is a relict of religion. Anti-mentalism grown musty, and materialism gone mouldy, are themselves not sweetly scented either.[8]

1.3.2 Making much of matter

This brings us to the reverse side of Bloomfield's rejection of mentalism: his acceptance of materialism (or mechanism) as a properly scientific basis for causal explanations of human conduct. Thus Bloomfield (1933: 33) stated that:

> The *materialistic* (or, better, *mechanistic*) theory supposes that the variability of human conduct, including speech, is due only to the fact that the human body is a very complex system. Human actions, according to the materialistic view, are part of cause-and-effect sequences exactly like those which we observe, say in the study of physics and chemistry.

Bloomfield (1933: 38) considered materialism to be less dangerous than mentalism. He judged mentalistic views dangerous because of their ability 'to tempt the observer to appeal to purely spiritual standards instead of reporting the facts'. But a scientist who accepted the materialistic theory 'is under no such temptation'. And this brought Bloomfield (1933: 38) to state 'that in all sciences like linguistics, which observe some specific type of human activity, the worker must proceed exactly as if he held the materialistic view. This practical effectiveness is one of the strongest considerations in favor of scientific materialism.'

Not all the doctrines that jointly make up materialism express exactly the same view on what the real world consists of. On the more extreme views, the real world consists of material things and nothing else. 'Extreme' materialism is conventionally taken to incorporate two fundamental theses. These Campbell (1967: 179) formulates as follows:

1 'Everything that is, is material.'
2 'Everything that can be explained can be explained on the basis of laws involving only the antecedent physical conditions.'[9]

The first tenet says, in effect, that there are no incorporeal souls or spirits, no spiritual principalities or powers, no angels or devils – no immaterial entities (Campbell 1967: 179). Nothing, therefore, can be explained by invoking such entities, a point captured in the second tenet of 'extreme' materialism. It is the two tenets quoted above that jointly form the backbone of Bloomfieldian materialism. The materialistic root of Bloomfield's conception of language, clearly, also lacks ontological originality.

But what does 'material' mean in this context? What is a material thing? How does one draw the line between what is material and what is not? As noted by Campbell (1967: 179), one can list properties of material things; for example, properties such as position in space and time, size, shape, duration, mass, velocity, solidity, inertia, electric charge, spin, rigidity, temperature, hardness, and the like. But, he adds, 'the list is open-ended.' From this follows that the questions formulated above 'have no determinate answers'. The distinction 'material *v.* nonmaterial' is in fact badly blurred. A similar point has recently been argued by Chomsky (1987a: 3–5) too; the argument will be considered in section 3.1.5 below.

Materialism has many maladies, of which Campbell surveys a variety. One of these is of particular relevance in the context of the present discussion: 'The most critical problem facing contemporary materialism is to provide an account of the mind which has some prospect of being at once adequate and compatible with materialism' (Campbell 1967: 187). The 'extreme' form of materialism adopted by Bloomfield, of course, could not address this problem in a satisfactory manner. There are forms of materialism, however, that do not construe this problem as a question of choosing between the mental and the material. Thus, Mario Bunge (1980: 21) contends that: 'one can talk about *mental phenomena* without leaving the biological ground: the mentalist vocabulary originally coined by religion and dualist philosophy begins to make, or is hoped to make, neurophysiological sense.'[10] And to make things even more interesting, there are not only forms of materialism that talk about the mental. There are also forms of mentalism – for example, those propounded by Chomsky and Fodor – that allow the mental to have a material basis, as we will see in chapter 3 below. Given these complexities, it may be useful to note that in the present discussion we are concerned with *Bloomfieldian* materialism and the *Bloomfieldian* materialist conception of language, not with materialism in one of its more sophisticated forms.

You have a nagging question, Dear Buyer? How all of this is going to help you master The Market? The point, really, is plain: though seemingly sane and seductively solid-looking, the form of materialism embraced by Bloomfield is much too crude a creed to be the basis of a sound conception of language. In fact, to base a notion of language on this form of materialism is to infect it at its very inception with a Degenerative Disease, known as Root Rot.

In the form of a caveat, Beguiled Buyer and Befuddled Blue, the message therefore is: Buyer, beware of rotten roots.

1.3.3 Ravaging reality

Bloomfield's materialist conception of language has been considered an instance of a more general philosophical view of what the world is composed of. This philosophical view or ontological theory has been characterized as 'nominalism' by Katz (1981). Stronger versions of nominalism hold that there are no abstract objects, no objects of thought, no objects other than those of sense perception (Woozeley 1967: 194). The world, on this view, is composed of physical objects and events, or units of sense experience.[11] Stronger versions of nominalism, moreover, hold that there are no universals in the form of categories or kinds of objects. The world, on this view, is composed solely of particulars: individual, unique objects.

In its extreme form, nominalism claims that 'there is nothing common to a class of particulars called by the same name other than that they are called by the same name' (Woozeley 1967: 203). On this extreme view, then, only names or words are universal. To avoid complete subjectivity, more moderate forms of nominalism, however, concede that the universality of words depends on the resemblance between things. Thus *table* is a universal (word) that can be applied to all individual objects that resemble each other in certain respects. But, there is no abstract universal category or kind 'table' that exists in itself independent of the word *table*. The core assumptions of more moderate versions of nominalism, in sum, are formulated as follows by Katz (1981: 22): 'Nominalism holds that only the sensible signs of language are real: the alleged use of them to name universals is nothing more than reference to space-time particulars with signs that apply generally on the basis of resemblance.' The view that there is nothing real beyond the observable – for example, disturbances in the air and scratches on solid surfaces – forms the basis for Katz (1981: 12, 23) calling the Bloomfieldian conception of language 'nominalist'. The nominalist nature of the Bloomfieldian conception of language will become clearer in the later chapters where we will consider non-nominalist conceptions of language.[12]

In its extreme form nominalism 'is so clearly untenable that it may be doubted whether anybody has actually tried to hold it'.[13] And in more moderate forms – those resting on the idea of resemblance – nominalism becomes difficult to distinguish from other ontological views of the world, views from which it is supposed to be distinct.[14]

What to think of nominalism? Well, Dear Buyer, there is a diagnostic device developed by the Order of Ordinary Ontologists. Who these would be? Labouring in labs and libraries, they are the lesser lights – practising scientists who see themselves as worrying about the wheelwork of the world, researching the recesses of reality, nosing around in the nebulous nooks of nature. But let us consider their list of 'Could-you-live-with' questions:

The Lesser Lights' Co(s)mic Check List

Could you live with:

1. *a universe uniformly inhabited by independent individuals?*
2. *planets patternlessly populated by particulars?*
3. *a world whirling around a non-existent nub?*
4. *sensibilia strangely stripped of structure?*
5. *a reality ravaged of all but its appearance?*

If you have answered 'No' to one or more of these loaded questions, then it is incumbent upon the Officers of the Order to communicate to you this weighty warning:

> *Buyer, beware of the nothingness behind the names of nominalism.*

Nominalism, indeed, they deem a decimating dogma – a dogma that wastes the world by denying reality all dimensions of depth and delicacy.

1.4 Sterilizing science

So what, then, is the second root of the Bloomfieldian conception of language? It takes on the form of a particular view of science and the methods of science, a view that has been labelled '(logical or neo-)positivist' and '(logical) empiricist'.[15] Of the various beliefs making up the Bloomfieldian view of science its aims and methods, three are of special interest to us:

1. To be meaningful, a scientific statement must report a movement in space and time (Bloomfield 1936: 90; Esper 1968: 187).
2. Abstract terms or concepts of scientific descriptions are no more than convenient fictions (Bloomfield 1933: 213; Katz 1981: 31, 38).
3. Science does not aim at giving a true representation of reality (Harris 1951: 72; Katz 1981: 26–7).

These three beliefs had an important part in the thinking of Bloomfield and Harris as they lay the foundations of a materialist conception of language. What we have to do, then, is to explore the ways in which these beliefs are linked to the materialism espoused by Bloomfield and Harris.

1.4.1 Mincing metaphysics

Bloomfield strongly believed in the idea that, to be scientifically meaningful, a statement has to report a movement in space and time. Thus, he (1936: 90) remarked: 'Statements that are not made in these terms are either scientifically meaningless or else make sense only if they are translated into statements about language.' He used *The world is known to me only through my perceptions* as an example of a scientifically meaningless statement, contending that: 'This statement is scientifically meaningless, for it directs us to no observation at any place or time; it predicts nothing.' On Bloomfield's view, however, such meaningless statements could be made meaningful. This could be done by translating them in a specific way into statements about language. Bloomfield (1936: 90) illustrated this point with reference to the sentence *Redness is a concept*: 'This makes sense only if it is translated into a statement about language, namely: *In the English language the word redness is a noun.*' But something more had to be done, as Bloomfield (1936: 90) added in a footnote:

> The term *noun* . . . must then be defined, for English grammar, and the term *word* for language in general, as technical terms of linguistics; this definition, moreover, must be made in terms of the postulates, undefined basic terms, and earlier definitions of linguistics – not by definitions of meaning and not in metaphysical terms.

The negative note on which these remarks end is particularly significant. It reflects a central concern of Bloomfield's: finding a means of ridding linguistics of metaphysical claims.

To Bloomfield, (animistic) mentalism could not form the basis of a 'scientific' conception of language. In his thinking, statements made in terms of such mentalistic expressions as 'meaning', 'ideas' etc. could not direct linguists to observations at any place or time. Such statements predicted nothing and had to be rejected as meaningless metaphysics. Only statements made in materialist or physicalist terms – referring to movements in space and time – could be considered scientifically meaningful from this perspective. So Bloomfield's view of what was scientifically meaningful and what was not was a powerful force that drove him and his followers to the conception of language as something material.

Bloomfield was not original in either his abhorrence of metaphysics or his adoption of a particular criterion for scientific meaningfulness. As he pointed out himself (1936: 90), these philosophical concerns represented a doctrine at which other scholars had earlier arrived: his friend Weiss and, in the 1920s, the logical positivists of the Vienna Circle. The latter included Schlick, Waissmann, Neurath and Carnap among others. Following Mach, these scholars viewed science as fundamentally the description of experience. Metaphysics, on their view, was a 'mess of verbiage' choking both science and philosophy to death. And so metaphysics had to be eradicated.[16]

Michael Scriven (1969: 195) gives a graphic account of what the logical positivists were after:

> The Vienna Circle or *Wiener Kreis* was a band of cutthroats that went after the fat burghers of Continental metaphysics who had become intolerably inbred and pompously verbose. The *kris* is a Malaysian knife, and the *Wiener Kreis* employed a kind of Occam's Razor called the Verifiability Principle. It performed a tracheotomy that made it possible for philosophy to breathe again. . . .

With the aid of the Verifiability Principle of Meaning, metaphysics was reduced to 'meaningless nonsense' or 'sheer gibberish', in the words of Karl Popper (1976: 80). In essence, this principle was an attempt at answering the question 'Under what conditions is a sentence cognitively or factually meaningful?' (cf. Ashby 1967: 245). And the principle stated that a statement must either be analytic or empirically verifiable in order to be meaningful (Ashby 1967: 240). This means that to be meaningful, a (non-analytic) statement must express a proposition that can, at least in principle, be shown to be true, false or to some degree probable by reference to empirical observations. In a parodied form the Verifiability Principle boiled down to the following: 'If [something] can't be seen or measured, it is not meaningful to talk about'.[17]

In terms of the Verifiability Principle, such statements of traditional philosophy as 'Reality is spiritual', 'The Absolute is beyond time', 'Beauty is significant form' are cognitively meaningless. Such sentences, it was contended, could not be verified on the basis of experience. Hence they represented 'metaphysical gibberish'. In assigning a central role to experience, the Verifiability Principle is obviously empiricist. It reflects the general epistemological position that, ultimately, our knowledge is based on experience that we get through our senses.[18]

We cannot consider here the intricacies and technicalities of the Verifiability Principle of Meaning.[19] It should be clear, however, that Bloomfield's idea of what is scientifically meaningful and what is not echoes the essence of this principle. And it may be expected that the former idea will also reflect the flaws of the latter principle, a point we will explore below.

You're turned on, as a duo, Buyer and Blue, by the ideal of a Sanitized Science stripped of all statements of a pseudoscientific sort? And you rather like Bloomfield's idea of using a variant of Verifiability as a Conceptual Cutter for carving away sediments of a supra-sensory sort? A clinically cleared-up conception of language is just what you're after too? I hate to douse your delight, but verifiability turned out, in the course of time, to be little better than a vice. It proved to be without real virtue both in more refined forms such as Carnap's Cutlass and in less expert editions such as Bloomfield's Blade.[20] *What's that? Would I care to elaborate? But of course.*

1.4.2 Knifing knowledge

The Verifiability Principle gave rise to a range of controversial philosophical questions: about its function, its status, its content, its application, and so on.[21] And it has been argued – by Hempel (1965b: 117), for example – that this principle is based on an untenable view of what the appraisal of scientific statements is about. What is at stake in such appraisal is not whether any individual statement considered in isolation is meaningful, verifiable, falsifiable or some such. What is at stake, rather, is whether a system or network of statements, called a 'theory' for short, can be given an empirical interpretation when considered as a whole. For deciding the latter question, there is no single, simple acid test. On the contrary, to arrive at a nonsimplistic answer to it in any particular instance, scientists in fact consider a whole range of properties of theories: the clarity and precision with which the theories are formulated, the explanatory and predictive power that the theories have in regard to observable phenomena, the formal simplicity of the theories, the extent to which the theories have been confirmed by experimental evidence, and so on.

The Verifiability Principle, moreover, turned out to be overly destructive: it was not aimed at metaphysics alone, but also posed a serious threat to respectable science. Scientific laws – laws which the positivist proponents of the principle accepted – were diagnosed by it as meaningless: 'For such laws, are, by the nature of the case, not conclusively verifiable; there is no set of experiences such that having these experiences is equivalent to the truth of a scientific law' (Passmore 1967: 55). And, there ultimately:

> was the sheer absurdity of the use of verifiability as a meaning criterion: how could one ever say that a theory was gibberish because it could not be verified? Was it not necessary to understand a theory in order to judge whether or not it could be verified? And could an understandable theory be sheer gibberish? (Popper 1976: 80)

So the *Wiener Kris* called Verifiability was an ill-designed instrument. It could not do the kind of cutting considered necessary for saving science and philosophy. Consequently, it had to be discarded as a defective device. Or, to continue in Scriven's (1969: 195) medical metaphor:

> when the populace begins to show signs of worshipping the device of deliverance, it is appropriate to point out that we can go on to better devices, indeed, that to fail to do so is to risk an infection that might prove just as fatal as choking to death on a mess of verbiage.

Present-day philosophers of science are not sold on the idea of sanitizing science. It is generally agreed that science is so shot through with metaphysics that surgical separation of the two is impossible. And what is more, it is argued, such separation would be bad for science. Core assumptions of science, assumptions without which scientific inquiry cannot proceed, are metaphysical in that they cannot be made subject to empirical tests. In support of this contention, Bunge (1977) lists such 'metaphysical hypotheses' of science as the following: 'There is a world external to the cognitive subject', 'The world is composed of things', 'Forms are properties of things', 'Everything changes', 'Nothing comes out of nothing and no thing reduces to nothing.'[22] So much, then, for general versions of Verifiability.

We still have to look at what Bloomfield did with his version of Verifiability in trying to manufacture a materialist conception of language that would be metaphysics-free. To dispel any doubts that may have remained about the empiricist essence of Bloomfield's endeavour, consider the following oft-quoted exposition that he (1939: 13) once gave of his view of science:

> we can distinguish science from other phases of human activity by agreeing that science shall deal only with events that are accessible in their time and place to any and all observers (strict *behaviorism*) or only with events that are placed in co-ordinates of time and space (*mechanism*), or that science shall employ only such initial statements and predictions as lead to definite handling operations (*operationalism*), or only terms such as are derivable by rigid definition

from a set of everyday terms concerning physical happenings (*physicalism*).

Bloomfield (1939: 13), moreover, made a quite curious claim about this view of science: 'this delimitation does not restrict the subject matter of science but rather characterizes its method.'

Noam Chomsky (1964), followed by Jerrold Katz (1964) and others, has strongly argued that this claim by Bloomfield cannot be accepted. The Bloomfieldian view of science, they contend, radically and ruinously restricts the range of phenomena that may form the 'subject matter' of science. In the case of linguistics, this view, in the words of Katz (1964: 129), reduces the subject matter to 'the corpus of elicitable utterances, behavioral responses to such utterances, and observable features of the context in which utterances occur'. Beyond the Bloomfieldian boundaries lies a whole range of significant linguistic phenomena to be accounted for: the infinity of the number of grammatical sentences of any language, the creativity of language use, the freedom of language use from stimulus control, and the appropriateness of the vast majority of used utterances.[23] In terms of a typical formulation of Chomsky's (1972a: 10):

> The normal use of language is innovative, in the sense that much of what we say in the course of normal language use is entirely new, not a repetition of anything that we have heard before and not even similar in pattern . . . The number of sentences in one's native language that one will immediately understand with no feeling of difficulty or strangeness is astronomical.

The Bloomfieldian materialist conception of language, moreover, provides no basis for and account of these and other related phenomena. Such an account has to refer to mental capacities, events and processes which lie beyond the empiricist Bloomfieldian boundaries of science. This is so because the former phenomena and the latter capacities, events and processes cannot be described in strictly behaviourist, mechanist, operationalist or physicalist terms. And for this positivist powerlessness there is a further price to pay. Without an adequate description of the mental capacities, events and processes just referred to, it is impossible to answer three fundamental questions. These questions, first raised by Chomsky, are in the words of Katz (1964: 134):

1 What is known by a speaker who is fluent in a natural language?
2 How is such linguistic knowledge put into operation to achieve communication?
3 How do speakers come to acquire this ability?

It will become clear in chapter 3 that, in the context of Chomskyan mentalism, these same questions are given the status of 'basic' questions.[24]

'Barren', Dear Buyer, this is the Seasoned Shopper's verdict on a conception of language that provides no basis for understanding the nature of knowledge of language, the nature of linguistic performance or the nature of language acquisition. Bloomfield's Blade turned out all wrong. It had been meant to be a Sharp Scalpel – just what the doctor had ordered for surgically slicing away the malignant metaphysical matter in the (animist) mentalistic conception of language. But in the event, Blinded Blue, it proved to be a blade woefully blunt, good only for bludgeoning – a Positivist Pole-axe that paralysed the patient, that pulped rather than purified the Product. So the Bloomfieldian moves to make mincemeat of meaningless metaphysics were, in the end, an emasculating empiricist exercise. It produced a linguistic science of stupendous sterility, a materialist conception of language infamous for its infertility. To sum it all up in a Market Moral for the Concerned Customer:

> *Sanitized science isn't sane science.*

Could I throw in a caveat for the Beginning Buyer too? But, of course, caveats I have many, the following being as good as any:

> *Buyer, beware of sterile seeds that send up shrivelling shoots.*

1.4.3 Fixing it with fictions

Bloomfield, we have seen, held a nominalist view of reality and a positivist/empiricist view of science. As for his view of reality: Bloomfield's materialism reflected the nominalist belief that there is nothing real beyond what can be sensed. Reality, on this belief, does not include abstract objects or categories. As for Bloomfield's view of science: his positivism/empiricism was embodied in his view of what is and what is not scientifically meaningful. To be scientifically meaningful, statements have to be made in terms that refer to observable movements in space and time.

One would expect Bloomfield's descriptions of languages to be strictly in accord with his nominalist and positivist/empiricist beliefs. This, however, is not the case. In some of his linguistic descriptions, Bloomfield was forced to use terms and expressions that were abstract in the sense that they did not denote entities that could be found in linguistic utterances. In being abstract, these entities violated Bloomfield's nominalism. And the statements made about these entities could not be verified with reference to experience. Hence, in violation of his empiricism, such statements were scientifically meaningless.

Bloomfield's (1933: 213) description of irregular English plurals such as *knives, mouths* and *houses* is a case in point:

> We can describe the peculiarity of these plurals by saying that the final [f, θ, s] of the underlying singular is replaced by [v, ∂, z] before the bound form is added. The word 'before' in this statement means that the alternant of the bound form is the one appropriate to the substituted sound; thus, the plural of *knife* adds not [-s], but [-z]: 'first' the [-f] is replaced by [-v], and 'then' the appropriate alternant [-z] is added.

In this description, the abstract terms that violate Bloomfield's nominalism are *before, after, first,* and *then*. They were problematic, since, in Bloomfield's (1933: 213) view:

> it goes without saying, for instance, that the speaker who says *knives*, does not 'first' replace [f] by [v] and 'then' add [-z], but merely utters a form (*knives*) which in certain features resembles and in certain features differs from a certain other form (namely, *knife*).

Terms such as *before*, *after*, *first* thus denote ordering relations (among rules) that could not be part of English on Bloomfield's conception of language. His solution to this embarrassing problem was to declare the ordering relations in question (descriptive) fictions:

> The terms 'before, after, first, then', and so on, in such statements, tell the *descriptive* order. The actual sequence of constituents, and their structural order (§13.3) are a part of the language, but the descriptive order of grammatical features is a fiction and results simply from our method of describing the forms.

This strategy of assigning embarrassing abstract terms the status of convenient fictions was adopted by various followers of Bloomfield.[25] Terms such as 'phoneme', 'morph', 'juncture', 'long component', 'noun', 'verb', 'sentence', 'sentence-form', 'construction type', 'transformation' were too abstract to denote anything that could be observed in utterances. To take care of the embarrassment caused by such 'abstractions' to their nominalist ontology, Bloomfieldians declared abstract terms 'convenient fictions', 'descriptive conveniences', 'purely logical symbols' etc.: useful as descriptive tools without having to be part of observable linguistic reality. The device of useful fictions, thus, enables the Bloomfieldian linguist to retain his belief in nominalism, and thereby his materialist conception of language. At the same time this notion allows him to use whatever abstract term he wishes in his descriptive work.

Using fictions to take care of the embarrassment caused by abstractions to a nominalist ontology is a move credited to Mach. Mach, a positivist *par excellence*, was deeply embarrassed by his recourse to molecules, entities that were too abstract to be observed. To save his sensationalism, he declared molecules to be a 'valueless image' representing a mere '*façon de parler*'.

> If hypotheses are chosen [so] that their subject can never appeal to the senses and therefore also can never be tested, as in the case of the mechanical molecular theory, the investigator has done more than science, whose aim is facts, required of him – and this work of supererogation is an evil . . . In a complete theory, to all the details of the phenomena details of the hypothesis must correspond, and all rules for these hypothetical things must also be

directly transferable to the phenomena. But then molecules are merely a valueless image. (Mach 1893: 59; quoted in Katz 1981: 31)

As a 'valueless image', molecules are useful tools for making computations about observable phenomena. And, having been declared 'fictions', molecules need not be shown to be part of the observable world. But having recourse to valueless images can hardly be reconciled with the Machian position that science should aim at giving a description of an observable reality. To say that something is a fiction is, in the words of Nagel (1961: 134), to say that it is 'not true of the facts'. And this is bad, unless it could be argued that truth did not really matter, a line of thought that we will pursue below.[26]

Ultimately, Dear Buyer, the Machian Machination of using fictions amounts to no more than a Façon of Face-saving. And we note the following Market Motto:

Fictions are tell-tale signs of tinker-toy science.

Flights into fiction are what one is forced into by clinging to nominalist beliefs. And a science tooled up with fictions can hardly be more meritorious than a science making use of Metaphysical Machinery. Of all people surely you, Dear Blue, should have a care or two for the commodity called consistency?

But, however that may be, you were wondering if I could couch the core of my concern in a caveat? No problem – that is all in the day's work to me:

Buyer, beware of fleshless fruits without flavour.

1.4.4 Trampling on truth

Nominalists embarrassed by abstract terms, then, have portrayed these as convenient fictions. Let us dig a little deeper into the consequences which this strategy has for the aims of science.

A first consequence concerns the nature of the relation between science (or scientific theories) and reality (or the world). A view widely held by ordinary scientists is that one of the aims of science is to give a true description of the world.[27] Fictions, however, do not purport to represent any aspect of reality at all. It follows, then, that if a scientist uses a considerable number of fictions, he cannot seriously claim to be describing the world or to be representing reality.

As noted by Katz (1981: 32), Harris (1970: 272, n. 5) realized this when he stated that the idea of theories in linguistics being put forth as true representations of reality 'has something of the absolutist postwar temper of social institutions, but is not required by the character and range of these tools of analysis'. Linguistic theories, to Harris, are not descriptions of anything. Rather, they are (sets of) tools for analysing corpora of utterances. From a conventional perspective, tools cannot be taken to be about an aspect of the world or of reality. So the use of too many fictions – as a means of dealing with embarrassing abstract terms – makes nonsense of selecting for science the aim of giving a description of reality.

A second and related consequence of the use of fictions concerns the status of truth in characterizing the aims of science. On the conventional view, scientists aim to give descriptions of reality that are true, correct etc. But if science does not make descriptive claims about the world or reality, science cannot make claims that aspire to being empirically true. And this was realized by Harris too, a point well made by Katz (1981: 26–7):

> Harris, unlike his fellow structuralists, conceived of linguistics as making no claim to strictly scientific truth. He thought of linguistics more in the way that some people think of literary criticism or artistic depiction, as illuminating aspects of their complex subject without involving a claim to be the sole truth. For Harris, the study of languages illuminates its subject matter by means of a variety of alternative treatments, none of which can claim a monopoly on truth.

It does not make sense to think of computational or analytical tools as being true or false. And Harris did not think of the resulting 'computations' or 'analyses' as being true of false either. The analyses resulting from applying Harris's theoretical tools to corpora of utterances took on the form of classifications or arrangements of utterances and their various component parts. These classifications were not considered true or false by Harris – merely more or less 'convenient', 'simple', 'consistent', 'compact' or 'useful' (Harris 1951: 8–9; 1970: 777). The following statement by Harris (1951: 72) gives a clear illustration of this point:

> The phonemes resulted from a classification of complementary segmental elements; and this could be carried out in various ways. For a particular language, one phonemic arrangement may be more convenient, in terms of particular criteria, than other arrangements. The linguistic requisite is not that a particular arrangement be presented, but that the criteria which determine the arrangement be explicit.

Note, here, moreover, how the use of convenient fictions led to a redefinition of the aims of (linguistic) science. In terms of this redefinition, science no longer aims at giving a true representation of (aspects of) reality. In terms of this redefinition, science essentially provides tools for classifying observable phenomena. Recall that the resort to fictions was a strategy for defusing the threat posed by abstract terms to nominalism. And recall that nominalism was manifested in linguistics in, among other things, the Bloomfieldian materialist conception of language as disturbances in the air. In sum: to enable the linguist to think of language as something material, a radical redefinition of the aims of (linguistic) science was required.[28]

You can live with the consequences of calling on convenient fictions to make the materialist conception of language tick? In fact, you demand to know what is wrong with renouncing reality and trampling on truth? Nothing of course, Bellicose Blue. Nothing is wrong, that is, as long as you don't care a fig about lowering the Sights of Science. Nothing, if you fancied fiction as much as fact, convenience as much as correctness. Nothing, if you are sanguine about science shrivelled up. But if you find all of these agreeable simply to keep your Nominalist Nose above water, to save your Sensationalist Skin, you are in trouble. Then, I fear, your game is up, as has been pointed out by Katz (1981: 38–9):

> *Only so much contrary practice can be explained away as* façon de parler. *Once all the interesting constructs in the theory turn out to be* façon de parler, *as was the case with Harris's transformational theory, the game is up. Once too much of the theory is construed as a mere piece of computing machinery with no implications for the subject-matter of the theory, the theory can no longer be taken to be about what it is supposed to be about according to the gospel.*

One could do as you suggest, Obstreperous Blue: one could, indeed, attempt to invoke instrumentalism to provide principled props for the position that theories are in essence mere tools for making computations and predictions about observable phenomena. But this won't help all that much. To see why not, we have to take a closer look at what instrumentalism is all about.

1.4.5 Insulating it with instrumentalism

Instrumentalism represents a cluster of philosophical positions that is concerned with the nature of the relation between scientific theories and the reality on which they are supposed to bear. The so-called instrumentalist position represents one of various views as to the cognitive or ontological status of theories.[29] Reduced to essentials, instrumentalism portrays theories as instruments, tools or computational devices for the organization of observations and the ordering of scientific laws. On the instrumentalist view, theories are not taken to describe an underlying reality. And as means of organizing observations, theories do not make claims that can be true or false. As tools of organization and computation, theories can only be more or less simple, economical etc.[30] The following remarks by Nagel (1916: 129) succinctly capture the essence of the various formulations of instrumentalism:

> The central claim of the instrumentalist view is that a theory is neither a summary description nor a generalized statement of relations between observable data. On the contrary, a theory is held to be a rule or a principle for analyzing and symbolically representing certain materials of gross experience, and at the same time an instrument in a technique for inferring observation statements from other such statements.

The merits of instrumentalism have been debated at length. It is not necessary to go into the details of this debate here. We will consider only a couple of general reasons that make the adoption of instrumentalism rather less than attractive. To begin with, there is a consideration of a historical sort. As Popper (1969: 114) points out, eminent physicists – including Bohr, Heisenberg and Einstein – embraced instrumentalism as 'a way out of the special difficulties' that arose in their theories. The general point is that leading scientists have not tended to adopt instrumentalism for principled philosophical reasons. They were driven to instrumentalism in an attempt to save threatened theories. Historically, instrumentalism thus has been an escape hatch for scientists haunted by problems of an empirical sort.

Instrumentalism, moreover, provides a solution to a scientist's difficulties by obscuring them. As is well known, theories that make truth claims about the world can under certain circumstances be refuted. But theories conceived of as instruments of computation or prediction are immune to refutation. In the words of Popper (1969: 112–13), 'An instrument may break down, to be sure, or it may become outmoded. But it hardly makes sense to say that we submit an instrument to the severest tests we can design in order to reject it if it does not stand up to them.' Instrumentalism makes it possible for a scientist, in other words, to retain a refuted theory as 'a calculating device with a limited range of applicability'. And, as Popper (1969: 113) notes: 'We may sometimes be disappointed to find that the range of applicability of an instrument is smaller than we expected at first; but this does not make us discard the instrument qua instrument – whether it is a theory or anything else.' A strict adherence to instrumentalism, then, will not spur on the scientist to subject his theories to searching tests. And instrumentalism cannot account for instances of scientific progress that have been made by means of the refutation of theories.

In addition to the problems pointed out above, there is still the matter of consistency to be considered. Calling in the aid of convenient fictions is a ploy that has a place in a descriptivist view of theories. The essence of this view, as noted by Nagel (1961: 118), is that science must 'merely describe' in a simple or economical way 'the succession of events'. Recourse to fictions is a means of fixing false descriptions. But calling theories 'instruments' is something completely different. Instruments, by their very nature, are not descriptive of anything. Having a maximally limited range of applicability does not turn an instrument into a fiction.

Considerations such as these have brought Nagel (1961: 134) to state:

> It does not follow, however, that on the instrumentalist view theories are 'fictions', except in the quite innocent sense that theories are human creations. For in the pejorative sense of the word, to say that a theory is a fiction is to claim that the theory is not true to the facts; and this is not a claim which is consistent with the instrumentalist position that truth and falsity are inappropriate characterizations for theories.[31]

So, Dear Buyer, one could try to patch up the nominalist underbelly of the materialist conception of language with the aid of fictions. But one cannot bestow propriety on this Plastering-over Procedure by intoning the name of instrumentalism. Instrumentalism, simply, is not the right sort of stuff for fixing Foundational Fissures caused by the use of fictions. Of course, Dear Buyer, this can be captured in a caveat for customers keen to recognize cracked conceptions for what they really are:

> *Buyer, beware of rifts roughly repaired with Philosophical Filler.*

So, Bellyaching Blue, if I were you I wouldn't be that keen on going instrumentalist.

1.4.6 *Spitting on speculation*

This brings us to the Bloomfieldian requirement that scientific descriptions must be, not speculative, but inductive. This requirement applies both to what Bloomfield called 'general grammar' and to particular grammars of specific languages. As for the former, Bloomfield (1933: 20) stipulated that the study of general grammar 'will be not speculative but inductive'. And he (1933: 21) elaborated: 'The only useful generalizations about language are inductive generalizations. Features which we think ought to be universal may be absent from the very next language that becomes accessible.' We have here a specific articulation of the meta-scientific belief that the inferential links between a theory and the phenomena on which it bears have to be simple and direct. Generalizations about phenomena have to be directly inferable from data about these phenomena by means of simple induction.

Influential Bloomfieldians applied this inductivist requirement to particular grammars too: grammatical descriptions had to be inductively linked to corpora of utterances. To ensure this, these Bloomfieldians attempted to devise simple analytical operations that could be mechanically performed on the utterances of a corpus in order to 'grind out a correct taxonomic grammar', to use a phrase of Katz's (1981: 35). These operations — including segmentation, identification, matching, classification and so on — had to be applied first at the most 'objective' level, that of the acoustic signal. From this concrete level, the operations had to be applied stepwise to higher levels of grammatical description. To avoid circularity, the units of a higher level (e.g. morphemes) could be established only after units of the immediately lower level (e.g. phonemes) had been identified. Proceeding step by step, linguists had to arrive at the various levels of grammatical description in a fixed order: phonemics, morphemics, syntax, discourse.[32] This step-by-step procedural approach to linguistic description embodies the belief that scientific inferences must be simple, direct, non-speculative.

But how does this belief tie in with the Bloomfieldian materialist conception of language? Calling the step-by-step methodological approach 'empiricist', Katz (1981: 35) has answered this question as follows: 'Nominalism fixes the character of the ground level, while empiricism makes sure that higher levels of grammatical classification are built up from the ground without anything entering into the construction above the ground level.' Bloomfieldians, in other words, invoked inductivism to enforce nominalism in its materialist manifestation. Speculative or non-inductive thinking could, as it were, put wrong ideas into the materialist's head. Being less direct, any speculative or non-inductive inferences could make the materialist lose touch with the 'ground level' of his observable reality. Accordingly, inductivism had to provide the inferential chains that anchored higher levels of grammatical description securely in sounds and scratches.

Note that inductivism and positivism/empiricism are not linked in the same way to materialism. Positivism/empiricism disallows claims about unobservable entities. In so doing, it rules out (animist) mentalistic claims as not scientifically meaningful. And thereby, in turn, positivism/empiricism more or less forces Bloomfieldians to believe in materialism. This is not the case with inductivism: a linguist can be an inductivist without being a materialist. That is, in contrast to positivism/empiricism, inductivism is not a root of the materialist conception of language. Moreover, a linguist can be a materialist without being a rigid inductivist. This is true, for example, of Harris. As has been noted by Hymes and Fought (1975: 1051), for Harris the 'inductivist idiom' meant that 'one needs an operational foothold in a corpus of data, but given that foothold one can take imaginative, inventive leaps.' Harris saw linguistics as an essentially mathematical science, a view not compatible with a rigid adherence to the belief that linguistic descriptions must be inductive, not speculative.[33]

The Bloomfieldian belief in induction reflects what has been called 'the Baconian view of science'. With reference to the essence of this view, Bacon remarked:

> But then, and only then, may we hope well of the sciences when in a just scale of ascent, and by successive steps not interrupted or broken, we rise from particulars to lesser axioms; and then to middle axioms, one above the other; and last of all to the most general . . . The understanding must not therefore be supplied with wings, but rather hung with weights to keep it from leaping and flying. (Bacon 1620; quoted in Bach 1965: 19)

Eminent scientists and leading philosophers of science have alike come to reject the Baconian view as an erroneous reconstruction of the logic of scientific inquiry. Significant scientific discoveries, it has been contended, cannot be made through Baconian induction or any other purely logical procedure. Imaginative, creative, intuitive leaps – of the kind disallowed by Bacon – are needed to arrive at the hypotheses, theories and laws which will provide the required understanding of the world.

Thus Einstein (1973: 299), one of the most eminent of scientists, rejected the idea of there being an 'inductive method which would lead to the fundamental concepts of physics'.[34] He (1973: 266) took the concepts and fundamental principles of scientific theories to be 'free inventions of the human intellect'. Leading to the laws of science, Einstein (1973: 221) saw 'no logical path': 'only intuition resting on sympathetic experience can reach them.' And, in Einstein's (1973: 334) view, a theoretical idea 'is produced by a creative act'.

Philosophers of science too have argued forcefully that the logic of scientific inquiry cannot be inductive. Popper and his followers have become famous for their efforts to dispel the 'Baconian myth of induction'.[35] Popper (1969: 46), for example, has argued that:

> the belief that we can start with pure observations alone, without anything in the nature of a theory, is absurd; as may be illustrated by the story of the man who dedicated his life to natural science, wrote down everything he could observe, and bequeathed his priceless collection of observations to the Royal Society to be used as inductive evidence. This story should show us that though beetles may profitably be collected, observations may not.

And, finally, there have been the linguists whose work has shown Bloomfield's belief in induction to be in error. Decisive, in this regard, has been Chomsky's disillusionment with step-by-step inductive data-processing procedures. His application of such procedures to corpora of utterances failed to yield adequate syntactic descriptions of the infinitely many sentences of the language: 'The failure of inductive, data-processing procedures at the syntactic level became more obvious the more I worked on the problem' (Chomsky 1975a: 30). 'The problem' here, as noted by Katz (1981: 35), is 'the difficulty of specifying the inductive step that, according to structuralist doctrine, takes the linguist from a finite corpus to a syntactic description of the infinitely many sentences of the language.'

So, does the Bloomfieldian belief in induction provide yet another reason for rejecting the materialist conception of language? Not necessarily. As we have seen, this belief was not an essential ingredient of the materialist conception of language. It was a meta-scientific mainstay of Bloomfieldian linguistics, though. The point is plain: what we have been doing all along is to inspect the materialist or Bloomfieldian conception of language and not Bloomfieldian linguistics as such – nor, for that matter, neo-Bloomfieldian, taxonomic, distributionalist or American structuralist linguistics. The materialist conception of language is but one of the components of Bloomfieldian linguistics which, in addition to that conception, included much else besides: assumptions about linguistic structure, meta-scientific beliefs such as the one about induction, methodological practices such as those of segmentation, matching and classification and so on.[36]

What am I getting at, then? Simply, Dear Buyer, that the Philosophical Fate of the materialist conception of language was not inextricably tied up with that of the Bloomfieldian belief in induction. The former did not of necessity have to go under along with the latter. Which is not to say that Insipid Inductivism was not used to supplement materialism in the staking out of a Sterilized Science. But, in the case of (neo-)Bloomfieldian linguistics, it was a different matter. This body of beliefs had to be buried along with the Bloomfieldian belief in Baconian induction.[37]

1.5 Getting a fix on physicalism

Having turned the Bloomfieldian materialist conception of language inside out, we can now get down to serious business, Dear Buyer. Indeed, we are ready to face the eternal question: To buy, or not to buy . . . Let me give it to you straight: I most certainly wouldn't take this conception as a cure for Ontological Angst.

No, Bleating Blue, you have not been led up the market path. Delving into the depths of the Bloomfieldian conception of language has most certainly not been a waste of time. On the contrary, for those who have to master The Market, it may well have been an enlightening exercise. We have learnt at least five general lessons from our meeting with the most Physicalist of Fellows:

1 *On the essence of language: it is not something of a stuff that can be sensed.*
2 *On constructing a conception of language: method does not make matter.*
3 *On appraising a conception of language: look at roots and fruits.*
4 *On metaphysical medicine: concreteness cannot be a cure.*
5 *On the nature of a conception of language: it is not a capsule crammed with dogma.*

As for the first and fifth lessons, more than enough has already been said for guiding even Blinkered Blues. But let me add a word or two about the others, reintroducing you en passant to another fiery Physical Family.

Lesson number two is about meta-metaphysics. A conception of language, as we noted in the introductory paragraph to this chapter, is a body of basic beliefs about the very nature or essence of language. We saw, moreover, that these beliefs are products of serious thinking about language itself. Once a linguist has arrived at a body of beliefs depicting language as made up of a certain kind of stuff, he can proceed to look for meta-scientific principles and methods that can be fruitfully used in the detailed investigation of the principles and properties of language(s). This is normal practice: in scientific inquiry, the nature of the stuff of which a thing is taken to be made up dictates the methods by which that thing can be further investigated.

Bloomfieldians, by contrast, did it the other way round. They proceeded from certain a priori *meta-scientific beliefs – beliefs in nominalism, empiricism and so on. And they allowed these beliefs to dictate to them what they should take to be the stuff making up the essence of language: empiricistically sanctioned sounds and scratches. Chances are slim that by reasoning in reverse in the manner of Metafix, a famous French Physicalist, one could construct a conception of language capable of capturing its nature or essence, a point borne out by the bankruptcy of the Bloomfieldian Business.*

The third lesson has been concretely taught. A conception of language cannot be better than the assumptions and presuppositions on which it is founded. That is why one has to dig up its roots. And a conception of language cannot be better than its empirical and conceptual consequences. That is why one has to taste its fruits. Heuristic fruitfulness, indeed, is a prized property for a linguistic ontology. Roots and fruits obviously, however, are not all that matter. Internal consistency – recall the mismatch between fictionalism and instrumentalism? – is another consideration that counts. And I will draw your attention to others as we make our way through The Market.

Lesson number four, I guess, must have been painful to you, Dear Buyer. But you simply have to accept that the world, as we sense it, forms no more than a small segment of what exists. This is why craving for a 'concrete' conception of language will actually aggravate your Angst. The concreteness of materialism is more than offset by the fictions it fosters and by the various Nuances of Nominalist Nothingness needed to keep it from collapse. As the Market's Medicine Man, 'the venerable village druid' Getafix will warn: 'There is no comfort in being hooked on (scratches in) stony stuff. Ontologically speaking, one Obelix is enough! Nor can one be healed by equating language with what can be heard. Don't fall for Cacofonix's idée fixe*!' No, for mending a Metaphysical Malady one needs an Abstracter Antidote, a prescription which you will yet come to appreciate, Long-suffering Shopper. (Incidentally, the fifth lesson listed above will also gall our Gauls, saying in effect that Dogmatix won't be allowed to run wild in The Market. And, contrary to the first and final principle of Asterix's Axiology, the philosophically fiercest fellows don't have the final word on The Market.)*

Learning these general lessons by no means exhausts the benefits that can be derived from getting to the bottom of the Bloomfieldian conception of language. Knowledge of the clockwork of this conception will allow more profitable probing of some of the other conceptions on The Market: not only the cognate conceptions of language constructed in harmony with the Bloomfieldian one, but also the competing conceptions created in violent confrontation with it. Without a sound understanding of the hidden springs of Bloomfieldian materialism, Dear Buyer, one simply has no hope of fathoming the layout and dynamics of The Market. But let us get down to just this, leaving unsold on the shelf the concrete, quick-fix conception of Menhir Metaphysix.

2

Billing Language as Behavioural

2.0 Messing on The Market

You have been wondering all along whether there really is any logic in the layout of the Metaphysics Market. But of course, Bothered Buyer. Sensible souls that they were, its Druid Designers meant The Market to be a statement in structural simplicity. Precisely one pair of cleverly conceived coordinates serves to order the display of what, on a superficial survey, seems to be a chaotic collection of conceptions of language. Fundamental is the Concreteness Coordinate. Along this, competing conceptions of language are astutely arranged from the completely concrete at the one end to the absolutely abstract at the other. Known also as the Abstractness Axis, this is the first line that we will follow, steadily step by studious step, in our appraisal of the metaphysical merchandise we are after. The second axis we will hit in chapter 5.

We started out – you should still be able to recall – by considering first of all the concretest of commodities: the Bloomfieldian materialist conception of language. A little less concrete than Bloomfieldian sounds and scratches is the action or behaviour of which they are the products. So let us look next at a cluster of conceptions in terms of which language is portrayed as something essentially behavioural.

The idea that language is something behavioural has been the staple food of generations of scholars and students on both sides of the Atlantic. Indeed, for decades it has been marketed for the masticating masses by the MacDonalds of Metaphysics. You sincerely hope, Distressed Buyer, that this Culinary Conception of language can do something for your Angst, for the Harrowing Hunger you happen to have for an answer to the question 'What is language in essence?' Or, that it would at least appease the persisting Positivist Pangs of our Boisterous Blue. There is only one way to find out, for Buyer and Blue alike: by getting one's teeth into this form of Philosophical Fast Food as it has been dished up on The Market – first by linguists, then by psychologists, and finally by philosophers.

2.1 Brunching on post-Bloomfieldian burgers

Language is something behavioural. This is the core of a cluster of conceptions of language that has traditionally been called 'taxonomic-behaviorist'[1] or 'post-Bloomfieldian'.[2] 'Behaviourist', however, is a multiply ambiguous term. So, as we proceed, it will become clear that not all conceptions in which language is something behaviour*al* are 'behaviour*ist*' in the technical sense of the term. The various post-Bloomfieldian conceptions of language to be considered in this section are, in fact, more aptly characterized as 'behaviour*al* conceptions'. Incidentally, the expression 'behavioural conception (of language)' should not be taken to mean that the conception itself has the property of being behavioural. The expression, rather, is shorthand for 'conception portraying language and languages as being behavioural in essence'. This applies, *mutatis mutandis*, to expressions such as 'materialist/mentalist/Platonist etc. conception (of language)' as well.

2.1.1 Munching the metaphysical meat

The question, obviously, is: What is meant by 'something behavioural'? Each of the various answers given to this question portrays the essence of language in a slightly different way. On a first portrayal, language is identified with a certain variety of behaviour. Kenneth Pike (1967: 26) has been a particularly strong proponent of this conception: 'It is concluded . . . that language is behavior, i.e. a phase of human activity which must not be treated as structurally divorced from the structure of nonverbal human activity.' The variety of behaviour in question is further characterized by

Pike as 'human', 'verbal' and 'structured'. He (1967: 26) contends moreover that 'language behavior and non-language behavior are fused in single events.' And he (1967: 26, 32) maintains that 'verbal and nonverbal elements may at times substitute structurally for one another in function.' On Pike's view, language and non-language behaviour, then, are both structurally and functionally analogous.[3] From this, he concludes that language and non-language behaviour must be 'handled by one approach'.[4]

Pike's identification of language with behaviour is absolute: language has no feature not present in behaviour. Dwight Bolinger (1968: 14) also says that 'language is behavior' and that 'the essence of language is a way of acting.'[5] But, in addition, he (1968: 15) provides for the existence of a 'thing-like' system that persists through time from speaker to speaker. This system, on Bolinger's (1968: 15) construal, 'goes by various names – competence, knowledge, *langue* – to distinguish it from performance, or speech, or *parole* or whatever else we may call its practical use at any given moment.' Clearly, Bolinger is careful not to conflate language and speech. Pike (1967: 536), by contrast, does not see any basis for such a distinction. Thus, he contends that: 'As more and more materials in speech begin to appear structured, the view that "language" as a structure differs from "speech" as activity is threatened.' This is one of the 'factors' that brings him 'to abandon the distinction between *la langue* and "la parole" proposed by Saussure'.[6]

On a first post-Bloomfieldian behavioural conception, then, language is identified with behaviour itself. On a second one, a language is portrayed as something more abstract than behaviour itself. On the latter conception, a language is a system of habits that controls language behaviour. This conception of a language has been propounded by post-Bloomfieldian linguists such as Charles Hockett (1958) and Robert Hall (1964).

To clarify the conception of a language as a (complex) set of habits, Hockett (1958: 137, 141) draws a distinction between acts of speech and habits. He (1958: 141) considers acts of speech – also called 'utterances' by him – to be historical events. These events are not habits but each of these events 'partly conforms to, reflects, and is controlled by habits'. Moreover, whereas acts of speech are directly observable, habits are not. Thus Hockett (1958:

141–2) states that: 'Acts of speech, like other historical events, are directly observable. Habits are not directly observable, they must be inferred from observed events, whether the inferring agent is a child learning a language or an analyst seeking to describe one.' In Hockett's view, language structure 'resides entirely' in habits. In addition to a speaker's 'structural' or 'linguistic' habits, Hockett (1958: 143–4) provides for 'habits of some other order' that affect a speaker's fluency. Habits of the latter sort, which are not 'language habits in the proper sense', may cause a speaker to stutter, to hem and haw, to vary the register of his voice, to change his quality of tone and so on. Hockett (1958: 144) considers it 'proper to ignore' habits of the latter sort in the study of language.

On Hall's elaboration of this behavioural conception, the 'oral-auditory' habits making up language have both an individual and a social side. Thus, Hall (1964: 19) contends that 'speech' habits are individual in that they are manifested in the habits, potential or actualized, of each individual speaker. As individual phenomena, these habits have their '*locus existendi*' in the individual brain. 'Speech' habits, in Hall's (1964: 17) view, are social 'in that they are not the product of individual free will, but are common to the entire group of persons who use the language.' Though 'speech' habits have their '*locus existendi*' in the speaker's brain, they are not mental entities. Hall (1964: 403) rejects a 'mental interpretation' of language, seeing no necessity for 'mental factors as necessary postulates for explaining linguistic phenomena'. And he (1964: 404) contends that 'the nonmentalist assumptions of modern linguistics are no different from the basis on which all other scientific work rests.'

You have been told that one can eat one's way out of one's Ontological Angst. Well, Dear Buyer, it has definitely been tried before. Just think of all those students, sucklings and seniors, who have been forcibly fed Post-Bloomfieldian Behavioural Burgers to subdue the disquiet induced by the question 'What is language in essence?' But Fast Food Fads in terms of which language is behaviour, habit or something similar have turned out not to be nourishing notions. To see why not, we will in due course inspect the make-up of the metaphysical meals on the MacDonalds' Menu.

Right now, we first have to consider a question of origin: Where did post-Bloomfieldians get the idea that language should be thought of as something behavioural? Who were the Conceptual Cooks responsible for the recipe of Behavioural Burgers?

2.1.2 Rummaging for the recipe

The paternity of the idea that language is behaviour is often attributed to Bloomfield himself. Thus, with reference to the roots of Pike's conception of language, Davis (1973: 173), for example, contends that: 'The tagmemic theory of language, like Bloomfieldian and post-Bloomfieldian theory, views language as a particular kind of human behavior. Bloomfieldian theory considered language as human vocal behavior with respect to a matrix of stimulus-response.' This view of the origin of the idea that language is behaviour cannot, however, be correct.

First, as noted by Hymes and Fought (1975: 1004), Bloomfield's view of language was not really influenced by the behaviourism he took over from Weiss: 'Weiss's views on behaviorism had perhaps more influence on others than they had on Bloomfield, and . . . insofar they were necessary to his linguistic work, the necessity appears to have been personal and social, rather than linguistic.' Bloomfield conceived of language as essentially something physical, not something behavioural.[7] What is more, Bloomfield himself stated explicitly that he had developed his ideas about language without reference to psychological positions of any kind.[8]

Bloomfield did, of course, invoke the notions 'stimulus' and 'response' to outline his view of meaning. Thus, consider the following schematic representation of Bloomfield's (1933: 26):

$$S \rightarrow r \ldots\ldots s \rightarrow R$$

Bloomfield took the meaning of the 'speech occurrence/event' $r \ldots\ldots s$ to consist in the (nonlinguistic) stimulus (S) of the speaker plus the (nonlinguistic) response (R) of the hearer.[9] But Bloomfield (1939: 18) did not consider this to be an essentially behaviourist definition of meaning:

> This [definition] holds good even under a mentalistic view: in this view it is merely supposed that the speaker's stimulus and the

> hearer's response are 'ideas', 'concepts' or the like, which may be postulated in more or less exact accommodation to the uttered speech-forms and serve to link these to the actually observable stimulus and response.

So even Bloomfield's use of the notions 'stimulus' and 'response' does not indicate that his thinking about language is behaviourist in a substantive sense. His use of these notions, specifically, does not indicate that he holds the view that language is behaviour.

Rather, as is clear from Esper's (1968: 186ff.) account, Bloomfield's behaviourism is of a meta-scientific sort: views about the nature of science.[10] These are the views, anti-metaphysicist, anti-mentalist, pro-positivist and pro-empiricist, towards which he was guided by Weiss. So, Bloomfield's behaviourism was of a meta-scientific and not a substantive sort.[11]

Who, then, in the context of American linguistics came up with the idea that language is a kind of behaviour? Pike (1967: 32) contends that the people who did so were scholars who looked at language from a cultural or ethnological perspective. For instance, Sapir (1949a: 166; 1949b: 32) – whose conception of language will be considered in some detail in section 5.4 below – treated language as 'symbolic behavior' and characterized it 'as strictly socialized a type of human behavior as anything'. He (1949b: 12), moreover, anticipated the idea that units of language behaviour and units of nonlanguage behaviour may constitute interchangeable parts of larger units of behaviour. And Kluckhohn (1949: 148) articulated the view of a large number of ethnolinguistically orientated scholars when he stated that 'language is just one kind of cultural behavior.'[12]

The origin of the idea that language is habit is equally elusive. Hall (1964: 17) refers to work by Twaddell for the view that 'language habits' are 'both below and above the control of the individual'. Twaddell (1949: 4), having referred to language as 'that odd human practice', does characterize language in terms of a notion of 'habit'. But he leaves this notion unclear in regard to both content and origin. The same is true of the way in which Whitney (1971: 11) used a notion of 'habit' when he remarked, more than a century ago,[13] that: 'The dominion of habit is not less powerful in language than in anything else that we acquire and practise.'

There is an additional, rather obvious, possibility to be considered in regard to possible source(s) of the behavioural conception of language espoused by American linguists: the general idea that language is behaviour, habit or something similar may have been taken over by linguists from behaviourist psychologists. For the greater part of the first half of the century, behaviourism – in the various forms developed by Watson, Thorndike, Tolman, Skinner, Hull and others – was the dominant school in American psychology. In so far as behaviourists did have a conception of language, they depicted it as something behavioural.[14] Their generally positivist view of science ruled out the possibility for language to be something mental. Language had to be something 'observable' such as verbal behaviour or something 'objectively' identifiable such as habits, dispositions or the like.[15] It seems plausible that this view of language could have rubbed off on linguists who worked in the same academic environment and intellectual climate as behaviourist psychologists.

Strangely, though, this apparently did not happen. As noted by Fodor et al. (1974: 24): 'until the early 1950s there was a curious lack of fruitful interaction between psychology and linguistics in the mainstream of American thinking.'[16] The reasons why linguists did not take over the behaviourist conception of language (behaviour) held by their psychologist colleagues are less than clear. Why behaviourist psychologists did not take over their linguist colleagues' views on language is easier to understand. The reason is to be found in the hardline empiricist view of science held by these psychologists. As noted by Newmeyer (1980: 11), this view was so extreme 'that it had no place even for the unobservable phonemes and morphemes of structural linguistics.' Only measurable responses of speakers were admissible in the descriptions of verbal behaviour.[17] So, until the fifties, American linguists and behaviourist psychologists had no significant intellectual interaction.[18] Consequently, the behavioural conceptions of language that were popular with post-Bloomfieldian linguists before the fifties could not have had their roots in behaviourist psychology.

The Post-Bloomfieldian behavioural conception of language is in a clear sense shallow in comparison to the Bloomfieldian materialist conception. Bloomfield, to begin with, did take the trouble to try to make clear what 'material(ist)' is supposed to mean. Recall in this connection what he had to say on the nature of noise, using physicalist phrases such as 'sound waves', 'displacement of matter' and the like to describe it. But post-Bloomfieldians have been studiously silent about what 'behaviour', 'habit' and so on is supposed to signify. They have not attempted to make clear how behaviour is supposed to differ from mere motion or accidental action, thereby making behaving a mysterious matter. And how habit differs from skill, practice and disposition – not even to mention knowledge how and knowledge that in this connection – is left unclear as well. This means that the post-Bloomfieldian behavioural conception of language is, from an ontological point of view, either empty or obscure.

Bloomfield, moreover, gave the reasons that propelled him toward portraying language as disturbances in the air. Post-Bloomfieldians, by contrast, have not attempted to lay bare the bases of their belief that language is behaviour, habit or something similar. On the whole, foundational matters receive little or no attention in textbook treatments of post-Bloomfieldian portrayals of language as something behavioural. Perhaps this view seemed to be so 'common-sensical', so widely held, so popular, that it was considered perfectly proper simply to assert it without further support.[19]

What this all adds up to? Well, my dear Famished Fellow, that a Post-Bloomfieldian Bash offers you the feeblest of fares: Behavioural Burgers, Habitual Hash and other such mysterious Metaphysical Mash. And, of course, Cordon Bleu Burgers: a Sensational Solid for patrons with a perversely positivist palate.[20] *As for Gastronomic Guidance, why not chew on the following consonant-crammed Culinary Caveat?*

Biter, beware of jaw-jarring junk.

Would I please refrain from belittling the belief that language is something behavioural? Especially not in its bare bones embodiment in basic books by post-Bloomfieldians who are anyway proud to present themselves as happy-go-lucky laymen in matters metaphysical. And you dare me, Bristling Blue, to turn my attention to the business of pros who are big on behaviour. By all means, Fulminating Fellow, let us get down to the beliefs of the Big Boffins of the Behaviourist Breed. Indeed, let us turn to the stuff of one B. F. Skinner who, for years and years, has ruled the Reinforced Roost.

2.2 Supping on psychological stuff

Within the framework of radical behaviourist psychology, B. F. Skinner (1957: 2) identifies language with verbal behaviour. He uses the term 'language' in quotation marks, indicating graphically that he does not consider language to be something distinct from behaviour. Skinner (1957: 2, 14) defines verbal behaviour as 'behavior reinforced through the mediation of other persons'. This formulation is intended to mean that a person's verbal behaviour is behaviour whose 'first effect is upon other men'. Verbal behaviour, that is, is 'effective only through the mediation of other persons'. Skinner includes in verbal behaviour the behaviour or 'practices' of individual speakers only. He excludes from it the verbal 'practices' of 'linguistic communities'. To come to grips with Skinner's conception of language we clearly have to take a closer look at the core notion of 'verbal behaviour'.

2.2.1 Stoking up on stimuli and responses

Verbal behaviour, in Skinner's (1957: 20) view, is made up of units that have traditionally been called 'responses'. He prefers the technical term 'operant' to 'response', an operant being a unit of behaviour which 'operates on the environment'. An operant has to be distinguished from an 'activity', which is 'primarily concerned with the internal economy of the organism'.

As units of behaviour, operants, moreover, are functionally related to one or more independent variables. More fully, Skinner (1957: 20) defines a unit of behaviour – verbal or nonverbal – as being 'composed of a response of identifiable form functionally related to one or more independent variables'. In short, verbal behaviour is made up of responses that are under the control of objectively identifiable stimuli.

Ultimately, verbal behaviour – and, therefore, language – reduces to muscular movement. Thus, Skinner (1957: 13) states that:

> Our subject matter is verbal behavior, and we must accept this in the crude from in which it is observed. In studying speech, we have to account for a series of complex muscular activities which produce noises. In studying writing or gesturing, we deal with other sorts of muscular responses. It has long been recognized that this is the stuff of which languages are made. . . .[21]

Skinner further characterizes verbal behaviour – and thereby language – in terms of what it is not. First, verbal behaviour is not identical to vocal behaviour. He (1957: 14) considers 'any movement capable of affecting another organism [to be] verbal'. Consequently, verbal behaviour includes much more than vocal behaviour:

> there are extensive written languages, sign languages, and languages in which the 'speaker' stimulates the skin of the 'listener.' Audible behavior which is not vocal (for example, clapping the hands for a servant, or blowing a bugle) and gestures are verbal, although they may not compose an organized language. The skilled telegraphist behaves verbally by moving his wrist. Some of these forms normally arise only after vocal behavior has been established, but this is not necessarily so. Writing and typing may be either primordially verbal or transcriptions of a prior vocal form. Pointing to words is verbal – as, indeed, is all pointing, since it is effective only when it alters the behavior of someone. The definition also covers manipulations of physical objects which are undertaken because of the effect upon people, as in the use of ceremonial trappings.

Vocal behaviour is verbal behaviour 'executed' by the complex musculature of the speech tract.

Secondly, verbal behaviour is distinct from the 'objective entities' produced by it. Skinner (1957: 7) observes that verbal behaviour leaves 'records' or 'traces': the sound stream of vocal speech, the words on a page, the signals transmitted on a telephone or telegraph wire. These may be studied as 'objective facts'. But Skinner (1957: 7) insists on preserving the distinction between an activity and its traces. The belief that 'speech has an independent existence apart from the behavior of the speaker' he considers an 'unfortunate' idea.

Thirdly, verbal behaviour has no aspect that needs to be described or explained with reference to 'events taking place inside the organism'. Skinner (1957: 5), accordingly disallows any recourse to ideas, images, meaning and so on in describing verbal behaviour and in explaining the causation of specific verbal responses. Verbal behaviour, in his view, can be causally explained in terms of notions such as 'stimulus', 'response' and 'reinforcement', terms taken over from experimental study of animal behaviour.[22] Skinner's fundamental theses, in sum, may be formulated as follows:

> external factors consisting of present stimulation and the history of reinforcement (in particular the frequency, arrangement, and witholding of reinforcing stimuli) are of overwhelming importance, and . . . the general principles revealed in laboratory studies of these phenomena provide the basis for understanding the complexities of verbal behavior. (Chomsky 1959: 27)

In a Skinnerian account of behaviour, verbal and nonverbal, no reference to anything mental is allowed. Concepts involving purpose, desire, intention, feeling and so on are eschewed. Mentalistic terms such as 'thinking', 'expectation', 'understanding' and, of course, 'mind' are considered pejorative. Explanations of behaviour of human beings and animals have to be stated in terms of concepts designating only physical things and events.[23] In sum: Skinner's conception of verbal behaviour (or language) is behaviourist in an explicit, technical sense. This conception of verbal behaviour (or language) should be sharply distinguished, therefore, from 'ordinary' behavioural conceptions of language held by post-Bloomfieldian linguists.

An Operant Orgy? I wouldn't rush off to one just yet, my dear Foraging Fellow. The Skinnerian conception of language is definitely not just what the doctor ordered for Ontological Angst. Quite a number of Conceptions Connoisseurs have tried the belief that there is no more to language than stimuli and paired responses. And they didn't take to the taste at all. When messing on The Metaphysics Market, one should first chew on a conception of language to make sure that it will go down well. So before swallowing the belief that language (behaviour) consists of S-R stuff, let us enquire why Epistemic Epicures have found it a Disagreeable Dish.

2.2.2 *Ripping into raw reinforcement and the rest*

Both Skinner's ideas on the nature of verbal behaviour and his approach to studying it were subjected to searching criticism by Chomsky (1959). The impact of this criticism was such that MacCorquodale (1970: 83), a staunch defender of behaviourism, observed: 'It . . . was a virtuoso performance whose echoes are still reverberating in psychology and whose dust has still not settled after 10 years.' Chomsky (1964, 1972a, 1975a,b) later extended his main points of criticism to behaviourist conceptions of language in general. This brought MacCorquodale (1970: 83) to observe that 'No behaviorist escaped untouched.' And on his (1970: 98) view: 'Nearly every aspect of currently popular psycholinguistic dogma was adumbrated in it, including its warlike tone: the new look is a frown.' Many linguists and psycholinguists, in fact, believe that Chomsky's criticisms effectively destroyed behaviourism as an intellectually respectable framework for the study of language (behaviour).[24]

So let us consider the essence of Chomsky's early criticisms of Skinner and also his subsequent extension of them to behaviourist conceptions of language in general. It will, of course, not be possible to consider all of Chomsky's criticisms of behaviourism. We will concern ourselves with the criticisms that bear on the belief that language is something behaviourist. Particularly relevant to our concerns are Chomsky's criticisms of Skinner's conception (also called a 'definition') of verbal behaviour as 'behavior reinforced through the mediation of other persons'.

First there are problems with the scope of this definition. On the one hand, Chomsky (1959: 43) argues, this definition is clearly too broad, both in its earliest form and in the refined form later proposed by Skinner (1957: 45). On both forms, Chomsky contends, the definition includes under verbal behaviour such examples as a rat pressing the bar in a Skinner-box, a child brushing his teeth, a boxer retreating before an opponent, and a mechanic repairing an automobile. Recall that Skinner considers '*any* movement capable of affecting another organism [to be] verbal' (1957: 14, emphasis added).

On the other hand, Chomsky (1959: 45) contends, Skinner's definition of verbal behaviour is too narrow: 'Exactly how much of ordinary linguistic behavior is verbal in this sense [of the definition] . . . is something of a question: perhaps, as I have pointed out above, a fairly small fraction of it, if any substantive meaning is assigned to the term "reinforced".' Chomsky (1959: 37ff.) argues that for much of ordinary linguistic behaviour there simply is nothing that could be identified as 'reinforcers' if this term is to have any objective meaning. For example, he (1959: 46) notes, a speaker will not be able to respond properly to *Your money or your life* 'unless he has a past history of being killed', having been killed before being the necessary 'reinforcer'. And Chomsky (1959: 37) discusses a great number of other cases in which Skinner has to use an essentially empty notion of 'reinforcement' in order to say that an instance of verbal behaviour has been reinforced.

Secondly, Chomsky (1959: 56–7) argues, Skinner's conception of verbal behaviour fails to reflect fundamental properties of much that has been considered typical instances of language behaviour. Chomsky singles out three of these properties: much of a speaker-listener's language behaviour is innovative; much is not related by means of generalization to what is familiar; much is not under the control of discernible stimuli. As for the innovative character of language behaviour, Chomsky (1959: 56) notes that speakers 'constantly read and hear new sequences of words'. And speakers recognize these as sentences and understand them despite their novelty. Turning to the role of generalization in language behaviour, Chomsky (1959: 56) observes that: 'It is easy to show that the new events we accept and understand as sentences are not related to those with which we are familiar by any simple notion of formal (or semantic or statistical) similarity or identity of grammatical frame.' He considers 'talk of generalization in this case' to be 'entirely pointless and empty'.

Addressing the matter of 'stimulus control', Chomsky (1959: 31) uses a variety of examples to show that verbal behaviour typically is not under stimulus control', if the latter notion is to have any objective content. Thus, if one were to respond verbally with *Dutch* to a particular painting, this utterance would be under 'stimulus (= the painting) control' in the Skinnerian sense. But, Chomsky observes, one could instead have responded with *Clashes with the wallpaper, I thought you liked abstract work, Never saw it before, Tilted, Hanging too low, Beautiful, Hideous, Remember our camping trip last summer* or any of a (potentially infinite) number of other appropriate utterances. In order to say that the latter responses are under 'stimulus control', Skinner has to extend the notion 'stimulus' to the extent that it loses all objectivity in its usage. This, Chomsky (1959: 32) concludes, means that: 'Stimuli are no longer part of the outside physical world; they are driven back into the organism. We identify the stimulus when we hear the response. It is clear from such examples, which abound, that the talk of "stimulus control" simply disguises a complete retreat to mentalistic psychology.' The ability of speakers to behave linguistically in an 'innovative' and productive way cannot, therefore, be captured by means of Skinner's basic notions 'stimulus', 'response' and 'reinforcement'. Dennett (1978: 67) generalizes this point of Chomsky's to apply to nonverbal behaviour too, observing that 'when someone behaves in a novel manner, there is a problem [for Skinner]. Pigeons do not exhibit very interesting novel behavior, but human beings do.'

Returning to Skinner's notions of 'stimulus', 'response' and 'reinforcement', Chomsky (1959: 30) observes that they are relatively well defined with respect to the bar-pressing experiments conducted in the laboratory study of animal behaviour. But, he argues, these notions have no clear, objective meaning when one attempts to apply them to (human) verbal behaviour. The vagueness of these notions makes it impossible to answer what Chomsky (1959: 54) calls 'the most elementary questions', including: 'What are in fact the actual units of verbal behavior?', 'How do we decide what stimuli are in "control" in a specific case?', 'When are stimuli "similar"?' Chomsky's problems with the vagueness of Skinner's fundamental notions of 'stimulus', 'response' and 'reinforcement' lead him to the general conclusion that 'with a literal reading . . . the book [i.e. *Verbal Behavior*] covers almost no aspect of linguistic behavior, and . . . with a metaphorical reading, it is no more scientific than the traditional [mentalistic] approaches to the subject matter, and rarely as clear and careful.'

To understand the innovative aspects of a person's language behaviour, Chomsky (1959: 56) contends, one must attribute to him/her an 'abstract ability', 'a grammar that each individual has somehow internalized'. Talk of 'stimulus generalization', in such a case of innovative behaviour not under the control of any discernible stimulus, 'simply perpetuates the mystery under a new title', according to Chomsky (1959: 42). At the root of Skinner's failure to come to grips with the 'innovative' aspect of language behaviour lies, in Chomsky's (1957: 28) view, the behaviourist belief that 'precise prediction of verbal behaviour involves only specification of the few external factors that he [i.e. Skinner] has isolated experimentally with lower organisms.' Complementary to this belief, Chomsky (1957: 28) notes, is Skinner's idea that 'the contribution of the speaker [to his/her verbal behavior] is quite trivial and elementary.'

In later work, Chomsky has generalized his fundamental criticisms of the Skinnerian conception of verbal behaviour to behaviourist conceptions of language as a class. He (1972a: 11–12) emphasizes his conclusion that the 'creative aspect of language use' cannot be accounted for within any behaviourist framework. The existence of this aspect turns, for Chomsky, on three observations. The first is that language use is innovative in the sense considered above and productive in the sense of being potentially infinite in scope.[25] The second observation is that the normal use of language is 'free from the control of stimuli, either internal or external'. And the third is that language use is 'appropriate to the situation'.

Chomsky (1972a: 4) argues that, if linguists are ever to understand the first two of these observations,

> then we must abstract for separate and independent study a cognitive system, a system of knowledge and belief, that develops in early childhood and that interacts with many other factors to determine the kinds of behavior that we observe; to introduce a technical term, we must isolate and study the system of *linguistic competence* that underlies behavior but that is not realized in any direct or simple way in behavior.

And, to Chomsky, the system of linguistic competence is qualitatively different from anything that can be described in terms of the concepts of S-R psychology.[26] Behaviourist psychology has no concept corresponding to his notion of competence, according to Chomsky (1972a: 72). Its characterization of verbal behaviour or 'language' is limited to a narrow and inadequate concept of what is learned, namely in the words of Chomsky (1972a: 72): 'a system of stimulus-response connections, a network of associations, a repertoire of behavioral items, a habit hierarchy, or a system of dispositions to respond in a particular way under specifiable stimulus conditions.' The 'creative aspect of language use' cannot be accounted for in such behaviourist terms.[27]

Thirdly, Chomsky (1959: 42, 57) rejects Skinner's view of the acquisition of verbal behaviour or, for short, language learning. Thus Chomsky (1959: 42) argues that 'It is simply not true that children can learn language only through "meticulous care" on the part of adults who shape their verbal repertoire through careful differential reinforcement'. Chomsky (1957: 43) agrees that reinforcement, casual observation, natural inquisitiveness, a strong tendency to imitate and the child's capacity to generalize are important factors in language acquisition. But, he argues, there are facts indicating that language acquisition involves the processing of information in a variety of 'very special and highly complex ways' which are poorly understood. These ways 'may be largely innate, or may develop through some sort of learning or through maturation of the nervous system'. The facts that conflict with the former behaviourist view of language learning – and that point to the latter special ways of learning – include, according to Chomsky (1959: 42, 57), the following: children acquire their language in an astonishingly short time; careful instruction by parents plays no significant role in language acquisition; this acquisition is to a large extent unaffected by children's intelligence; language acquisition takes place in a comparable way in all children; on the basis of exposure to concrete utterances, children acquire a grammar that is highly abstract and complex.[28]

Facts such as these suggest to Chomsky (1959: 57) that human beings are somehow 'specially designed' to acquire language. But Skinner's view of the acquisition of verbal behaviour denies the possibility of a child's making any contribution to language learning. This denial, Chomsky (1959: 58) contends, 'permits only a superficial account of language acquisition, with a vast and unanalyzed contribution attributed to the step called "generalization" which in fact includes just about everything of interest in this process.' On Skinner's conception of verbal behaviour, Chomsky concludes, language acquisition is just as much of a mystery as the innovative and productive aspects of language use.

Over the years, Chomsky (e.g. 1972a: 72–3, 1975b: 15–17) has fleshed out his criticisms of Skinner's view of the acquisition of verbal behaviour so as to apply to behaviourist theories of language learning in general. In essence, Chomsky's first major point of criticism of behaviourist accounts of language learning is one of logic: before one can have a concept of 'learning' one must have an adequate concept of 'what is learned'. Thus, he (1975b: 16) points out: 'Where it [i.e. an adequate concept of "what is learned"] is missing, the basic questions of "learning theory" cannot even be formulated.' The reason why these theories fail is that they proceed from an insufficiently rich characterization of the complexity and abstractness of 'what is learned', of what Chomsky calls 'the underlying competence'. This is why these theories make the unrealistic claim that language is learned by means of such simple mechanisms or operations as association, conditioning, generalization, abstraction and induction.

Chomsky's (1972a: 72) second major point of criticism of behaviourist accounts of language learning is that an adequate concept of 'what is learned' 'lies beyond the conceptual limits of behaviorist psychological theory'. The reason for this is that 'behaviorist psychology has quite consciously accepted methodological restrictions that do not permit the study of systems of the necessary complexity and abstractness.' In an undiluted form, these restrictions rule out all entities that are not publicly observable, including of course the mind and its contents. In section 2.4 below we will see that the restrictions flow from an ontology that is essentially materialist and from a view of science that is essentially empiricist. Chomsky's second major criticism of behaviourist theories of language learning and behaviour, thus, is ultimately of a meta-scientific sort.[29]

In closing, let us turn again to Chomsky's (1957: 32) point that Skinner's 'talk of "stimulus control" simply disguises a complete retreat to mentalistic psychology.' In his 'Skinner Skinned', Dennett (1978) offers Skinner an alternative but equally unattractive option.

He (1978: 56) notes that what bothers Skinner about mentalistic explanations of behaviour is the *ease* with which they can be 'concocted': 'One falls back on the "miracle-working mind", which, just because it *is* miraculous "explains nothing at all".' Dennett considers this to be an 'ancient and honorable objection vividly characterized by Molière as the *virtus dormitiva*'. On being asked to explain what it was in opium that put people to sleep, the learned 'doctor' in *Le Malade Imaginaire* cites its *virtus dormitiva* or sleep-producing power. Skinner, on Dennett's reading, thinks that all mentalistic explanation is infected with the *virtus dormitiva*.

Dennett (1978: 67), however, proceeds to argue that to account for a person's responses to new stimuli – e.g. my handing over my wallet when held up for the first time – Skinner has to posit an 'external *virtus dormitiva*'. That is, in Dennett's (1978: 67) view, Skinner

> has no record of any earlier experiences of this sort, but *infers* their existence, and moreover *endows* them with an automatically theory-satisfying quality: these postulated earlier experiences are claimed to resemble-in-whatever-is-the-crucial-respect the situation that they must resemble for the Skinnerian explanation to work.

That is, Skinner must arbitrarily assume that I hand over my wallet because I must in the past have had some experiences that reinforced wallet-handing-over-behaviour in circumstances like these. A mentalistic (intentionalist) explanation of this behaviour in terms of my *wanting* to save my skin and my *believing* that I am being threatened is for Skinner infected with an internal *virtus dormitiva*. Given, however, the nature of the arbitrary assumptions about earlier experiences required by Skinner's non-mentalistic explanation, this explanation is infected on Dennett's analysis with an external *virtus dormitiva*.

Ontological Angst not being an imaginary malady, you don't take turning Molière's Metaphysics back on to The Skinned Skinner to be a laughing matter. And you would like to point out, Bristling Blue, that:

1 *The behaviourist spread includes rather more than Raw Reflexology.*
2 *The MacDonalds Men have no exactly taken Chomsky's criticisms lying down.*

Before I go any further, you insist, I must address these matters. But by all means, Beside-yourself Blue; that is just what I had in mind (if you'll excuse my mentalese).

2.2.3 Diversifying the diet

Behaviourism, G. E. Zuriff (1985: 1) has argued, is not simply the science of behaviour developed by behaviourists since the turn of the century. Rather, on his view, it is the conceptual framework underlying that science. And this framework he (1986: 687) characterizes in an inclusive way:

> First, it is a philosophy of science dictating standards for posing psychological questions and for the methodology, explanations, and psychological theory involved in answering them. Second, behaviorism is a philosophy of mind that makes certain assumptions about human nature and the working of the mind. Third, there are several very general empirical hypotheses that constitute a background theory for all behavioral theories. Fourth, behaviorism is an ideology, recommending goals for behavioral science and its application.[30]

On this characterization, behaviourism is a diversified body of beliefs manifested in a variety of forms, branches, schools, theories and so on.

The oldest family of behaviourist beliefs is that of philosophical behaviourism. In Kaufman's (1967: 268) view, it is as old as reductive materialism. The most celebrated theory of this sort, Kaufman contends, is Hobbes's attempt to interpret all mental states as matter in motion. Philosophical behaviourism has two branches: analytical behaviourism and logical behaviourism. Analytical behaviourism is a philosophy of mind maintaining that all mental terms can be analysed in terms of behaviour.[31] In doing so, it rejects the two-substance metaphysical doctrine known as Cartesian dualism, a point to which we will return in section 2.3.1 below. Logical behaviourism, by contrast, is, on Zuriff's (1985: 7–8) reconstruction, a philosophy of science. In terms of Hempel's (1969: 165) characterization, this philosophy of science includes the work that was done in the 1930s and 1940s by logical empiricists on the nature and status of the social sciences in relation to other branches of scientific inquiry.[32]

A younger family of behaviourist beliefs is alternatively called 'scientific behaviourism' and 'psychological behaviourism'. Scientific behaviourism, on Kaufman's (1967: 268) analysis, starts with the work of J. B. Watson. In attempting to establish psychology as a science, Watson contended that states of consciousness are too private to study scientifically. On his view, only observation of behaviour is able to provide the necessary data for scientific psychology. Scientific or psychological behaviourism has taken on a great many forms. Some of the more general forms – interlinked in various ways – are: eliminative behaviourism, methodological behaviourism, radical behaviourism, molar behaviourism, molecular behaviourism, reflexology, mediation theory, interbehaviourism and purposive behaviourism.[33] And in terms of a different kind of taxonomy, a distinction has been drawn between classical behaviourism, neobehaviourism, and neo-neobehaviourism.[34]

Recently, moreover, ideas from various of the above-mentioned forms of behaviourism have been collectively 'reformulated' as 'reconstructed behaviourism'. This recent form of behaviourism is due to Zuriff (1985: 1, 3–4; 1986: 687): taking into consideration the entire scope of behaviourism – roughly from 1910 to the present – he has reconstructed its conceptual framework in a 'logical scheme': 'In this reconstruction, the fundamental premise is that psychology is to be a natural science, and the major corollaries are that psychology is to be objective and empirical' (Zuriff 1986: 687).

There is no question, then, that behaviourism has been a doctrine characterized by considerable internal diversity. Equally true, however, is that this diversity has been constrained in crucial ways by certain basic ideas, as noted by Taylor (1967: 516), for example: 'Behaviorism has taken a number of forms and gone through a number of transformations, but certain basic ideas have remained throughout the changes.' The most basic idea is that the mind does not have the same reality as the brain or body. The central subject of inquiry of psychology is taken to be behaviour. And, in accounting for behaviour, claims imputing reality to mental states, events or activity have to be avoided.[35] As will be shown in section 2.4 below, at a meta-level all forms of behaviourism are 'underlied by characteristics of positivism', to use a formulation of Zuriff's (1985: 261).

As for the first matter you raised towards the end of section 2.2.2: nobody in The Market can afford to be dazzled by mere diversity, Unbending Blue. Chomsky's criticisms of the Skinnerian conception of language cannot be countered by simply saying that there are many, many other forms of behaviourism. And by trading on the hopeful implication that some of these forms will miraculously prove to be immune to these criticisms.

What to make of the Conceptual Cocktail mixed by Zuriff? Concocted of assorted astringent stuffs distilled by Watson, Skinner, Tolman, Hull and others, it has been found far from drinker-friendly by friends and foes alike, as the following judgements indicate:

> *Zuriff has produced 'yet another variation and repetition of the [Watsonean] manifesto' (Epstein 1986: 702).*
>
> *'Zuriff has done us a disservice by exhibiting behaviorism mainly as a midden of past metatheoretical muddles' (Rozeboom 1986: 714).*
>
> *Zuriff has 'resurrected . . . every nitwit idea ever proposed by behaviorists' (Schnaitter 1986: 715).*

A caveat for those with a taste for Philosophical Firewater? Anything to please you, Shaking Shopper:

In Conceptual Cocktails, a kick is not as good as a cure!

Which is to say that the markings of a well-conceived conception of language are not forthcoming from Zuriff's Moonshine Metaphysics.

2.2.4 *Defending the dish*

Over the years, various scholars have attempted to defend the behaviourist conception of language against criticisms by Chomsky and like-minded cognitive psychologists.[36] Though often spirited, these defences have, for a number of general reasons, failed to convince nonbehaviourists that the criticisms in question are less than devastating.

First, defenders of the behaviourist conception of language have failed to make clear what they would accept as a refutation of their beliefs about the nature of language (behaviour). This has prompted, for example, Marshall (1986: 7) to remark:

> Zuriff's conclusion – 'while Chomsky's theory may force a development within S-R psychology, it does not refute it, or, at least, a sophisticated version of it' (p. 149) – impels one to inquire what Zuriff would acknowledge as a refutation. And at this point one moves from science to ideology, as Zuriff himself is well aware (p. 3).[37]

The same basic point was made nearly a quarter of a century ago by Koch (1964: 6): 'I am not even sure what a "refutation" (of behaviorism) would mean . . . I do not see what, in [sic] final analysis, can be done for a truly obstinate disbeliever in mind or experience, even by way of therapy.'

Secondly, interlinked with this problem of irrefutability, is that of behaviourists' remarkable 'adaptability'. Thus, behaviourists have curiously contended that they can accept Chomsky's concepts of 'competence' and 'generative grammar' as 'a functional description of stimulus and response classes' or as 'a kind of hypothetical construct'.[38] This move in effect immunizes the behaviourist conception of language (behaviour) against some of Chomsky's most telling points of criticism, specifically against those relating to behaviourists' inability to account for the productivity and novelty of language behaviour. But this immunity is bought at a price: on the one hand, by stripping the technical terms 'competence' and 'generative grammar' of substantive, empirical content; on the other hand, by making empty claims in terms of obscure notions such as 'response class'. Thus, Chomsky (1972a: 92) has observed:

> The defect [i.e. the inability to account for linguistic productivity] can be overcome, he [i.e. Salzinger] argues, by making use of the notion 'response class'. True, it cannot be that each response is reinforced, but the class of acceptable sentences constitutes a response class, like the set of bar-presses in a particular Skinnerian experiment. Unfortunately, this is empty verbiage until the condition that defines membership in this class is established. If the condition involves the notion 'generation by a given grammar', then we are back where we started.[39]

Behaviourists' general strategy of using terminological means to defend, apparently at all costs, their most basic beliefs was noticed years ago by Koch (1964: 7) too: 'The usual device is a shifting use of an extraordinarily non-particulate and crassly defined technical vocabulary.' This 'device' allows behaviourists, in Koch's words, to 'artfully conceal discrepancies between precept and practice'. With the aid of this 'device', even the most flawed conception of something can be indefinitely maintained.[40]

Thirdly, in defending their conception of language, behaviourists have relied heavily on arguments in terms of 'what might be the case', 'what can be done', 'what is not necessarily so'. Consider as a case in point the following remarks by Zuriff (1985: 149): 'It might prove necessary to include a transformational grammar, but this step does not necessarily violate behaviorist standards. A generative grammar can be interpreted as a structural description of functional stimulus and response classes.' Of this form of argument, or rather rhetoric, Hamlyn (1985: 703) has aptly observed:

> Something has to be preserved, it seems to be suggested; there are such and such possibilities of doing so. But surely what is wanted is the truth – the correct way of understanding the situation, not merely how it might be understood if we were determined to observe supposed criteria of scientific acceptability of a positivist kind.

The 'what might be' form of argument – in conjunction with empty terminology – can, of course, be used to fix just about any flaw in a conception of language.

Fourthly, it has been argued that in defending their beliefs on verbal behaviour (or language), behaviourists have deliberately avoided addressing Chomsky's real criticisms. This has been done by changing these criticisms into claims which Chomsky has not argued and by defending behaviourism against such straw men. These points have been argued by, for example, Erwin (1978: 91) with reference to the most extensive defence of Skinner's views, namely that by MacCorquodale (1970). Thus, referring to MacCorquodale's incorrect 'reduction' of Chomsky's criticisms of the Skinnerian conception of verbal behaviour, Erwin (1978: 91) observes that:

> MacCorquodale (1970, p. 84) admits that none of the preceding criticisms is explicitly stated by Chomsky, but contends that his review 'adumbrates' them. However, he provides no evidence for this claim, and it is not plausible. Neither Chomsky's conclusion nor his supporting arguments rest on any of the preceding criticisms . . . it should be made clear that refuting the preceding criticisms would not in itself answer any of Chomsky's arguments.

Yet, as noted by Erwin (1978: 90), MacCorquodale's defence of Skinner's views is now being cited by behaviourists 'as satisfactorily answering Chomsky's arguments'.

For general reasons, then, behaviourists' defence of their conception of language (or verbal behaviour) has been found to lack credibility.[41] Behaviourists, specifically, have not been able to convince their critics that the nature of 'what is learned' – that is, language – can be captured by modifying behaviourism in essentially terminological ways. The unwillingness or inability of behaviourists seriously to address criticisms of their most fundamental assumptions seems to have elicited two general sorts of reaction from the critics. The first is a lack of interest in further debate. This, for example, has been Zuriff's (1985: 720) experience: 'It is perhaps a sign of behaviorism's decline that nearly all the antibehaviourists invited by BBS [*Behavioral and Brain Sciences*] to review *Reconstruction* [Zuriff 1985] did not deign to do so.' The second is that of dismissive denouncement: both long ago, when Koch (in Wann 1964: 162) reacted as follows in a debate with behaviourists: 'I would be happy to say that what we have been hearing could be characterized as the death rattle of behaviorism, but this would be a rather more dignified statement than I should like to sponsor, because death is, at least, a dignified process.' And more recently, when Hamlyn (1985: 705) portrayed Zuriff's defence of behaviourism as 'an attempt to shore up what ought to be abandoned forever'.

Clearly, Dear Buyer, dressing Behaviourist Burgers with Wordy Whip will not make up for the Mental Meat they miss. There is indeed more to defending a dish than reflexively rewording its recipe. Once the empty expressions have been expunged, all behaviourist conceptions of language, including the Brewed-again Brand, are seen to share the same Skin-ner Skewing:

> *All, all is but skin;*
> *There's no mind within.*
> *Yes, insides are forever out;*
> *Just outsides will be always in.*[42]

2.3 Feeding on philosophical fare

The view that language is something behavioural has been defended by some linguistic philosophers too. Of particular interest in this regard are two related but distinct kinds of linguistic philosophy that were dominant in Britain in the forties and fifties. The first is the later philosophy of Ludwig Wittgenstein; the second the ordinary language philosophy of Gilbert Ryle, J. L. Austin and other Oxford philosophers.[43] These, however, are not the only philosophies that have portrayed language as something behavioural. Of the various others that have done so, Quine's philosophy has perhaps been the most influential. Many leading philosophers who consider language something behavioural simultaneously take it to be something social too. The idea that language is something social will be considered in chapter 5 below. But let us proceed to the later Wittgenstein's conception of language.

2.3.1 Biting into behavioural bangers

The ideas of both the later Wittgenstein and the ordinary language philosophers are complex and susceptible to diverging interpretations. Here we can consider only the ontological oulines of the conception of language attributed to these scholars.[44]

In his later work, represented by *Philosophical Investigations*, Wittgenstein espoused various views on the nature of language. On one of these, it is claimed, Wittgenstein considers language to be 'a bewildering variety of complex human *activities*, undertaken with multifarious purposes' (emphasis added).[45] The view that language exists as activities – also called a 'practice' – is still advocated by present-day Oxford philosophers. Thus Baker and Hacker (1984: 285) contend that: 'A language is a *normative* practice, a practice of using signs according to rules. It is also a *social* practice. It exists in the activities of language users in a community. . . .' The practice mentioned in this quotation is normative in the sense that speakers are guided by rules. On Baker and Hacker's (1984: 259ff.; 1985: 62ff.) reading of Wittgenstein, rules tell speakers what ought to be done. But speakers determine what is done. Moreover, rules are created by the free will of speakers and may be modified or annulled by them. And rules can be consulted and broken by speakers: a rule is 'not a set of rails down which one is forced'. Rules cannot be consulted, followed and violated unless they can be publicly expressed and tabulated. This, moreover, means that rules must be more or less transparent and consciously known to speakers.

Baker and Hacker (1984: 256) hold a behaviourist view of the acquisition of language as well, claiming that 'language use *begins* (with children) as imitative, reactive and habitual behaviour'. They, moreover, claim that 'the roots of the mastery of language lie in *training*.' This is consonant with Wittgenstein's view that teaching and training are important in language learning.[46]

Chomsky (1964: 24–5) considers Wittgenstein to have a '(taxonomic-)behaviorist' view of the nature of language. In the context of this study, however, it would not be wholly accurate to say that the Wittgensteinian views on language jointly constitute a conception of language in the conventional sense. Recall that a conception of language is conventionally taken to be an answer to the question 'What is language in essence?' (cf. Katz 1981: 46; section 1.1 above). But Wittgenstein and ordinary language philosophers were not concerned with determining the essence of language, number, knowledge, truth, existence and so on – at least, not if this essence had to be captured by means of analysis with complete exactness in terms of defining properties. For in Wittgenstein's view:

> in philosophy a rigorous demarcation of such concepts as language, proposition, number, object, property, etc. is otiose precisely because in this sense of 'explain', philosophy explains nothing. It should not be seen as a system of hypotheses from which deductions are to be made. This takes away the main reason for seeking a strict definition of language. (Baker and Hacker 1980: 344–5)

Wittgenstein contended that words such as 'language', 'Satz', 'number', and so on are not 'explained' by giving '*Merkmal*-definitions. Rather, such words are 'explained' by giving examples to which they apply and by pointing to overlapping similarities between these examples. These similarities Wittgenstein compared to the resemblances holding between members of a family.[47] So Wittgenstein's means of elucidating the meaning of 'language' is that of family resemblance characterization, not of '*Merkmal*-definition'. He judged the question 'What is language?' to be formulated in a misguided form since it looks like a quest for the impossible: a sharp definition in terms of one or more '*Merkmale*'.[48]

Ordinary language philosophers adopted a similar approach to the question 'What is language?', as is clear from the following remarks by Stuart Hampshire (1966: 267):

> we do not in philosophy need to state precisely what are the necessary and sufficient conditions for calling a signalling system a language; for we are not particularly concerned with defining the word 'language'. Nor are we concerned with a systematic classification of the different grammatical forms of language; the interest of contemporary philosophers in forms of speech neither is, nor should be, scientific or systematic.

A fundamental concern of these philosophers, rather, was to describe the ordinary uses of words, expressions and idioms in particular languages. By doing so, they hoped to dissolve philosophical problems caused by the misuse of ordinary language. As noted by Katz (1966: 75), Wittgenstein considered conceptual confusions and metaphysical speculations to be symptoms of such misuses. And the therapy for such philosophical confusions consists in detailed description of the actual use of the words or expressions whose misuse caused them. The philosophical confusions and speculations concerning the existence of a spirit or mind are a case in point. It is through the misuse and literal understanding of mentalistic expressions that philosophers are misled into postulating a spirit or mind.[49] Wittgenstein's later philosophy, thus, has a strongly negative thrust: ridding philosophy of meaningless metaphysics and mythology.

The concern of Wittgensteinians with normative rules that guide the 'activities' of speakers is, ultimately, a *philosophical* concern as well. Thus Baker and Hacker (1985: 54) state that: 'Philosophy is concerned with rules of grammar, rules for the use of expressions, only in so far as they shed light upon particular philosophical problems. . . .' Philosophy aims, not at producing a grammar, but at resolving philosophical questions. For example, the Wittgensteinian philosopher would be concerned with the different rules for the use of sensation and perception words to dissolve conceptual puzzles and to resolve confusions about perception and speakers' knowledge of the world. This philosopher, Baker and Hacker (1985: 55) explain, would point out that it makes sense to say 'I see better, more distinctly, than you' but not 'I feel pain better, more distinctly, than you'. Wittgenstein, in their (1985: 55) words, considered grammar:

> [to be] the account book of language. Its rules determine the limits of sense, and by carefully scrutinizing them the philosopher may determine at what point he has drawn an overdraft on Reason, violated the rules of an expression and so, in subtle and not readily identifiable ways, traversed the bounds of sense.

The fact that Wittgensteinians have portrayed language as something behavioural does not make them psychological behaviourists. Indeed, Wittgenstein himself denied that psychology concerned him: 'I conceive of understanding, in a sense, behaviouristically – What is behaviouristic in my conception consists only in that I do not distinguish between "outer" and "inner". Because psychology does not concern me.'[50] Rather, Wittgenstein and such ordinary language philosophers as Ryle have been considered 'philosophical' or 'analytic(al)' behaviourists.[51]

As manifested in the work of Ryle, analytical behaviourism may be reduced to a negative and a positive thesis. The negative thesis asserts that everyday talk about the mind does not entail the mind–body dualism defended by Descartes. It is the incorrect use of mentalistic language – expressions taken to refer to mental attributes, processes, states, events and so on – that contributed to Descartes's mistake of regarding 'the soul as some special sort of object, ontologically distinct from physical objects, belonging to a category of objects that are nonspatial, immaterial, and knowable only through introspection' (Katz 1966: 84). The positive thesis is that everyday mentalistic language can be analysed as referring to material objects and their behaviour. Thus, Ryle (1949: 25) remarks that 'when we describe people as exercising qualities of mind, we are not referring to occult episodes of which their overt acts and utterances are effects; we are referring to those overt acts and utterances themselves.' In support of this thesis, Ryle analyses the ordinary use of various mentalistic words. He tries in particular to show how words that apparently refer to mental life, including emotion and feeling, can be understood as referring to 'witnessable activities'.[52] In sum: analytical behaviourism rules out, as a matter of principle, the possibility that either language or grammar could be something mental.

Why can't I work up an appetite for ordinary Oxbridge Bangers – to your taste the one conception of language not filled with Philosophical Fat and Mythological Meat? Cutting down on Conceptual Calories, I would agree, Baffled Blue, could possibly cure a cardiac condition. But that is not the point of putting a metaphysics meal on The Market; rather, the point is to fill a void caused by the absence of an answer to the question 'What is language in essence?' And for filling this void, the watery wisdom cooked up in Colleges by Kilojoule-Counting Conceptioneers won't do much. I should go a little deeper into the reasons for my dissatisfaction with the British Brother of the Behaviourist Burger? This is a sensible suggestion, Dear Buyer; never take a marketeer's word simply on trust.

2.3.2 Weighing the Wittgensteinian wurst

The views of Wittgenstein and ordinary language philosophers do not make up a full-blown conception of language.[53] We will consider three reasons why this is so, reasons discussed in a perceptive manner by Katz (1966).

First, as already noted above, Wittgenstein was not concerned with isolating the essence of language. In particular, he argued that it is impossible to capture this essence in terms of a definition that spells out the properties that are necessary and sufficient for something to be language. Katz (1966: 72) observes, however, 'that Wittgenstein offers no specific arguments for his position that we cannot expect to find definitions which express a necessary and sufficient condition for applying a given word.' All that Wittgenstein does, Katz points out, is to show that certain 'simple-minded' definitions are not acceptable for the application of certain words. 'Game' is Wittgenstein's famous example of a word whose various uses ought rather to be characterized in terms of the notion of a 'family resemblance'. But, Katz argues, Wittgenstein fails to establish that there is no condition that is necessary and sufficient for a word such as 'game' to be applied correctly. And, Katz (1966: 73) concludes:

> he [i.e. Wittgenstein] neither provides a reason why a statement of the family resemblance is the best we can do, nor does he try to analyze his cases to show that they amount to more than multiple senses of the same orthographic element, such that some of the simple-minded definitions he considers work for some senses and others work for other senses.

Katz's basic points carry over to 'language'. It has not been shown that the essence of 'language' cannot be captured by means of a '*Merkmal*'-definition. Wittgenstein has not furnished any principled reasons why characterizations of the essence of language have of necessity to be vague.

Secondly, the view of language held by ordinary language philosophers is not linked systematically enough to the reality on which it is supposed to bear. This view, we saw, is concerned with linguistic details, with properties of individual, isolated words and expressions. As noted by Katz (1966: 88), this concern with specific facts of natural language 'went hand in hand with a failure to take into account the complex structural organization in which such facts are systematized in actual languages.' The most important reason for this failure lies, on Katz's analysis, in the antitheoretical orientation of ordinary language philosophy. This orientation is, according to Katz (1966: 88–9), a reaction 'to the logical empiricist's excesses in theory construction, and . . . to the theoretical systems developed in some traditional metaphysical enterprises.'

A theory of linguistic structure forms an essential link between a conception of language and the deeper and more systematic aspects of linguistic reality. In the case of ordinary language philosophers' view of language, this link or coupling is absent. This view, consequently, could play only a limited heuristic role in exploring less superficial and more systematic aspects of this reality. Ordinary language philosophers did make fragmentary descriptions that provide insight into especially the meaning of words and expressions.[54] Much of what is regular and systematic at less superficial and more complex levels of language, specifically syntax, has, however, been beyond their reach because of their unwillingness to formulate a theory of linguistic structure.

As a consequence Wittgensteinians have an oversimplified view of language, a view in which the complexity and abstractness of language is seriously underestimated. And this has caused their conception of the nature of language learning and the rules of (philosophical) grammar to be simplistic. Recall that in Wittgenstein's view, teaching and training are crucial to language learning. Speakers of a language, moreover, are claimed to have conscious knowledge, publicly expressible, of rules of grammar. But from careful work that has been done in generative syntax particularly, it has become clear that fundamental aspects of linguistic structure are too abstract to be taught or to be learned by means of training. Ordinary speakers simply do not have any conscious knowledge of the grammatical rules underlying such aspects of linguistic structure. In sum: the fact that ordinary language philosophers do not (wish to) have a theory of linguistic structure has insulated their view of language from corrective pressures exerted by more abstract aspects of linguistic reality.[55]

Thirdly, Katz (1966: 90) notes, ordinary language philosophers' aversity to having a theory of linguistic structure reflects something deeper: 'a thoroughgoing distrust of generalizations'. He quotes Ryle, who articulated this distrust by saying that 'in philosophy, generalizations are unclarifications.' Generalizations are considered to come between a philosopher and the so-called facts, preventing him/her from seeing the facts for what they really are. The core of the 'methodological' position of ordinary language philosophers is characterized as follows by Katz (1966: 90):

> Contrary to the scientific view that explanation consists in the systematization of detailed facts in the form of generalizations that reveal their underlying organization, the ordinary language philosopher's view . . . seems to be that explanation in philosophy consists in overthrowing generalizations by showing that the facts they purport to cover do not fit nicely as instances.[56]

Wittgensteinians, thus, were concerned with finding counter-examples to generalizations. But their view of the methodological role of counter-examples was less than sophisticated. They failed to appreciate that counter-examples bear in the first place on the *formulation* of generalizations. They, moreover, did not see that counter-examples have the positive role of indicating the direction in which generalizations should be revised. Katz's (1966: 91) formulation of these two shortcomings in ordinary language philosophers' view of counter-examples deserves being quoted in full:

> Counter-examples are indeed conclusive against the *formulation* of a generalization, but this does not mean that the generalization which we seek to formulate is wrong or that every feature of the formulation shares equally in the guilt. The ordinary language philosopher also fails to appreciate the role of counter-examples to indicate the direction in which the formulation of a generalization should be revised, not just to accommodate them, but to increase the degree to which the generalization reveals the underlying organization of the facts.

A conception of language, it was noted, has to make systematic contact with linguistic reality. For this purpose, we have seen above, an adequate theory of linguistic structure is required. Even more essential, however, is a proper methodology for analysing and interpreting the facts of linguistic reality. An approach – whether 'philosophical' or 'purely linguistic' – that does not properly appreciate the role of generalizations and counter-examples has to be sterile. Its conception of language cannot guide fruitful exploration of the reality on which it is supposed to bear. And such a conception is immune to the corrective pressures exerted by this reality.

It is interesting to note in this connection the following disclaimer by Wittgenstein: 'it is, rather, of the essence that we do not seek to learn anything *new* by it [i.e. philosophy of language]' (quoted by Katz 1966: 90). This may be an extreme formulation, not acceptable on a literal reading to many ordinary language philosophers. Its general tenet, however, helps us to understand why ordinary language philosophy could not shed much light on the nature of language.[57]

One can understand why Wittgensteinian Word-Watchers are averse to Conceptual Corpulence caused by the consumption of mushy metaphysics and mythology. But, as an alternative, Philosophical Frailty and Theoretical Thinness pose just as big a hazard to the health of the Conceptions Consumer. This is why practitioners of preventive metaphysics won't prescribe the buying of a conception of language on which language has no definable essence, on which a theory of linguistic structure belongs to the realm of religion, and on which generalizing about language(s) is seen as an exercise in generating obscurity. So, to sum it up in a clinician's caveat specially for you, Dear Buyer:

> *Buyer, beware: the alternative to Ontological Obesity canot lie in Metaphysical Malnutrition.*

You would like to point out, Dear Blue, that a Wittgensteinian Work-out is not the only way of becoming linguistically lean, philosophically fit. Could it be that I have never heard of the Quinian way of fighting Philosophical Flab? But I have, Dear Blue. And for our Buyer's sake, we will take the briefest of looks at the Quinian conception of language.

2.3.3 Dishing up dispositions

In his *Word and Object* (1960), the American philosopher W. V. O. Quine presents a number of views on language that can be collectively taken to constitute a behaviourist conception of language. For, on a particular reconstruction by Chomsky (1968: 54ff.) it would seem that Quine (1960: 11) proposes that language is 'a fabric of sentences variously associated to one another and to non-verbal stimuli by the mechanism of conditioned response'. Quine (1960: 27), moreover, characterizes language as 'the complex of present dispositions to verbal behavior, in which speakers of the same language have perforce come to resemble one another. . .'.

Quine's view of language learning is behaviourist too. He (1960: 9) considers language learning to be the learning of (a network of) sentences. And sentences can be learned by three means, all of which are behaviourist: by 'direct conditioning' of a whole sentence to some sensory stimulation; by 'association' of sentences with other sentences; and by building up sentences from learned parts by 'analogy' with the way in which those parts have been previously seen to occur in other sentences. And in all of this, Quine (1960: 82) assigns to 'reinforcement' a central role: 'It remains clear in any event that the child's early learning of a verbal response depends on society's reinforcement of the response in association with the stimulations that merit the response, from society's point of view, and society's discouragement of it otherwise.' Quine (1960: 82) explicitly describes his view of language learning as 'congenial enough to Skinner's scheme. . .'.

Quine's conception of language and its learning has been severely criticized by Chomsky. To Chomsky (1968: 64–5) the description of language as 'a complex of present dispositions to verbal behavior' seems 'rather perverse'. On the one hand, Chomsky (1968: 57–8) argues that Quine's shifting use of the term 'dispositions' makes it all but impossible to determine what he means by 'disposition' and 'language'.[58] Hence in this context, in Chomsky's view, 'disposition' is an essentially empty notion. On the other hand, Chomsky (1968: 65) rhetorically asks: 'what point can there be to a definition of "language" that makes language vary with mood, personality, brain lesions, eye injuries, gullibility, nutritional level, knowledge and belief, in the way in which "dispositions to respond" will vary under these and numerous other irrelevant conditions.' Underlying the 'dispositional' characterization of language, Chomsky suggests, is the typical behaviourist confusion of what a person does or is likely to do and what he knows. Quine, on Chomsky's reading, therefore confuses performance with competence in characterizing language as a complex of dispositions to behave. Belonging to the realm of performance, the notion of 'dispositions to behave' is not appropriate for characterizing the nature of language. Thus, Chomsky (1975b: 23) has remarked that:

> The notions 'capacity' and 'family of dispositions' are more closely related to behavior and 'language use'; they do not lead us to inquire into the nature of the 'ghost in the machine' through the study of cognitive structures and their organization, as normal scientific practice and intellectual curiosity would demand.[59]

In Chomsky's view, the proper way to exorcise 'the ghost in the machine' is to determine the structure of mind and its products.

Since Quine's conception of language learning is essentially behaviourist, it has all the shortcomings discussed in section 2.2.2 above. And Chomsky (1968: 64) finds the entire notion of 'learning sentences' to be 'almost unintelligible'. He (1968: 64) justifies this judgement with the aid of a concrete example:

> Suppose that I describe a scene as rather like the view from my study window, except for the lake in the distance. Am I capable of this because I have learned the sentence: 'This scene is rather like the view from my study window, except for the lake in the distance'? To say this would be as absurd as to suppose that I form this and other sentences of ordinary life by 'analogical substitution', in any useful sense of this term.

When we learn a language, we obviously do not 'learn sentences' or acquire a 'behavioural repertoire' through training. Rather, Chomsky (1968: 64) contends, we 'develop certain principles . . . that determine the form and meaning of indefinitely many sentences'.[60]

The criticisms by Chomsky and others have left Quine strangely unmoved. Thus, recently, he (1990: 37–8) reaffirmed his behaviourist stance:

> I hold further that the behaviorist approach is mandatory. In psychology one may or may not be a behaviorist, but in linguistics one has no choice. Each of us learns his language by observing other people's verbal behavior and having his own faltering verbal behavior observed and reinforced or corrected by others.

And Quine's (1990: 38) theory of meaning has remained uncompromisingly behaviourist too: 'There is nothing in linguistic meaning beyond what is to be gleaned from overt behavior in observable circumstances.' It is not clear what would persuade Quine to give up the behaviourist beliefs quoted above.

If, Slimming Shopper, you don't want to pursue philosophical firmness at the risk of becoming epistemically emaciated, here is a Dietary Directive you should heed:

Buyer, beware: dispositions make for a decimating diet.

At last, then, we are ready for diagnosing the deepest drives of Behaviourist Brokers and for dissecting these in broad daylight. (You cannot have failed to notice, Dear Buyer, that The Market is a rather poorly lit place.)

2.4 Boiling it down to the basics

What, then, has brought behaviourist psychologists to portray language as essentially something behavioural? The hard core of the answer lies in Zuriff's (1985: 261) statement that '[i]n many ways behaviorism can usefully be understood as a psychological version of positivism.' That is, on an alternative characterization of his, the behaviourist conceptual framework is 'underlied by characteristics of positivism'. Thus, behaviourist psychologists portray language as something essentially behavioural because they ultimately believe in positivism. In a suitably modified form, this applies to many behaviourist philosophers or analytical behaviourists too. But what does it mean to say that someone's positivist philosophy drives him/

her towards a characterization of language as behaviour, activity, a practice, habits or dispositions? This is the general question that will concern us below. In answering it, we will consider those 'characteristics of positivism' that, on Zuriff's (1985: 261ff.) reconstruction, underlie the behaviourist conceptual framework.[61]

First, behaviourists share the positivist rejection of what Zuriff (1985: 271; 1986: 698) calls 'metaphysicalism'. Acting in a typically positivist spirit, behaviourists have been concerned with the demarcating of 'positive knowledge'. This is to be done by discriminating between beliefs that deserve to be called 'knowledge' and beliefs that should be discarded as 'metaphysical' because they 'generate endless disputes that thwart the purposes of intellectual inquiry'. Behaviourist 'anti-metaphysicalism' boils down to the denial of the existence of the mental – particularly a 'consciousness' – as a real entity. This anti-mentalism precludes on *a priori* grounds the possibility that behaviourists could characterize the essence of language in non-empty mentalist terms.

Secondly, complementary to behaviourists' anti-mentalist doctrine is their simplistic materialist ontology. In a typically positivist way, 'matter is considered the sole constituent of the universe', to use a formulation of Zuriff's (1985: 271). Expressed in ontological jargon, this means that behaviourists such as Watson, Skinner, Rorty and Quine are eliminative materialists: they claim that there are no mental states and events. To physical monists, of course, the essence of language cannot consist in any sort of stuff other than matter. And to those who are psychologists, there is no substantive option other than that of depicting language as something behavioural, behaviour (or the behavioural) being considered a form of matter.

Thirdly, behaviourists' materialism is in consonance with the deeper positivist commitment to a nominalist ontology. As noted by Zuriff (1986: 699), the distinction between appearance and reality is rejected by behaviourists. Specifically, they believe that there is no deeper (level of) reality beyond the 'realm of observation'. They concede that much of our knowledge consists in abstract concepts or abstractions. But these are not taken as referring to 'transcendents' in a realm beyond experiences. Reification – characterized by Zuriff (1985: 269) as the 'treating of an abstract term as the name of [a] substantial entity with an independent existence of its own'

– is considered extremely dangerous. It misleads the scientist 'into asking fruitless questions, pursuing futile lines of investigation, and formulating specious explanations'. The myth of 'the ghost in the machine' is, on Ryle's analysis, a product of reification. And, on Zuriff's view, reification or hypostatization, as he also calls it, underlies the view that grammar represents a distinct mental entity. So, given their nominalist stance on abstract concepts, behaviourists cannot locate the essence of language in any realm other than that of the observable.

Fourthly, behaviourists, in keeping with the positivist tradition, adopt an empiricist epistemology. This means, in Zuriff's words (1986: 698), that: 'The positivist preference for knowledge based on direct experience expresses itself in behaviorism as the emphasis on experimentation, direct observation, and scientific empiricism.' This epistemology is intended to ensure that scientists will not speculate about the 'metaphysics' of unobservable events in the organism. And as Zuriff (1986: 698) sees it, this empiricist 'attitude also underlies the behaviorist insistence that theoretical terms be securely linked to observables'. Behaviourist epistemology, in addition, has a pragmatist flavour. Specifically, the truth of a statement and the meaning of a concept are, as Zuriff (1986: 698) notes, 'matters of their usefulness rather than transcendent properties of words'. As a consequence, behaviourists do not view theories as sets of statements that express true or false statements. Instead, theories are taken to be instruments that may be more or less useful for predicting and controlling behaviour. And, ultimately, science is viewed, in the words of Zuriff (1985: 268), as an instrument aiming to achieve a 'pragmatic validity', as 'an instrument of adaption'. More fully, Zuriff (1985: 250) says: 'Science is defined in behaviorism as those methods which the behavioral science [sic] determine to be most effective in enhancing the knower's ability to predict, control and therefore adapt to the environment.' But to return to the central issue: given their empiricist epistemology, behaviourists are forced to portray the essence of language as a stuff that can be investigated by means of their 'positive', 'objective' methods.

The behaviourist conception of language, clearly, is essentially an aprioristic one. It has its bases in metaphysics – a situation that is rather paradoxical, given behaviourists' aversion to metaphysics.

Behaviourists' anti-metaphysicalism, anti-mentalism, materialism, nominalism and empiricism represent doctrines that are essentially metaphysical. These doctrines cannot really be justified with what behaviourists consider 'empirical means of investigation'. The claims which these doctrines express are not 'established on direct experience', to use a behaviourist catchphrase.[62] Yet, behaviourists have allowed these doctrines to force them to depict language as something essentially material. These doctrines, moreover, place behaviourists in a scholarly straight-jacket: they are not allowed to reflect freely on the nature of language, nondogmatically looking for every possible means of justifying or refuting whatever ideas such reflection may yield. These doctrines, thus, have had a stifling effect on what Koch (1964: 20) has called behaviourist's 'problematic curiosity'.

A conception of language dictated by philosophical doctrines must inevitably reflect the limitations of these doctrines. And in the preceding discussion of the Bloomfieldian materialist conception of language, it was shown that the forms of materialism, nominalism, empiricism and instrumentalism associated with logical positivism have been considered fundamentally flawed.[63] Instead of reviewing these general flaws once again, let us rather focus on a more specific additional problem with which behaviourists have grappled unsuccessfully for decades: giving an adequate definition of 'behaviour'.

The difficulties with defining 'behaviour' become clear when one considers certain questions on which behaviourists have failed to agree.[64] These questions should be viewed against the background of what Kaufman (1967: 269) considers the commonsense definition of 'behaviour' as 'any movement of an organism'.

1 Does the terms 'behaviour' also apply to the physiological processes of or physiological events in an organism?[65]
2 Should the effects produced by movements be considered part of behaviour as well?[66]
3 Must a movement be involved in something an organism is *doing*, in some *action* he performs, in order to constitute behaviour?[67]
4 Can everything that a human organism does be viewed as behaviour?[68]

5 Should such unobservables as 'pain', 'intentions' and so on to which reference has to be made in describing certain actions of a person be considered part of his/her behaviour?[69]

On the answers to these and similar other questions, behaviourists have disagreed for decades.[70]

In this connection, Zuriff (1985: 93), a committed behaviourist, has remarked that:

> Even for behaviorists, among whom there is general consensus that the goals of psychology are the prediction and control of behavior, criteria cannot be formulated in a universally agreed way. First, there is no common opinion on what is meant by the 'behavior' to be predicted and controlled.

This means that the nature of the primary stuff that language is supposed to consist of on the behaviourist conception is unclear. And we have seen above that this holds true for such secondary behavioural entities as dispositions as well. In sum: the metaphysical doctrines held by behaviourists dictate to them that language can only be something behavioural, yet the exact nature of this something is unclear to them.

Anti-metaphysicalism, materialism, nominalism and empiricism, then, make up the Bare Bones of the behaviourist conception of language. And, Dear Buyer, they represent reflexes of the most basic ingredient of all, positivism. In this respect, the behaviourist conception of language is identical to the materialist one propounded by Bloomfield. Yet, the latter conception did not taste nearly as bad as the former. No, Beaming Blue, you have not caught me in the act of perpetrating a paradox. You see, when Bloomfield got hooked on positivism, it was still a fairly fresh philosophy that held out, at least initially, some promise of progress. But by the time that many behaviourists selected positivism as the basis of their Burgers and Bangers, it had already gone sour. This is what Koch (1964: 5) means when he observes that 'Psychology is . . . in the unenviable position of standing on philosophical foundations which began to be vacated by philosophy almost as soon as the former had borrowed them.' And, with reference to their methodological beliefs, Koch (1964: 22) points out that the behaviourist

> *began to become bereft of his extracurricular [i.e. positivist] methodological supports very shortly after he discovered them. Behaviorism has stood pat on a few issues dissected out of the methodology of science anywhere from twenty to thirty years ago. But philosophers and scientific methodologists have not stood pat.*

So, Dear Buyer, if yours is a stomach that cannot stand Stale Stuff, behaviourist conceptions of language will only aggravate your Angst.

2.5 Washing it down with a word of warning

So much, then, for eating out ontologically on The Market. Behaviourism, you would agree, Abstinent Buyer, is far too feeble a fare to feed one philosophically, to ease the sense of Epistemic Emptiness caused by the question 'What is language in essence?' But we have learned some general lessons:

1. *On the essence of language: it is not of any known Behavioural Brand.*
2. *On constructing a conception of language: relate it rigorously to reality.*
3. *On appraising a conception of language: test it for Ontological Opacity.*
4. *On the nature of conceptions: essences are of the essence.*

On lesson number one we need not dwell much longer. Though language might, unexpectedly, turn out to be something behavioural, this wouldn't be within the behaviourist ontology that we have considered. Behaviourism, as we know it, has no future on The Metaphysics Market, Burbling Blue. We have indeed reached 'the end of the long and boring behaviourist night', to quote an On-duty Ontological Oracle (cf. Bunge 1980: ix).

Let me refresh your memory as regards the core of the second lesson, Dear Buyer. The beliefs making up a conception of language may legitimately be highly abstract, but they cannot be Free-Floating Flotsam. They have to be tied down tightly to the reality that they are supposed to be about. For this, we have seen, two kinds of conceptual couplings are required: theories of linguistic structure and associated epistemologies for exploring this reality. A theory of linguistic structure has to ensure that the just-mentioned beliefs are ultimately grounded in the full complexity of linguistic reality, including the realm that is hidden from the naked eye. The task of an epistemology is to ensure that this grounding is done in accordance with respectable canons of intellectual inquiry. A conception of language which is not carefully coupled to linguistic reality has the fabric of fiction. It may well sound 'commonsensical', 'clever' or the like, but it fails in its fundamental function: informing us about the essence of something 'out there', a something called 'language'.

The third lesson, Buyer and Blue, is perhaps the most important of all. A conception of language on which language is made up of an ontologically opaque stuff fails in its foremost function. Accordingly, in characterizing this stuff, it does not pay to be cryptic. It won't do simply to say that language is behaviour, action, practice, habit or disposition, full stop. Rather, the nature of these stuffs has to be carefully characterized. And these stuffs have to be distinguished from one another in a non-arbitrary manner.

Let me illustrate the general point with the aid of a final example, the Firthian conception of language. Inspired by the anthropologist Bronislaw Malinowski, J. R. Firth and such followers of his as M. A. K. Halliday have also characterized language as something behavioural. Halliday (1973: 51), for example, has contended that 'If we regard language as social behaviour . . . this means that we are treating it as a form of behaviour potential. It is what the speaker can do.' Halliday goes on to equate 'behaviour potential' in the case of language with 'meaning potential'. Language, therefore, is 'what the speaker can mean'. And, Halliday (1973: 52–3) tries to explain, the Firthian notion of 'meaning potential' is not the same as the Chomskyan notion of 'linguistic competence':

> *A word or two should be said here about the relation of the concept of meaning potential to the Chomskyan notion of competence, even if only very briefly. The two are somewhat different. Meaning potential is defined not in terms of the mind but in terms of the culture; not as what the speaker knows, but as what he can do – in the special sense of what he can do linguistically (what he 'can mean', as we have expressed it). The distinction is important because 'can do' is of the same order of abstraction as 'does'; the two are related simply as potential to actualized potential, and can be used to illuminate each other. But 'knows' is distinct and clearly insulated from 'does'; the relation between the two is complex and oblique. . . .*

This sounds eminently reasonable to you, Dear Buyer? But do you have any idea of how 'potential' is supposed to differ from 'ability', 'skill', 'capacity', 'habit' or 'disposition'?[71] *And are you capable of locating 'potential' in the scheme of things, given that 'potential' exists neither in the mind nor in actual behaviour? Moreover, within what kind of ontology does it make sense, Dear Frowning Fellow, to lump 'potential' and 'actualized potential' together as being of 'the same order of abstraction'? Halliday has been rather less than forthcoming about these matters. So do we really know what sort of stuff 'potential' is supposed to be? Do we have any reason not to despatch 'potential' to the ontological limbo?*[72]

Lesson number four deals with a meta-matter, our conception of conceptions. This is a lesson – you will recall, Dear Buyer – which we learned when looking at the winding Wittgensteinian way of thinking about things. The lesson is all about being maximally clear, accurate and non-arbitrary when constructing a conception of something. To deride the pursuit of essential properties as 'naive', to denounce the search for necessary and sufficient conditions as 'vulgar', is a way of taking evasive action. To do this, Buyer and Blue, amounts to relinquishing the responsibility of being as clear, accurate and non-arbitrary as one can about what something really is. To those wary of waffle, conceptions, accordingly, are about essences.

Suppose, counterfactually I guess, we were all to agree with Noam Chomsky (1975a: 40) that behaviourism is 'a dead end, if not an intellectual scandal'. Where then would we turn for a conception of language which even this most consummate of Conception Cooks would consider kosher? The time, Dear Buyer and Blue, is ripe for inspecting the conception held by this Master Metaphysician himself.

3

Selling Language as Soul

3.0 Magnifying mind

You can't make sense of what you think you hear? A muffled mixture of intoning and droning, chanting and canting, praying and a weird kind of braying. Would I care to comment on why sacramental sounds are to be heard in, of all places, a market. Well, if I may remind you, Baffled Buyer, this is not your ordinary kind of market. Here, after all, metaphysics makes up the merchandise. What is more, as I have hoped you would observe for yourself, we have been travelling further up along its Abstractness Axis. Our ascent, then, has brought us to the sector in which language is offered for sale as part of a soul of sorts. And what you are hearing, improbable as it may sound, is an ontological liturgy variously given voice by Cardinal Conceptioneers in chapel-like kiosks. (In this town, steep(l)ed as it is in transcendental tradition, even markets are expected to sport spires!) Although they differ in many dimensions of their creeds – which range from done-up dualism to matured monism – the basic message common to these Fellows of the Frock rings out clearly: the Miracle of Mind is just the right medicine for allaying the Angst induced by the question 'What is language in essence?'

In the inner circle, sitting at the feet of the Makers of Mind, are the middle men, the Mentalist Missionaries, eager to go out and spread the word that there is money in Mind. That is, for those who are willing to join the flock by investing in intentionality, functionalism, emergentism, biologism, quantum gravity or some other up-market form of mentalism. Listening on the fringes, there are Lay Linguists and assorted other Secular Shoppers who, despite their agnostic ancestry, have not been able to bring themselves to fall for physicalism or to buy behaviourism. Having been driven up the Abstractness Axis too, they are ready to listen to the lessons of Liturgical Linguistics, to consider the message that language, in essence, is embodied in a state, structure or module of Mind.

By all means, Dear Blue, do feel free to slip in your 'small question'. Why from the Critical Customer's point of view the idea that language is something mental should not be rejected out of hand as an Ontological Opiate ruinous to the user's rationality? The answer, of course, depends on what 'mental' is supposed to mean. As for its meanings, listed on The Market there are many, from A(vram's) to Z(arathustra's). We obviously have to restrict ourselves to a couple of the more sophisticated senses that seem to have a future beyond the confines of Folk Philosophy and Faculty Fiction.

To begin with, we will attend the exegetic exercises conducted by a Mentalist in the Mosaic Mould, the one who led his people to liberty out of Behaviourist Bondage and Empiricist Enslavement, into which they had been enticed by Philosophers of the Flesh(pots). In addition to being Leader and Liberator, he is Legislator too: in his teachings, you will come to see, he regularly refers to tables brought down from Mount Meta a couple of millenia ago. Having listened to the Mosaic Monologues, we will proceed to look at the roots of the religion, the sectarianism it has spawned, the updating of its dogma and the holy war it has unleashed.

The trick, of course, will be to see where the Mentalist Message is essentially empty, delicately deceptive, deeply divine or dangerously deluded. It is just possible, Unbelieving Blue, that you and other Disrespectful Detractors will be amazed to see what mentalism amounts to without its mask of mystery. So, I urge you to practise perseverance as you prepare yourself to receive the revelations that our Modern Moses is about to make.

3.1 Generating the gospel

Both language in general and individual languages are mental entities. This is the core of the conception of language that has been developed by Noam Chomsky. For close on thirty years this Chomskyan conception of language has been the topic of vigorous debate by all sorts of scholars interested in the question 'What is language in essence?' In the eyes of some linguists, the Chomskyan conception of language has even achieved the status of 'the current orthodoxy in linguistics'.[1] Yet this conception of language has been understood less than well, even by leading scholars. It is therefore of considerable importance to go in some detail into questions such as the following: In what sense is (a) language a mental entity to Chomsky? Why does he portray (a) language as mental? What are the (alleged) shortcomings and merits of the Chomskyan conception of language? As a run-up to considering these questions, let us briefly consider two classes of conceptions of language that Chomsky has rejected.

3.1.1 Crusading against commonsensicality

Chomsky (1986: 15ff.; 1988a: 37) has recently drawn a distinction between 'the intuitive, pretheoretic common-sense notion of language' and various 'technical concepts that have been proposed with the intent of developing an eventual science of language'.[2] On Chomsky's account, the common-sense notion departs in several ways from the technical ones. First, the common-sense notion of language has 'a crucial sociopolitical dimension'. Thus, Chomsky observes, Chinese is spoken of as 'a language' despite the fact that the various 'Chinese dialects' are as diverse as the various Romance languages. The sociopolitical dimension of the common-sense notion of language is expressed by the well-known witticism that a language is a dialect with an army and a navy.[3] Chomsky, however, is doubtful that any coherent accout of language can be given in such sociopolitical terms. Rather, he (1986: 15) remarks: 'all scientific approaches have simply abandoned these elements of what is called "language" in common usage.' Chomsky (1988a: 37), thus, does not consider language a social phenomenon, if 'social' is to have the common-sense meaning of ordinary usage. He also considers it objectionable to say that language, as some kind of social phenomenon, is 'a shared property of a community'. This is so because, on his view, in ordinary usage there is no clear answer to the question 'What kind of community?'. In chapter 5 we will return to various social conceptions of language and to Chomsky's criticisms of them.

Secondly, Chomsky (1986: 16) notes that the common-sense notion of language has 'a normative-teleological element' which has also been eliminated from 'scientific approaches'. This normative-teleological element is not to be identified with the judgements of prescriptive grammar. Rather, the 'normative-teleological' element is present in judgements of the progress made by a foreigner or child learning English. Chomsky (1986: 16) observes that

> We have no way of referring directly to what that person knows: It is not English, nor is it some other language that resembles English. We do not, for example, say that the person has a perfect knowledge of some language L, similar to English but still different from it. What we say is that the child or foreigner has a 'partial knowledge of English,' or is 'on his or her way' toward acquiring knowledge of English, and if they reach the goal, they will then know English.

Again, Chomsky doubts whether it is possible to give a coherent account of this aspect of the common-sense notion of language. He (1988a: 37) stresses that serious inquiry into language requires conceptual precision. This entails that linguists have to refine or replace the concepts of ordinary usage, just as physicists assign a technical meaning to such terms as 'energy', 'force' and 'work' that departs from the imprecise and rather obscure meaning of ordinary usage.

So, Dear Buyer, should you wish to progress from Lay Linguist to Ordained Ontologist, there are lessons in liturgical locution to be learned. Couching conceptions in mere Common Cant can, indeed, create confusion. You too, Ordinary-language Blue, would have to learn to speak in Technical Tongues. Otherwise,, the Missionaries of the Mosaic Movement may not bother to bring you in from the Outer Ontological Darkness. And, unfortunately, Beseeching Buyer, it is strictly forbidden to keep your own common-sense conception of language, simply supplementing it with a technical one. Such Doctrinal Duplicity, the Linguist-Legislator will insist, is absolutely forbidden by the first of The n Commandments for Conceptioneers which I will now recite for the sake of all Sinful Shoppers:

The First Commandment for Conceptioneers
Thou shalt have no other conception(s) before me.

So, you will have to curb the commonsensicality that you have so carefully cultivated, my Dear Blasé Blue. And come to grips with the Mosaic Moral that the conceptioneer's Path to Pandemonium is paved with Homey Heresies and Folksy Facts. Incidentally, the First Commandment outlaws Ecclesiastic Eclecticism too, as an -ism perversive of the Product – a point to which we will return.

3.1.2 Exorcising externality

Let us consider next a major class of 'technical' conceptions of language that has been rejected as fundamentally flawed by Chomsky (1986: 19–21). In terms of these conceptions, language is something external to the mind/brain. These conceptions portray language as what Chomsky (1986: 20) calls 'externalized language' or 'E-language', a 'construct' that is 'understood independently of the properties of the mind/brain'.

If (an) E-language is not associated with a speaker-listener's mind/brain, what is it then? It has been viewed in descriptive linguistics and behavioural psychology and so on, Chomsky (1986: 19) says, as 'a collection of actions, or utterances, or linguistic forms (words, sentences) paired with meanings, or as a system of linguistic forms or events.' Thus, in Saussure's structuralism, a language was taken to be a system of signs, specifically a system of sounds and an associated system of concepts. Bloomfield and his followers had a concept of E-language too, considering a language to be the totality of utterances that can be made in a speech community.[4] And, more recently, David Lewis (1975) defined a language as a pairing of sentences and meanings over an infinite range. To give one more example, under the E-language 'rubric', Chomsky (1986: 20) includes the notion of a language as a collection (or system) of actions or behaviours of some sort.

From the point of view of E-language, Chomsky (1986: 20) notes, a grammar is a collection of descriptive statements concerning an E-language. Technically, a grammar may be regarded as a function that enumerates the elements – sentences, speech-events and so on – that jointly make up the E-language. And a linguist is free to select any such grammar as long as it correctly identifies the E-language, a point to which we will return below. Universal grammar (UG) is, in the E-language perspective, a theory that makes statements that are true of many or all human languages. As observed by Chomsky (1986: 20), some linguists held these statements to express a set of conditions to be satisfied by the E-languages that count as human languages. Other linguists – Chomsky mentions Martin Joos, William Dwight Whitney, and Edward Sapir as examples – appeared to deny that an enterprise such as universal grammar was possible. Joos (1957, preface), for example, maintained that 'languages could differ from each other without limit and in unpredictable ways.' This, in essence, is to say that there are no linguistic universals.

Chomsky has dealt in some detail with what he judges to be flaws in the concept of E-language.[5] At the basis of this judgement, lies Chomsky's contention that the technical concept of E-language is in a dual sense too far removed from reality. As for the first, Chomsky (1986: 26–8) argues that E-language is too far removed from the psychological, ultimately biological, mechanisms involved in the acquisition and use of language. He (1986: 26) maintains that 'languages in this [E-language] sense are not real-world objects but are artificial, somewhat arbitrary and perhaps not very interesting constructs.' What is more, Chomsky (1986: 30–31) claims, an E-language is not 'given'. What is given to the child is some finite array of data on the basis of which the child's mind constructs a mental grammar, or an I-language, as will become clear in section 3.1.3 below. For reasons such as those mentioned above, Chomsky (1986: 31) consequently considers E-language to be 'derivative', relatively 'remote from data and mechanisms'. Thus to him (1986: 25) 'the object of study in most of traditional or structuralist grammar or behavioral psychology is . . . an epiphenomenon at best.'

The 'artificial' or 'epiphenomenal' character of E-language(s) has various consequences that are unattractive to Chomsky. On the one hand, because an E-language is an artifact, it can be characterized in various ways. Hence, Chomsky (1986: 26) contends that 'there is no issue of correctness with regard to E-languages.' Questions of truth and falsity, he (1986: 20) maintains, do not arise. And Chomsky (1986: 26) argues that ultimately 'We can define "E-language" in one way or another or not at all, since the concept appears to play no role in the theory of language.' On the other hand, Chomsky (1986: 25) claims, in terms of the notion of E-language, languages are ill-defined in having no determinate boundaries. In a more superficial sense, it is unclear in the case of many expressions or sentences – e.g. *Give it me* – whether they are contained by a particular E-language or not. That is, it is not clear which objects do and which do not belong to the set making up a particular E-language. In a deeper sense too, E-languages are vague or indeterminate. Chomsky (1987a: 33) argues this point by referring to so-called 'semi-grammatical sentences' such as *the child seems sleeping*. He asks whether this expression is in the language or outside it and contends that either answer is unacceptable. On his view, an English speaker interprets it instantaneously 'in a perfectly definite way' that is quite different from the way in which it would be interpreted by a monolingual speaker of Japanese. This leads Chomsky to conclude that the expression cannot simply be excluded from the set 'E-English', in spite of the fact that it is 'plainly not well-formed'. But, Chomsky claims, speakers of English and Japanese will also differ in how they interpret some sentence of Hindi. And, he (1987a: 33) proceeds: 'Therefore we conclude that all languages fall within English, a conclusion that makes no sense.' All of this makes the status of E-language quite obscure to Chomsky (1986: 25): 'the bounds of E-language can be set in one way or another, depending on some rather arbitrary decisions as to what it whould include.'

This brings us to the second respect in which Chomsky (1986: 27) considers the concept of E-language too far removed from what is real: it is not sufficiently close to the common-sense notion of language.[6] In support of this claim, Chomsky (1986: 27) observes that when people speak of a person knowing a language they do not mean that he or she knows an infinite set of sentences or sound-meaning pairs (taken in extension) or a set of behaviours or acts. Rather, they mean that the person knows 'what makes sound and meaning relate to one another in a specific way, what makes them "hang together"'.

In sum: Chomsky has two major criticisms of concepts of E-language: their 'artificial' character and their deviation from the common-sense concept of language.[7] He (1986: 28) judges the consideration involved in the first to be 'the clearer and more important'. It is not to be expected that the concepts that are appropriate for the description and understanding of the physical world will include 'the sometimes similar concepts of normal discourse'.[8]

What the Mosaic Mentalist teaches, then, is that to get to the essence of language one has to follow a rigorous routine of renouncing things that are not real. One has to lead a linguistic life of not exalting externality, a life in line with

> The Second Commandment for Conceptioneers
> *Thou shalt not make thyself a conceptual model of anything artificial.*
> *Thou shalt not bow thyself down to anything epiphenomenal.*
> *Thou shalt not serve sets or systems about which the truth cannot be told.*

I guess you are wondering where such an exacting exercise in abstinence will lead to, Bothered Blue. The Linguist-Leader's answer, as you will directly see, is: internal life.

3.1.3 Invoking internality

In terms of a second major class of 'technical' concepts, language, in essence, is 'internalized language' or 'I-language'. An I-language, Chomksy (1986: 22) states, is 'some element of the mind of the person who knows the language, acquired by the learner, and used by the speaker-hearer.' To study I-language is in Chomsky's (1986: 24) view to study 'the system of knowledge of language attained and internally represented in the mind/brain'.[9] To portray language as I-language, rather than E-language, involves a conceptual shift. This shift is characterized by Chomsky (1986: 24) as a 'shift in the focus of attention from actual or potential behavior and the products of behavior to the system of knowledge that underlies the use and understanding of language, and more deeply, to the innate endowment that makes it possible for humans to attain such knowledge.' The question, then, is: What is the nature of the knowledge and endowment referred to in these remarks by Chomsky? To answer this question, Chomsky ascribes certain properties to a particular human mental faculty, the so-called language faculty. Specifically, as a 'mental organ' or 'module' of mind, the language faculty has two states that are of special significance.[10] So let us consider what Chomsky has to say on the ontology of each of these states.

The first significant state of the language faculty is the initial state, which is taken by Chomsky to be 'genetically determined'.[11] That is, the initial state of this faculty incorporates the so-called genetic language programme, or genetically encoded linguistic principles, representing the child's innate linguistic endowment. The language faculty is in its initial state in a child that has not had any linguistic experience in the sense of having been exposed to utterances of or data about his/her language.[12]

The initial state of the language faculty is described by a U(niversal) G(rammar). This is a linguistic theory expressing a system of conditions that identify the I-languages that, on Chomsky's (1986: 23) formulation, are accessible to humans, given their biological endowment. From this point of view, Chomsky (1980a: 29) takes the subfield of universal grammar to be 'a study of the biologically necessary properties of human language'. These are the genetically determined properties that are, in Chomsky's (1980a: 28) words, 'characteristic of the human species'.

The basic statements of the theory of UG, also called 'linguistic universals', express claims about biologically necessary properties of human language.[13] Chomskyan linguistic universals, by implication, do not express claims about so-called logically or conceptually necessary properties that 'language as such' must have. Properties of language are, on Chomsky's (1980a: 28–9) formulation, logically or conceptually necessary if they are properties 'such that if a system failed to have them we would simply not call it a language.'[14]

The second significant state of the language faculty is an attained, stable state.[15] This state develops or grows out of the initial state under the 'triggering' and 'shaping' influence of the child's linguistic experience.[16] This development or growth has conventionally been called 'language learning' or 'language acquisition'. It is the attained, stable state of the language faculty that incorporates what Chomsky has characterized as 'knowledge of a language'.[17]

On Chomsky's (1980a) analysis, knowledge of language has various defining properties. It is, for example, unconscious knowledge;[18] it is neither grounded (or justified) nor *a priori* knowledge but, rather, caused knowledge;[19] it is distinct from a speaker-hearer's ability or capacity to use his/her language.[20] In the present ontological context, however, to Chomsky the central property of knowledge of language is that it exists as a mental state: to know a language is to be in a mental state. The obvious question is 'What kind of mental state?' Chomsky's early (1980a: 44ff.) reply was: 'I assume . . . that to be in such a mental state is to have a certain mental structure consisting of a system of rules and principles that generate and relate mental representations of various types.' As a result of a second conceptual shift, Chomsky (1986: 146, 150–1) has recently changed his characterization of knowledge of language (or, rather, grammar). He does not think of knowledge of language as a rule system anymore, but rather as a system of principles with fixed parameters. Thus, Chomsky (1985: 150–1) states:

> The language that we then know is a system of principles with parameters fixed, along with a periphery of marked exceptions. What we know is not a rule system in the conventional sense. In fact, it might be that the notion of rule in this sense, like the notion of E-language (so it seems), has no status in linguistic theory. One can formulate algorithms that project rule systems from a choice of values for the parameters of UG, but it is not obvious that this is a significant move or that it matters how it is done.[21]

A theory of the attained, stable state of the language faculty is called a '(particular) grammar'. Chomsky (1986: 23) considers the statements expressed by a grammar to be 'statements of the theory of mind about the I-language, hence statements about the structures of the brain formulated at a certain level of abstraction from mechanisms.' The mechanisms referred to in these remarks are physical mechanisms underlying the use and acquisition of the language. And the structures of the brain mentioned by Chomsky are 'specific things in the world, with their specific properties'.[22] Because Chomsky (1986: 26–7) considers states and structures of the mind/brain to be 'real and definite', the statements made by a grammar about these are either true or false. This applies to the statements of both a particular and a universal grammar.

In sum: in terms of Chomsky's concept of I-language, an individual I-language is something in the speaker's mind/brain. On a more recent formulation of Chomsky's (1988a: 36), this something is a cognitive system represented in the mind/brain of a particular individual. Ontologically, therefore, Chomsky (1986: 18) locates a language within the framework of individual psychology. He (1988a: 36) uses the term 'language' to refer to an individual phenomenon. In terms of Chomsky's concept of I-language, what is universal in language is something in the biological make-up of the human species, specifically the genetically determined aspect of the human mind/brain. As for the shift in perspective from the technical concept E-language to the technical concept I-language, Chomsky (1986: 28) sums it up as a shift towards realism in two respects: 'toward the study of a real object rather than an artificial construct, and toward the study of what we really mean by "a language" or "knowledge of language" in informal usage (again, abstracting from sociopolitical and normative-teleological factors)'.

So: to reach the Conceptioneer's Canaan, where the essence of language is said to be crystal clear, one has to travel the Road of Realism. Or so the Linguist-Liberator teaches. And while pursuing the pillar of Functionalist Fire, Dear Buyer, one will be sustained by Mentalistic Manna and Realist Refreshments from a rock. As for the route from externality to internality, with its detours through stretches of desert dogma, our Moses of Mass is said to know it from personal experience. It has been alleged[23] *that he himself once proceeded from a concept of E-language: 'From now on I will consider a language to be a set (finite or infinite) of sentences, each finite in length and constructed out of a finite set of elements' (Chomsky 1957: 13).*

The following remarks too may be construed as evidencing a further case in which the Mosaic Mentalist was seemingly seduced by se(c)tarianism: 'For our own purpose we can think of a language as a set of structural description of sentences, where a full structural description determines (in particular) the sound and meaning of a linguistic expression' (Chomsky 1977: 81).[24] *(By the way, Dear Buyer, could you think of any worthy 'purpose' that would be served by thinking of language as an artifact, an epiphenomenon?) The Mosaic Mentalist, however, firmly rejected allegations that, even in moments of youthful abandon, he on occasion served the Conceptual Calf called 'externality', as we will come to see in section 3.5.2 below.*

You are wondering, Bemused Blue, why it is of such importance to deny all entanglement with externality, even liaisons of long ago. The answer, I suggest, may be quite simple. How could anyone making much (out) of Mind on The Market, let alone a mentalist in the Mosaic Mould, confess to having broken:

> The Seventh Commandment for Conceptioneers
> *Thou shalt not, adulterously, deal in any dogma devoid of Mind.*

Incidentally, Dear Buyer, the shift from a concept of E-language to a concept of I-language is an example of what may be characterized as a Conceptions Conversion; Bloomfield's reverting from Wundtian mentalism to Weissian materialism being another example. Given the fervour of the convert, this could explain the harshness of the Linguist-Legislator's judgement of Latter-day Platonists who, as a result of a Counter-Conversion, have been singing the praises of a conception of language that is essentially externalist. But more about this in chapter 4.

3.1.4 Anointing an abstraction

Over the years Chomsky has taken considerable care to say clearly what he takes knowledge of (a) language to be. But in so doing, has he also said clearly what he takes language to be? More fundamentally, does Chomsky draw a distinction between a speaker-hearer's knowledge of (a) language and the language known by the speaker-hearer? Or is this a spurious distinction within Chomsky's thinking? It is to questions such as these that we next turn.

In Chomsky's recent writings, various formulations may be found in which he seems to identify both (the) I-langauage and '(the) language' with (a system of) knowledge of language. Consider three typical cases:

> *The system of knowledge attained – the I-language* – assigns a status to every relevant physical event, say every sound wave. (Chomsky 1986: 26, emphasis added)

> *language seems to be best understood as a cognitive system, a system of knowledge* represented in the mind. . . . (Chomsky 1987a: 17, emphasis added)

> *The language now constitutes one of the many systems of knowledge* that the person has come to acquire, one of the person's cognitive systems. (Chomsky 1988a: 36, emphasis added)[25]

Other formulations, however, seem to suggest that Chomsky does draw a distinction between 'language' and knowledge of language or the mental representation of such knowledge. As a case in point, consider the following: 'During the past 5–6 years, these efforts have converged in a somewhat unexpected way, yielding a rather different conception of *the nature of language and its mental representation*' (Chomsky 1986: 5, emphasis added). The emphasized part of this quotation seems to indicate that Chomsky does not consider 'language' and its mental representation to be identical.[26]

So, if '(a) language' is distinct from knowledge about it, what then is '(a) language' to Chomsky? The answer, it seems, is this: an abstraction from a mental state or from I-language. Thus consider the following remarks by Chomsky:

> Suppose we analyze the notion 'H knows language L' in relational terms, that is, as involving a relation R (knowing, having, or whatever) holding between H and *an abstract entity L.* (Chomsky 1986: 22, emphasis added)

> Taking knowledge of language to be a cognitive state, we might construe the 'language' as an *abstract object*, the 'object of knowledge,' an *abstract system* of rules and principles (or whatever turns out to be correct) that is an image of the generative procedure, the I-language, represented in the mind and ultimately in the brain in now-unknown 'more elementary' mechanisms. Since

> the language in this sense is completely determined by the I-language, though *abstracted* from it, it is not entirely clear that this further step is motivated, but perhaps it is. (Chomsky 1988b: 21, emphasis added)

The mind, as conceived of by Chomsky, is of course itself abstracted from something else, namely the brain (a point that will be pursued further in section 3.1.5 below). Moreover, (the) I-language is an abstraction as well:

> It is natural to take L to be I-language, Jespersen's notion of 'structure', regarding this as *an entity abstracted from a state of the language faculty*, the latter being one component of the mind. (Chomsky 1986: 23, emphasis added)

> The *I-language is abstracted* directly as a component of the state attained. (Chomsky 1986: 26, emphasis added)

This means that '(a) language' is an abstraction from an abstraction. But what is the nature of an entity that has been abstracted from an abstracted mental state or I-language? Of what kind of stuff is the second abstracted entity supposed to consist? Is it still a mental entity, perhaps 'more abstract' only? Note in this connection that, by abstracting mind from the brain, Chomsky moved from one ontological level, the material, to another one, the mental. Does one also get such a shift when '(a) language' is abstracted from (a state of) the mind? And what aspects of the mental state from which '(a) language' is abstracted are 'suppressed' by means of such further abstraction? What is to be gained by doing this? Questions such as these are not dealt with explicitly by Chomsky, except when he (1988d: 21) remarks that 'Since the language in this sense is completely determined by the I-language, though abstracted from it, it is not entirely clear that this further step is motivated, but perhaps it is.' But this remark is hardly more than an expression of puzzlement.

Chomsky's answer to one question, though given obliquely only, seems clear, however, This question can be framed in various ways: Is it possible to say anything of substance about '(an) abstracted language' that cannot be said about the state of the mind from which it has been abstracted? Are there any facts about or principles of the former that do not hold of the latter? The indirect answer to these questions lies in the fact that Chomsky does not appear to say anything of substance, either at the level of facts or at the level of principles, that applies to '(an) abstracted language' but not to the mental state from which it has been abstracted. And Chomsky does not provide for a novel kind of theory – new in addition to particular and universal grammars – that would express claims about '(an) abstracted language' only.

Note, though, that by saying that '(a) language' is an abstraction, Chomsky does not mean that it is abstract in a Platonist sense. An object is abstract in a Platonist sense if it has no spatial, temporal or causal properties.[27] Chomsky (1986: 33), in fact, has explicitly rejected the idea that '(a) language' could be 'an abstract "Platonic" entity that exists apart from any mental structures'. Thus, he (1986: 33) has contended amongst other things that: 'There is no initial plausibility to the idea that apart from the truths of grammar concerning the I-language and the truths of UG concerning S_0 there is an additional domain of fact about P[latonic]-language, independent of any psychological states of individuals.' We will return to these views of Chomsky when examining the conception on which (a) language is a Platonic abstract object.[28] For now, it is sufficient to note that by calling '(a) language' an abstraction, Chomsky does not say that it is abstract in the sense of having no spatial, temporal or causal properties. As a matter of fact, Chomsky's calling '(a) language' an abstraction does not seem to contribute substantively to drawing an ontological distinction between '(a) language' and either knowledge of language or the mental state(s) in which such knowledge is embodied. So abstracted from knowledge of language or from the mental state in which it is embodied, '(a) language' is something terminological, something undefined in regard to substance. It is against this background that I will further use the expression 'the Chomskyan conception of language'.

So what's happened to the Promised Land where the essence of (a) language is supposed to be truly transparent? Is it perhaps no more than a mirage machinated by a Prodigious Prophet? Would it not have been better to have stayed behind in the Desert of Defunct Doctrine to dance around the Artifactual Calf? Would

I not say that even artificiality and epiphenomenality are to be preferred to mere terminological technicality? In accordance with which of the Commandments for Conceptioneers would the serving of sets be more sinful than the anointing of abstractions of a second degree?

Getting hot under the collar – or should I say 'cassock' – Belligerent Blue? But could you keep your cool for one moment more before buying into the 'epi' rather than the empty. The final revelation by the Mosaic Mentalist is upon us.

3.1.5 Beatifying the body

What we still have to do then is to take a closer look at Chomsky's notion of 'mind'. What does he take the mind to be? What, to him, is it that makes something 'mental'? How does he distinguish between the mind and the brain? The essence of Chomsky's (1987a: 1) answer to these questions is that 'Talk about mind is simply talk about the brain at some level of abstraction that we believe to be appropriate for understanding its essential properties.'[29] At the level of abstraction referred to above, Chomsky and others seek to identify what he (1987a: 2) calls 'cognitive systems': systems of knowledge, belief, understanding and interpretation. These systems are systems by virtue of functional and structural principles or, as Chomsky (1987a: 2) puts it: 'by virtue of the specific function that the system plays in the life of the organism, and by virtue of its specific principles, concepts, and structural properties, and the integration of its elements.'

The above-mentioned cognitive systems, principles and so on must, however, be realized in physical mechanisms of the brain. But talk about the mind is not talk about these physical mechanisms. That is, the claims about the mind and its (cognitive) systems and states abstract away from their physical bases. And such abstract characterization is proper even at a stage when the physical mechanisms are unknown. For Chomsky (1988b: 3) takes 'the abstract [i.e. mental] objects we construct [when characterizing the brain at the level of function and structure] to be real insofar as they enter into explanatory theories that provide insight and understanding'. He (1986: 38) considers it the task of the brain sciences to discover the mechanisms of the brain that are the physical realization of the mind, its systems and their states.[30] It is important to note, though that even if such physical mechanisms are discovered, Chomsky (1987a: 5–6) is 'unlikely to abandon the mentalistic level of inquiry and discourse'. To act thus would be to act in the same way as chemists who have not ceased to discuss 'abstractly construed' molecules, elements, the periodic table and so on.

To Chomsky, the mind is therefore something functional and structural. It has, on his view, no substance distinct from that of the brain. In this respect, Chomsky (1987a: 4) departs from the Cartesians, who posited a second substance, a *res cogitans*, which they called 'mind'. This second substance, or 'thinking substance', they took to be distinct from the body and separate from it. Chomsky (1980a: 105) is careful to point out that there is no further ontological import to his references to mind, mental representations and so on. He (1987a: 1) considers his 'mentalistic terminology [to bear] no dubious metaphysical burden'. He is not a dualist in the Cartesian or any other metaphysical sense.[31]

Chomsky (1987a: 3–5), in fact, considers it misleading to think of the so-called mind-body problem – the problem of relating the mind to the brain – as a philosophical problem, one that lies 'outside of the physical sciences'. He is even doubtful as to whether there is such a problem. Thus, Chomsky (1987a: 4) argues that this problem can be formulated coherently only to the extent that there is a fairly definite notion of body in the sense of 'physical entity'. Only if there were such a notion could one ask whether some phenomenon fell within its range. If there is no definite notion of 'body', then clearly no phenomenon can be claimed to be beyond the body's limits.

Chomsky (1987a: 5; 1989: 5) contends that there is no longer a definite concept of body. The Cartesians had one, a kind of contact mechanics 'restricted to the ways in which physical entities interact by pushing, pulling, colliding and so on'. But Chomsky argues, their notion or theory of body collapsed when Newton appealed to the principle of 'action at a distance' in order to account for such phenomena as the fall of bodies and the motions of the planets. Such action was due to a force that exceeded the limits of Cartesian contact mechanics. Indeed, initially, it was considered an 'occult force' or 'mysterious principle'.

The abandonment of the Cartesian theory of body has had profound consequences, in Chomsky's (1987a: 5) view:

> We no longer have a definite concept of body. Rather, the theory of body – or physics – now includes whatever concepts are necessary to account for events in the physical world: forces, massless particles, waves, strings in 10-dimensional space, or whatever. We can therefore no longer coherently ask whether some phenomenon falls outside the range of 'body'. We can only ask whether our current concepts of 'body' are adequate to account for this phenomenon;. . . .

Given these views, the mind-body problem cannot even be formulated in classical terms. And no new terms in which to formulate this problem coherently have to date, in Chomsky's opinion, been proposed.

The problem that Chomsky (1987a: 5) does see is rather different:

> it is the two-fold problem of investigating the phenomena of mind on the one hand, and seeking to relate them to the main body [sic] of the natural sciences on the other, by discovering the physical mechanisms that exhibit the properties and principles that we find in our inquiry into the mind. It may be that current physics suffices for this task, or it may be that it does not, as so often has been the case in the past.

Suppose that physics turns out to be incapable of accounting for the properties and principles of mind – that is, suppose that current concepts of 'body' are inadequate to account for mental phenomena. In this event, Chomsky (1987a: 5) contends, 'we must extend and modify our basic physics, much as Newton extended Cartesian mechanics to account for the motion of the heavenly bodies'.[32] The result would be a more adequate concept of body, not a new, metaphysical, concept of mind. Mind would remain something functional and structural without a distinct substance.

Suppose further that a given mental phenomenon stubbornly resisted explanation by means of subsumption under drastically extended notions of body. That is, suppose that scientists kept on failing to find a way to modify their 'basic physics' in order to account for this phenomenon. Even under such circumstances Chomsky would not be forced to introduce a new sort of mind, a mind of a substance distinct from that of the body. The reason for this is that Chomsky (1988c: 13) provides for the possibility that some of the questions that scientists can pose might 'lie beyond the scope of human intelligence'. Such questions he (1980a: 6) refers to as 'mysteries'.[33] Mysteries, in Chomsky's (1980a: 6) view, are questions that 'simply lie beyond the reach of our minds structured and organized as they are, either absolutely beyond those limits or at so far a remove from anything that we can comprehend with requisite facility that they will never be incorporated within explanatory theories intelligible to humans.' In support of the provision which he makes for the existence of mysteries, Chomsky (1988c: 13) cites Karl Popper's (1969) observation that it is 'clearly mistaken' to suppose that 'our quest for knowledge must succeed'.[34]

Consider now again the recalcitrant mental phenomenon mentioned above. Given the notion of a 'mystery', Chomsky need not regard this phenomenon as pointing to the existence of a substantive kind of mind, i.e. a mind distinct in substance from the body. He could maintain that this phenomenon simply reflects the existence of yet another mystery about the body.[35] Given this line of reasoning, it is not clear what, if anything, would compel Chomsky to give up the view that (a) language is something abstracted from ultimately the body.

Having forsaken the Fleshpots of Physicalism to follow The Linguist-Liberator to the Land of Milk and Mind, you now feel a deep sense of ontological disillusionment. The trek along the Abstract Axis has brought you somewhere that you fear to be ontologically neither here nor there. I can understand, Balked Buyer, that Beefless Body, despite its being beatified, is not exactly the Meaty Mind of the metaphysical kind that you expected to find. And that a language faculty of Fleshless Function could not cure the distress induced by the question 'What is language in essence?' All of which is rather ruinous to our ameliorative Mosaic Metaphor.

But, then, a metaphysical mind of dualist design cannot provide the right kind of cure for your Ontological Angst either. For (psychophysical) dualism, our On-Duty Ontological Oracle will pronounce, should be considered a Dodoesque Doctrine. And for saying so, he (Bunge 1980: 16–21) will rapidly recite ten reasons of which the first is that (psychophysical) dualism is fatally fuzzy in failing to give a precise characterization of the notion of a mind. Dualists, on his view, at best offer examples of mental states (e.g. a happy mood) or mental events (e.g. a perception). But they do not state what is in such states of and changes in the mind. Dualists, moreover, fail to elucidate the notion of 'correlation' that they use standardly in the expression 'mental states (or events) have neural correlates.' This brings our Master-at-Metaphysics to pronounce dualism a 'nonhypothesis'.

> *Because dualism in either of its main versions – parallelism and interactionism – is imprecise, it can hardly be put to empirical tests. It tells us that whatever we introspect or retrospect is mental, and whatever is mental has some 'neural correlate'. So, dualism labels instead of explaining, and remains always on the safe side of vagueness.*[36]

So, Dear Buyer, if you simply must take Mentalistic Medicine for relieving your pain, the most potent potion, I fear, is a Placebo plied in the Sacramental Section of The Market.

3.2 Founding the faith

What has brought Chomsky to portray language as something mental? What are the roots of Chomskyan mentalism? These are the questions to which we turn next. Here we will examine two main roots of Chomskyan mentalism: the Cartesian belief that language is a 'mirror' of 'the essence of human nature', and Chomsky's faith in 'the standard practice of the natural sciences'. A number of the secondary roots of the Chomskyan conception of language will be identified *en passant* in section 3.3 below.

3.2.1 Hallowing humanity

Chomsky (1987a: 6–7) notes that the study of language is central to two kinds of inquiry. On the one hand, it is central to traditional

Western philosophy and psychology, 'which have been concerned with understanding the essential nature of human beings'. In the context of contemporary scientific inquiry, on the other hand, it is central to certain endeavours which attempt to understand human nature 'in the light of what we now know or may hope to learn about organisms and about the brain'.

Chomsky (1987a: 7) furnishes various reasons why language has been and will continue to be of significance for the study of human nature. The first is that language appears to be a 'true species property'. That is, Chomsky considers language in its essentials to be unique to the human species and to be 'a common part of our shared biological endowment'. Secondly, Chomsky notes that language enters in a crucial way into thought, action and social relations. And, thirdly, he considers language 'relatively accessible to study'; in this regard, language differs markedly from other essentially human attributes such as 'problem solving' and 'artistic creativity'. And so Chomsky (1987a: 55; 1987b: 8), following the Cartesians, has come to view the study of language as a means of understanding 'the essential nature of human beings', 'language [being] a kind of "mirror of mind", reflecting the essential properties of mind'.

From this perspective, Chomsky (1987c: 11) considers the central problem of the theory of language to be that of explaining how people can speak and understand sentences that are new in their own experience or in the history of the language. Chomsky views this phenomenon not as exotic, but rather as the norm in the ordinary use of language. It represents to Chomsky (1987c: 11) 'the creative aspect of language use':

> the commonplace but often neglected fact that the normal use of language is unbounded in scope, free from identifiable stimulus control, coherent and appropriate to situations that evoke but do not cause it (a crucial distinction), arousing in listeners thoughts that they too might express in the same or similar ways.

The question then is how the unbounded scope of the normal use of language, its freedom from stimulus control, and its coherence and appropriateness to situations can be accounted for. Not, Chomsky has argued, by considering language to be something external to the mind/brain: whether as something physical in a

Bloomfieldian sense (see section 1.2 above) or as something psychological in a behaviourist sense (see section 2.2 above). Over the years, Chomsky (1959: 56; 1972a: 11–12, 72; 1987a: 10; 1987b: 2ff.; 1988c: 11) has argued forcefully that the 'creative aspect of language use' cannot be accounted for within any behaviourist framework. That is, the unbounded scope of the normal use of language, its freedom from stimulus control and its appropriateness to situations cannot be understood by considering language to be a system of stimulus-response connections, a network of associations, a repertoire of behavioural items, a habit hierarchy, a system of dispositions to respond in a particular way under specifiable stimulus conditions, an ability or a skill (see sections 2.2.2 and 2.3.3 above). To account for the unbounded scope of the normal use of language and for its freedom from stimulus control, Chomsky (1959: 56) has contended, one must attribute to a person something abstract that he/she has internalized. To understand these phenomena, Chomsky (1972a: 4) has argued, linguists must isolate a cognitive system, a system of knowledge or, more technically, a system of linguistic competence. This system underlies behaviour, Chomsky believes, but is not realized in any direct or simple way in behaviour. Chomsky, in short, portrays language as something mental. If language is viewed in this way, its study can provide a means of understanding 'the essential nature of human beings'.[37] It is therefore from a concern with the latter pursuit that Chomsky's mentalist conception of language ultimately springs.

That language is 'a mirror of mind' and, as such, reflects the essential properties of mind is considered by Chomsky (1987a: 55) to be 'a traditional idea'. Central to the thinking of the Cartesians in particular, it was 'enriched' in the course of the eighteenth and nineteenth centuries. During the first half of the twentieth century, however, linguists and psychologists on the whole were not seriously concerned with understanding 'the essential nature of human beings'. And, as noted by Chomsky (1987c: 12), the phenomenon of 'the creative aspect of language use' was not seriously addressed by these scholars until the mid-1950s. Their lack of concern with these matters, Chomsky (1987c: 12) contends, was due to the influence of the behaviourist conception of language as a system of habits, dispositions or abilities.

This state of affairs was changed by what Chomsky (1987a: 50, 54–5; 1987b: 2, 6–8; 1987c: 14; 1988b: 2) calls the 'cognitive revolution'. Getting underway in the mid-1950s, this revolution was concerned with the states of the mind/brain that entered into thought, planning, perception, learning and action. The mind/brain was considered an information processing system that formed abstract representations and that carried out computations in which they were used and modified. This approach, Chomsky (1987b: 2) observes, stands in sharp contrast to the behaviourist study of the shaping and control of behaviour. The latter study systematically avoided consideration of the states of the mind/brain that entered into behaviour. Rather, it sought – though unsuccessfully – to establish direct relations among stimulus situations, contingencies of reinforcement and behaviour. The barrenness of the behaviourist approach is caused, on Chomsky's (1987b: 2) diagnosis, by its refusal to consider 'the major and essential component of all behavior, namely the states of the mind/brain'.

The rise of generative grammar is looked upon by Chomsky (1987a: 55) as a major factor in the cognitive revolution. It 'resurrected' traditional ideas, particularly the Cartesian idea of language as a 'mirror of mind'. And it reaffirmed the importance of coming to grips with 'the creative aspect of language use' in attempting to understand the essence of language and mind. This led to an important conceptual shift: the shift from the conception of language as an externalized object to that of language as an internalized object.[38] Guided by the latter conception, the study of language has pursued three 'central questions':

1 What is/constitutes knowledge of language?
2 How is such knowledge acquired?
3 How is such knowledge used?[39]

To see what was involved in the cognitive revolution and in the first conceptual shift referred to above, it is instructive to compare the way in which behaviourists would have standardly answered these three questions and the way in which Chomskyan mentalists answered them prior to the second conceptual shift. Here are the respective answers as summarized by Chomsky (1987a: 64, 67; 1987b: 20, 24):

1 What is knowledge of language?
Behaviourist answer: 'it is a system of habits, dispositions, abilities.'
Mentalist answer: 'language is a computational system, a rule system of some sort. Knowledge of language is knowledge of this rule system.'

2 How is language acquired?
Behaviourist answer: 'by conditioning, training, habit formation, and "general learning mechanisms" such as induction'.
Mentalist answer: 'the initial state of the language faculty determines possible rules and modes of interaction. Language is acquired by a process of selection of a rule system of an appropriate sort on the basis of direct evidence. Experience yields an inventory of rules, through the language acquisition device of the language faculty.'

3 How is language used?
Behaviourist answer: 'language use is the exercise of an ability like any skill, say, bicycle-riding. New forms are produced or understood "by analogy" to old ones.'
Mentalist answer: 'the use of language is rule-governed behavior. Rules form mental representations, which enter into our speaking and understanding. A sentence is parsed and understood by a systematic search through the rule system of the language in question.'

As pointed out by Chomsky (1987a: 67; 1987b: 24), the first conceptual shift associated with generative grammar was a shift of focus away from behaviour and its products to the system of knowledge in the mind/brain that underlies behaviour. He considers this shift of focus 'extremely productive' in two senses: it not only led to a rapid increase in the range of empirical phenomena investigated; it also, on Chomsky's view, led to many new theoretical discoveries, including the construction of explanations for facts that had gone unnoticed before.[40]

Founding the Faith may seem, then, mainly a matter of digging up Descartes and dusting him down, Dear Buyer. In fact, however, this rooting ritual was carried out in a peculiarly post-hoccy way. In terms of Chomsky's (1987a: 55) own account, modern mentalism was conceived in the 'cognitive revolution' of the 1950s. And only later was it (re)rooted in the Cartesian Creed that language is a 'mirror of mind' reflecting the essence of man's Hallowed Humanity. Since we are dealing here with an exercise in excavation, however, let us not bury ourselves in dry-as-dust details of 'before' and 'after', Dear Pit-Side Spectator. If you really savour the idea of man's embodying a soul, albeit but a soul of sorts, then let Chomsky command your respect as, with the assistance of the Resurrected René, he continues to spearhead the Creativity Crusade against those Forces of the Flesh that would gladly downgrade ours to a Soulless Species, on a paltry par with key-pecking pigeons and maze-running rats. Disdaining to bow down before the Behaviourist Baal, he has been the one to expose the emptiness of the Externalist Effigy, stripping from the Mindless Man Model all semblance of reason and intellectual respectability.

3.2.2 Sanctifying science

The other main root of the Chomskyan conception of language as something mental is Chomsky's faith in 'normal scientific practice' or 'the standard practice of the natural sciences'. Properly pursued in the study of 'the creative aspect of language use', this practice may be relied upon to reveal the most adequate scientific conception of language.

Chomsky (1982: 14; 1987b: 1) believes that cognitive scientists should attempt 'to assimilate the study of language to the main body of the natural sciences'. Questions of mind/brain, including questions of language, he (1987b: 12) contends, should be approached 'in the spirit of the natural sciences'. This means, he (1988b: 3) maintains, that answers to the three fundamental questions – 'What constitutes knowledge of language?', 'How is such knowledge acquired?', and 'How is such knowledge put to use?' – should be integrated within the natural sciences. But adopting the approach of the natural sciences in the study of language is, to Chomsky, tantamount to adopting a mentalistic approach. Thus he contends that:

> A mentalistic approach to the study of behavior in terms of the cognitive systems that underlie it is not only in accord with normal

> scientific practice, but also a step towards assimilating the study of behavior into the main body of the natural sciences. (1987a: 6)
>
> . . . mentalism falls strictly within the standard practice of the natural sciences applied in this particular domain. (1987b: 1; cf. also 1987a: 50)
>
> Mentalism, in short, is just normal scientific practice, and an essential step towards integrating the study of the phenomena that concern us into the more 'fundamental' natural sciences. (1987c: 2)

What, then, in Chomsky's view is involved in following 'normal scientific practice' in the study of linguistic phenomena? Its goal, Chomsky (1987b: 1) assumes, is to formulate principles 'that enter into successful and insightful explanation of linguistic (and other) phenomena that are provided by observation and experiment'. The pursuit of such explanatory principles has both a negative and a positive side. Let us consider them in turn.

The negative side consists, as Chomsky (1987b: 1) puts it, in 'abandoning dogmas that are entirely foreign to the natural sciences and that have no place in rational inquiry'. To him, this means rejection of the dogmatic imposition of *a priori* limits on possible theory construction. Chomsky (1987b: 1; 1982: 14) singles out two such irrational limits, namely those of behaviourism and operationism. Loosely, the first of these limits outlaws theoretical concepts and principles whose empirical import cannot be specified with reference to behavioural data alone. The second limit disallows theoretical concepts and principles whose content cannot be linked to behavioural data by means of publicly observable operations or measuring procedures.[41]

On the positive side, as Chomsky (1986: 23; 1987b: 1–2) understands it, the pursuit of explanatory principles means that it is proper to formulate abstract concepts or 'notions'. Chomsky (1987b: 1–2) elucidates the nature of such 'abstract inquiry' with reference to nineteenth-century chemistry, 'which sought to explain phenomena in terms of such abstract notions as elements, the periodic table, valence, benzene rings, and so on – that is, in terms of abstract properties of then-unknown, perhaps still unknown mechanisms'. Such 'abstract inquiry' is viewed by Chomsky as 'an essential preliminary and guide for the subsequent inquiry into physical mechanisms'.

Chomsky (1987b: 2) considers the mentalistic study of language to be quite similar in approach and character to the 'abstract inquiry' into chemical elements. The statements of a grammar Chomsky (1986: 23) takes to be similar to the statements of a physical theory. Both the former and the latter characterize certain entities and their properties 'in abstraction from whatever may turn out to be the mechanisms that account for these properties. . .'. Statements about I-language, Chomsky (1986: 23) moreover contends, are true or false much in the same way that statements about the chemical structure of benzene or about the valence of oxygen are true or false.

The epistemological stance adopted by Chomsky (1989: 5) on truth and falsity is 'essentially the standpoint of the working scientist'. The latter standpoint, he notes, represents what Richard Popkin (1979) has called the 'constructive skepticism' of Gassendi and Mersenne in their reaction to the sceptical crisis of the sixteenth and seventeenth centuries. On Popkin's account, constructive scepticism recognized that 'the secrets of nature, of things-in-themselves, are forever hidden from us.' And it accepted that 'absolutely certain grounds could not be given for our knowledge.' But, it maintained, we do 'possess standards for evaluating the reliability and applicability of what we have found out about the world'.[42]

Procceding from these assumptions, mentalists, Chomsky (1989: 5) explains, 'will inquire into the cognitive faculties themselves, regarding them as just another part of the natural world that we hope to understand. . .'. Chomsky does not see in the 'lack of indubitable foundations' a sufficient reason for rejecting the 'working assumption' that there is an 'objective reality to be discovered', though, admittedly, a reality that can at best be grasped in part only.

What the 'standard practice of the natural sciences' or 'normal scientific practice' means to Chomsky is, in a nutshell, the following: Its goal is to formulate explanatory theories – theories whose principles give insight into phenomena. In pursuing such explanatory principles, one should not place *a priori* limits – for example, of a behaviourist or operationist kind – on theory construction; to do so would be mere dogmatism. Rather, one should feel free to postulate abstract properties: properties which are abstract in that they characterize the function and the structure of mechanisms that are still unknown at a physical level. And one should take a constructively sceptical stance on the truth of the claims made by such 'abstract inquiry'.

The foregoing in effect means to Chomsky that, in studying the linguistic phenomena considered in section 3.2.2, one cannot have an intellectually more respectable conception of language than that yielded by the pursuit of 'normal scientific practice'. That is, Chomsky's faith in this practice is a co-determinant of the mentalistic import of his conception of language.

Dear Buyer, I have to make what could be considered a 'confession'. (To symbolize his solidarity with the Sacramental Scene, a Conceptions Counsellor every so often has to engage in a spiritual speech act when doing his thing. So here it comes.) Just conceivably, in presenting to you Chomsky's ontology and its roots, I may occasionally have used in the italics mode some expression that conjured up the picture of a man full of faith, brimming with belief. But – and this is where perhaps I have misled you, unintentionally of course! – he has faith in things after a fashion only, as a memorable exchange between him (1987d: 48) and one James Peck reveals:

JP: *Do you have a deep faith in reason?*
NC: *I don't have faith in that or anything else.*

Even so, if you are hoping, Beliefless Blue, that NC will yet turn out to be a Fully Faithless Fellow like yourself, you hope in vain. To see why, consider the exchange immediately following the one just quoted:

JP: *Not even in reason?*
NC: *I wouldn't say 'faith'. I think . . . it's all we have. I don't have faith that the truth will prevail if it becomes known. But we have no alternative to proceeding on that assumption, whatever its credibility may be.*

So, perhaps one should rather say that NC is a man whose faith was fixed by default. And come to think of it, if the Speaking Species can make do with a soul of sorts, what on earth (or in heaven) is full-blown faith needed for, Bemused Buyer?

3.3 Reforming the religion

The mentalistic core of the Chomskyan conception of language, we have seen, is rooted in 'traditional ideas', specifically in certain 'enriched' Cartesian ideas. And, as will be explained below, other, ontologically somewhat more peripheral, components of this conception have antecedents in beliefs held by Plato and Humboldt. But neither the former ideas nor the latter beliefs figure in an unmodified form as 'building blocks' of the Chomskyan conception of language. So let us briefly consider some of the major ways in which the core and ancillary components of this conception of language differ from the ideas and beliefs to which they go back.

In terms of the ontological core of the Chomskyan conception of language, language is something mental, a faculty of mind. In this respect, the Chomskyan conception of language is essentially Cartesian. And there are important similarities between the Cartesian and the Chomskyan concept of mind. Let us consider these as they are seen by Chomsky.[43]

The first similarity concerns the way the mind 'works'. Thus Chomsky (1987b: 5) states that 'we must resort to a representational theory of mind of the Cartesian sort, including the concept of the mind as an information-processing system that computes, forms and modifies representations. . . .'[44] The second similarity between the Cartesian and Chomskyan concept of mind concerns the doctrine of innate ideas. As phrased by Chomsky (1987b: 5), 'we must adopt something like the Cartesian concept of innate ideas, biologically determined properties of the mind/brain that provide a framework for the construction of mental representations, a framework that enters into our perception and action.'[45]

As noted in section 3.1.5 above, however, there is also a fundamental difference between the Cartesian and Chomskyan conceptions of mind. This concerns substance: on the Cartesian conception, mind and body represent different substances. As observed by Chomsky (1982: 6), Descartes 'postulated two substances, body and mind, held them to be distinct, and raised various questions about the nature of their interaction'. Chomsky (1982: 6–7; 1987a: 28; 1988b: 12) considers this Cartesian distinction – and the dualism associated with it – to be 'rational' but 'untenable'. It was 'rational' in the sense that the Cartesians found phenomena – thought, consciousness, the use of language – that could not be accounted for in terms of the principles of their contact mechanics and sought to explain these phenomena in terms of extra-mechanical principles. Or, as Chomsky (1982: 7) succinctly puts it: 'The *principle of mind* was introduced to account for the limitations of mechanism – it was supposd to be a new creative principle standing alongside the mechanical principle – and a new kind of substance, mind, was needed as a basis for it.' But the Cartesian two-substance metaphysics has become 'untenable' because of the collapse of the concept of body that was construed in terms of a version of contact mechanics. As noted in section 3.1.5 above, Chomsky argues that this concept of 'body' was made to 'disappear' by the Newtonian revolution. And, he (1982: 9) goes on to contend, 'What replaced it [i.e. the Cartesian concept of "body"] was the concept of the *physical world* which simply incorporates *whatever we understand*.' This means to Chomsky that whatever things physicists 'devise' form part of the physical world or the concept of 'body' 'as long as they contribute to an intelligible picture of nature'. This is why he sees no need to postulate a distinct kind of substance for whatever is attributed to mind.

Let us next consider one of the ontologically ancillary components of the Chomskyan conception of language that also represents a modified version of a traditional idea, one with an antecedent in the thinking of Plato. As we saw in section 3.2.1 above, one of the fundamental questions addressed by Chomskyans is the question of how language is acquired. Chomsky (1987b: 11) considers this question to be a special case of 'Plato's problem': How do we come to have such rich and specific knowledge, or such intricate systems of belief and understanding, when the evidence available to us is so meagre?[46] This problem is discussed in the Platonic dialogues where Socrates sets out to show that a slave boy knows the truths of geometry despite the fact that he has had no instruction in geometry.

In similar vein, Chomsky (e.g. 1980a: 166; 1986: 6–8) has argued over the years that for many properties of the system representing a speaker's knowledge of his native language, there is no evidence in his childhood experience of the language.[47] Chomsky accordingly has framed the problem of language acquisition in a Platonic cast: How can children come to know their native language on the basis of severely limited experience or evidence about the language?[48]

But let us return to Plato's problem. Plato had an answer to it: anamnesis, that is the doctrine of reminiscence, recollection or remembrance. In terms of this doctrine, there are certain kinds of knowledge which are acquired neither on the basis of sensory experience nor by means of instruction. Rather, what happens is that these kinds of knowledge are recalled under certain circumstances as knowledge that we had in an earlier existence.[49]

Following Leibniz, Chomsky (1987b: 12) considers Plato's answer to be 'on the right track' but agrees that it has to be 'purged of the error of preexistence', as Leibniz puts it. Negatively, this purging entails a rejection of the belief that the 'immortal soul' is the mechanism by which knowledge is 'remembered' from an earlier existence. And, positively, on Chomsky's (1987b: 12) view, what this purging involves, in a modern idiom, is 'reconstructing Platonic "remembrance" in terms of the genetic endowment of human beings'.

Applied to the Chomskyan problem of language acquisition, this approach has led to the postulation of a language faculty that incorporates in its initial state a 'genetic language programme' or 'genetically encoded linguistic principles' which represent the child's innate linguistic endowment. Under the 'triggering' and 'shaping' influence of the child's linguistic experience, Chomsky contends, the initial state of the language 'grows' or 'matures' into a stable state which represents the mature speaker's knowledge of his language. In short, the genetic component of the Chomskyan conception of language represents a modernized version of the Platonic doctrine of anamnesis and of the Cartesian concept of innate ideas. In this context, a person 'remembers' something or 'knows' something 'innately' in the sense that he has inherited it genetically.

We turn, finally, to a component of the Chomskyan conception of language that represents, in a modified form, an idea attributed to Wilhelm von Humboldt. Chomsky (1988b: 5) observes that, at an intuitive level, 'a language is a particular way of expressing thought and understanding the thought expressed.' If this intuition is rephrased within the theory of mind developed in the cognitive revolution of the fifties, Chomsky (1988b: 5) contends, 'a language is a particular generative procedure that assigns to every possible expression a representation of its form and its meaning, insofar as these are determined by the language faculty. . .'.

But the view that language is a generative procedure, Chomsky (1988b: 4) notes, has an antecedent in Wilhelm von Humboldt's idea that 'language is a system that makes infinite use of finite means.'[50] Chomsky points out, however, that Humboldt was unable to give a 'clear account' of this 'correct idea', leaving it 'vague' and 'unformed'. And, consequently, he was unable to use this idea as the basis for research into language. Recent developments in modern logic and mathematics, though, have yielded conceptual tools that enable the infinite use of finite means to be studied 'with considerable clarity and understanding'. That is to say, as Chomsky (1987a: 16–17; 1987c: 13) explains, these developments have provided the formal means by which Humboldt's basic idea can be captured as a manifestation of 'properties of discrete infinity'.[51] Specifically, these developments have made it possible for Chomsky (1987b: 7) to propose that 'A generative grammar of a language . . . is a formal system that states explicitly what are these finite means available to the mind/brain, which can make infinite, unbounded use of these means.'[52]

From an ontological point of view, however, it is important to note that Humboldt did anticipate the distinction between E-language and I-language. Chomsky (1988b: 4) accordingly remarks that 'Crucially, Humboldt regarded language not as a set of constructed objects, say utterances or speech acts, but rather as a process of generation; language is *eine Erzeugung*, not *ein todtes Erzeugtes*.' Chomsky (1987b: 4) cautions, though, that it was not possible in Humboldt's day to distinguish performance clearly from linguistic competence in the sense of possession of knowledge. In Humboldt's work, specifically, there is no clear distinction between, on the one hand, the abstract generative procedure that assigns structural descriptions to all expressions and, on the other hand, the actual *Arbeit des Geistes* by means of which thought is expressed in linguistic performance. The development of the proper distinction had to await the early work on generative grammar.

The particulars we have been looking at, Dear Buyer, point to a deeper pattern: reform, revival, resurrection and the like are part and parcel of the life-cycle of real religions. After all, to create a New Rage Religion, the Mosaic Mentalist has practised certain

> Rites of Reform
> *Biologize (what was buried long, long ago as) baseless belief.*
> *Mathematize (what was misunderstood as) a murky message.*
> *Scientize (what has sent many to sleep as) a stale sermon.*

By using the rites of this recipe – the first for souping up substance, the second for freshening up form and the third for pepping up preaching – the Leading Liturgist has managed to come up with a make of mentalism fully in phase with functionalist market forces. Indeed, ideas interred as irredeemable, Dear Blue, he has ritefully reanimated within a contemporary conception of language for which even Militant Materialists seem content to clunk down hard cash on the counter.

3.4 Slumbering sectarianism

Chomsky, of course, is not the only contemporary scholar to portray language as something mental. A variety of linguists, psychologists, philosophers and other sorts of 'cognitive scientists' have held similar beliefs. But few have attempted to develop these beliefs into a full-blown conception of language, one that is well enough articulated and motivated to stand up to serious comparison with the Chomskyan conception in regard to content and relative merits.[53] Among the few exceptions, the most notable has been Jerry Fodor, dubbed 'The Complete Cognitivist' by Howard Gardner (1985: 81). Fodor, despite having been strongly influenced by the views of Chomsky, has a mentalist conception of language that differs in a specific way from the Chomskyan one. So, not only is Fodor's conception of language interesting in its own right, it also provides a contrastive perspective on the Chomskyan conception. It will therefore be worth our while to take a look at Fodor's conception of language.

Like the Chomskyan conception of language, Fodor's has Cartesian roots. Thus, Fodor (1981: 1) points out that his theory of mind 'looks a lot like . . . Descartes', blending, as it does, elements of mentalism and nativism'. Specifically, as also noted by Gardner (1985: 84), Fodor believes that mental states really exist, that they can interact with one another, and that they can be studied by means of the empirical methods of psychology, linguistics and other cognitive sciences. But, like Chomsky, Fodor does not believe that there are two substances, mind and matter. So Cartesian dualism forms part of the 'ontological baggage' that Fodor (1981: 1, 2) has 'thrown overboard', to use one of his own evocative phrases.

Fodor, moreover, holds a position on 'what linguistics is about' that has been articulated by Chomsky and (the earlier) Katz (1974). Calling this position 'the Right View', Fodor (1985a: 148–9) summarizes it as follows:

> (a) Linguistic theories are descriptions of grammars. (b) It is nomologically necessary that learning one's native language involves learning its grammar, so a theory of how grammars are learned is *de facto* a (partial [?]) theory of how languages are learned. (c) It is nomologically necessary that the grammar of a language is internally represented by speaker/hearers of that language; up to dialectical variants, the grammar of a language is what its speaker/hearers have in common by virtue of which they are speaker/hearers of the *same* language. (d) It is nomologically necessary that the internal representation of the grammar (or, equivalently for these purposes, the internally represented grammar) is causally implicated in communication exchange between speakers and hearers in so far as these exchanges are mediated by their use of the language that they share; talking and understanding the language normally involve exploiting the internally represented grammar. (n. 4 omitted)

Katz, incidentally, has come to reject 'the Right View' in favour of 'the Wrong View', as we will see below.

The basic tenets common to Chomsky's and Fodor's linguistic ontology instantiate, on Katz's analysis, the general ontological doctrine of conceptualism. According to conceptualism, universals are mental or mind-dependent. This means that, if there were no minds, there could be no universals, in the same way that there could be no thoughts, imagery or memories.[54] To be a conceptualist about language is, accordingly, to hold that there is no such thing as (a) language independent of speakers' psychological states (cf. Cummins and Harnish 1980: 18). Chomsky (1982: 14) himself has pointed out that the past quarter of a century has seen 'a shift to a representational theory of mind, and to a mentalist or *conceptualist* interpretation of the study of language' (emphasis added). But to date he has not spelled out in general ontological terms what he takes conceptualism, as opposed to realism and nominalism, to be.[55]

Now, returning to the main issue, how does Fodor's mentalist conception of language differ from the Chomskyan one? One of the more fundamental difference ties in with Fodor's (1983: 38ff.) functional taxonomy of cognitive mechanisms or systems (or psychological processes, as he also calls these). Within this taxonomy, Fodor draws a distinction between transducers, input systems and central processors (or systems). Informally, the function of transducers and input systems is to so represent the world as to make it accessible to thought. Transducers, Fodor (1983: 42) contends, specify the distribution of stimulations at the 'surfaces' (as it were) of the organism. In traditional terms, transducers are sense organs that translate physical energy into neural firing patterns but that do so without changing the information content of the translated physical energy. In a more contemporary idiom, transducers may be said to input proximal stimulus configurations and to output modality-specific representations. As input to transducers, these configurations are not (yet) computationally patterned; as output from transducers, these representations are in a symbolic format.[56]

Input systems (input analysers or interface systems) operate on the specifications that are the output from transducers. Specifically, input systems 'deliver representations that are most naturally interpreted as characterizing the arrangement of *things in the world*'. On the basis of this function, Fodor describes input systems as 'inference performing systems'. More technically, he (1983: 42) contends, 'the inferences at issue have as their "premises" transduced representations of proximal stimulus configurations, and as their "conclusions" representations of the character and distribution of distal objects.' Fodor (1983: 44ff.) considers perceptual systems to be instances of input systems. In the case of vision, for example, he (1983: 47) considers mechanisms for colour perception, for the analysis of shape and for the analysis of three-dimensional spatial relations to be typical input systems.

The mental representations 'inferred' by input systems serve as input to central processors or systems. The function of these central processors or systems, as characterized by Fodor, is to fix beliefs about what the world is like. More specifically, Fodor (1983: 104) assumes that

> the typical function of central systems is the fixation of belief (perceptual or otherwise) by non-demonstrative inference. Central systems look at what input systems deliver, and they look at what is in memory, and they use this information to constrain the computation of 'best hypotheses' about what the world is like.

Fodor (1983: 103) assumes that when people talk pretheoretically about such mental processes as thinking and problem solving, they have in mind the operation of such central systems. In addition, Carston (1988: 43) mentions fantasizing, daydreaming, and mental rehearsals of forthcoming interaction as 'less utilitarian' activities possibly carried out by central systems.

Returning to input systems, Fodor (1983: 47ff.) considers them to be modular. Mental modules, so goes Fodor's account, (more or less) share nine properties that are mutually relatively independent.

1 Input systems are domain-specific: each system specializes in processing input on a particular topic or in a particular domain (Fodor 1983: 47ff.; Dennett 1984: 286).
2 The operation of input systems is mandatory: a system automatically and involuntarily applies whenever it can apply (Fodor 1983: 52ff.).
3 There is only limited central access to the mental representations that input systems compute: 'inter-levels' of input representation are relatively inaccessible to consciousness (Fodor 1983: 55–60).

4 Input systems are fast: the activities carried out by input systems are among the fastest of our psychological processes (Fodor 1983: 61–4).
5 Input systems are informationally encapsulated: they do not have access to all the information that the organism internally represents (Fodor 1983: 64ff.).
6 Input analysers have shallow outputs: the information encoded by these outputs are highly constrained and typically are phenomenologically salient (Fodor 1983: 86–97).
7 Input systems are associated with fixed neural architecture: they are neurally 'hardwired' (Fodor 1983: 98–9).
8 Input systems exhibit characteristic and specific breakdown patterns: the pathologies of input systems are caused by 'insult' to specialized, 'hardwired', circuits (Fodor 1983: 99–100).
9 The ontogeny of input systems exhibits a characteristic pace and sequencing: a great deal of the developmental course of input systems is endogenously determined (Fodor 1983: 100–101).

Central systems or processes, by contrast, are non-modular. Fodor (1983: 101ff.) has argued that they are (relatively) global or domain-neutral, conscious, unencapsulated, slower, less automatic and lacking in fixed neural architecture.[57]

Where, then, does language fit into Fodor's taxonomy of cognitive systems? Language, in Fodor's (1983: 44, 47) view, like the perceptual systems, has the functional and other properties of input systems. Switching from 'language' to 'language mechanisms' (p. 44) and later to 'language processing mechanisms' (p. 48), Fodor (p. 44) contends to begin with that these mechanisms typically have the function of an input system. This involves more than the obvious point that utterances are themselves objects that have to be perceptually identified. More interesting, Fodor (1983: 44) maintains, is that 'Understanding a token sentence presumably involves assigning it a structural description, this being part and parcel of computing a token-to-type relation; and that is precisely the sort of function that we would expect an input system to perform.' Next Fodor (1983: 47ff.) argues that 'language'/'language processing mechanisms' has/have (most of) the non-functional properties of input systems as well, properties not shared by central cognitive systems. These are the above-mentioned nine properties that make a system modular. Accordingly, Fodor contends that 'language'/'language processing' is domain-specific, fast and mandatory, encapsulated or impenetrable to extralinguistic beliefs, generally inaccessible to the central systems, innately specified, fixed in regard to neural architecture, relatively fixed in regard to growth pattern across individuals, and patterned in regard to breakdown.

Fodor's portrayal of 'language'/'language (processing) mechanisms' as an input system has an antecedent in a view of psychological reality that he shares with Janet Fodor and Merrill Garrett. With respect to semantic representations, Fodor, et al. (1975: 515) express this view within the framework of the following condition: 'Semantic representations are psychologically real in the sense that, given appropriate idealizations, understanding a sentence requires the recovery of its semantic representation.' As noted by Katz (1981: 96–7), this means that semantic representations – as well as other levels of representation in grammars – have to figure in on-line computations in the comprehension of sentences.

Joan Bresnan (1978: 3) and other 'cognitive scientists' who work within the framework of lexical-functional grammar have adopted a related position on psychological reality.[58] The essence of this position is that a grammar cannot be considered psychologically real if there is no evidence that it can be successfully 'realized'. Thus, Bresnan states that

> we should be able to define for it [i.e. a realistic grammar] explicit realization mappings to psychological models of language use. These realizations should map distinct grammatical rules and units into distinct processing operations and informational units in such a way that different rule types of the grammar are associated with different processing functions.

If the grammatical distinctions of a grammar were not 'realized' in this way in a psychological model, Bresnan would not be willing to say that the grammar 'represent [s] the knowledge of the language user in any psychologically interesting sense'. Plainly, whatever such a grammar described, it would not be a language.

The idea that grammars are not psychologically real unless they characterize (operations in) the process of speech processing is not held only by scholars who work within the framework of lexical-functional grammar. As noted by Alexander George (1989a: 99), this idea is shared by, amongst others, Kintsch (1974) and Soames (1985). The idea in question, moreover, has various other versions. Thus George (1989a: 99) distinguishes two use-orientated positions on the 'psychological significance' of grammars that are weaker than Bresnan's. The first 'demands only that grammars be explicitly represented in some internal system of mental representation that is causally effective during language use.' The second 'does not require that the grammar be explicitly represented in order to be psychologically significant; it demands only that the information contained in the grammar be realized in a particular state that is causally influential in the operation of some processes responsible for the perception or production of speech.' George does not furnish examples of scholars holding the former position; he considers Peacocke's (1986, 1989) view of psychological significance to instantiate the latter position.[59]

This discussion of various positions on psychological reality/ significance is more than a mere digression. Certain scholars take language to be whatever is described by psychologically real/ significant grammars. Given the criteria for psychological reality/ significance considered above, such scholars would maintain that language is something in (volved in) a 'parser' and/or a 'producer'. That is, these scholars would have a conception of language related to Fodor's.

But let us return to the main question, namely: How does Fodor's mentalistic conception of language differ from Chomsky's? Chomsky (1988b: 15; 1989: 2) seems to understand Fodor as contending that 'the language', 'the grammar' or 'the language faculty' is a parser: 'It is sometimes argued that the language (or "grammar") should be *identified* with the parser, taken as an input system in something like Jerry Fodor's sense.' Chomsky, however, disagrees with such an identification. And he maintains that languages are not 'designed for parsability'. He (1988b: 15) observes that 'With only a slight air of paradox, we may say that languages, as such, are not usable. If some expressions are not parsable, as is often the case, they are simply not used, and the language is no worse for that.' Chomsky cites the well-known fact that so-called 'ungrammatical' or 'deviant' sentences are often 'quite readily parsable' and 'even perfectly intelligible'. In addition, such sentences may be quite properly used in appropriate circumstances. Chomsky's example is 'the knife cut the meat with a sword', uttered as referring to Mack the Knife.

Chomsky, accordingly, is not agreeable to *identifying* 'the language (faculty)' with 'the parser'. His (1989: 2) position is that there are input and output systems *associated with* the language faculty. He does not indicate, however, whether or not he takes these systems to have the properties assigned by Fodor to input systems. Nor does he indicate whether or not the language (faculty) is a central system in Fodor's terms. And, to my knowledge, Chomsky has not indicated in general terms whether or not Fodor's distinction between input systems and central systems provides a useful framework within which to clarify the nature of language as something mental.[60] But Chomsky has made it clear why he considers the conception of language as a parser to be flawed: this conception is incompatible with the existence of sentences that are ungrammatical but parsable. This means that Chomsky judges this conception of language to be empirically inadequate.

The way in which Fodor seems to arrive at the idea that 'language' is an input system is problematic from a general conceptual point of view as well. Recall that in his list of putative input systems Fodor (1983: 44) includes one he calls 'language'. But when he (1983: 44) begins to discuss the function of his putative input systems, he switches from 'language' to 'language mechanisms'. And when he comes to discuss the non-functional properties of these input systems, he (1983: 44) executes yet a further switch, using 'language processing mechanisms' in place of 'language mechanisms'. Unfortunately, he has not found it necessary to consider the ontological consequences of the arbitrarily executed double switch from 'language' to 'language mechanisms' and from there to 'language processing mechanisms'. Through these switches (on-line) language processing has been assigned, in what seems to be an essentially nonreasoned way, the status of the empirical locus of a particular conception of language.[61] And, in the process, the status of the fundamental distinction between linguistic competence/knowledge of language and performance has been obscured. In portraying language as an input system, Fodor does not make clear what has happened to what he (1985a: 149) has called elsewhere 'the internally represented grammar'.[62] This is particularly unfortunate, since both the idea that there is an internally represented grammar and the distinction between competence and performance form part of 'the Right View' of what linguistics is about. And, as we have seen above, Fodor has been a defender of this view.

Would I say that, by trafficking in the trinity of Transducer, Input System and Central Processor, Fodor turns himself into a False Functionalist Prophet? By no means, Dear Buyer. On my reading, such 'trafficking' amounts to little more than singing a slightly different spiritual song. Indeed, looked at from a dispassionate distance, the ontological differences between Fodor and Chomsky are seen to be of a slumbering sectarian sort, not representing any radical rift in the religion. And their conceptions of language have a great deal in common. Like the Chomskyan language faculty, Fodorian input systems are all in(side) the mind. In short, the conceptions of language of both Chomsky and Fodor are mentalistic to the core. Recall that, in more general ontological terms, Katz has contended that, moreover, both Chomsky and Fodor are sporting conceptualist caps. And, neither Chomsky nor Fodor holds a conception of language in terms of which language is a distinct entity: whereas Chomsky (apparently) identifies language with knowledge of language, Fodor (apparently) identifies it with mechanisms of language processing. And so Entrepreneurs in Exegesis, engaging in just a touch of exaggeration, have been able to claim that both Chomsky and Fodor hold a conception of language *that is essentially empty.*

Incidentally, while Chomsky and Fodor treat each other with tolerance in a spirit of believe and let believe, the way they deal with Rival Religionists is a different story. Consider, for instance, Fodor's (1983) chapter on 'Four Accounts of Mental Structure', on which Dennett (1984: 286) comments as follows:

> *The chapter is full of insights, but in the author's zeal to leave no view unbranded, it gives off the weird incense of religious war: The True Faith of the Neocartesian is enunciated at length, the*

> *Four-Point Creed of the Associationist ('of either the classical mentalist or more recent learning-theoretic' persuasion) is formulated (on p. 27), and we are told, for instance, that 'environmentalist biases provide a main motivation for the computational associationist's constructivism' (p. 35). Those who have little faith in refutation-by-classification ('But that's just a variety of -ism!') will take this chapter's many lessons with a grain of salt.*

And, of course, there are many examples of the meting out of Chomskyan Chastisement to those who have dared to break one of the n *Commandments, as I will show you in a minute.*

But let us first recall an incident involving a Bunch of Bad Boys and a Batch of Biblical Bears. One day the Boys – who were very bad indeed and, I suppose, a little bored into the bargain – were overcome by a desire to poke fun at an elderly gentleman, none other than a famous prophet. And prophets, as everyone knows, have access to rather special systems of censure for dealing with abusive attention. So the Profaned Prophet faced the woods and summoned the Bears – that were very Biblical indeed and, I suppose, a little bored into the bargain – to set upon the flippant little devils and teach them a lesson or two. (No fewer than 42 of them were that day torn to pieces.) Which goes to show that pulling a prophetic or patriarchal leg has always tended to be a high-risk business.

True enough, the bears that roam the Metaphysics Market are not feared for their jaws and claws. But the Market does harbour a species of Prophet Protectors who are no less deadly in the way they go for the joker's jugular. These are the Serious Scholars who take literally what was meant to be treated lightly, analysing it in a way that is warranted to wipe the wit out. So, Dear Buyer, should you feel an inclination to believe that Chomskyan ontology is on a par with religion, let me urge you to study Neil Smith's (1989: 198ff.) serious and censorious analysis of a humorous suggestion to similar effect.

3.5 Waging war over the word

For nearly three decades, the Chomskyan approach to the study of language has been the target of vigorous and diverse criticisms.[63]

Newmeyer (1986: 8), in fact, has assigned Chomsky the status of 'the most attacked linguist in history'. Of the criticisms involved, a significant number have been directed at the beliefs making up the Chomskyan mentalistic conception of language.[64] These criticisms are meant to reveal various kinds of vitiating flaws in the Chomskyan view that language and languages are mental entities or, more technically, certain states of the module of mind called the 'language faculty'.

For expository purposes, these criticisms may be viewed as belonging to three types. Criticisms of the first type, in essence, say that language is not something mental but rather something else: something behavioural (e.g. a system of habits, a set of dispositions etc.), something social (e.g. a practice, a set of conventions etc.), something abstract (e.g. a Platonic entity), something autonomous (e.g. a Popperian World Three object), and so on. These criticisms are essentially contrastive: their force depends on the merit of the alternatives with which the Chomskyan conception of language is being compared. This means that these criticisms have to be assessed in the context of a critical appraisal of the alternative conceptions of language involved in the comparison. This is done in an indirect way in chapters 1–5 of the present study. And a more direct comparative appraisal of the Chomskyan conception of language and the major alternatives to it will be presented in chapter 6.[65]

Criticisms of the second type are not intended to undermine the general idea that language is something mental. Rather, these criticisms question some specific ontological aspect of Chomskyan mentalism. For example, instances of this type of criticism question the existence of a separate language faculty or attack the way in which Chomsky characterizes the two significant states of this faculty. As a matter of fact, we considered an implicit criticism of this type above: Fodor's portrayal of language as a mental input system or parser. In section 3.5.1 below we will look at various explicit instances of criticisms of this type.

Criticisms of the third type form very much of a mixed bag. Indeed, what they have in common is little more than a 'negative' property: their main thrust differs from that of both of the other types. A scholar could criticize the Chomskyan conception of language for being internally incoherent, for example, without necessarily thereby denying that language is something mental or necessarily thereby claiming that Chomsky has been mistaken in his characterization of a specific aspect of (one of the states) of the language faculty. In section 3.5.2 below we will consider representative instances of the second type of criticisms of the Chomskyan conception of language.

Neither section 3.5.1 nor section 3.5.2 aims at giving an exhaustive survey of the types of criticisms being distinguished here. An attempt at exhaustive coverage would be misguided in any case: many criticisms of the Chomskyan conception of language are too obscure, uninformed, ill-directed or poorly argued to merit in-depth consideration.

3.5.1 Misprising the module

Central to the Chomskyan conception of language, as we saw in section 3.1.3 above, is the belief that people have a distinct language faculty, a mental 'organ' with two states of special significance. The first or initial state is said to incorporate the genetic language programme that represents the child's innate linguistic endowment. The second state, the attained or stable state, represents what Chomsky has characterized as '(unconscious) knowledge of a particular language'.

Let us then consider five of the classic criticisms of the language faculty or the specific states attributed to it by Chomsky. I first formulate these criticisms in a sort of 'archi' -form, and then show how they have been fleshed out by leading psychologists, philosophers or linguists.

1 The child's acquisition of his/her language can be accounted for by invoking general (ized) learning or ontogenetic mechanisms. Consequently, there is no need to assume the existence of a distinct language faculty that has an innate or genetically determined state.

This is the essence of a widely held objection to the Chomskyan conception of language. Let us consider three of the specific versions in which it has been put forward.

Putnam (1983: 295) has contended that 'our cognitive repertoire . . . *must* include *multipurpose* learning strategies, heuristics, and so forth.' And he (1983: 296) has remarked, moreover, that 'Once it is granted that such multipurpose learning strategies exist, the claim that they *cannot* account for language becomes highly dubious. . . .' The existence of such multipurpose learning strategies would clearly make it unnecessary to postulate a distinct language faculty with a state that is genetically equipped for language acquisition.

Responding to Putnam, Chomsky (1983: 320) has pointed out that Putnam has failed to give any hint of what 'the general mechanisms for learning' are. And Chomsky (1983: 320) continues:

> To invoke an unspecified 'general intelligence' or unspecified 'multipurpose learning strategies' is no more illuminating than his reference, at one point, to divine intervention. We have no way of knowing what, if anything, Putnam has assumed. The point is worth stressing, since it illustrates a common fallacy in discussions of this sort. The use of words such as 'general intelligence' does not constitute an empirical assumption unless these notions are somehow clarified.

This brings us to Piaget (1983: 31), who has contended that Chomsky's 'hypothesis of innateness is not mandatory'. This is to say that

> the 'innate fixed nucleus' would retain all its properties of a 'fixed nucleus' if it were not innate but constituted the 'necessary' result of the constructions of sensorimotor intelligence, which is prior to language and results from those joint organic and behavioral autoregulations that determine this epigenesis.

That is, Piaget claims that what can be explained on the assumption of genetically encoded principles or fixed innate structures can be equally well explained as the 'necessary' result of constructions of sensorimotor intelligence.

Chomsky (1983: 36) has rejected Piaget's criticism by pointing out that there are no substantive proposals involving 'constructions of sensorimotor intelligence' that offer any hope of accounting for the phenomena of language that demand explanation. And

Chomsky does not see any initial plausibility to Piaget's suggestion either. That is, on Chomsky's (1980a: 207) reading

> the literature contains no evidence or argument to support this remarkable factual claim [about the relative explanatory power of constructivism], nor even any explanation of what sense it might have. Again, we see here an instance of the unfortunate but rather common insistence on dogmatic and unsupported factual doctrines in the human sciences.

The 'phenomena of language' referred to by Chomsky above include those associated with the so-called poverty of the stimulus. In his (1980b: 42) view, the stimulus (or evidence) for language acquisition is impoverished in the sense that it contains no evidence at all for certain properties and principles of (the grammars of) the languages acquired by children.

An example, recently used by Chomsky (1986: 7–8), may serve to clarify further the notion of 'poverty of the stimulus'. Consider the manner in which (1) and (2) are interpreted:

I wonder who [the men expected to see them] (1)
[the men expected to see them] (2)

Although both (1) and (2) include the clause '[the men expected to see them]', the two instances of the pronoun *them* are interpreted quite differently. In (1), it may be interpreted as referring to the people denoted by the (antecedent) expression *the men*; in (2) it cannot be understood as referring to these people. (In (2) the referent of *them* is determined by what Chomsky calls 'the situational or discourse context'.) Chomsky claims that these facts about the interpretation of (1) and (2) 'are known without relevant experience to differentiate the cases' (1986: 8). In Chomsky's view, that is, the stimulus is impoverished in the sense that it contains no evidence for the principle – currently formulated within binding theory – which the child has to 'acquire' in order to be able to interpret (1) and (2) correctly. What Chomsky would require, then, is for Piaget to give an explanation of how children would be able to acquire this principle in terms of 'constructions of sensorimotor intelligence'. In the absence of such an explanation

Piaget's criticisms of the Chomskyan language faculty would lack the required power.[66]

Quine and many other scholars have expressed, in an empiricist spirit, the belief that language is acquired by means of one or more of such general mechanisms as conditioning, association, generalization, abstraction or induction. This empiricist approach holds, on Chomsky's (1965: 58–9) interpretation, that

> language is essentially an adventitious construct, taught by 'conditioning' (as would be maintained, for example, by Skinner or Quine) or by drill and explicit explanation (as was claimed by Wittgenstein), or built up by elementary 'data-processing' procedures (as modern linguistics typically maintains), but, in any event, relatively independent in its structure of any innate mental faculties.

The existence of general empiricist learning mechanisms such as those mentioned above would undermine Chomsky's grounds for postulating a distinct language faculty. Chomsky, however, has forcefully argued that empiricist approaches of language acquisition cannot account for the poverty of the stimulus. Like Putnam's 'multipurpose language strategies' approach and like Piaget's constructivist approach, that is, empiricist approaches cannot give an account of how children acquire abstract principles of language for which the stimulus contains no evidence at all.

2 The stimulus is not as poor as Chomskyans make it out to be. Consequently, there is no need to assume the existence of a language faculty with genetically encoded linguistic principles.

This criticism proceeds from the assumption that children acquire their language on the basis of the modified speech which mothers, fathers and caretakers use when talking to young children.[67] Referred to as 'motherese', 'caretaker speech' or 'baby talk', this speech is assumed, moreover, to be richer than the stimulus considered too impoverished by Chomskyans. If this were true – as believed, for example, by Cromer (1980: 16) – the grounds for assuming a genetically based language faculty would be less than compelling. Chomsky (1980b: 42), however, maintains that there is no evidence that the simplified data offered to children in the form of 'motherese' constitute the stimulus on the basis of which children actually acquire their language. And there is evidence, he claims, which shows that such simplified data or motherese could even make language harder for children to acquire and language acquisition more of a problem for linguists and psychologists to explain. By avoiding apparently complex constructions, motherese could impoverish the database for language acquisition even further. At the same time it would turn the acquisition of such constructions into a greater problem. In sum: the criticism under consideration is potentially powerful in regard to thrust, but it proceeds from factual assumptions that are too dubious.

3 Knowledge, by definition, cannot be innate. Consequently, the idea that there is a state of the language faculty that comprises innate knowledge of language has to be rejected. (Alternative formulation: So, the idea that some knowledge of language is innate has to be rejected.)

We have here the gist of a conceptual or philosophical criticism of Chomsky's epistemological characterization of the initial state of the language faculty. Chomsky (1980a: 95) observes that it is standardly argued that, for a belief to qualify as knowledge, it must be justified. That is, a person holding this belief must have good reasons for being certain that what is believed is in fact the case. Innate knowledge, obviously, fails this condition, as has been contended by Edgley (1970: 28ff.), for example.

Chomsky (1980a: 96–9; 1980b: 51), however, has rejected the idea that justification or grounding in reasons constitutes an appropriate basis for a condition for what have been considered paradigm cases of propositional knowledge. And he (1980b: 51) argues that, if this condition is accepted, 'then central cases of what have been called "knowledge" will be excluded'. He maintains that 'Knowledge comes in many varieties, and for crucial elements of our knowledge the traditional empiricist paradigm [requiring grounding in good reasons] seems to me inadequate.' Chomsky (1980a: 95ff.) discusses in some detail two cases of knowledge that cast serious doubt on the above-mentioned empiricist condition. The first is a child's (unlearned) knowledge that an object in parabolic motion passing behind a screen will emerge at a specific point. The second is the child's (unlearned) knowledge that a linguistic expression has a certain property, for example the correct interpretation of the expressions presented as (1) and (2) above. Such cases of unlearned, unjustified knowledge diminish on Chomsky's view the force of the standard argument against innate knowledge.[68]

4 Knowledge of language must, by definition, be conscious knowledge. Consequently, the belief that there is a state of the language faculty that comprises unconscious/tacit/implicit knowledge must be rejected. (Alternative formulation: So, the belief that knowledge of language may be unconscious/tacit/implicit must be rejected.)

This is a standard objection to Chomsky's epistemologically phrased characterization of the attained, stable state of the language faculty. Recall that in Chomsky's view (1980a: 69) the speaker also knows the rules of the mental grammar of his language, the principles governing the operation of the rules, and the 'innate schematism' of the language. But, he contends, the speaker cannot become aware by introspection of what he knows specifically of these rules, principles and 'innate schematism'. These are 'inaccessible to consciousness'. Conscious knowledge, by contrast, is accessible, non-implicit knowledge.

To avoid terminological confusion, Chomsky (1980a: 70) introduced the term 'cognizing' to refer to tacit knowledge, reserving the term 'knowing' for conscious knowledge; 'Thus, "cognizing" is tacit or implicit knowledge . . . [and] . . . has the structure and character of knowledge, but may be and in the interesting cases is inaccessible to consciousness.' Cognizing, thus, appears to Chomsky (1986: 269) 'to have all the properties of knowledge in the ordinary sense of the term, apart, perhaps, from accessibility to consciousness'. And he would like to say that 'cognization' is 'unconscious or tacit or implicit knowledge'.

Returning to the criticism stated as (4) above: it has been contended by various scholars that one cannot attribute knowledge – specifically if it is to be embodied in a system of rules – to a person unless this knowledge is accessible to consciousness. Searle (1976), for example, has claimed that 'It is a general characteristic of attributions of unconscious mental states that the attribution presupposes that the state can become conscious. . . .' And Davis (1976: 78) has stated in similar vein that 'a necessary condition for someone to know the rules which govern some activity is that he must be able to say or show us what the rules are. . . .' The gist of the criticism in question, then, is that the belief that knowledge of language (as embodied in a system of rules) is unconscious knowledge contains an internal contradiction.[69] If this criticism were correct, Chomsky's epistemologically phrased characterization of the attained state of the language faculty would indeed be seriously flawed.

Chomsky (1980a: 241–4) has reacted to the criticism in question by attacking a general principle on which it is based: the principle of accessibility. On his (1980a: 241) formulation, this principle expresses the belief that 'the contents of mind are in principle open to reflection and careful thought if only the barriers of dogma, superstition, or psychic disorder are removed.' Chomsky (1980a: 244) argues, however, that there is no reason to suppose that we have any access to the principles that enter into our knowledge and use of language. In arguing this, he aligns himself with such scholars as Vico, Joseph Priestly, John Stuart Mill and C. G. Jung, all of whom insisted that the basic principles of the psyche are inaccessible to introspection.

In keeping with his rejection of the principle of accessibility, Chomsky (1980a: 131) observes that Searle offers no argument at all for the position that knowledge of language cannot be tacit. In Chomsky's view, Searle merely stipulates that mental states must be accessible to consciousness. And, Searle claims without argument that 'otherwise' attribution of mental states loses 'much of its explanatory power'. Chomsky argues that the latter statement is 'simply false'. He concludes, moreover, that Searle's condition that a person must be aware of the rules that enter into his behaviour 'remains sheer dogmatism, supported by no kind of argument'.

Observe that, within the Chomskyan framework, three claims must be clearly distinguished from one another: (a) the claim that knowledge of language is unconscious knowledge, (b) the claim that knowledge of language is embodied in a system of rules, and (c) the claim that the actual use of language constitutes a case of rule-following. From an ontological point of view, the first claim is fundamental: accordingly, there is no contradiction or inconsistency in doing what Chomsky did when he significantly changed his position in regard to the second and third claims but retained, unchanged, his position in regard to the first claim. Recall, that as a result of the second conceptual shift in Chomskyan linguistics, rules no longer have a substantive status within the Chomskyan conception of language. Rather, rules are now taken by Chomsky (1988b: 17–18) to be epiphenomena, principles and parameters being the basic structural components of language(s).

The claims represented as (b) and (c) above were also criticized on various counts, especially in the seventies and early eighties. Though some of the resulting criticisms were interesting, we will not consider them here: they do not seem to carry over in any straightforward way to the principles-and-parameters conception of language currently held by Chomsky.[70] It is not clear precisely how Chomsky sees the 'mechanics' of language use in terms of this conception of language, a point that we will return to in section 3.5.2 below.[71]

5 Linguistic intuition yields insufficiently firm evidence about (the knowledge of language that constitutes) the attained, final state of the language faculty. Consequently, there is no source yielding sufficiently reliable evidence about the form and contents of the attained, final state of this faculty.

The alleged shortcomings of linguistic intuition as a source of evidence for claims expressed by grammars about the linguistic competence of speaker-hearers formed a topic of prolonged and often heated debate, particularly in the sixties and seventies.[72] Rephrased in the contemproary idiom, the gist of this epistemologically based criticism would be that, because of problems with assessing the relevance and reliability of individual linguistic intuitions, Chomskyan claims about the character and contents of the I-language cannot be properly tested and justified. If this were true, the status of the I-language would be in jeopardy. There would be little point in having a linguistic ontology that provided for entities the claims about which were, essentially, arbitrary. This would make the I-language an entity not amenable to normal scientific inquiry.

Before considering the merit of the criticism in question, let us get a little clearer about the nature of linguistic intuition and the judgements based on it. Native speakers of a language are claimed to arrive at linguistic judgements by means of two 'methods' or 'processes': intuition and introspection. Pateman (1987: 135) has recently characterized intuition as a process that 'gives us causally related indexical or symptomatic evidence for the character of underlying psycholinguistic (or, more generally, psychological) processes'. Accordingly, he takes individual intuitions to be 'reports of appearances' that provide 'causal evidence' of a subjective sort about out minds. Introspection represents to Chomsky (1980a: 140ff.) the 'reflection', 'analysis' or 'careful thought' to which 'accessible' elements of the contents of the mind may be subjected.

Pateman (1987: 135), moreover, has made an interesting attempt to establish a link between the distinctions *intuition v. introspection* and *I-language v. E-language*:

> In Chomsky's terms (Chomsky 1986, ch. 2), intuition provides evidence for the character of I-languages (internalized languages), whereas introspective judgement – exercised, for example, when a foreigner asks me whether you can say P in English – provides evidence for the character of E-languages (externalized languages).

Being products of the causal efficacy of the I-language, linguistic intuitions are thus taken to provide a 'window' on the I-language. The form of the argument is a familiar one: the inference of 'hidden' properties of a causal agent from evident properties of its results or products.

It has been argued, however, that given some linguistic judgement by a native speaker – e.g. that *Colorless green ideas sleep furiously* constitutes a bizarre utterance – there is no principled way to determine whether this judgement bears on the I-language English rather than on some other cognitive or perceptual mechanism. Nor, the argument proceeds, is there an adequate way of determining the correctness of such judgements.[73]

Suppose that this argument were sound.[74] It would then still not follow that there is no source of sufficiently firm evidence about the attained state of the Chomskyan language faculty. This would follow only if linguistic intuition were the sole source of evidence about this state of the language faculty. But, Chomsky (e.g. 1986: 36–7) has argued, there in fact are a variety of sources of evidence about both states of the language faculty:

> In principle, evidence concerning the character of the I-language and initial state could come from many different sources apart from judgments concerning the form and meaning of expressions: perceptual experiments, the study of acquisition and deficit or of partially invented languages such as creoles (n. 25), or of literary usage or language change, neurology, biochemistry, and so on.

And, Chomsky contends, linguists cannot know in advance just how informative any one of such various kinds of evidence will be in regard to any one of the various significant states of the language faculty. Moreover, he expects that a broader range of evidence will enable linguists to identify in just what respects 'informant judgements' (as he calls them) are useful or unreliable and why this is so. A broader range of evidence, on his view, will also compensate for errors introduced under the working assumption that informant judgements give linguists 'direct evidence' about the structure of the I-language. Given the above considerations, the contention that (the attained state of) the language faculty is ontologically an inadmissible entity in not being amenable to normal scientific investigation is a rather less than compelling criticism.

In conclusion: Chomsky's views of the various states of the language faculty have been the target of a great many criticisms with ontological import. The five discussed above exemplify but do not exhaust criticisms of the kind in question. To mention but one further example of the same type: Kenny (1984: 138) has criticized Chomsky for misidentifying the nature of knowledge of language. On Kenny's view knowledge of a language is an ability, an abstraction from behaviour. Because of this misidentification, Kenny contends, Chomsky is confused about what it is that he, i.e. Chomsky, is studying. We will return in section 5.5 below to Chomsky's reaction to the criticism that he has failed to see that knowledge equals ability.

You now have a better idea what Dennett was talking about when he referred to 'religious war'? Indeed, Dear Buyer, our Moses is known as a man inclined to mete out rough retribution. Like Piaget and Searle, many others have been burnt by his Brimstone Brand of rhetoric. Take the case of Inhelder et al. (1974: 10), the Piaget Parish Priests who had the impertinence to proclaim that Chomskyan nativism 'does not help to solve any problem; all it does is to transfer the question from the psychological to the biological level by formulating it in terms of biological development.'

The Mass Mentalist countered with a Searing Sermon, asserting for instance that no one would take such an argument seriously if Inhelder and her Partners in Pontification advanced it in the case of physical development, say that of the general structure of binocular vision. And he (1980a: 209) concluded his condemnation with the following clincher: 'the arguments they put forth are in no way empirical but rather purely a priori. All of this again simply constitutes another chapter in the history of dogmatism.' The pungency that pricks our nostrils here, Buyer and Blue, is no waft of the 'weird incense' detected by Dennett; it marks an altogether starker, more sulphuric, stuff.

3.5.2 Mocking Moses

We come, next, to those criticisms of the Chomskyan conception of language that are not intended primarily to undermine the idea that people have a distinct language faculty or 'organ'. From this mixed bag we select four typical instances for closer inspection.

1 The Chomskyan conception of language does not provide an adequate basis for accounting for certain logical relations between sentences. Consequently, this conception places 'crippling limitations on the scope of linguistics'.

This criticism, which has been offered by Katz and Postal (1989: 8ff.), may be illustrated with reference to pairs of sentences such as the following:

John killed Bill. (3)
Bill is dead. (4)

Like Chomksy (1988c: 8), Katz and Postal (1989: 4) consider (3) and (4) to be related in terms of entailment. That is, if (3) is true, then (4) is necessarily true 'in virtue of natural language'. In other words, (3) necessarily entails (4), the necessity being of a logical kind. And Katz and Postal (1989: 4, 22) consider this to be an 'actual fact', which 'uncontroversially form[s] part of the domain of NLs' [natural languages] and, accordingly, falls within the (explanatory) 'scope of linguistics'.

But, Katz and Postal argue, this fact cannot be accounted for in terms of the Chomskyan mentalistic conception of language. Though the specifics of their argument are complex, its outlines are relatively simple. Katz and Postal (1989: 9ff.) argue that, to make possible an account of the fact in question, the *logical* law of entailment must be enabled to 'apply' (or 'refer') to the senses of the sentences (3) and (4). But in terms of the Chomskyan conception of language, sentences, their structures and their senses are *psychological* objects. Katz and Postal, moreover, assume that the objects to which logical laws apply and those laws themselves can hardly belong to different ontological levels.

Against this background, Katz and Postal (1989: 10) construe the following 'paradox':

> If senses are parts of the grammatical structure of NL sentences, and if linguistics both deals with the grammatical structure of sentences and is psychological, then senses are psychological. But if senses are psychological and the laws of logic refer to them, then these laws are also psychological. Consequently, logic is psychological, contradicting the accepted view in philosophy that logic is nonpsychological.

Katz and Postal (1989: 10) see three ways out of this 'paradox', only one of which they claim to be open to Chomskyans who wish to retain the view that language is something psychological: that of denying both that logic applies to natural language and that natural language sentences have any grammatical properties of significance for logic. On their view, this way out of the 'paradox' renders incomprehensible the fact that logical reasoning is defined on the meanings of natural language sentences. Moreover, they consider it to 'fly in the face' of such 'evident logically relevant' features of natural language semantics as quantifier scope, analytical entailment and contradiction. Giving up the assumption that there is an overlap between the senses of natural language sentences and logical objects would mean to them a retreat to the 1957 position that linguistic theory does not incorporate a semantic theory. And they (1989: 10) consider 'This option [to be] unattractive and unmotivated because it sacrifices some of the subject matter of linguistics and all of its logical relevance simply to save an ideology [i.e. that language is something psychological].' In short: Katz and Postal's criticism boils down to the claim that natural language has logical properties that cannot be accounted for on the basis of the belief that language is something psychological.[75]

How forceful, then, is this criticism by Katz and Postal of the Chomskyan conception of language? Though of an interesting sort, it is less than compelling, the problem being that it turns on too many controversial assumptions. These include the following:

1 that the necessity involved in the relation between (3) and (4) is indeed of a logical sort;
2 that, to account for logical properties of natural language sentences, the laws of logic must 'apply' directly to the senses or grammatical structures of such sentences;
3 that the 'subject matter' or 'scope' of a field can be delimited in an *a priori* way.

Let us consider the third assumption in some detail in order to see what it is that makes it controversial.[76]

The question is whether 'logical facts' of the sort in question do indeed 'uncontroversially form part of the domain of NLs' and, by definition, fall within the 'scope of linguistics', necessarily constituting part of its 'subject matter'.[77] There are various problems with Katz and Postal's affirmative answer to this question.

The first is of an exegetic sort. They (1989: 19) contend that Chomsky agreed that the 'logical fact' in question belongs to 'a core of facts defining grammatical study'. In support of this contention they quote the following remark by Chomsky (1986: 36): 'In actual practice, linguistics as a discipline is characterized by attention to certain kinds of evidence that are for the moment relatively accesssible and informative: largely, the judgments of native speakers.' This remark by Chomsky seems to me to be saying something about the practice of linguistic inquiry: it gives

Chomsky's view of how linguistic inquiry is actually practised, not of how he would *define* grammatical study in principle in an *a priori* way. Moreover, in the context from which Katz and Postal have taken this remark, Chomsky does not specifically mention 'logical facts' of the kind in question as a kind of evidence to which linguistics gives attention.

There are similar problems of exegesis with Katz and Postal's treatment of a second remark by Chomsky (1986: 37): 'If a theory of language failed to account for these judgments, if would plainly be a failure; *we might* [emphasis added by Katz and Postal], in fact, conclude that it is not a theory of language, but rather of something else.' Katz and Postal (1989: 20) express their 'basic accord' with this remark but add that 'the emphasized hedge should be replaced by "we would have to".' But the need for suggesting this replacement clearly shows that the remark quoted gives no support to the claim that Chomsky too considers 'logical facts' to form uncontroversially part of the core of facts that *define* grammatical study.

In the passage from which Katz and Postal quote the remarks represented above, Chomsky (1986: 37) adopts a rather different position on the delimitation of the scope or 'realm' of a field of inquiry: 'As in the case of any inquiry into some aspect of the physical world, there is no way of delimiting the kinds of evidence that might, in principle, prove relevant.' And:

> But we cannot know in advance just how informative various kinds of evidence will prove to be with regard to the language faculty and its manifestations, and we should anticipate that a broader range of evidence and deeper understanding will enable us to identify in just what respects informant judgments are useful or unreliable and why, and to compensate for the errors introduced under the tentative working assumption, which is indispensable, for today, and does provide us with rich and significant information.

The latter remark by Chomsky, interestingly, follows immediately on the second one quoted by Katz and Postal.

It seems clear then that Chomsky would not agree with Katz and Postal's (1989: 2) claim that it is possible to specifiy in an *a priori* way 'a collection of facts which uncontroversially form part of the domain of NLs'. Nor, it seems, would he agree with the claim that the inability of a conception of language to provide a basis for accounting for an arbitrary subset of such a collection of facts necessarily constitutes a serious flaw.

This means that Chomsky would resist what Fodor (1985b: 147–8) has called 'the Wrong View' of linguistics. On Fodor's characterization the Wrong View maintains:

> (a) that there is a specifiable data base for linquistic theories; (b) that this data base can be specified antecedently to theory construction; (c) that the empirical content of linguistic theories consists of what they have to say about the data base; and (d) that the data base for linguistics consists of the corpora of utterances that informants produce (or, in some versions, would produce given specified forms of prompting).

Fodor suggests that if (d) were modified so as to read 'the data base for linguistics consists of the intuitions (about grammaticality, ambiguity and so on) that informants produce or would produce', then one gets the view of linguistic inquiry common to Stich (1985) and the later Katz (1977).

Fodor (1985a: 150–1) proceeds to argue that the view that the scientist can stipulate what data are to count as relevant to the (dis)confirmation of his theories is simply not plausible, given the way that real science is conducted. He takes this to be a point of utmost methodological seriousness since it implies that 'either the Wrong View misdescribes linguistics or what linguists do is somehow an exception to the methodological principles that other sciences endorse.' And Fodor (1985a: 151) goes on to make the stronger point that: 'Any science is under the obligation to explain why *what it takes to be data* relevant to the confirmation of its theories *are* data relevant to the confirmation of its theories.' This condition, Fodor (1985b: 152) points out, can be met on the view that language is something psychological: intuitions can be used to confirm grammars because grammars are internally represented and actually contribute to the etiology of the speaker/hearer's intuitive judgements. The Wrong View, Fodor (1985a: 152) notes, can say ony 'We do it because we have always done it', or, 'We do it by stipulation.'[78]

It seems to me, therefore, that Katz and Postal have not shown that 'logical facts' such as the ones in question 'uncontroversially' constitute part of the subject matter of linguistics. And even if we accepted for argument's sake that they have, this would still not necessarily reflect negatively on the Chomskyan conception of language. To see why not, note that Chomsky has drawn a distinction between *linguistic theory* and (*the field of*) *linguistics*. Thus, he (1965: 3) introduced the idealizations of 'an ideal speaker-listener' and 'a completely homogeneous speech community' by stating that 'Linguistic theory is concerned primarily with an ideal speaker-listener, in a completely homogeneous speech community. . .'. 'Linguistic theory', in this statement, refers to theories of grammar, i.e. to theories of competence or theories of knowledge of grammar. 'Linguistic theory' in this statement is not being used as a synonym for 'the field of linguistics'. Thus, Newmeyer (1983: 75) observes that:

> the opening words of the paragraph are 'Linguistic theory is concerned', not 'The field of linguistics is concerned'. Chomsky has consistently used the term 'linguistic theory' to refer to theories of grammar (i.e. theories of competence) rather than to refer to *any* work (theoretical or nontheoretical) involving language study.

Invoking the distinction in question, Chomsky (1980a: 25) has argued, for example, that certain kinds of data about linguistic variation in real speech communities are irrelevant to the concerns of linguistic theory as a theory about the language faculty.[79] In similar vein, Chomsky would be able to argue that, even if the 'logical facts' in question did fall within the scope of linguistics, they were nevertheless irrelevant to a theory about the nature and states of the language faculty.

In its present form, then, Katz and Postal's criticism of 1 cannot be taken to reveal a real flaw in the Chomskyan conception of language.

2 The Chomskyan conception of language is 'plagued by' several distinct 'contradictions'. Consequently, it is internally inconsistent.

This is the core of a second criticism levelled by Katz and Postal (1989: 57) at the Chomskyan conception of language. They (1989:

44ff.) diagnose four such 'contradictions', which will be briefly outlined below. Katz and Postal base their diagnosis of these 'contradictions' on what they consider to be conflicting statements in relatively recent writings of Chomsky's.

First 'Contradiction': Being psychobiological, all grammatical and grammatically determined properties are contingent, but some are necessary. Katz and Postal (1989: 44–5) cite various formulations of Chomsky's indicating to them that he 'claims that NL [i.e. natural language] is a feature of *contingent* mind/brains'.[80] They (1989: 45–6) subsequently quote a number of statements by Chomsky to the effect that there exist some (natural language) sentences that are analytic, i.e. sentences which, purely by virtue of the meanings they express, determine truths which are necessary.[81] Being necessarily true, Katz and Postal argue, is not a contingent property of sentences. The 'paradox' that they construe in this regard accordingly has the same basis as the criticism represented as 1 above.

Second 'Contradiction': Grammars (in the sense of I-languages) are physical objects, and hence have spatial location, but are also sets (in the sense of generative grammars), and hence lack spatial location. Katz and Postal (1989: 44–5) again present various quotations from Chomsky's writings to show that he takes an I-language to be a 'difinite real-world object, situated in space and time' and that this space-time location is in the mind.[82] To construe the 'paradox' under consideration, they claim that Chomsky takes a generative grammar to be by definition a set of strings of symbols. Moreover, they quote a passage from Chomsky (1986: 34) in which he says that 'sets are not in the mind/brain.' This indicates to Katz and Postal (1989: 49) 'a contradiction' in Chomsky's position, which consists in equivocating over whether I-languages are abstract, mathematical objects or whether they are physical objects. In the former case I-languages would be analogues to computer programs; in the latter case I-languages would be analogues of physical states of computers which instantiate programs.[83]

Third 'Contradiction': Sentential objects exist in minds/brains, hence are finite in number, but are also infinite in number. Katz and Postal (1989: 53–4) contend that certain remarks of Chomsky's indicate that on his view there are infinitely many I-(language) sentences.[84] But his (1980a: 221) belief that 'the grammar itself is finite, represented in a finite brain' limits the I-sentences to a finite number. This is so because on Katz and Postal's (1989: 53) construal 'an infinite number of I-sentences includes sentences too large to be "represented in the brain".'

Fourth 'Contradiction': Sentences are internal (mental) objects but also are external (acoustic) objects. Katz and Postal (1989: 48) quote remarks by Chomsky which, they hold, indicate that he operates with a notion of 'sentences' in terms of which sentences exist in mental representations.[85] To construe the 'paradox' in question, they subsequently quote a remark by Chomsky that portrays sentences as physical entities.[86] Whereas entities that form part of mental representations are internal, entities portrayed as physical events are external.

Chomsky's remarkable skill in dissolving what seem like contradictions in his work and his amazing ability to deflate what seem like crippling criticisms have been commented on by many (e.g. Gardner 1985: 14; Botha 1989a; Smith 1989: 206). So it would not be prudent to consider the four 'contradictions' outlined above to be real contradictions before having seen Chomsky's reaction to them. And it would not be wise to accept at this stage Katz and Postal's (1989: 55) claim that 'These contradictions can be eliminated but at a cost almost as damaging as the contradictions themselves.' What Katz and Postal (1989: 57) have done, however, is to furnish substantial evidence for the contention that there are tensions within the Chomskyan conception of language. These tensions, it has been claimed, are caused by the fact that Chomsky's mentalistic conception of language retains elements of a 'formalistic' E-language conception of language that he held in an earlier phase of his thinking (Botha 1989a: 72–3). Many years ago, Steinberg (1975: 220–1) put the point as follows:

> His original conception regarding the nature of the relationship between a theoretical grammar and a speaker was actually a formalistic, not a mentalistic one. During this formalistic phase, Chomsky did not regard the rules of his theoretical grammar as

representing knowledge held by speakers. Only certain aspects of the output of the theoretical grammar were regarded as psychologically significant. This formalistic type of theory was held by Chomsky until about 1959, at which time his views began to change.

In Katz and Postal's (1989: 21) phraseology, the tensions under consideration have been created by 'two separate agendas' in Chomsky's thinking. The first, nonmentalistic, 'agenda' they take to underlie Chomsky's (1986: 36) remark that linguistics is characterized in actual practice by attention to certain kinds of evidence: largely the judgements of native speakers. The second, mentalistic, 'agenda' underlies Chomsky's (1986: 3) position that generative grammar is concerned with those aspects of form and meaning that are determined by the language faculty, taken to be a particular component of the human mind. Chomsky (1986: 28–9), however, has emphatically rejected the allegation that he ever held a nonmentalistic, E-language, conception of language. The evidence adduced by Chomsky in support of this response includes historical considerations of an accidental sort that are hard for relative outsiders to appraise 30 years later.[87]

3 It is not clear how I-language figures in language production and perception. Consequently, the Chomskyan conception of language is underdeveloped from an ontological point of view.

Prior to the second conceptual shift, as we have seen, the notion of 'rules' was central to Chomsky's thinking about language: coming to know a language (or, rather, a grammar) was seen as the acquisition of a rule system, and using a language was viewed as the following of rules. Subsequent to the second conceptual shift, however, knowledge of language is taken to be knowledge of a system of principles with parameters fixed. And acquisition of language is insightfully characterized as the fixing of these parameters. But Chomsky has not yet provided a clear account of what the use of language would entail if it were no longer considered to be a matter of rule-following. To put it in positive terms: Chomsky has still to spell out how language production and perception can be conceived of in terms of principles and parameters. He (1986: 151, 243) has noted that the second conceptual shift suggests that questions of the use of language merit 'substantial rethinking'. And he has speculated in general terms on the possibility that parsers could be based on lexical properties and principles of universal grammar that 'determine structures from them'. But, as for specifics, Chomsky has to date left unclear what language use would entail if it had to be characterized in terms of his principles-and-parameters conception of language.

4 In terms of the Chomskyan conception of language, there is no difference of substance between language and knowledge of language. Consequently, this conception of language is either empty or provides for a spurious distinction.

As we noted in section 3.1.4 above, Chomsky seems to draw a distinction between 'language' and 'knowledge of language'. But it is not at all clear that this is more than a terminological distinction. That is, from certain remarks made by Chomsky the inference may be drawn that he does not conceive of language as something that is substantively distinct from knowledge of language. And from other remarks, indicating that this distinction may involve more than terminology, it is not clear what substance it has. These and other unclear aspects of the Chomskyan distinction between language and knowledge of language were discussed in some detail in section 3.1.4 above.

Katz and Postal (1989: 11–13) have a more negative view of this aspect of the Chomskyan conception of language. They do give Chomsky credit for diagnosing a fatal flaw in American structuralism: the failure to distinguish between knowledge of a natural language (i.e. competence) and the exercise of that knowledge (i.e. performance). But they (1989: 11–12) proceed to contend that 'Conceptualism's mistake [where conceptualism includes the Chomskyan conception of language] is the parallel failure to draw the further distinction between knowledge of an NL [i.e. natural language] and the object it is knowledge of, the NL itself.' Without this distinction, they argue, everything about a natural language becomes a contingent matter of human psychology. This, they believe, leaves no place for 'necessary connection in grammatical structure', for example. A conception of language that fails to distinguish between knowledge of natural language and the natural language which is known makes it impossible to specify the grammatical structures of sentences in a way that enables these to play a role in logic. Consequently, the laws of logic cannot apply to these structures to account for 'logical facts' such as those about the logical necessity of the relationship holding between *John killed Bill* and *Bill is dead.*

As we saw above, it cannot be stipulated antecedently that the Chomskyan conception of language has to provide the kind of account of 'logical facts' that Katz and Postal have in mind. If there were no other kinds of facts to be captured by drawing the distinction between language and knowledge of language, the factual basis for criticizing Chomsky for not drawing this distinction is rather shaky. What is the point, it may be asked, of drawing distinctions that have no factual import? On the other hand, there must be something conceptually amiss with a theoretical conception that implicitly provides for a spurious distinction between what should be relatively fundamental notions.

Given that religion is to bring one happiness, how happy should one be about the Chomskyan (non)distinction between language and knowledge of language? Could we possibly approach a Practising Prophet for a pronouncement on how to feel or not to feel about the matter? Well, Dear Buyer, we can always turn to the Complete Cognitivist and Charismatic Conceptualist – the man who is so much more than a mere missionary marketing modularity. Indeed, while doing sterling stunt work as a stand-in for Overworked Oracles, he has established himself as a constant source of quips about the quintessence of the human condition.

Thus one day, in the style of his famous forebear Jerra Truth-Star, spake the Substitute Sage – with wonted wisdom, nor wanting in wit – on the relations which obtain between happiness and, mirabile dictu, *the drawing of distinctions: 'If only we made all the distinctions that there are, then we should all be as happy as kings. (Kings are notoriously* very *happy)' (Fodor 1985b: 1). From this precious profundity, how are we to derive the answer we are after? Well, Dear Buyer, this is where Nonsequiturian Nomology comes into play. The Law of Excluding the Excessive enables us to make the impeccable inference that, if kings made even one distinction too many, they would be less than* very *happy. Assuming further as axiomatic that everybody would like to share in the notoriety of kings, the Second Law of Liturgical Licence sanctions the inference that nobody should want to draw a nondistinction between language and knowledge of language. Drawing distinctions in the absence of things that can differ is definitely not the road to Blue-blooded Bliss.*

3.6 Getting rid of the ghost

Both Chomsky's and Fodor's portrayal of language as something mental may be subjected to nontrivial criticisms of an ontological sort. This seems to be clear from the discussion in sections 3.4 and 3.5. One potential point of criticism, however, cannot be made: that Chomsky and Fodor have in Cartesian fashion taken the mental to represent a distinct, 'ghost-like', substance. Chomsky and Fodor are both monists in the sense of not postulating the existence of some substance distinct from matter.

Chomsky, we have seen, believes in an open-ended concept of 'the body' or 'matter'. And, he believes, one cannot have a more respectable conception of something than that yielded by the pursuit of 'normal scientific practice'. The consequence of these two beliefs Salkie (1990: 80) neatly captures as follows: 'Whatever science proposes about body or mind thus becomes part of the "material world", in the only reliable sense of that term.' Chomsky, thus, is ultimately a materialist, a 'scientific monist' as Salkie would have it.[88] Recall, however, that in his study of language and mind, Chomsky is concerned with the 'material world' at an abstract level. This is the level of function and structure, not that of the 'physical realization' of brain mechanisms. And Chomsky (1987a: 5–6) considers it unlikely that the abstract mentalistic level of inquiry and discourse will be abandoned, even if the pertinent 'physical mechanisms' are discovered. Recall also that Chomsky (1988c: 13) is unwilling to predict that the natural sciences will someday 'annex' all mental phenomena.

In the final analysis, Chomsky's linguistic ontology is a function of his view that the 'standard practice of the natural sciences' offers the most reliable means of fathoming reality. And his ontology and epistemology are quite closely interlinked, as Salkie (1990: 80) notes too: 'His [i.e. Chomsky's] belief in the unity of science lies behind his belief in the unity of being.' Linking ontology and epistemology in certain direct ways, however, can be disastrous. This we have seen in our examination of Bloomfieldian materialism in chapter 1. The question (to be pursued in note 20 to chapter 6) accordingly is whether Chomsky's linguistic ontology is also at risk on account of its being so directly interlinked with his epistemology.

Fodor, too, has been characterized as a 'physicalist'. In Rey's (1991: xii) account, Fodor's version of physicalism involves three basic commitments:

(1) all events (and objects) are identical to or composed of physical events,
(2) for every exemplified property there are physical conditions which are sufficient and explanatory of the exemplification of that property,
(3) all basic laws are laws of physics.

Fodor's physicalism, however, is weaker than traditional brands of physicalism. On the one hand, Fodor does not require that there be bi-conditional bridge laws linking the phenomena of a special science such as psychology to the underlying phenomena of physics. On the other hand, he considers *ceteris paribus* clauses to play an ineliminable role in specifying the laws of the special sciences. Rey (1991: xii) takes this to mean that

> Fodor doesn't regard such clauses as short for some description of appropriate boundary conditions that will be spelled out once the science matures. Rather, they are a way of indicating that apparent exceptions to the law are to be explained by interference from other quarters that may not be (and usually are not) specifiable within the terms of the law itself.

Finally, like Chomsky, Fodor has an open-ended idea of what constitutes 'the physical'. Thus, explicating Fodor's views, Rey (1991: xii), observes: 'There is always a reasonable worry about just what constitutes the "physical": the phenomena cited in *present* physics. Some as yet unspecified future, ideal physics?' Given this 'open-mindedness', it is understandable why Fodor, like Chomsky, has not taken the mental to be a substance distinct from the material.[89]

3.7 Saying 'selah'

Tired of being treated to a Moses-Managed Metaphysics, Weary-seeming Window-Worshipper? And well you may be! But before we say 'Selah' and take a break, the story that language is part of a soul of sorts may fittingly be sealed with seven sayings. Each of these is meant to capture a general lesson that you and our Fast-fading Blue and, indeed, I myself may learn from the goings-on in the Sacramental Section of The Market.

1 *On the essence of language: it remains a jealously guarded secret.*
2 *On knowledge of language: it has to be based in the body.*
3 *On constructing a conception of language: breathe new life into buried beliefs.*
4 *On appraising a conception of language: test it for internal tensions.*
5 *On deconstructing 'language': it does not pay to treat it all the way like an Ontological Onion.*
6 *On the scope of a conception of language: beware of the Omnipotent Octopus.*
7 *On crusading against conceptualism: 'all they that take the sword shall perish with the sword.'*

The first four lessons have been properly preached, you would agree, Dear Buyer. It could be useful, however, to look a little closer at Ontological Onions, Omnipotent Octopuses and Sticky Ends.

Lesson number five, then, is about the Chomskyan procedure for penetrating to the essence of language. Here are its steps. Start by peeling away the outermost layer comprising such 'common-sensical' crudities as sociopolitical beliefs: it is conceptually so coarse as to be good for next to nothing. Next remove the E-language layer of externalist assumptions as unfit for conceptual consumption too. In this way, you get to the deeper, more delicate layer of I-language/knowledge of language which is tastily internalist, an intrinsic ingredient of a conceptualist linguistic ontology. But having committed yourself to peeling as the proper procedure for penetrating to the core of language, you are left with no option but to carry on. So, finally, remove the innermost layer of I-language/knowledge of language. To your dismay, where you expected to find language, there is nothing. Language, like an ordinary onion, is to be found – so it would seem – in what one cuts away to get to its contentless core. So, perpetual peeling away at 'language' won't purchase the conceptualist the happiness he is after.

In defence of Ontological Onions, however, I must say that they are not nearly as dangerous as the octopuses of lesson number six. Professionals in the business of constructing conceptions can't stand a reality that is chaotically cut up into a diversity of disconnected domains, each of which is reigned over by a distinct conception in splended isolation. Understanding reality ultimately requires conceptual unification, or so it is believed. So a conception of language is standardly required to embrace in its explanatory scope a fairly wide range of phenomena or 'facts' that all seem to manifest aspects of language. But, pushed to its limits, the observance of this requirement could turn a conception of language into an Ontological Octopus with arms enveloping too many of the phenomena that are commonsensically (or antecedently) considered 'linguistic'. The price for Ontological Omnipotence is Explanatory Impotence, as the recent history of linguistics has shown.[90] *And being obsessed with this brand of omnipotence may, alas, be conducive to the cobbling together of a conception in terms of which language is a Metaphysical Monster imitating in regard to internal incongruity a particular Biblical Beast: the one which, though it had seven heads, ten horns, the feet of a bear and the mouth of a lion, still contrived to look like a leopard.*

Which brings me to the topic of lesson number seven, the fate of Militant Metaphysicists who have challenged Chomsky at conceptual combat. It truly is a tale in the Old Testament tradition of death and doom, gore and gloom. That is, as far as the fortunes of Chomsky's Ontological Opponents are concerned. Not wanting to upset your emotional equilibrium with particulars of punctured personalities and ruptured reputations, I will simply ask Howard Gardner (1985: 214) to sum it all up in the driest of manners: 'Chomsky has rarely been defeated in argument on his own ground. . .'[91]

So what have I really been saying, then? That the Chomskyan conception of language is best left unbought on the shelf? No, not at all, Dear Buyer. For one thing, The Book of Good and Bad Buys is simply not yet ready for final balancing. Before we are going to be able to attempt any Act of Apocalyptic Appraisal, we will have to inspect several more conceptions of language which are for sale on The Market. So, rather than consign the Chomskyan conception to the flames right now, let us put it on ice. It will keep while we complete the preparations for our Eschatological Exercise, which will call for us to deal with the last things and with the things that last. Selah.

4

Pushing Language as Platonic (not to Mention Popperian)

4.0 Levitating language

Good, clean philosophical fun – can we have some of that here, please! Not that we're demanding anything, Downbeat Buyer, beyond what we doubly deserve. No, make that 'triply deserve'. After all, didn't we have to face the Philistine fatuousness of old-fashioned physicalism? Didn't we have to bear to the full the boredom of barren behaviourism? Didn't we have to submit to the mystery of modern mentalism? So here's what I suggest. We go right on up the Abstract Axis, making the ascent to its apex, because there we will be epistemically entertained by Magician Metaphysicists who conjure up (an image of) language as something absolutely abstract. The sight of languages being plucked out of top hats like so many realist rabbits, or Platonist pigeons, should go some of the way at least towards meeting our need for metaphysical amusement. And rest assured, the magic will be strictly white. Ah yes, it's quite some time now since Occult Ontologists were once and for all banned from practising their murky magic on The Metaphysics Market.

The choice, basically, is between two shows, Dear Shopper. For connoisseurs of conjuring – on the one hand – capable of appreciating refined routines, the Athenian Abstractists will advance the most amusing answer to the question 'What is language in essence?' If you haven't already guessed it, the founding father of this philosophically fleet-fingered family performed under the stage-name of Plato the Perfectionist. Ancient Audiences were captivated by this conjurer and his distinctive transforming trick: taking nothing that they could notice, and then turning it into – hey Plato! – an abstract object. And it is after this philosophical fashion that more than two millennia later a couple of our contemporaries, the Magicians of Manhattan, carry on their cultivated conceptual crafts.

Philosophically less sophisticated folk – on the other hand – may go for the sort of wizardry that is worked in a more worldly way. Such more mundane meta-amusement is provided by World 3 Wand Wavers, Popperian Prestidigitators and assorted Common Conceptual Contortionists. Being not really interested in just any abracadabra conception of language, we won't, however, seek our epistemic entertainment in the fare offered by philosophical fork benders and fire-eaters. Nor will we let ourselves be enticed to attend such metaphysical one-man shows as those staged by Montague the Magnificent, Hans-Heinrich the Handy and sundry other solo sorcerers.

(Incidentally, many a Master Metaphysicist uses assistants-in-training for such menial metaphysical tasks as oiling hidden philosophical flaps and springs, opening and closing secret conceptual compartments, keeping epistemological escape ways clear and marking metaphysical cards. Only Thingumajig Magicians, though, conceal in their audiences conceptual confederates, stooges whose job it is to make their masters' mediocre magic work.)

But now let us sneak a peek at how Platonists and Popperians practise their profession: levitating languages so that these float, as it were, above time and space.

4.1 Performing Platonist passes

Language is an abstract object. This is the ontological core of a conception of language that has been alternatively called 'realism', 'Platonism' or 'Platonic realism'. The best-articulated version of this linguistic ontology is due to Jerrold Katz and his associates Paul Postal, Terence Langendoen and Thomas Bever. As noted by Katz (1981: 19, n. 17), various other linguists and philosophers have been attracted to realism but have refrained from developing it in a systematic way or from accepting its full implications.[1]

Before considering the Platonist conception of language, let us briefly look at Platonism from a more general philosophical perspective. As noted by Ryle (1967b: 334), it is not easy to capture the 'essence' of Platonism since it comprises a variety of doctrines: ontological, epistemological, ethical and so on. In quite general terms, however, Ryle characterizes Platonism as a metaphysical philosophy concerned with a transcendent reality. With this, Ryle observes, goes a rationalistic belief in the power of thought to grasp transcendent realities directly. But let us consider some of the specific ontological and epistemological doctrines that have been dubbed 'Platonist'.

Central to our concerns is the Platonist ontological theory of universals. Known as 'realism', the essence of this theory in the words of Woozley (1967: 195) is that 'universals exist in themselves and would exist even if there were no minds to be aware of them. . . .' Realists consider universals to be 'public somethings' that would be available for discovery even if there were nobody to discover them. Conceptualists, by contrast, believe universals to be in the mind: if there were no minds, there could be no universals. Universals, on a conceptualist construal, have the same status as thoughts, memories, mental images and dreams, none of which can exist in a mindless world.

The realist theory of universals can be understood against the background of a distinction drawn by Plato between what Popper (1977: 43) has called three 'worlds': a world of 'visible objects', a world of 'affections or states of the soul' and a world of 'intelligible objects'. This last world is a transcendent one; its 'intelligible objects' – called also 'forms', 'ideas' or 'essences' – are those objects which general or universal concepts denote. The Good, the Beautiful and the Just are in Popper's (1977: 43) phrasing 'the most important essences in his [i.e. Plato's] world of intelligible forms or ideas'. In addition, this world contains the natural numbers. Plato's world of intelligible objects is not man-made: he conceived of it as timeless, immutable and of divine origin.

Associated with Platonic realism is an epistemological theory that provides for a faculty of (intellectual) intuition. The function of this faculty is to acquire a priori knowledge of whatever it is that makes up transcendent Platonic reality. Conventional Platonists have considered the knowledge acquired by this faculty to be infallible. This Platonist epistemology goes back to Plato's postulation of an 'eye of the soul'. For Plato, as noted by Popper (1977: 44), this 'mental eye' is the seat of the faculty of intellectual intuition. It can 'see' an idea, essence or object that belongs to Plato's intelligible world. And, in Popper's (1977: 44) phraseology, 'Once we have managed to see it, to grasp it, we know this essence: we can see it in the "light of truth". This intellectual intuition, once it has been achieved, is infallible.' Against this background we can now go on to explore the Platonist conception of language.[2]

In this section, we will focus on Katzian Platonism, the version of realism that has been explicitly and energetically promoted by the so-called New York School as superior not only to Chomskyan mentalism but, indeed, to all other linguistic ontologies.[3] The basic questions we will consider are the following: What does it mean to say that language is an abstract object? Why is language considered abstract by Katz and his associates? What form of science is linguistics, given the view that language is something abstract? What methodology has been adopted by Platonists for investigating language as an abstract object? What are the merits and shortcomings of the Platonist conception of language?

4.1.1 Concealing conceptual compartments

Platonist linguistic reality is populated by sentences, individual languages and, possibly, something called '(natural) language (in general)'.[4] And these entities are abstract objects, objects that are not physical, mental, biological or social. In slightly less negative terms, Katz (1981: 181) characterizes abstract objects as being 'objective, timeless, placeless entities that we discover and learn about'.[5] An abstract object is 'objective', Katz (1981: 186) explains, in the sense that 'no one person has a special relation to it.' That is, no person has privileged access to it in the way that he/she may have to psychological states, events, etc. that occur in his/her consciousness. Abstract objects, moreover, are changeless in the sense of not 'being different at different times'. Rather, abstract objects are cohesive in the sense of 'having logically inseparable basic properties'.

But let us consider the three kinds of abstract linguistic entities mentioned above. As for sentences, Katz (1984: 18) believes that they can be thought of in the same way that Platonist mathematicians conceive of numbers. This means to Katz (1984: 18) that 'Sentences . . . are not taken to be located here or there in physical space like sound waves or deposits of ink, and they are not taken to occur either at one time or another or in one subjectivity or another in the manner of mental events and states.' Rather, Katz takes sentences to be 'abstract' and 'objective'. Sentences, he (1984: 18) claims, are 'entities whose structure we discover', not entities that we create. And, on Katz's view, we discover the structure of sentences 'by intuition and reason, not by perception and induction'.

On the Platonist view, because sentences cannot have either spatial or temporal location, they cannot have material properties either. This timeless and 'spaceless' nature of sentences Katz and Postal (1989: 7) illustrate with reference to the sentence *Flying planes can be dangerous.* They observe, that is, that it is just as impossible for this sentence to occur on Christmas day in AD 2000 as it is for this sentence to be in Bethlehem. And since sentences are not located in either time or space, Platonists believe, they cannot be involved in causal interactions: sentences are not caused by anything and sentences cannot cause anything (cf. Katz and Postal 1989: 5–6). Concretely, what this means to Katz and Postal (1989: 8) is that, for example, the sentence *Flying planes can be dangerous* cannot be caused by vocal-tract movements. Nor can this sentence cause crystal to break.

Continuing to clarify the abstract nature of sentences, Katz and Postal invoke Peirce's distinction between types and tokens. As timeless and 'spaceless' entities not involved in causation, sentences are types in terms of this distinction. As an abstract type, however, a sentence may have various concrete tokens that take on the form of written or spoken utterances. The text above, for example, includes two written utterance tokens of the sentence type 'Flying planes can be dangerous'. In contrast to sentence types, utterance tokens are material objects located in space and time. The properties of utterance tokens, moreover, are caused – by vocal-tract movements in the case of spoken utterances. And utterance tokens can act causally on things – produced at a sufficiently high pitch they can, for example, cause crystal to break.[6]

To clarify the nature of abstract objects further, Katz and Postal have drawn a distinction between Platonic abstract objects and abstract(ed) or ideal objects of the kind constructed in empirical inquiry.[7] In terms of a definition given by Katz (1981: 55), 'An ideal object is a construction resulting from the idealization of actual objects and it is used to make statements about them [i.e. the actual objects] without undue complication.' Completely frictionless planes and perfectly rigid rods are typical examples of the ideal objects constructed by physicists. These ideal objects abstract away from those features of actual surfaces and bodies, respectively, which would unnecessarily complicate the statement of the laws of physics governing these actual objects. In linguistics, likewise, Chomsky's ideal speaker-listener is an ideal object too: it abstracts away from actual speaker-listeners by leaving out of consideration, for instance, so-called performance features that would needlessly complicate the statements of 'grammatical laws'.[8]

Platonic abstract objects, by contrast, are not idealizations or ideal objects. That is, they are not the products of any abstracting away from the complicating features of actual objects. And they are not constructed as the means by which to simplify the laws of a discipline. Katz (1981: 56) emphasizes the point that Platonic abstract objects differ in ontological kind from the physical and psychological objects represented in ideal objects. Platonic abstract objects, he contends, are like the *actual* objects of empirical science in that they are things of which the statements of a science may be true.

This brings us to the second kind of objects populating Platonist linguistic reality. The status of being components of this reality has been explicitly assigned by Platonists not only to sentences but also to individual languages (Katz 1981: 76; 1984: 24; Katz and Postal 1989: 30ff.). Recently, Katz and Postal (1989: 29), for instance, have reiterated the Platonist position that 'NLs [= natural languages] are taken to be real things.' But beyond portraying languages as abstract, Platonists have had relatively little to say about their distinctive ontological properties. In an early characterization, Katz (1981: 9) depicted a language as 'a timeless, unchangeable, objective structure'. And, in a more linguistic vein, he (1981: 172) also described different languages as 'different systems of expressive forms associated with an invariant semantic structure. . . .' More recently, Platonists in their characterization of individual languages have replaced the earlier notions of 'structure' and 'system' by the notion of 'collection'. Katz and Postal (1989: 27ff.), for example, have portrayed languages as being 'collections of sentences understood (or regarded) as abstract objects'. And certain mathematical properties of such collections have been discussed at length by Langendoen and Postal (1985).[9] But the question whether there is an ontologically significant difference between a 'system' or 'structure' on the one hand and a 'collection' on the other hand has, as far as I know, not been considered explicitly in recent Platonist writings. The clarity of the Platonist notion of 'a natural language', of course, has not been enhanced by this.

The ontological status and properties of a third kind of abstract object that may form part of Platonist linguistic reality is rather unclear. Certain formulations by Platonists suggest that, in addition to sentences and individual languages, '(natural) language (in general)' is also a component of this reality. For example, Katz (1981: 76) states that 'The second, and stronger claim [of Platonism] is that sentences and *language* are abstract objects and thus linguistics is about abstract objects' (emphasis added). This formulation may be read as indicating that language, as opposed to individual languages, may form a distinct part of Platonist linguistic reality. Other formulations, however, seem to suggest that sentences and languages are the only inhabitants of this reality. Thus, characterizing linguistic theory, Katz (1984: 24) uses the phrase 'linguistic theory, being about natural languages collectively. . . .' Formulations such as this leave the ontological status of the putative Platonist object 'language' rather less than clear. This object, that is, may be something derivative in being nondistinct from 'natural languages collectively'.

The matter is not made any clearer by Katz's (1981) discussion of the 'nature of language', 'the essential properties of natural languages' and 'linguistic universals'. In his (1981: 229) words, Platonism has 'an alternative conception of the nature of *language* and linguistic universals' (emphasis added). Elaborating on this point, Katz (1981: 229) switches, however, from 'language' to 'languages': 'We claim that the essential property of natural languages is that their grammatical structure constitutes an effable correlation of sentences with senses.'[10] And in his formulation of the Platonist notion of 'linguistic universal', Katz (1981: 229) uses the expression 'every a natural language' rather than '(natural) language (in general)': 'A grammatical feature F is a linguistic universal if every natural language has F and a natural language could not be effable without having F.'[11] But, in an earlier passage, Katz (1981: 225) states that properties such as effability require 'another conception of the nature of *language*, one on which the properties conceived to be part of the nature of *language* are properties without which *language* would not be what it is' (emphasis added).[12] In a technical ontological discussion, one must assume, the use of 'language' instead of 'languages' is not a matter of arbitrary terminological variation. Katz, however, has not divulged the reasons for his choice of terminology.

There is a particular formulation which suggests more strongly that Katz (1981: 231) considers 'language' to be something distinct from 'languages': 'Some [properties] are definitional, entering into our concept of *the abstract object natural language*, while others, no less inseparable, are not' (emphasis added). But Katz has refrained from indicating the respect(s) in which 'the abstract object natural language' is ontologically distinct from individual natural languages regarded as abstract objects. He (1981: 222) does state that 'the ontological category for natural languages taken collectively cannot be different from the ontological category for them individually'. This remark seems to say no more than that both individual languages and 'languages taken collectively' are abstract objects. It does not answer questions such as the following: Is 'the abstract object natural language' an entity that is distinct from 'individual languages taken collectively'? In ontological terms, what does it mean 'to take individual languages collectively'?

It is possible, though, that the answer to the question 'What is "the abstract object natural language"?' is a quite straightforward one. Namely: 'the abstract object natural language' is whatever it is that is described, characterized, etc. by a Platonist linguistic or grammatical theory. Adopting this approach to find out what 'the abstract object natural language' really is, one 'simply' has to get to the bottom of the Platonist conception of 'a linguistic or grammatical theory'. Let us attempt to do just this, taking as our point of departure the distinction drawn by Katz and other Platonists between a (generative) grammar and (a) linguistic/grammatical theory.

Katz's (1981: 55) characterization of a (generative) grammar is unambiguous in regard to ontological import: 'A generative grammar for a language L is a theory of the grammatical structure of the sentences of L, and these are abstract objects.'[13]

By contrast, the various characterizations that Katz and other Platonists have given over the years of (a) linguistic/grammatical theory and, thereby, of linguistic or grammatical universals are much less transparent.

Consider first a relatively early characterization given by Katz (1981: 55):

(C1) A linguistic theory is a theory of the grammatical universals of language, that is, a theory of the essential common structure of natural languages.

If 'the abstract object natural language' were identical to what a linguistic theory is a theory of, this object would in terms of (C1) be exhaustively made up of grammatical universals. And grammatical universals are equated with the essential common structure of natural languages, a point which may be represented as follows for the sake of later reference:

(E1) grammatical universals = the essential common structure of natural languages.

This relatively simple picture is complicated, however, by a later characterization given by Katz (1984: 43) of 'linguistic theory' and 'a correct linguistic theory':

(C2) Linguistic theory, on the Platonist view, is a theory of the invariances in the grammatical structures of all natural languages . . . A 'correct linguistic theory' states all invariances and essential properties of natural language in the simplest way.

As for its first statement, the characterization (C2) differs from (C1) in two respects: in (C2), 'language' is replaced by 'languages' and, significantly, in (C2) the idea of essentiality appears to have lost its status as a criterion for linguistic universals. The latter point, in a nutshell, may be represented as follows:

(E2) grammatical universals = the invariances in the grammatical structures of all natural languages.

The second statement of (C2), however, reintroduces the idea of essentiality but, through the use of 'and', it nevertheless broadens the Platonist notion of linguistic or grammatical universals. In the form of an equation:

(E3) grammatical universals = all invariances and essential properties of natural language.

In terms of the characterization (C2), 'the abstract object natural language' would be made up of 'all the invariances in the grammatical structures of all natural languages' plus 'all essential properties of natural language'. The characterization (C2) seems therefore to have (at least) two consequences. First, it does not seem to matter whether or not the intended 'invariances' concern essential or non-essential aspects/features of the grammatical structures of natural languages. Nor, secondly, does it seem to matter whether or not the intended essential properties are invariant. What these two consequences of (C2) may mean is unclear to me.

But the Platonist notions of 'grammatical/linguistic theory' and 'grammatical/linguistic universals' have been made even more opaque by the following recent characterization offered by Katz and Postal (1989: 13):

(C3) grammatical theory on the realist view is an explication of NL universals. It is a theory of the principles which hold for all sentences of all NLs and of those holding for all full collections of such sentences . . . The universal grammatical principles are either clauses of the definition of 'NL sentence' or [clauses] of the definition of 'NL'. . . .

The characterization (C3) differs from (C2) in various respects. First, in terms of (C3), 'the abstract object natural language' – if (C3) did in fact provide for the existence of this object – would be made up not of 'invariances in grammatical structure' and 'essential properties of language' but of 'principles which hold for all sentences of all NLs and of those holding for all full collections of such sentences'. It may be that the expression 'principles . . .' is intended to be synonymous with 'invariances . . .' and 'essential properties. . .'. But Katz and Postal do not say so. Secondly, 'universal grammatical principles' are portrayed not as parts or properties of a distinct abstract object somewhere 'out there' in a Platonic reality but as clauses of the definition of the notion 'NL sentence' and the notion 'NL'. This, obviously, is ontologically significant. In terms of an equation-like formulation, the essence of (C3) boils down to the following:

(C4) NL universals = the principles which hold for all sentences of all NLs and those holding for all full collections of such sentences = clauses of the definition of 'NL sentence' or of the definition of 'NL'.

We can now return to the question that triggered our examination of the Platonist notions of '(a) grammatical/linguistic theory' and 'grammatical/linguistic universals', namely: Is the entity called by Katz 'the abstract object language' something distinct from 'all natural languages taken collectively'? The various characterizations offered by Platonists of the notions of '(a) grammatical/linguistic theory' and 'grammatical/linguistic universals' do not provide a clear answer to this question. On the contrary: given these characterizations, one may conclude that the Platonist notions of '(a) grammatical/linguistic theory' and 'grammatical/linguistic universals' are themselves in need clarification.

Katz, of course, has anticipated modifications of the Platonist conception of 'linguistic universals'. Thus, referring to 'effability', he (1981: 231) has stated that 'Since there is no reason to think that this property alone defines natural language, completion of the definition of natural language, like the enumeration of the full set of linguistic universals, is a matter for future studies.' But Platonists have refrained from explaining and justifying the various changes that they have made in (the formulation of) their characterization of the notion of 'grammatical/linguistic universals'.

In sum: Platonist linguistic reality incorporates sentences and individual natural languages. Whether this reality, in addition, includes '(natural) language (in general)' or 'the abstract object language' as a distinct entity is unclear. So are the properties that may individuate this entity ontologically.

Thing Theurgy performances such as the one we have just watched essentially involve two tricks being done in tandem, Spell-bound Buyer. First, just to get the show on the road an alchemical act is presented by means of which, to the roll of realist drums, what ordinary ontologists would consider to be nothing is transmuted into sentences by Prime Practitioners of the Neoplatonist Arts.[14] *Next, muffled by the strains of metaphysical music, follows a magical move in which levers are thrown so as to set in motion the revolving realm of Platonist linguistic reality. And so, metaphysically mesmerized by its rapid rotation, the audience soon becomes unable to see whether, like sentences and like languages, 'language (in general)', though concealed in some third compartment, is also an inhabitant of this linguistic reality. It is this now-you-see-it-now-you-don't realist routine, Benumbed Blue, that induces the state of stupefaction in which many a seeker of the essence of language is unable to make out the ontological obscurities of the Platonist object 'language (in general)'.*

4.1.2 *Motivating the magic*

Why would Katz and other Platonists like to think that (a) language is an abstract object? Among the beliefs in which the Platonist conception of language is rooted, four are basic:

(B1) A conception of language or foundational position must account more adequately than its rivals do for all the facts of 'linguistics proper'.
(B2) The facts that fall within the domain of 'linguistics proper' include the fact that, if certain sentences are true, certain others are necessarily true, and also the fact that certain sentences are true in virtue of their meaning.
(B3) For facts such as those mentioned in (B2) to be accounted for, the laws of logic have to apply to the senses of sentences.
(B4) The laws of logic cannot apply to the senses of sentences unless these senses and laws have the same ontological status, namely the status of abstract objects.

The beliefs (B1)–(B4) have been discussed in various Platonist studies, the most recent of which is a joint paper by Katz and Postal (1989).[15]

As for (B1), it is a meta-belief expressing a general condition that should be met by any foundational position, linguistic ontology or conception of language. As formulated by Katz and Postal (1989: 5), (B1) actually represents only the tip of a submergred meta-mountain. That is, underlying this belief there are various more basic assumptions, not all of which are stated explicitly by Katz and Postal. The more basic assumptions include:

(A1) It is in principle possible to state *a priori* the (categories of) facts that fall within the domain or scope of a discipline.
(A2) Linguists, or at least a majority of leading linguists, agree that certain (categories of) facts fall within the scope of 'linguistics proper'.
(A3) The linguists referred to in (A2) agree that it makes sense/ is wise, in a foundational context, to draw a distinction between 'linguistics proper' and whatever forms of linguistics this has to be distinguished from.
(A4) The linguists referred to in (A2) agree about what it is – simplicity, deductive or explanatory depth, etc. – that makes one linguistic account of 'the facts' more adequate than the alternatives.

To some of these assumptions we will return below.

As for (B2), the facts included in the domain of 'linguistics proper' are, in Katz and Postal's (1989: 4) view, 'facts about NL sentences, covering every aspect of sentential structure, *viz.* syntactic, morphological, phonological and semantic. They are revealed in the judgments that fluent speakers make about their structure.' And, as specified in (B2), there facts include facts about semantic relations like 'analytic entailment' and semantic properties like 'analytic'.[16] The relation of analytic entailment is illustrated by Katz and Postal (1989: 4) with reference to the sentences *John killed Bill* and *Bill is dead* between (the senses of) which it holds. If the first of these sentences is true, then in virtue of natural language the second is necessarily true. the property of analyticity, in turn, is illustrated by Katz and Postal (1989: 4) with reference to the sentence *Whoever is persuaded to sing intends/decides to sing*. The proposition expressed in this sentence is, on Katz and Postal's formulation, 'a truth of meaning independent of empirical fact'. In short, then, the facts referred to in (B2) are facts involving necessary truth.

Regarding (B3), the semantic theory developed over the years by Katz and his associates has always assumed what Katz and Postal (1989: 9) call 'a substantive relation between NLs and logic'.[17] They observe that definitions of semantic properties like 'analytic' and of semantic relations like 'analytic entailment' provide an account of one class of facts about logical implication. And since analytic entailments are valid, Katz and others have found it reasonable to suppose that the senses of natural language sentences contain semantic information essential to the theory of implication. The semantic theory in question has assumed, in other words, that senses provide at least part of the propositional information on the basis of which logical laws apply to natural language sentences. That is, it is assumed that there is an overlap between what Katz and Postal (1989: 9) call 'aspects of grammatical form' and 'logical principles', respectively.[18]

As for (B4), it is closely interlinked with the assumption, just mentioned, of an overlap between the senses of sentences and the laws of logic. Thus, Katz and Postal (1989: 9) state:

> acceptance of an overlap between the senses of NL sentences and logical objects involves linguists in foundational issues at least to the extent of committing them to a *common* ontological position for linguistics and logic. For the objects to which logical laws apply and those laws themselves can hardly belong to different ontological realms.

For example, if logical laws are not psychological, the objects to which they apply cannot be psychological either, and vice versa.

Following Frege (1967), Platonists have argued that logical laws cannot be psychological. If they were, they could not be the laws of necessary connection that they are. As Katz and Postal (1989: 10) put it: 'If logical laws were "laws of thought", that is, empirical laws about contingent things, they would be contingent and, like laws in physics and other natural sciences, could possibly be false. But, being necessarily true, logical laws could not possibly be false.' Rather, laws of logic have conventionally been assigned a realist status. That is, these laws have been considered abstract objects: objective, timeless, placeless entities not involved in causation. But if laws and the objects to which they apply must have the same ontological status, then (senses of) sentences have to be considered abstract objects. This is the core of the justification furnished by Katz and Postal for their Platonist conception of language.

In terms of Chomskyan conceptualism, Katz and Postal (1989: 10) claim, the senses of sentences have to be psychological (or biological). To account for facts about analyticity and analytical entailment, Chomskyans would therefore have to adopt a psychological conception of logic too. Katz and Postal (1989: 10), however, consider 'Frege's arguments against psychologism too compelling to contemplate defending a psychological view of logic'. Consequently, they (1989: 15) contend, Chomskyan conceptualism cannot explain such facts as the validity of analytic inferences like that from *John killed Bill* to *Bill is dead.* And so, according to Katz and Postal, Chomskyan conceptualism fails to satisfy the condition embodied in the belief (B1).[19]

Katz and Postal (1989: 11) maintain that the inability of conceptualism to provide an explanation for the logicosemantic facts in question springs from a particular 'mistake'. This mistake takes the form of a 'failure' which is parallel to the failure by American structuralism to draw a distinction between the knowledge of a natural language (competence) and the exercise of that knowledge (performance). The failure to draw the competence-performance distinction has led to an 'adulteration of grammar' with such 'extraneous facts' as memory limitations. Katz and Postal (1989: 11–12) go on to argue that 'Conceptualism's mistake is the parallel failure to draw the further distinction between knowledge of an NL and the object it is knowledge of, the NL itself.' Without this distinction, they claim, grammar is still being adulterated by various extraneous factors. These are the particular features of information representation and processing in the human mind/brain. By taking grammars to be theories of epistemic states, Katz and Postal (1989: 12) contend, conceptualism makes everything about a natural language a contingent matter of human psychology. Consequently, there is no place for necessary connection in grammatical structure. Given, however, the distinciton between knowledge of a natural language and the natural langauge that is known, the grammatical structure of sentences can be specified in a way that enables them to play a role in logic, Katz and Postal argue. And, they go on (1989: 12) to comment, 'Just as C's [= Chomsky's] competence/ performance distinction provided a basis for a psychological formulation of the foundations of linguistics, the distinction between linguistic knowledge and its object provided one for a realist formulation.' Accordingly, Katz (1981: 77) considers his main criticism of conceptualism to be parallel to Chomsky's main criticism of nominalism (as embodied in American structuralism): 'the constraints imposed put too low a ceiling on the abstractness of grammars for them to be optimal.'

Katz (1981: 77–8; 1984; 34) has noted that the fundamental distinction drawn by Platonism between the knowledge that speakers have of their language and the languages that speakers have knowledge of is simply a special case of a more general epistemological distinction: the distinction between the knowledge that we have of things and the things that we have the knowledge of. Various disciplines provide for special cases of this distinction. In mathematics, for example, a distinction is drawn between an ideal calculator's knowledge of the natural numbers and the natural numbers themselves. And, in logic, a distinction in drawn between an ideal reasoner's knowledge of implication and the implication relations themselves. Katz (1984: 34) observes that 'Platonism is in part an attempt to be consistent in our treatment of the special sciences by drawing the same distinction between knowledge and its object in the case of linguistics that we drew, as a matter of course, in the parallel cases of logic and mathematics.' In Katz's (1981: 78) view, the Platonist position thus does not have to produce a justification for treating linguistics differently from mathematics and logic, a justification that to him 'seems not to be available'.

You are right, Dear Buyer. The justification put forward by Platonists for their conception of language has about it, undeniably, a ring of reasonableness. But, Buyer, beware: in the end, magic owes its power to what is hard to hear or see. And in keeping with this counsel, alas, adroitly articulated justifications too have to be closely considered for what they may conceal. So it is of some interest that, in justifying their Abstractist Act, realists have kept the assumptions (A1) and (A4) cleverly out of sight. But before contemplating the consequences of this concealment, we need to attend to another matter first.

4.1.3 Siting the show in science

What kind of discipline is linguistics? This is one of the questions engendered by the Platonist distinction 'language *v.* knowledge of language' and by the assumption that languages are abstract objects. Like other sciences that study an object as opposed to knowledge of this object, Platonist linguistics is construed not to be a form of psychology. Thus, with reference to mathematics and logic Katz (1981: 78) observes: 'There is no temptation to conflate the psychological study of the ideal calculator's knowledge of number with the mathematical study of numbers, or to conflate the psychological study of the ideal reasoner's knowledge of implication relations with the logical study of implication relations.' And he goes on to ask rhetorically: 'But, if there is a clear distinction in these disciplines, why conflate psychological study of the ideal speaker's knowledge of a language with the grammatical study of the language?' (cf. also Katz 1984: 34 for these views). Accordingly, one of the two basic claims made by Platonism is, in Katz's (1981: 76) words

> that linguistics is not a psychological science, that its theories are not about states of mind, mental events, or their neurological realizations, but about sentences and languages directly in the way that we ordinarily take linguistics to be about sentences and languages.[20]

In arguing that linguistics is not a psychological science, Platonists do not mean to question the legitimacy of the study of knowledge of language or linguistic competence. Thus Katz and Postal (1989: 13) remark:

> Naturally, realists acknowledge the legitimacy of questions about competence, just as conceptualists acknowledge the legitimacy of questions about performance. But according to realism, the study of the competence belongs to the empirical field of psycholinguistics rather than to the formal discipline of linguistics.

Note that the second one of the statements justs quoted contains *inter alia* the core of the positive part of the Platonist answer to the question 'What kind of discipline is linguistics?' Given the distinction between knowledge of language and language, and given the assumption that languages are abstract objects, linguistics is a formal science. But what does this mean?

To begin with, Katz (1984: 27) assigns linguistics the status of 'a branch of mathematics'. Like the mathematician, Katz (1981: 212–13) maintains, the linguist sees his task as that of constructing a theory 'revealing the structure of a set of abstract objects'. Linguistic theories, on the Platonist view, are '*a priori* systematizations' of facts about natural language sentences.[21] This means that linguistics is not an empirical enterprise.[22] But this does not mean to Platonists that linguistics is not 'scientific', is 'devoid of intellectual interest' or does not pursue truth (cf. Katz 1981: 2, 3, 46; 1984: 19; Katz and Postal 1989: 19, 37). Thus, reacting to a criticism voiced by Chomsky, Katz and Postal (1989: 19) remark:

> The last phrase of (14), which mentions 'true theories', amounts to the gratuitous conclusion that failure to interpret talk about NLs as talk about psychological structures abandons interest in true theories. This has as little ground as would a claim that failure to interpret talk about real numbers as talk about psychological structures abandons interest in true (mathematical) theories. In linguistics, as in logic and mathematics, realists abandon interest in true theories of *psychology*, but this does not mean they abandon interest in true theories. True theories of psychology are abandoned in order to pursue true theories of NLs, implication and numbers.

This brings us to the epistemological means adopted by realists for the pursuit of true theories of natural languages. If these means are not the means of empirical science, what can they be? How is it possible to obtain *a priori* knowledge of abstract objects, objects neither located in time and space nor involved in causality? The essence of the answer given by Katz (1981: 193) is that 'Platonists invoke intuition to play essentially the same role in their account of *a priori* knowledge that perception and introspection play in accounts of *a posteriori* knowledge.' In Katz's (1981: 195) view, perception, introspection and intuition are mental faculties 'issuing in acts of apprehension'. That is, these three mental faculties provide people with basic knowledge. These three faculties differ in his view principally in terms of the kinds of objects about which they provide such knowledge. In perception, he contends, people observe physical objects: objects in the external world. In introspection, people observe objects of subjective experience: their own thoughts, feelings, emotions etc. And in intuition, Katz asserts, people grasp abstract objects: numbers, sets, sentences etc. In his view, both intuition and perception involve internal representations of objects. These representations he considers to be the source of knowledge. But, he believes, neither in the case of perception nor in the case of intuition do they represent something psychological. What is represented in both cases, Katz (1981: 196) claims, is 'something objective'. Introspection, by contrast, he considers to be a matter of obtaining 'mental meter readings'. The important point to Katz (1981: 196), therefore, is that 'Though the source of an intuition is psychological, its import concerns objective matters of linguistic, logical, or mathematic fact.' Finally, Katz (1981: 199) assumes that, like perception and introspection, intuition is fallible: there can be genuine instances of erroneous intuition.[23]

Katz's (1981: 200–2) Platonism differs in an important respect from traditional Platonism in regard to the way the faculty of intuition 'works'. Traditional Platonism has modelled its account of intuition on perception: intuitive knowledge depends on the knower's establishing some form of direct contact with the objects of knowledge. That is, the traditional Platonist account requires a causal relation between a perceiver and the perceived object. Katz (1981: 201), however, notes that abstract objects could not occur in such a causal relation: 'Being objective, abstract objects do not occur as a constituent of the conscious experience of a knower, and, being aspatial and atemporal, they cannot act on a knower through a causal process to produce a representation of themselves in the manner of sense perception.' Hence, Katz (1981: 202) prefers an alternative, Kantian, account of intuition. On Kant's account, Katz observes, intuitive awareness is not conceived of as a causal effect of an external event. Rather, intuitive awareness is considered 'the effect of an internal construction'. Katz (1981: 203) stresses that what is 'internally constructed' is not abstract objects themselves, but rather internal representations of abstract objects. The internal representations may or may not correspond to the abstract objects outside people. It is for this reason that Katz considers intuitions to be fallible.

Like research in mathematics and logic, linguistic research begins, according to Katz and Postal (1989: 36), with 'a finite number of basic facts provided by intuition'. And each type of research generalizes to infinite collections. In logic, for instance, research begins with intuitions about implication relations among propositions, consistency relations among propositions, and so on. These intuitions, they claim, involve a very small, finite number of cases which are generalized to principles about all propositions, principles such as those involved in Modus Ponens. Likewise, Katz and Postal (1989: 36) maintain, linguistic research begins with 'a finite, in fact extremely small number of facts', facts such as those about analyticity and analytical entailment considered above. And these facts, similarly, are generalized to infinite collections of sentences. The grammars that result from the 'projection' of the initial or early facts are, as Katz (1984: 23) notes, 'revisable in the light of later intuitions and canons of theory construction'. Truth or correctness in the case of Platonist grammars is assumed by Katz and Postal (1989: 31) to be essentially 'a matter of factual coverage and simplicity'.

Sure, Bottled-up Blue, let fly and speak your mind about what you term 'tricky talk about intuition'. Indeed, the thought has occurred to me too that what is involved in the grasping of abstract objects is not intuition but rather illusion. But don't expect Manhattan Magicians to buy the suggestion that their Abstractist Act is an exercise in illusionist magic. Indeed, a certain Performing Platonist going by the cryptic stage-name of J. the Fey has various ways of handling mistrustful members of an audience who dare to doubt the existence of intuition. For instance, on one occasion – I recall it vividly – this Resourceful Realist turned dramatically to the wings and summoned on to the stage a witness, Ram the Ham, reputed to be able to receive mathematical messages broadcast to us (or should that be 'beamed down'?) from the Platonic Plane:

> *People without first-hand experience [of mathematical intuition] or people with doubts about the interpretation of intuition can examine*

> *the remarkable case of Ramanujan, an Indian postal clerk who discovered huge amounts of mathematics for himself without even a rudimentary knowledge of mathematical proof. (Katz 1981: 193–4)*

You find the Indian connection disconcerting? Well, so do I, so do I. But I won't go so far as to say that resorting to the establishment of a New York–New Delhi Axis has reduced Platonist epistemology to a Realist Rope Trick. Not just yet, anyway.

4.1.4 *Appraising the abstractist act*

So far, there has not been a coherent debate about putative merits and flaws of the Platonist conception of language. On the one hand, this conception of language has been criticized by a variety of scholars who cannot be considered Chomskyans. Strangely, though, Platonists on the whole have failed to respond to these criticisms. On the other hand, Chomsky himself has so far refrained from directly subjecting the Platonist conception of language to systematic criticism. The rather cryptic critical comments that he has made on this conception of language have the character of asides scattered about in his various accounts of the foundations of conceptualism. Curiously, Platonists, notably Katz and Postal (1989), have taken great pains to collect and rebut these insufficiently explicated criticisms. Below we will consider six of the more important points of criticism against the Platonist conception of language.[24]

1 Several aspects of Platonist linguistic ontology have not been sufficiently well explicated.

Two examples should suffice to illustrate this point of criticism. First, Dillinger (1984a: 17) has observed that Katz (1981) does not specify the possible relations between the 'three independent kinds of reality: material, mental and mathematical'. Dillinger does not consider it sufficient for Katz to say that mental and mathematical objects can be linked by the 'knowledge of' relation which is 'simply left undefined. Nearly ten years after the publication of the book reviewed by Dillinger, Katz and Postal (1989: 34) still find themselves obliged to observe that

> It is, of course, hard at present to say what this relation consists in [i.e. the relation in which internal rules representing knowledge of language stand to the collection of sentences as sound-meaning-pairs], because the 'knowledge of' relation is as complex as the 'exercise of' relation linking competence and performance.

Secondly, as noted in section 4.1.1 above, the Platonist notion 'the abstract object natural language' is obscure in regard to ontological import. Specifically, it is unclear whether a Katzian Platonist linguistic reality, in addition to including sentences and languages, also includes '(natural) language (in general)'. And it is equally unclear what the individuating properties of this putative object might be.

2 It is dubious whether particular individual languages denoted by terms such as 'English' or 'French' can be taken to exist as abstract objects of a Platonist sort.

Versions of this criticism have been offered by both Pateman (1983: 283; 1987: 51) and Carr (1990: 122–3). It is based on the observation that 'the act of intuition' does not yield direct judgements about languages such as English or French considered as wholes. In this regard, then, languages are unlike sentences: there are no direct data on the basis of which particular individual languages can be linguistically defined. To put it another way: in terms of the 'knowledge of' relation, there are no intuitive data for the explanation of which a linguistic theory has to use concepts such as 'English' or 'French'.

Carr (1990: 123) contends, accordingly, that Katz (1981: 77, 79) is mistaken in using the 'knowledge of' relation to justify 'French' etc. as linguistic objects. One can take the 'knowledge of' relation as having sentences and their properties as its object, Carr maintains, without having to claim that 'French' etc. are linguistic objects. And he (1990: 123) concludes: 'In having knowledge of a given set of sentences and their properties, or the grammar which underlies these, it is an arbitrary matter whether we refer to that grammar as "French", "Spanish", or whatever.' Note, incidentally, that if the existence of an abstract linguistic object has to be justified by means of invoking the 'knowledge of' relation, it is dubious whether what Katz has called 'the abstract object natural language' can be claimed to exist in the realm of Platonist linguistic reality. No evidence has been offered that non-linguists, through 'acts of intuitive apprehension', have knowledge of this putative Platonist object.

3 The idea that languages are sets or collections of sentences is flawed in fundamental ways.

This point embodies Chomsky's criticisms of the conception of 'E(xternalized)-language'. In terms of this conception, a language is something external to the mind/brain. As Chomsky (1986: 20) puts it, 'E-language' is a 'construct' that is 'understood independently of the properties of the mind/brain'. On this conception, Chomsky (1986: 19) observes, a language has been viewed as a collection or system of actions, events, utterances or linguistic forms such as words or sentences.[25]

Chomsky's various criticisms of the notion of 'E-language' have been taken by Katz and Postal (1989) as applying to the Platonist conception of language as well. And they have attempted a systematic rebuttal of these criticisms. For the purposes of the present discussion, Chomsky's criticisms of the notion 'E-language' may be reduced to the following three:

(1) E-language is 'artificial' or 'epiphenomenal' in that it is too far removed from the psychological, ultimately biological, mechanisms involved in the acquisition and use of language (Chomsky 1986: 26–8). As a consequence, an E-language can be characterized in various ways. Hence, Chomsky (1986: 26) contends, 'there is no issue of correctness with regard to E-languages.' No questions of truth or falsity, he (1986: 20) maintains, arise here.

Katz and Postal (1989: 34) consider Chomsky's (1986: 27) remark that 'E-language, however construed, is farther removed from (psychological) mechanisms than I-language, at a higher order of abstraction' to be 'incoherent':

> If E-languages do not exist ('are not real-world objects'), then they cannot be further removed from anything, and no distance measure can relate *them* to (presumably psychological) mechanisms. And if they *do* exist, the realist claim is granted and it hardly matters that E-languages represent 'a higher order of abstraction'.

And to Chomsky's point that there is no issue of correctness with regard to E-languages, Katz and Postal's (1989: 31) overly brief response is 'that correctness is a matter of factual coverage and simplicity.'

(2) In terms of the notion of 'E-language', languages are ill-defined in having no determinate boundaries (Chomsky 1986: 25). In a more superficial sense, it is unclear in the case of many expressions or sentences, e.g. *Give it me*, whether they are contained by a particular E-language or not. In a deeper sense too, E-languages are vague and indeterminate. Chomsky (1987a: 33) argues this point by referring to 'semi-grammatical sentences' such as *The child seems sleeping*. He asks whether this expression is in the language or outside, and maintains that either answer is unacceptable. All of this makes the status of E-language quite obscure in Chomsky's (1986: 25) opinion: 'the bounds of E-language can be set in one way or another, depending on some rather arbitrary decisions as to what it should include.'

As regards the more superficial sense in which Chomsky considers E-languages to have indeterminate boundaries, Katz and Postal (1989: 38) reply that 'the problem is the same for conceptualist and realist alike because it lies at the level of linguistics proper [as opposed to the study of the foundations of linguistics].' In their view, many cases of apparent indeterminacy 'reduce to questions about distinct closely related NLs sharing many sentences'. So, they presume, everyone would judge that British English contains this sentence and American English does not. Katz and Postal's response to Chomsky's point that E-languages are indeterminate in a deeper sense as well is too detailed to represent in full here. The essence of their position, however, is that there is no dispute about the fact that *The child seems sleeping* is ill-formed. Realists, consequently, say that this string is not part of the relevant E-language. And to account for the interpretation of such 'semi-sentences', Katz and Postal argue, both they and Chomsky would have to appeal to auxiliary hypotheses of a nongrammatical character.

(3) The concept of E-language is too far removed from what is real; that is, it is not sufficiently close to the common-sense notion of language. In support of this claim, Chomsky (1986: 27) observes that when people speak of a person knowing a language they do

not mean that he or she knows an infinite set of sentences or sound-meaning pairs (taken in extension) or a set of behaviours or acts. Rather, they mean that the person knows 'what makes sound and meaning relate to one another in a specific way, what makes them "hang together"'. Katz and Postal (1989: 34) consider these remarks by Chomsky as being 'not really relevant to the issues between conceptualism and realism'. In any event, they contend, these remarks are based on a misconception, 'the illicit supposition that the fact in which knowledge of an NL consists is nonrelational'. For, they argue, if this fact is relational, 'then knowing an NL does mean knowing an infinite set of sound/meaning pairs.'[26]

4 Platonists have not given a satisfactory account of how people can come to have knowledge of abstract objects.

In Katz's view, let us recall, abstract objects are objective. This means that they do not form part of a person's subjective, conscious experience. Hence, a person cannot come to know anything about abstract objects by means of introspection. Katz believes moreover that abstract objects, being aspatial and atemporal, cannot act causally on a person's senses. Hence, a person cannot come to know anything about abstract objects by means of perception. These points, Katz (1981: 201) summarizes as follows: 'Being objective, abstract objects do not occur as a constituent of the conscious experience of a knower, and, being aspatial and atemporal, they cannot act on a knower through a causal process to produce a representation of themselves in the manner of sense perception.' The question then is: How can a person, e.g. a linguist, possibly get to know anything about abstract linguistic objects? This, of course, is a question about the epistemology needed by Platonists for investigating abstract linguistic objects. And various scholars, e.g. Itkonen (1983a: 242) and Carr (1990: 120–1), have argued that the epistemology proposed by Katz is unsatisfactory.

As observed in section 4.1.3 above, the epistemology proposed by Katz (1981: 201ff.) for acquiring knowledge of abstract (linguistic) objects is essentially a Kantian theory of pure intuition. In terms of this theory, we have seen, intuitive awareness is not a causal effect of an external event, but the effect of an internal construction (Katz 1981: 202). That is, on a Kantian theory, a person is able to construct a mental representation of an abstract object.

To flesh out the Kantian conception of pure intuition for the special case of the apprehension of the grammatical structure of sentences, Katz proposes three further 'components'. The first is a Chomsky-like nativist theory of how speakers of natural language acquire their knowledge of its grammar. On this theory of Katz's (1981: 204), there is an *a priori* source for the universal conditions that must be sufficient (a) for the construction of the abstract notion of a sentence of a natural language and (b) for the construction of the less abstract concepts of 'English sentence', 'French sentence' etc. as well as for their intuitive instantiations.

Given the distinction between knowledge and its object, Katz (1981: 204) contends, the mental representation of the grammatical structure of a sentence may diverge from the grammatical structure of the sentence in the language. In Katz's (1981: 205) phrasing 'such mental representations can, and probably do, contain errors of omission and commission about the structure of sentences of the language.' In order to explain how intuition compensates for such errors or misrepresentations, Katz proposes two further components for his theory of intuition. One component – the second component of his 'fleshed out' theory of Kantian intuiton – corrects for such errors on the basis of what Katz (1981: 205) depicts as 'an innate notion of the "knowledge of" relation'. He assumes that the faculty of intuition has access to this innate notion and that it utilizes the distinction between knowledge and its object 'to compensate for [mental] misrepresentations of grammatical structure'. The other 'corrective' component – the third component of Katz's 'fleshed out' theory – is based on the assumption that people have an innate idea of an abstract (linguistic) object. Intuition, in Katz's (1981: 205) terminology, 'sculpts' a person's innate idea of the abstract object 'sentence' into the concept of a sentence *in concreto*.[27] So what Katz assumes is, in short, that the ontological characteristics of the object that grammatical knowledge is knowledge of are specified by the innate idea of an abstract object.

The interaction between the three components of his epistemology is depicted as follows by Katz (1981: 205):

> Using both the 'knowledge-of' relation and the idea of an abstract object, the faculty of intuition can operate on principles reflecting the form tacit grammatical rules take in humans and depsychologize them, reconstructing representations of sentences as concrete concepts of abstract objects. These two further components seem sufficient, since they can rectify the respects in which a speaker's tacit rules misdescribe facts about the language and construct concepts of abstract objects that properly describe sentence structure.

As outlined above, Katz's theory of intuition accounts for only those intuitions based on tacit knowledge. He (1981: 205–6) 'extends' this theory by assigning also to explicit knowledge, i.e. 'knowledge acquired in scientific pursuits', the role of 'input to the faculty of intuition'. Katz (1981: 206) believes that 'Intuitions based on tacit knowledge come first ontogenetically but as soon as explicit knowledge is acquired it feeds back into the faculty of intuition.' By means of this extension Katz provides for a source of intuitions about abstract objects postulated in the context of 'advanced theories'.

Katz's theory of intuition is problematic in various respects. First, Katz's explication of this highly intricate theory is at a level of generality and abstraction that leaves many specific points unclear. It is because of this, it seems, that Itkonen (1983a: 242) has maintained that this 'rather exotic apparatus' of Katz's does not give a satisfactory account of how people can come to have knowledge of something that has no causal relation to them. Thus, Itkonen remarks, Katz's account does not explain 'why there should be so good a fit between abstract objects, on the one hand, and innate ideas and internal representations, on the other'. Recourse to 'the innate idea of an abstract object' does not really contribute much to the solution of this problem. For, as Carr (1990: 121) has observed, Katz leaves it unclear how people are supposed to come to possess their innate knowledge of the concept 'abstract object'. This is a problem for Carr (1990: 121), 'especially when one considers that abstract objects are not available for causal interaction during the evolutionary process'.

Secondly, Katz (1981: 206) does not see his account of the operation of the faculty of intuition as representing 'an actual model'. His account is, in his own view, the product of having performed the 'philosophical task' of explaining 'how we can have inner representations of grammatical abstract objects without there having to be a causal relation of some sort between the subjective representation and the objective sentence.' Katz considered it 'fanciful' to think of providing 'at this time' an 'actual model' of the set of 'operating rules' of the faculty of intuition. Accordingly, he was not obliged to present any factual evidence in support of his theory of intuition.

Ten years later, however, Katz has still not presented an 'actual model' which could be subjected to empirical appraisal. In the absence of such an 'actual model' supported by factual evidence, non-Platonists will remain sceptical about the ability of people to come to have knowledge of abstract objects. And this scepticism will, understandably, extend to the existence of such objects. It is the absence of such an 'actual model' that has made it possible for Allan (1983: 679) to 'remain skeptical of his [Katz's] refurbishment of the immortal soul'. And possible for Dillinger (1984a: 302) to pose the rhetorical question: 'How is intuition to be distinguished from delirium, religious enlightment or dreams?'[28]

5 The Platonist conception of language is heuristically not relatively fruitful.

In terms of non-Platonist linguistic ontologies such as conceptualism, languages are acquired and used (utterances in them are produced and perceived), languages are subject to change and variation, languages are influenced by contact with other languages, and so on. That is, languages are believed to be ontologically integrated in a wider linguistic reality. Given this belief, it is required that a conception of language should be heuristically fruitful in the sense that its adoption leads to a better understanding of phenomena such as language acquisition, speech production and perception, language change, linguistic variation, language contact and so on. Conversely, such phenomena are viewed as potentially valuable sources of independent evidence about the nature and structure of language and languages. In sum: a conception of language that forms the core of such a non-Platonist approach is epistemically exposed to the corrective pressure and substantiating impact of evidence from a wide variety of sources.[29] On the Platonist conception of language, by contrast, it is not languages that are involved in the processes or phenomena indicated in the list above. Rather, it is knowledge of languages. Witness Katz (1981: 9): 'The language is a timeless, unchangeable, objective structure: knowledge of language is temporal, subject to change and subjective.' And: 'Language acquisition and language change thus involve a change in people's knowledge of language, with concomitant changes in their relationship to the linguistic structures in this infinite range [of languages].' Katz (1981: 9) considers the study of languages to be 'the study of these linguistic structures'. And he considers this study to be 'distinguishable from the study of human (or other) knowledge of them, its acquisition, use, or change'. The former study he labels 'linguistics (proper)'; the latter, 'psychology'.

On the Platonist view, then, languages are ontologically relatively isolated and claims about language(s) epistemically relatively insulated. Against this background, it is understandable why the Platonist conception of language has not been instrumental in linguists gaining a better understanding of the linguistic processes or phenomena listed above.[30] Moreover, data about such phenomena have not been used as independent evidence in support of the idea that languages are abstract objects. These observations, probably, form the basis for Fodor's (1985a: 160) view that:

> unlike the Platonistic linguist, the psycholinguist thinks that other kinds of data can constrain the choice of grammars too. He is therefore professionally interested in how languages are learned, how utterances are understood, whether there are linguistic universals, whether transformations are innate, how cognition affects language, how language affects cognition, aphasic speech, schizophrenic speech, metaphorical speech, speech production, speech acts, and, in short, all that stuff that got people interested in studying languages in the first place. Go ahead, be a Platonist if you like. But the action is all at the other end of town.

As a consequence, Fodor (1985a: 159) states, 'deep down nobody is remotely interested in it [Platonism].'

Platonists may contend that it does not follow from their beliefs that languages are ontologically isolated in an absolute sense. Nor, they may maintain, is it the case that their conception of language is epistemically insulated or heuristically unfruitful. In support of these contentions they may argue, for example, that, via knowledge of language, abstract linguistic objects are indirectly 'involved' in the above-mentioned linguistic processes or phenomena. And data about these processes or phenomena may be brought to bear indirectly, via theories of linguistic knowledge, on the Platonist conception of language. In this connection, Katz and Postal (1989: 13) have stated that 'realists can entertain the possibility of inferences from features of competence to features of NLs [natural languages], just as conceptualists can entertain the possibility of inferences from features of performance to features of competence.'

How it is possible to draw inferences from features of competence to features of natural languages, however, is not explained by Katz and Postal. Specifically, what is unclear is how data, facts etc. obtained by conceptualists in the *empirical* study of competence can, as a matter of principle, be used by Platonists in the *formal, non-empirical* study of natural languages. Katz and Postal's analogy in the remarks quoted above breaks down in a crucial respect. The study of features of competence, and the study of features of performance, are both taken to instantiate empirical inquiry. This means that, unlike inferences from features of competence to features of natural languages, inferences from features of performance to features of competence do not have to 'leap across' the epistemological divide separating empirical science from formal science. In the final analysis, Platonists have to show that Dillinger (1984a: 302) is wrong in claiming that 'interpreting linguistic theories in terms of abstract objects unrelated to mind or matter [and thereby turning linguistics into a branch of mathematics] makes all the rest of science, from anatomy to zoology, absolutely irrelevant to linguistics.'[31]

6 In developing and defending their linguistic ontology and in criticizing alternative ontologies such as conceptualism, Platonists make use of stipulation at crucial junctures.

Let us consider four examples of the meta-practice mentioned in 6. The first example involves the way in which Platonists go about defining the 'subject matter' or fixing the 'scope' of a discipline. Recall that in section 4.1.2 above we saw that, in arguing for Platonism and against conceptualism, Katz and Postal proceed from the implicit assumption (A1): It is possible to state *a priori* the (categories of) facts that fall within the domain or scope of a discipline. In line with this assumption, they state that all linguistic theories have to account for, amongst other things, facts about analyticity and analytic entailment. And they proceed to argue that, whereas linguistic theories based on a conceptualist conception of language cannot do this, linguistic theories based on a Platonist conception can. Therefore, they conclude, the Platonist conception is to be preferred to the conceptualist one.

This line of argumentation embodies what Fodor (1985a: 147–8) has called 'the Wrong View' of linguistics. On Fodor's characterization, it will be recalled, the Wrong View maintains

> (a) that there is a specifiable data base for linguistic theories; (b) that this data base can be specified antecedently to theory construction; (c) that the empirical content of linguistic theories consists of what they have to say about the data base; and (d) that the data base for linguistics consists of the corpora of utterances that informants produce (or, in some versions, would produce given specified forms of prompting).

Fodor suggests that if (d) were modified so as to read 'the data base for linguistics consists of the intuitions (about grammaticality, ambiguity and so on) that informants produce or would produce', then one gets the view of linguistic inquiry common to Stich (1985) and the later Katz (1977).

Fodor (1985a: 150–1) proceeds to argue that the view that the scientist can stipulate what data are to count as relevant to the (dis)confirmation of his theories in simply not plausible, given the way that real science is conducted. He takes this to be a point of the utmost methodological importance since it implies that 'either the Wrong View misdescribes linguistics or what linguists do is somehow an exception to the methodological principles that other sciences endorse.'

Of course, if the assumption (A1) is to be disallowed, and if facts about analyticity and analytical entailment do not necessarily bear on the adequacy of linguistic theories and on the conceptions of language underlying these, then Katz and Postal's main argument for a Platonist linguistic ontology loses much of its force.

The second example of the use of stipulation by Platonists concerns the relevance of the evidence they use for the justification of linguistic theories. Recall that this evidence consists of linguistic intuitions of native speakers. Katz (1981: 71) has even assigned intuitive evidence the status of 'direct evidence', saying thereby that it takes priority over other kinds of evidence.

Recall that Fodor (1985a: 151), however, has argued that any science is under an obligation to explain why *what it takes to be* data relevant to the justification of its theories *are* indeed data relevant to the justification of its theories. A scientist typically meets this condition by exhibiting a causal chain that runs from the entities that a theory posits, via the instruments of observation, to the psychological states of the observers. If the scientist is unable to connect the observations to the postulated entities by means of such a causal chain, he has no warrant to appeal to those observations as evidence for (or against) his theories.

Fodor (1985a: 152), moreover, observes that these general considerations apply, *mutatis mutandis*, to linguistics:

> In particular, an adequate linguistics *should explain why it is that the intuitions of speaker/hearers constitute data relevant to the confirmation of grammars.* The Right View meets this condition. It says 'We can use intuitions to confirm grammars because grammars are internally represented and actually contribute to the etiology of the speaker/hearer's intuitive judgments.' The Wrong View says only: 'We do it because we have always done it', or 'We do it by stipulation.'[32]

Being unable to establish a causal chain between abstract entities and native speakers' linguistic intuitions, Fodor observes, Platonists have to *stipulate* that linguistic intuitions are relevant to the justification of their linguistic theories. The ontological belief that linguistic entities are abstract thus forces Platonists to introduce an arbitrary element into their epistemology.

The third example of the use of stipulation by Platonists concerns the conditions on the basis of which conceptions of language or foundational positions should be appraised. In the introductory section of their paper, Katz and Postal (1989: 5) have the following to say about these conditions:

> To establish the superiority of any foundational position, one would have to meet the following general condition:
>
> (10) Show that the position
> a. provides a coherent account of the nature of the objects linguistics proper is about;
> b. offers a more adequate account than its rivals of all the facts in linguistics proper.
>
> (10a) requires a consistent account of the foundations of linguistics. (10b) requires that the account sacrifice a minimum of unchallenged facts in the domain of linguistics proper.

Katz and Postal's (10a) and (10b), needless to say, are not the only conditions that may be used for appraising a conception of language or foundational position. Of the various other conditions that have figured prominently in foundational debates, I mention two only:

(C1) A conception of language/foundational position should be heuristically fruitful.
(C2) A conception of language/foundational position should not necessitate the adoption of an obscure or obviously flawed epistemology.

(C1) played an important role in Chomsky's incisive critique of Bloomfieldian physicalism and (Skinnerian) behaviourism. He argued persuasively that, if these conceptions of language were adopted, no progress could be made in gaining new insights into or a better understanding of important aspects of linguistic structure, language acquisition and language use (Chomsky 1964; Botha 1989b; and chapter 2). Platonists such as Katz and Postal, of course, have accepted Chomsky's criticisms of physicalism and behaviourism (Katz 1981: 2, 12; Katz and Postal 1989: 4). It is therefore strange that they do not consider a condition with the gist of (C1) when embarking on a comparative appraisal of realism and conceptualism. They simply stipulate that their (10a) and (10b) are the conditions pertinent to their critical exercise.[33]

Turning to (C2), this condition (as we saw above) has been invoked by various scholars in their appraisal of Platonism. And Katz (1981: 193) himself has noted that 'chief' among the 'doubts' about the respectability of the philosophical basis of Platonism 'is the fear that Platonism does not mesh with an acceptable epistemology'. Accordingly, he uses a whole chapter of his 1981 book in an attempt 'to mitigate these doubts as much as possible by developing an [intuitionist] account of how humans obtain *a priori* knowledge of abstract objects'. But when selecting conditions for establishing the 'superiority' of foundational positions, Katz and Postal (1989: 5) simply stipulate that these should be their (10a) and (10b), making no mention of a condition with the general thrust of (C2). It is tempting to speculate that Katz and Postal's refraining from the use of either (C1) to (C2) in their comparative appraisal is somehow linked to the fact that Platonism has not turned out to be heuristically fruitful or to be associated with an 'acceptable epistemology'.[34]

For the fourth example of the objectionable use of stipulation by Platonists, we consider yet again Katz and Postal's condition (10b). This condition gives rise to a question: What is it that makes one (grammatical/linguistic) 'account' of 'the facts' more adequate than its rivals? That is: What are the criteria of adequacy for a comparative evaluation of rival grammatical/linguistic theories? Elaborating on (10b), Katz and Postal (1989: 3) mention one such criterion, which may be restated as (CA1).

(CA1) An account A1 is more adequate than an account A2 if A1 'sacrifices' fewer unchallenged facts in the domain of 'linguistics proper' than does A2.

In discussing the 'issue of correctness' as it arises in Platonist linguistics, Katz and Postal (1989: 31) state that 'correctness is a matter of factual coverage and simplicity'. Presumably, by 'factual coverage' Katz and Postal mean a criterion of adequacy such as (CA1) and by 'simplicity' one that may be stated as (CA2).

(CA2) An account A1 is more adequate than an account A2 if A1 is (in some sense) simpler than is A2.

But Katz and Postal give no reasons for choosing (CA1) and (CA2) from among the stock of criteria that have been used by present-day linguists for appraising grammars and linguistic theories.[35] It is sufficient to cite here two other criteria belonging to this stock, criteria which Chomskyan linguists have considered to be particularly important:

(CA3) An account A1 of linguistic facts is more adequate than an account A2 if A1 has greater deductive depth than does A2.

(CA4) An account A1 of linguistic facts is more adequate than an account A2 if A1 uses unifying principles whereas A2 uses superficial generalizations.

Both (CA3) and (CA4) are keyed to gaining deeper insight into or better understanding of facts rather than to providing wider coverage of them.[36] Why Katz and Postal prefer the criteria of adequacy (CA1) and (CA2) to alternatives such as (CA3) and (CA4), they do not explain. They simply stipulate (CA1) and (CA2).

Which brings us back to The Market and, this time, to the Theatre of Thaumaturgism. Reviewing a sizzling solo show by Katz (1981), the disrespectful detractor called Dillinger (1984a: 301–2) has dressed down this Master of Miraculous Metaphysics for dexterously dealing himself diverse criterial cards in order to demonstrate that Platonism is the 'proper' ontological interpretation for linguistic theories:

> *Essential to this argument is that the sense of 'proper' remain obscure, as it does, throughout the book. 'Proper' can thus be made to indicate a set of criteria specific to logical and mathematical theories and which, of course, no factual theory will be able to meet,* e.g. *maximal absolute simplicity and abstractness. With the cards stacked in this way, the conclusion is inevitable: the argument holds, abstract objects must exist, and linguistics is a kind of mathematics. This is what is touted as 'an approach [that] can expect to settle ontological controversies non-arbitrarily and without begging philosophical questions' (pp. 12–13)!*

Being a trumping trick in Katzian Conceptual Cards, then – as Catching-on Customer, you have anticipated all too accurately – Stacking by Stipulation amounts to pure magic. Dillinger (1984a:

302), incidentally, felt that our Artist-at-Arcanery would have done better to perform a spell binding speech act: 'Abracadabra would surely have been more to the point.'

4.2 Practising Popperian prestidigitation

The ontology propounded by Karl Popper (1972, 1977) contains the rudiments of a conception of language. In terms of this conception, language is an 'objective' entity autonomous of a 'self-conscious mind'. The Popperian conception of language differs in important ways, however, from the Platonist one defended by Katz and his associates. In this section, we will consider the Popperian conception of language, first in the rudimentary form it has in Popper's own work and then in the more fleshed-out form in which it has recently been defended by Carr (1987, 1990). Obviously, two matters of special interest to us will be, first, the basic differences between the Popperian and Platonist conceptions of language and, secondly, the relative merits of the Popperian conception.

4.2.1 Working World 3 wonders

Popper's ontology makes provision for three worlds, which it portrays as interacting with one another.[37] World 1 is the world of physical things and of states of physical things: molecules, clouds, animals, plants, brains, and so on. World 2 is the world of mental states, including not only states of consciousness and psychological dispositions but also 'unconscious states'. What Popper calls 'the self-conscious mind' is, accordingly, located in World 2. World 3 in the world of products of the human mind: stories, explanatory myths, tools, scientific theories and problems, social institutions, works of art. World 3, on an equivalent formulation, is the world of 'culture' and of 'objective knowledge'. Many World 3 objects, however, Popper (1977: 38) contends, 'exist in the form of material bodies, and belong in a sense to both World 1 and World 3.' As examples, he cites sculptures, paintings and books. Concerning books he (1977: 38–9) observes: 'A book is a physical object, and it therefore belongs to World 1; but what makes it a significant product of the human mind is its *content*: that which remains invariant in the various copies and editions. And this content belongs to World 3.' In addition, Popper (1977: 41–2) provides for 'unembodied World 3 objects' as well. For example, with the invention of natural numbers, Popper observes, there came into existence odd and even numbers 'even before anybody noticed this fact or drew attention to it'. Until their existence was noticed, odd and even numbers, then, were instances of 'unembodied World 3 objects'.

Being products of human thought, World 3 objects are 'man-made'. But, Popper (1977: 40) maintains, they nevertheless have 'a certain degree of autonomy': 'they may have, objectively, consequences of which nobody so far has thought and which may be *discovered*; discovered in the same sense in which an existing but so far unknown plant or animal may be discovered.' Once made by man, that is, World 3 objects 'begin to have a life of their own', to use Popper's (1977: 40) words. Popper emphasizes his view that World 3 objects are 'objective' in that they have this autonomy in relation to the (subjective) thought – belonging to World 2 – of which they are products.

Popper (1972: 153) considers the relationship between the three worlds 'one of the fundamental problems of this pluralistic philosophy'. He maintains that the three worlds are so related that, on the one hand, World 1 and World 2 can 'interact' and, on the other hand, World 2 and World 3 can 'interact'. This implies that the second world, namely the world of subjective or personal experiences, can interact with each of the other two worlds. It also implies, however, that the first and the third world cannot interact 'save through the intervention of the second world'.[38]

That World 3 exists 'in reality', Popper (1972: 159) contends, is clear 'from its tremendous effect on the first world [i.e. World 1], mediated through the second world [i.e. World 2]'. This contention reflects his (1977: 10) belief that (unobservable) things are real 'if they can causally act upon, or interact with, ordinary real material things'. The same belief underlies the sufficient condition/criterion for 'being real' which Popper (1977: 39) expresses as follows: 'interaction with World 1 – even indirect interaction – I regard as a decisive argument for calling a thing real.' To illustrate the validity of this condition/criterion, Popper (1972: 159) cites, among other things, the impact of atomic theory (a World 3 object) on our inorganic and organic environment (World 1 objects).

Popper (1977: 43) notes that his World 3 corresponds in some ways to Plato's world of intelligibles, a world to which we were introduced in section 4.1 above. But he denies that he is a Platonist (1972: 122–3, 154; 1977: 43–4) and points out various differences between the two 'abstract' worlds.[39] These include the following differences:

Plato's world of intelligibles	*Popper's World 3*
Divine in origin, eternal	Man-made, the products of human thought
Immutable	Changing
Contains essences	Essences 'play no significant role'
Does not contain problems, conjectures or theories	Contains problems, conjectures and theories (true and false)
'Grasped' by means of infallible intuition	'Grasped' by making or remaking its objects

As for the last difference, Popper (1977: 44) admits that there is something like intellectual intuition, but does not consider it infallible. For 'grasping' a World 3 object, Popper contends, people do not have 'an intellectual sense organ' or 'eye of the mind'. Rather, the 'grasping' of a World 3 object is 'an active process' in that it entails 'the making, the recreation, of that object'. This process Popper (1977: 44) illustrates by means of examples such as those he presents in the following terms:

> In order to understand a difficult Latin sentence, we have to construe it: to see how it is made, and to re-construct it, to re-make it. In order to understand a *problem*, we have to try at least some of the more obvious solutions, and to discover that they fail; thus we rediscover that there is a difficulty – a problem. In order to understand a *theory*, we have first to understand the problem which the theory was designed to solve, and to see whether the theory does better than do any of the more obvious solutions.

Popper's (1977: 45) view of the 'grasping' of World 3 objects assumes, therefore, the 'ability to produce certain World 3 objects, especially linguistic ones'. In turn this ability, on his view, is 'no doubt the result of practice'. So Popperians, let us note, differ from Platonists as regards the nature of the epistemological means necessary for acquiring knowledge of objective/abstract objects: Platonists, we saw in section 4.1.3 above, postulate for this purpose a special faculty of intuition.

Popper's choice of the 're-construction' of a difficult Latin sentence to illustrate the activity of 'grasping' gives an indication also of where languages fit into his trialist ontology. He (1977: 49) believes that 'the various languages are man-made: they are cultural World 3 objects, though they are made possible by capabilities, needs, and aims which have become genetically entrenched.' Here we have a fundamental difference between the Popperian and the Platonist conception of language: on the latter conception languages are not man-made objects. Platonists, we have seen, believe that languages belong to an eternal, unchanging ontological realm with which people cannot interact causally.

In line with his 'third world' view of language, Popper (1977: 45) portrays language learning as 'not natural but cultural and social'. As a 'World 3 learning process', Popper (1977: 48) claims, the learning of a particular language 'is not a gene-regulated process and therefore not a natural, but a cultural process'. And he (1977: 49) believes that 'every normal child acquires language through much active work.'[40]

In earlier pronouncements, Popper (1972) was less clear about the 'worldly' status of languages. In certain passages, he (1972: 159–60) expresses the view that 'human language' is part of the third world:

> According to the position which I am adopting here, the third world (part of which is human language) is the product of men, just as honey is the product of bees, or spiders' webs of spiders. *Like language* [sic] (and like honey) human language, and thus larger parts of the third world are *the unplanned product of human actions*,[9] though they may be solutions to biological or other problems.

In other passages, however, 'human language' is portrayed as belonging to all three worlds. Thus Popper (1972: 157) contends:

> This, it seems, was first seen by the Stoics who developed a marvellously subtle philosophy of language. Human language, as they realized, belongs to all three worlds.[6] In so far as it consists of physical actions or physical symbols, it belongs to the first world. In so far as it expresses a subjective or psychological state or in so far as grasping or understanding language involves a change in our subjective state,[7] it belongs to the second world. And in so far as language contains information, in so far as it says or states or describes anything or conveys any meaning or any significant message which may entail another, or agree or clash with another, it belongs to the third world. *Theories, or propositions, or statements are the most important third-world linguistic entities.*

Popper's use of expressions such as 'marvellously subtle' and 'realized' seem to indicate that he accepts the view of the Stoics that 'language' belongs to all three worlds. From the examples he (1972: 157) uses for elucidating this 'trialist' conception of language, it is clear that he takes the 'linguistic entities' belonging to the third world to be units of 'objective logical content', units of 'information' or 'message' units. These, Popper (1972: 20) states, are used in 'descriptive' and 'argumentative' functions. In his earlier work, in sum, Popper seems to have an E-language conception of language: a language is a collection of entities, important amongst which are units of (objective) content.

When in his later work Popper (1977) portrays language as World 3 objects, it is not clear whether he is talking about units of 'objective logical content' only. He does not explicitly invoke the traditional threefold distinction of concrete utterances as units of (physical) substance, sentences as units of (linguistic) form or structure and propositions as units of (logical) content. In fact, it is not clear whether he sees the need to distinguish between speech/*parole*/performance/or the like on the one hand and language/*langue*/competence/or the like on the other hand. Though Popper talks in the 'product' mode about language (units), he does not explicitly draw a distinction between an underlying linguistic system and the products that result from the use of such a system. Nor does the distinction between individual languages and language in general figure in Popper's linguistic ontology in any principled way. Popper, in fact, appears not to be well aquainted with fundamental conceptual distinctions standardly drawn in linguistics. And he has made no attempt to justify his conception of language *vis-à-vis* the major conceptions of language that have been entertained by leading twentieth-century linguists.

It is on account of such limitations in its conceptual well-foundedness that I have called Popper's conception of language 'rudimentary'. It also has limitations of a more serious kind, however: limitations which arise from flaws in Popper's trialist ontology. These further limitations, though, are more interesting to consider with reference to a version that makes slightly better contact with present-day linguistic theory and linguistic ontology. So let us move on to Carr's fleshed-out Popperian conception of language.

Understanding metaphysics as practised in the magical mode is a matter, Conceptions Customer, of seeing through the spectacle and its splendour the hollowness of the hocus-pocus. Especially spectacular, of course, is the adroit juggler's act of keeping all three worlds aloft at one and the same time. And truly impressive, too, in Sir Karl's Conceptual Cabbalism, are the Producing Passes and Remaking Routines by which to 'grasp' those wondrous World Three Things. And yet. And yet: the details of how all this is done suggest that much of Magical Metaphysics boils down to tricks that in themselves are both relatively trivial and quite traditional.

Take, for example, our Nimble-knuckled Knight's illustration of the activity of 'grasping'-by-remaking. Specifically, I have in mind here the so-called re-construction of an unidentified, 'difficult' sentence from Latin, a language – please note – of which in our day the Making and Remaking Rules have to be systematically taught and consciously learned. Instead of Latin, why not take a language such as English, of which many of our contemporaries are native speakers, who acquire the language naturally and use it naturally? Why not select for the purpose of illustration a 'simple' sentence such as Sir Karl is too clever to expect us to catch out? *The structures, rules and principles which are 'grasped' through remaking – why not explicitly represent them as those involved in the 'production' and interpretation of this sentence? But, of course, when it comes to getting out of a metaphysical mess, shortchanging an audience on specifics is, needless to say, the oldest of extraction tricks. That every native speaker of English can 'make' this sentence is probably true, Dear Blue. But, and here comes the Conceptual Catch, 'making a sentence' does not equal 'making out how a sentence is made'.*

4.2.2 *Withdrawing into the world of wizardry*

In a recent study, Philip Carr (1990) pursues the question 'Can we reasonably speak of linguistic realities?' In answer to this question, he proposes a Popperian meta-theory for theoretical linguistics or, as he calls it, 'an autonomist metatheory for the generative enterprise'. The generative enterprise, on Carr's (1990: 33) construal, is built on a particular 'metaphor', namely 'the notion that "a language" is a set of sentences'. And on his (1990: 33) view, 'the notion "rule" counts as a central metaphor in the generative linguist's attempt' to 'describe the mechanisms in the underlying linguistic reality'.

Carr's meta-theory – which is meant to be superior to Chomskyan 'psychologism' – has two components. The first is an epistemology in terms of which linguistic theories consist of potentially falsifiable propositions that attempt to describe the above-mentioned underlying linguistic reality. The second is a Popperian ontology in terms of which 'linguistic realities' (or objects) *are not* (a) psychological entities as argued by Chomsky (e.g. 1986) and Fodor (e.g. 1985a); (b) social norms as Itkonen (e.g. 1978) would like to believe; (c) dualistic objects with a naturalistic (or biologistic) side and a social (or sociopolitical) side as suggested by Pateman (e.g. 1987); or (d) abstract objects of a Platonic sort as proposed by Katz (e.g. 1981) and others. Rather, on Carr's (1990: 124–41) Popperian linguistic ontology, 'linguistic realities', *are* 'speaker-external', 'public', 'autonomous', 'objective' objects to be found in Popper's World 3.

According to Carr (1990: 37), the linguistic realities/objects just referred to include 'rules and sentences and thus languages'. The status of 'language in general' as a putative linguistic object inhabiting Popper's World 3 is left unclear by Carr. He (1990: 43–4) does, however, attempt to elucidate the nature of sentences as 'linguistic realities' by invoking 'the sentence/utterance distinction' as defended by Burton-Roberts (1985). For this distinction to be upheld, it has to be assumed that sentences are abstract objects which do not exist in a context. Sentences, on Burton-Robert's portrayal, are not events and 'do not occur'. Moreover, in Carr's (1990: 43–4) phrasing:

> We cannot attribute spatial location to them [i.e. sentences], and yet it is perfectly reasonable to say that they are linguistic realities whose properties we may investigate. The ontological status here attributed to sentences fits rather naturally with the idea of objective knowledge, [that is,] with the notion that linguistic objects exist in a public space as intersubjective objects of mutual knowledge, and not as objects in physical space.

Recall, that, as we saw in section 4.1.1 above, Platonists such as Katz and Postal also operate with an explicit distinction between (abstract) sentences and (concrete) utterances.

Linguistic objects, on Carr's (1990: 41–2) ontology, are not only abstract; they are 'public' as well. Reduced to its essence, his argument for the latter claim runs as follows:

1 The lexicon is a public object in the sense that 'the individual does not know all of the existing lexical morphemes of the language, and that this set of morphemes is definable only over sets which constitute members of communities' (p. 42).
2 'If lexical meaning is indeed reasonably described as a public, speaker-external state of affairs . . . then sentence meaning too has this ontological status' (p. 42).
3 'Thus the rules for semantic interpretation are public, and so are rules in general' (p. 42).
4 'And, if linguistic rules are public, so are the objects which they define: sentences and their sub-parts' (p. 42).
5 'Thus the syntactic, phonological and semantic rules may be said to enjoy the same intersubjective status' (p. 42).

On this ontological interpretation of the 'generative enterprise', Carr (1990: 42) considers it proper to say 'that a language, constituted by its rules, is a public object.'

How credible, then, is Carr's claim that 'linguistic realities' are 'autonomous', 'objective' objects located in Popper's World 3? Let us appraise this claim in terms of two of the minimal conditions which any theory of 'linguistic realities' – or, to put it more mundanely, any conception of language – must meet:

(C1) The 'roots condition': no conception of language should be based on general ontological assumptions which are seriously flawed.

(C2) The 'fruits' condition: a conception of language should be heuristically fruitful or, at least, more fruitful than its competitors.[41]

Let us take up the 'fruits' condition first. According to Carr (1990: 3), Chomsky's mentalist (or 'psychologistic') ontology probably continues to be held by the majority of linguists.[42] Consequently, one of the things which Carr has to show is that, in regard to heuristic fruitfulness, his own autonomist ontology is superior to Chomsky's mentalist ontology. This means in turn that Carr has to show amongst other things that there are one or more classes of linguistically significant generalizations or facts which cannot be captured within Chomskyan mentalism but which can be captured within his own autonomist ontology. Carr (1990: 46, 127) does seem to recognize the importance of this condition. In this connection, he (1990: 46) refers in general terms to 'ambiguities [of strings] in themselves', 'to generalisations about rules and sentences' and to 'phonological generalisations which are not phonetic'. And he (1990: 128–38) proceeds to argue – *contra* Ohala (1974), Vennemann (1974), Hooper (1976) and Donegan and Stampe (1979) – that 'there are phonological generalisations which are not phonetic generalisations and therefore that there are phonological objects which are not phonetic objects.' Carr (1990: 138–41), moreover, argues – *contra* Givón (1984) – that there are 'linguistic realities' of a syntactic sort that 'cannot be reduced to facts about discourse, or communication in general'.

But these arguments of Carr's are beside the point. What he has to show is that the phonological and syntactic regularities or generalizations in question cannot be expressed in terms of Chomskyan linguistic theories *because of* the mentalist (or biologistic) import of recent versions of Chomskyan ontology. And he has to show, of course, that these regularities or generalizations can be captured by 'purely' or 'autonomously' linguistic accounts *because of* the autonomist import of Popperian ontology. It is futile to argue against Chomskyan mentalism by attempting to discredit 'concretist' or 'reductionist' accounts of linguistic phenomena. Obviously, 'ontological mentalism' does not equal 'concretist phoneticism' or 'reductionist pragmaticism'.[43] The *form* of argument which Carr should have used is that within whose framework Katz and Postal (1989) attempt to show that there are facts about logico-semantic properties of sentences which cannot be accounted for by Chomskyan mentalism.[44]

The 'fruits' condition (C2) may be applied in reverse as well. When so applied, it requires Carr to show that it is possible to capture within the framework of his nonpsychologist, autonomist ontology all the *kinds* of significant generalizations or facts which can be accounted for within Chomskyan mentalism. Carr does not, however, attempt to do this. Such an attempt would require detailed linguistic analysis, an undertaking which in its turn would require, amongst other things, a well-articulated theory of linguistic structure. To establish a linguistic ontology as heuristically fruitful requires much more than meta-scientific argumentation, a point generally poorly undertstood by proponents of (new) conceptions of language.[45] In sum: Carr has failed to show that his autonomist ontology passes the 'fruits' condition in either of its two directions.[46]

Let us take up next the 'roots' condition for linguistic ontologies: how sound are the Popperian bases of Carr's autonomist ontology? Obviously, this ontology of Carr's cannot be sane if its Popperian bases are less than sound. Now, Popper's 'three-tiered', 'trialist' or 'dualist-interactionist' ontology has come in for some rather destructive criticisms. Let us consider a few of these.

First, Dennett (1979: 97) has argued that Popper's dualism 'has been composed as an alternative to a materialism no sane materialist holds'.[47] This means that Popper has not discredited 'the reigning orthodoxy among philosophers of mind'. A reason for this, Dennett (1979: 91) suggests, is that Popper's work – and that of Eccles too – 'fails to make serious contact with the best theoretical work of recent years'. Dennett (1979: 92) observes, moreover, that Popper 'does not usually manage to extend his appreciation of depth and intricacy to the works of other authors, who almost invariably are drastically underestimated by him.' But this means that Popper has made the required sort of case not even for postulating the existence of his World 2.

Secondly, Cohen (1979: 303) has found Popper's claims about the 'interaction' between the World 1 brain and the World 2 self-conscious mind to be 'empty'. He (1979: 303) argues as follows:

> The self-conscious mind, they say, integrates sensations, measures time, initiates body-movements, corrects recollections, and diagnoses perceptual illusions. But how does it do all those things? or even any one of them? To that question we are given no answer. We are not offered any hypothesis whatever about the structure of the self-conscious mind. We are not told what it is that enables the self-conscious mind to perform certain activities and unfits it to perform others. And it is a symptom of this emptiness of the Popper–Eccles hypothesis that it is sterile. It generates no new testable predictions because, as an explanation, it really has almost nothing to say.

These criticisms are justifiable because Popper and Eccles adopt Popper's methodology, which excludes any sharp differentiation between science and philosophy. Eccles (1977: 375), moreover, has claimed explicitly that their hypothesis about the unconscious mind 'belongs to science because it is based on empirical data and is objectively testable'. The further question, of course, is this: How could one even begin to make a credible case for the existence of World 3 products of a World 2 mind if questions such as Cohen's can be raised about such a mind?

Thirdly, Popper's notion of interaction is obscure in crucial ways. For instance, Dennett (1979: 94) has asked 'What kind of causal interaction can this be between a [World 2] thinking and a [World 3] theory?' He observes that 'we are not told' by Popper. And he continues: 'Popper waves his hands about how modern physics has vacated all the old-fashioned philosophical ideas about causation, but does not give a positive account of this new kind of causation. . . .' Also Beloff's (1978: 270–1) 'main worry' about Popper's trialist ontology concerns the way the key notion of 'interaction' has been 'deployed' by Popper. Essentially, Beloff –

who is generally quite sympathetic to Popper – is worried by the fact that:

> if we take the term 'interaction' literally, we may define it as a two-way causal process between two distinct entities. Now, the entities of World 3 are, as Popper clearly states, timeless abstractions. How, then, can a timeless abstraction actively participate in what, by definition, is a temporal process? The answer, surely, is that it can not. . . .

Beloff comes to the conclusion that Popper's notion of 'interaction' cannot be taken literally. This means that, from the point of view of perspicacity, the criterion adopted by Popper for assigning existence to World 3 objects is in poor shape.

Strangely, in fleshing out the Popperian conception of language, Carr has failed to consider 'roots' criticisms such as those by Dennett, Cohen, Beloff and Mortensen. Carr, in fact, has even compounded some of the problems concerned. Thus, he (1990: 81) arbitrarily conflates Popper's notion of 'interactionism' with a homonymic but distinct notion which, on Shaphere's (1969: 155) analysis, plays a role in *physical* reasoning, that is, in the context of a materialist ontology that does not provide for ontological domains similar to Popper's World 2 and World 3. Shaphere (1969: 156) notes specifically 'that what counts as an "interaction" is also specified on *scientific* grounds' (emphasis added). Carr fails to notice that 'interaction' within this context does not involve the curious kind of causality that he and Popper have to appeal to.

'Interaction(ism)', within Popper's trialist ontology, is an obscure notion. As a consequence, Popperians lack the epistemological means for obtaining (scientific) evidence about, amongst other things, World 3 linguistic entities. In this connection Carr has refrained from attempting to make sense of Popper's view that linguistic entities such as sentences can be 'grasped' by 'making' or 'recreating' them. And as we will see below, Popperians cannot fall back on ordinary linguistic intuition as a source of direct evidence about World 3 linguistic entities.

In sum: such criticisms of Popper's ontology as those by Dennett, Mortensen, Cohen and Beloff clearly indicate that the roots of

Carr's autonomist theory of linguistic realities are seriously flawed. Having failed both the 'roots' condition (C1) and the 'fruits' condition (C2), this linguistic ontology cannot be considered a serious alternative to Chomskyan 'psychologism'. Carr, in fact, is not in a particularly good position to criticize Chomskyan ontology in an incisive way: he appears not to be sufficiently well-informed about the basic beliefs constituting the more biologized version of mentalism espoused in Chomsky's more recent writings. Thus, contrary to what Carr seems to believe, these writings (e.g. Chomsky 1987a,b,c, 1988a,b,c,d, 1989) make it clear that Chomsky does *not* take (a) languages to be sets of sentences (Carr 1990: 33, 36, 42, 54, 103, 123, 126, 139); (b) rules to be real linguistic objects (1990: 33); or (c) I-languages to be systems of rules (1990: 49). We have seen that, in Carr's view, 'the notion that "a language" is a set of sentences' is 'the metaphor on which the "generative enterprise" is built' (1990: 33), and 'the notion "rule" counts as a central metaphor' of the 'generative enterprise' (1990: 33). These views may be true, by stipulation or definition. But if so, then Chomsky, strange to say, is no (longer) a practitioner of the 'generative enterprise'.[48]

Moreover, given the way in which considerations focusing on explanatory adequacy, on the poverty of the stimulus and on parameter-fixing have recently been invoked in the justification of Chomskyan linguistic analyses, Carr is wrong to believe (a) that 'considerations as to psychological plausibility rarely seem to figure in grammatical descriptions' (1990: 119), and to believe (b) that 'Chomskyan GB theory . . . may effectively be divorced from its psychological interpretation' (1990: 127). Because Carr is mistaken about (a) and (b) he errs, too, in thinking that autonomist linguistics can have the same evidential basis as Chomskyan linguistics (1990: 56). He is, moreover, incorrect in assuming that grammaticality judgements have the same status within the evidential bases of these two approaches. As we saw in section 4.1.4 above, because the Chomskyan language faculty is central to the aetiology of such judgements, they constitute in a principled way relevant evidence about the nature and properties of this faculty. Since nonpsychological, autonomous linguistic objects clearly cannot be involved in this way in the aetiology of grammaticality judgements, Carr, by contrast, has to stipulate that judgements of the latter sort constitute evidence about objects of the former kind. As regards recourse to intuitive linguistic judgements, Popperians face, contrary to what Carr seems to believe, the same problem as Platonists (see also Fodor 1985a: 151).

Carr's criticisms of Chomskyan mentalism, in fact, boil down to a few very general remarks. Taking over a point that Botha (1979) made about a mid-seventies version of Chomskyan mentalism, Carr complains that Chomskyan mentalism is 'ontologically indeterminate': Chomsky, he (1990: 89) alleges, has not actually come up 'with anything in the way of coherent proposals for dealing with the dualist/physicalist problem'. But Carr fails to consider the question whether this complaint applies to Chomsky's late-eighties version of mentalism, which differs from the earlier one in being much more biologistic. Carr is disturbed, moreover, by the fact that Chomsky has not been able to rid his mentalism of all reductionism, 'reductionism' being a dirty word in the Popperian vocabulary. But to discredit Chomskyan mentalism, one has to take apart the real thing – the more highly biologized, late-eighties conception of language – and show that it has specific flaws of a crippling sort.[49]

Should you itch to try your own hand at a little Popperian Prestidigitation, Dear Buyer, do think again about what it demands. Requiring philosophical flexibility and epistemological elasticity, it is a most demanding form of magic; actively 'grasping' World 3 objects is definitely not an Arthritic Act. And much more seriously, it may scar your sanity. Thus you will be able to recall that on Dennett's diagnosis, Popper's work 'fails to make serious contact with the best theoretical work of recent years'. And I myself have been forced to suggest above and elsewhere (Botha in press: 13–14) that Carr's contact with work highly relevant to his concerns is surprisingly slight. What we have here, Concerned Customer, are symptoms of a withdrawal by Popperian Wizards into yet another World, a scholarly world of their own. Conceptually, of course, it will be curtains for those Popperians who, on this retreat, cross the boundary by which the weird and wonderful realm of magic, ranging from white and mild to black and wild, is marked off from the realm of madness.

4.3 Bowing out to bouquets and boos

Levitational Linguistics, then, delivers lots of good laughs, Doubled-up Buyer. But at the same time some serious lessons may be learned at the Apex of the Abstractness Axis of The Market. Let me list you five of these lessons:

1 *On the essence of language: it cannot be arcanely abstract.*
2 *On linguistic objects: they cannot be Mathematical Maroonees.*
3 *On establishing a conception of language: it needs extensive epistemological exposure.*
4 *On means for learning about language: Extra Eyes, Sixth Senses and Grasping Gestures are the means, and marks, of magic.*
5 *On ontology in general: the more Worlds, the more Woes.*

Let me say something more about the core of these lessons, primarily with reference to the Platonist conception of language, the Popperian one not being of matching significance.

Collectively, the first four lessons mean that, in its present form, Platonic realism is not the remedy for the Ontological Angst caused by the question 'What is language in essence?' True, Dear Blue, Katzian Platonism has the distinct virtue of proceeding from an explicit conceptual distinction between languages and knowledge of language. For this, the Manhattan Magicians deserve bouquets from all of us. But the kind of abstractness they attribute to language makes it an arcanum, unfathomable by less problematic epistemological means. It is pointless to create for this purpose special means, such as Kantian intuition, that are in effect more mysterious than language itself. The kind of abstractness in question, moreover, turns languages into Conceptual Castaways, cut off causally by an ontological ocean from the mainland of linguistic processes, events and states which they naturally inhabit. Neither our understanding of languages nor our understanding of those linguistic phenomena can benefit from our instituting this sort of insularity.

Lesson number five warrants a special word, Dear Buyer. Its underlying logic is transparent, or so one would have hoped. Clearly, the more Worlds one postulates, the more vexing becomes the problem of accounting for the 'interactions' among them, especially if some of those Worlds are ontologically rather exotic. And the more difficult it becomes, too, to shun esoteric epistemological means for exploring those Worlds. So, as far as the creating of Worlds is concerned, conceptual conservatism would seem to commend itself as a prudent policy.

If you had been taking all of this for granted anyway, Conservative Customer, I have a last little surprise for you: it has in fact been proposed that Popper's framework should be 'extended' to include not three Worlds but four! The proponent being a linguist, no less. Missing from Popper's 'framework', Geoffrey Leech (1983: 51) maintains, 'is a world of societal facts . . . intervening between his second (subjective) and his third (objective) worlds. Thus Popper's objective "third world" becomes, in this redefinition, a "fourth world". . . .' No, Dismayed Blue, Leech seems not to have reckoned with the possibility that by multiplying Worlds he may make himself even more dependent on magic as a metaphysical means. So it may well be that I speak for many a Magician Metaphysicist as I cite, in closing, the lament of Marlowe's tormented Doctor Faustus: ''Tis magic, magic that hath ravished me.'

5

Stocking Language as Social Stuff

5.0 Offering *objets de couture*

Allow me to introduce you to the Mods of The Market. They, Curious Customer, are the Conceptions Consumers who would die rather than do things believed to be ontologically untoward. Such as fraternizing with philosophically frumpy physicalists, breaking burgers with bearded All Bodies behaviourists, rubbing s(h)oul(der)s with myth-mongering mentalists or trading tricks with abracadabra abstractists. It is these People-in-Pursuit-of-Polish who believe that a conception of language must bear the benchmarks of à la mode metaphysics, must be a creation of the Cardins of Conceptual Haute Couture. Finely tuned to the dernier cri, these are the people who throw their money about after such bits of belief as the Quinean Quip that language is a social art. (One has to admit, Perceptive Patron, that his quip has a catchily sophisticated ring to it, its elegance being enhanced by just the right touch of conceptual obscurity). And it is they, strangely enough, who believe that to be conceptually cool one has to take language to be something social in essence.

The Market, of course, caters for the philosophical fads and fancies of all. So Beau Blue, if you too are attracted to the idea that language is something social, it is time that we set out along the Social Scale, the second major conceptual coordinate along which conceptions of language are ordered on The Market. At the one end of the Scale, we find those conceptions that portray language as something intrinsically individual, Chomskyan mentalism being the paradigm case. At the other end are clustered those conceptions on which language is something social in essence. This is the area, crowded by customers as it is, that we will next explore.

But who are the Conceptual Couturiers credited with having created the more classy 'social' conceptions of language? As for Linguistic Lines: on the Continent the trend was set for years, of course, by the Salon de Saussure with its Durkheimian Design, whereas from America there emerged, in true Frontier Fashion, the Cultural Cut of the Sapirean Saloon, to be followed much later by the New Look (Socio-)Linguistics of the Labovian Lodge. Philosophical Fashions, by contrast, have mostly been variations on the Wittgensteinian view that language is a social practice, one of the better known being a conception cut from Common-sense Cloth by a Carfax Couturier going by a name so understated that it does not even appear on the labels. But let us try on some of the social conceptions of language individually, Chic Shopper, looking for loose threads, slipped stitches, separated seams and fatigued fabrics hidden by a stylish surface.

5.1 Flocking after a fashion

The belief that language is something social has for more than a century been pupularly held by linguists. Thus, Koerner (1975: 793) observes that: 'Ever since the appearance of Whitney's books in the 1860s and 1870s it has been almost universally recognized that language is a product of society, a social institution.' And the belief in question has not been restricted to linguists, as is clear from the following remarks by Katz (1981: 7): 'Quine can introduce his book [*Word and Object*] with the sentence "Language is a social art" – that is, he can say it without support – because this view is so widely held. We see it endorsed across the spectrum from popular writers on language to sophisticated linguists.'

Sociologists, obviously, have held a 'social' conception of language too, as has been recently observed by Pateman (1987: 57): 'it has seemed wellnigh obvious to many linguists (and all sociologists) that languages are social facts. . . .' The fashionability of the belief that language is something social, thus, appears to be well documented. But what is 'social' supposed to mean in a principled ontological context? What has been the ontological justification for portraying language as a social object (and, correspondingly, languages as social objects)? And what are the limitations of the most important 'social' conceptions of language? These are the questions that we will consider below – with reference to linguists in sections 5.2–5.4 and philosopers in sections 5.5–5.7. In section 5.8 we will examine one of the flaws marring all 'social' conceptions of language, whether proposed by linguists or by philosophers.

It is time to clear up a misunderstanding or two, Dear Buyer. The idea that language is something social has not been bought by Fashion Conscious Customers only. No, a variety of other Conceptions Consumers, who don't care a fig for philosophical fashionability, have been forking out money for it too. Quite a number of these seem to have done so because of their inability to see a particular false assumption for what it is. For your attention, Unconvinced Customer, let me state it as

> The Function Fallacy
> *Function fixes fabric.*

Given this assumption, and given the fact that language fulfils various important functions in society, it is a foregone – but false – conclusion that, ontologically, language is something social in essence.

Could I please put my finger on the flaw in this fateful assumption? But of course, my dear Frowning Fellow. You agree, I take it, that things which are essentially material, mental or biological are regularly used to perform functions in society? You agree for example, I take it, that concrete objects, abstract ideas and biological mechanisms are used by people for social ends? But does this social use of these objects, ideas and mechanisms turn them into social things? I trust, Scowling Scholar, that these questions will make you reappraise the beau monde belief that 'Language is as it is because of the functions it has evolved to serve in people's lives' (Halliday 1978: 4).

5.2 Styling it à la Saussure

Ferdinand de Saussure, on various accounts, portrayed language as something that is essentially social: more specifically, a social 'phenomenon', 'fact' or 'institution'.[1] Like other aspects of Saussure's linguistic thinking, however, his linguistic ontology is less than fully perspicuous. And such serious Saussure scholars as Koerner (1973: 45ff.) have questioned the accuracy of the way in which the remarks made by Saussure in his *Cours* (1916) on the 'social character of language' have been construed ontologically. It would be pretentious to attempt to give an exegesis of these remarks here; more prudent would be to consider the way in which they have been understood by Koerner (1973) and other more careful scholars such as Kaldewaij (1986).

At the basis of Saussure's linguistic ontology lies his tripartite distinction '*langue* v. *parole* v. *langage*'. In terms of Spence's (1957: 1) synoptic formulation, *la langue* is 'a system of signs existing in the minds of the members of a speech community'.[2] *La parole*, also on his summary formulation, is 'the free-speech activity of the individual, the use he makes of *la langue*'.[3] *Le langage* is the global phenomenon of language (in general), including both *la langue* and *la parole*.[4]

As used by Saussure to clarify the distinction between *langue* and *parole*, neither 'social' nor 'individual' is, on Koerner's (1973: 55, 59) reading, a technical term: 'expressions like "social" versus "individual" are never taken up as technical terms, but [are] used in a comparatively unspecificed sense '(1973: 58). The 'rather general meaning' attached by Saussure to 'social', moreover, 'would change with the angle from which he [i.e. Saussure] viewed linguistic phenomena'. Thus, on Koerner's reading, Saussure considers *langue* to be 'social' in the following senses:

1 It is 'collectively based': existing only in the collectivity of the '*masse parlante*'; based on a '*consentement collectif*'; having its source in the '*ésprit collectif*' of a given community; set up by a '*masse sociale*' (Koerner 1973: 54, 55, 58, Kaldewaij 1986: 18–19).
2 It is a 'conventional' thing and, as such, is 'learned' through social interaction (Koerner 1973: 54, 55, 56).

3 It is 'semiological in character' or 'communicative in nature' (Koerner 1973: 56; Kaldewaij 1986: 57).
4 It is 'subjected to the inertia of society' in that changes are adopted in a conservative way by the speech community (Koerner 1973: 55–6).

Two general points should be noted in connection with 1–4 above. First, as 'social' is used by Saussure, it is only in the 'collectivity' sense of 1 that 'social' has a direct bearing on the ontological status of *langue*. As used in 2, 'social' bears on the way in which *langue* is acquired. And as used in 3 and 4, 'social' bears on the function of *langue* and on the mode in which *langue* changes, respectively. Secondly, the ontological import of core notions (for example, '*masse parlante/sociale*', '*consentement/ésprit collectif*') is not clarified by Saussure in any rigorous way. This is a shortcoming shared by other social conceptions of language, a point to be taken up again below.

Koerner (1973: 45, 49, 52, 53, 54), moreover contends that *langue* is not considered by Saussure to be 'social' in the Durkheimian sense of constituting an external constraint on the individual in his speech acts.[5] On the contrary, as Koerner (1973: 52) observes, Saussure more than once noted 'the individual's liberty in the speech act'.[6]

Various linguists, including Wells (1947) and Kaldewaij (1986), have considered the possibility that Saussure may have used the term 'social' to indicate that (the concept of) *langue* has the status of an idealization. Viewed as an idealization, *langue* would abstract away from irrelevant individual and dialectal variants found in the community that uses the language. Kaldewaij (1986: 19) following Wells (1947) notes, however, that assigning *langue* the status of an idealization would be inconsistent with remarks such as the following by Saussure (1983: 100): 'So the notion of a linguistic state can only be an approximation. In static linguistics, as in most sciences, no demonstration is possible without a conventional simplification of the data.'[7] From this passage, Kaldewaij observes, it is clear that Saussure concedes that idealization has to be used in synchronic linguistics. But Saussure sees the use of idealizations as a necessary evil, as something not to be encouraged. This presumably makes it unlikely that he would assign the status of an idealization to so fundamental a concept as *langue.*

There are other ways too in which the ontological status of Saussure's *langue* is less than transparent. As we have seen above, the *Cours* contains a variety of remarks portraying *langue* as something social. But the *Cours* also contains remarks portraying *langue* as something psychological, as has been noted by various scholars. Salverda (1985: 17), for example, comments as follows:

> As for psychology, note that for De Saussure '*tout est psychologique dans la langue*' (CLG 21). This holds not only for the *signifié*, but also for the *signifiant* or *image acoustique* (CLG 98). The whole language sign is an '*entité psychologique*' (CLG 99). Also, the *langue* was seen as the product of the natural '*faculté linguistique*' of human beings (CLG 26–27). The *langue* itself was an object existing in the mind or brain of every speaker of the language community (CLG 38), a kind of collective mental property.[8]

Relevant in this context, too, is Saussure's (1983: 77) characterization of *langue* as 'the whole set of linguistic *habits* which enables the speaker to understand and to make himself undertstood' (emphasis added).[9] On a conventional construal, habits, of course, are psychological entities.

In connection with Saussure's linguistic ontology, then, questions such as the following arise: What does 'psychological' mean to Saussure? Is *langue* essentially psychological or essentially social? Or is *langue* ontologically mixed? How could *langue* be social and psychological at the same time? Or do we have ontological confusion here on Saussure's part? The answers to these questions are not clear, a fact that has given rise to a variety of conflicting interpretations of what Saussure 'really' meant by alternatively calling *langue* 'psychological' and 'social'.

A first, conservative, interpretation – put forward by Kaldewaij (1986: 18, 20), for example – is that Saussure uses 'psychological' nontechnically and in a negative sense: to contrast his conception of *langue* with conceptions of language as something physical or something logico-philosophical. On a second, more speculative, interpretation, Saussure's various uses of the term 'psychological' have been taken to indicate that his conception of *langue* is actually a mentalistic one. In this regard, Salverda (1985: 17), following Dik (1983: 8), concludes: 'Thus, De Saussure takes a clear mentalist position, giving a realist psychological interpretation of the object of linguistics. . . .' On this construal, the question arises as to what a 'collective mental property' could be. Salverda notes that Saussure could not have derived an answer to this question from the individual associationist psychology in the work of Paul. Saussure, on Salverda's interpretation, 'seems to have preferred the more social psychology of collective representation proposed by Durkheim'. The problem with this interpretation is that Koerner (1973: 52) has argued strongly – against Doroszewski – that, in the few cases where Saussure uses the term, *representation* 'has no particular technical meaning [e.g. the Durkheimian one] attached to it. . .'.[10] So, the ontological status of Saussure's *langue* as something essentially psychological is quite opaque.

A third interpretation would be that what Saussure takes to be essential (or central) to *langue* is neither social nor psychological. This, in fact, is Koerner's view. He (1973: 56–9) argues that it is the semiological or sign character of *langue* that Saussure took to be its 'central' aspect. Thus, Koerner (1973: 58–9) observes that

> Language as a system of signs and its mechanism constitute the central aspects of Saussurean theory, and social aspects of language are referred to whenever necessary (e.g. for the explanation of certain features of language change), but hardly amount to much more than commonplace observations and appear to be used as superficial coating of matters which are intrinsically linguistic in nature.

Koerner (1973: 57) deals at length with 'Saussure's emphasis on the semiological over and above the sociological aspect of language and its study'. In particular, Koerner (1973: 56) argues that 'Saussure appears to have claimed that language is a social fact just because of its semiological character.' The expression 'the semiological character' refers to two aspects of *langue*: (a) its communicative function and (b) the means used in this function, namely (a system of) signs. From neither (a) nor (b) it can be inferred in a straightforward way that, as far as ontological substance is concerned, *langue* is in a technical sense something 'social'.

In sum: the conception of language which has been attributed to Saussure is in various ways opaque and arbitrary. As an ontological characterization of *langue*, this conception is quite shallow, possibly because Saussure considered ontological questions to lie outside linguistics proper.[11] Consequently, it cannot be cited in support of the contention that there is a clear Saussurian sense in which language can be ontologically construed as something essentially social. Nor, for the same reason, can this conception be cited in support of the contention that language is essentially something psychological or autonomous.

So far, we have looked at some of the general ways in which Saussure's linguistic ontology is problematic. This ontology, in addition, exhibits various more specific shortcomings, it has been claimed. An interesting subset of these – discussed, for example, by Kaldewaij (1986: 19) and Pateman (1987: 58–9) – reflects tensions that exist between the phenomenon of linguistic variation and the concept of *langue*. On the one hand, Saussure (1983: 13) recognizes the phenomenon of linguistic variation, as is clear from the following statements: 'All the individuals linguistically linked in this manner will establish among themselves a kind of mean: all of them will reproduce – doubtless not exactly, but approximately – the same links to the same concepts.'[12] On the other hand, Saussure portrays *langue* as a self-contained, homogeneous system that exists perfectly in collectivity only. To account for the former variability, *langue* – in the sense of a particular language system – could be equated with a dialect or sub-dialect. This is what Saussure (1983: 89–90) seems to suggest when he characterizes the object of synchronic linguistics in the following terms:

> The object of synchronic study does not comprise everything which is simultaneous, but only the set of facts corresponding to any particular language. In this, it will take into account where necessary a division into dialects and subdialects. The term *synchronic*, in fact, is not sufficiently precise. *Idiosynchronic* would be a better term, even though it is more cumbersome.[13]

But then the object of synchronic linguistics would not be *langue*, for as Saussure (1983: 13) sees it, 'the language is never complete in any single individual, but exists perfectly only in collectivity.'[14]

So, in a nutshell, Saussure seems not to have been able to reconcile the view of *langue* as something essentially social with the pehomenon of 'idiosynchronic' linguistic variation. This means, of course, that in regard to empirical import Saussure's 'social' conception of language is at variance with an important aspect of linguistic reality.

In our italicized inspection of the Social Scene, couldn't we capture the more fundamental fallacies on which (once) fashionable 'social' conceptions of language have floundered? Splendid idea, Dear Buyer! Here is a second false assumption to chew on:

> The Freestyle Fallacy
> *The essence of language(s) can be insightfully characterized by using 'social' in an informal, nontechnical sense.*

The Saussurian experience has taught us the exact opposite. After all, styling characterizations of the essence of things freely and informally in a nontechnical form makes for something that we can all live better without: an obscuring ontology. So much, then, for what has also been affectionately nicknamed Ferdi's Foible.

5.3 Lining it with Labovian lore

William Labov, too, believes that the phenomenon of 'idiosynchronic' linguistic variation poses a serious problem for a Saussurian linguistic ontology. Thus, Labov (1972: 108) claims: 'the very concept of *idiolect*, of course, represents a defeat for the Saussurian notion of *langue* as the general possession of the speech community.'[15] At the same time, however, Labov (n.d.: 9) clearly wishes to retain the idea that *langue*, 'as the common property of the speech community', is what linguists are studying. This requires him to reconcile the notion of *langue* with what Pateman (1987: 59) calls 'the reality of linguistic variation'. To do this, Labov (e.g. 1977) proposes a new kind of linguistic rule, so-called variable rules, for describing what he calls 'the regular patterns of the speech community'. He does not consider it the aim of linguistic analysis to describe 'the idiosyncrasies of any given individual'. How successful, then, has Labov been in his attempt to rescue the idea that *langue* is 'a common property of the speech community'? It is with this question that we will concern ourselves below.

Labovian variable rules characterize in a statistical way the use of a variable linguistic feature or form (e.g. the copula) in a particular speech community (e.g. that of the speakers of the Black English Vernacular).[16] Such rules specify the frequency or frequencies with which such a variable feature or form will be affected (e.g. by contraction and deletion) in the presence of such factors as social class, age, sex, race and level of formality. The essence of the difference between a variable rule and an obligatory categorial rule of the conventional sort is characterized as follows by Bickerton (1971: 460). An obligatory rule says: 'When you recognize environment X, use feature Y.' A variable rule, by contrast, says: 'When you recognize environment X, use feature Y Z% of the time.'

In regard to the ontological import of variable rules, Labov (1977: 125) has made a number of strong claims, including the following two:

(C1) Variable rules are 'a part of the speaker's knowledge of the language'.

(C2) Variable rules are not 'statistical statements or approximations to some ideal or true grammar', but represent 'quantitative *relations* which are the form of the grammar itself'.

Both these ontological claims of Labov's have come in for severe criticism (e.g. Bickerton 1971, 1973; Wolfram and Fasold 1974; Kay and McDaniel 1979; Newmeyer 1983: 77–80; Wardhaugh 1986: 181–5; Pateman 1987: 60–2).

As for (C1): critics take variable rules as giving statistical summaries or 'capsulizations' of observed behaviour of a speech community. That is, variable rules express claims about a group. Yet, in terms of (C1), such rules are claimed to belong to individuals. Bickerton (1971: 460–1) and others have argued that Labov leaves it quite unclear what the idea of 'knowing a variable rule' entails for the mind of the individual speaker. On the one hand, it is unclear how the information summarized by variable rules could be acquired by children learning the language. The essence of Bickerton's (1971: 460) discussion of this acquisition problem is neatly summarized as follows by Newmeyer (1983: 80): 'Since speech communities are clearly *not* homogeneous, different members of it would have to be assumed to have the ability to calculate identical probabilities for the variables involved on the basis of exposure to different frequencies!' As we will see directly below, this assumption has rather questionable ontological implications.

On the other hand, as Bickerton (1971: 460–1) shows, it is unclear how variable rules would 'operate'. Quite exotic assumptions would have to be made about the underlying mental processes required to keep the individual's variable rule behaviour within the statistical limits set in the rule(s) for his group. Commenting in general terms on these assumptions, Bickerton (1971: 461) observes that:

> Labov's results are AS IF the processes I have just described somehow actually took place, and if those results came about in any other way, the onus is on him to show the means. Meanwhile, though our ignorance of the mind is still immense, one may hazard a guess that the processes just described are beyond its unaided and individual power. Yet 'something' must be adjusting individual behaviour to conform with certain norms, and, if we rule out the mind of the individual, we are left with some kind of supra-individual entity, i.e. a 'group mind'.

Returning to the above-mentioned problem of accounting for the individual's acquisition of variable rules: accounting for this acquisitional feat, too, would seem to require the postulation of such a 'group mind'. Since, as Newmeyer (1983: 80) notes: 'Variable-rule advocates seem to have placed themselves in the position of implicitly endorsing a theory of language acquisition that guarantees that any two speakers in the community will be led to hypothesize the same rule.' The Durkheimian notion of a 'group mind' has been treated with a considerable measure of scepticism. Rex (1961: 46) takes the view that the concept of *a* 'group mind' is not necessarily 'illegitimate'. He is willing to permit recourse to this concept 'provided that its meaning is made clear and statements about it [are] made in a verifiable form'. Durkheim's use of this concept, however, fails on Rex's view to meet these conditions, thereby representing no more than 'the reification of the concept'. Parsons (1968: 357) is even less attracted to this concept than Rex, judging it to be 'merely a metaphysical assumption'. The notion of a 'group mind' is unable, therefore, to provide the necessary link between what is claimed to be social and the minds of individuals.[17]

As for (C2): variable rules, it has been argued, do not represent quantitative relations that exist as part of a social linguistic reality. Rather, such rules are artefacts of Labov's methodology. Pateman (1987: 60), for instance, comments as follows:

> Labov's methodology is to collect speech data from individuals, subject variation in the data (e.g. phonetic realization of a phoneme, most famously /r/) to statistical analysis to establish linguistic and objectivistically defined social correlates of the variation, and then write variable rules which will generate the appropriate variant for any linguistic or social context. Why the variable rule should be regarded as other than an artefact of the methodology – a theoretical fiction – is completely unexplained.

Labov (1977: 127) himself sees neither his methods nor his 'enlargement' of the concept of 'rule of grammar' as 'radical revisions of generative grammar and phonology'. But, in terms of their ontological consequences, these methods and this 'conceptual enlargement' represent the most radical kind of 'revision' conceivable. The use of the (qualitative) methods and the concepts of 'generative grammar and phonology' do not entail the postulation of rules that are fictitious in the way that Labovian variable rules are on Pateman's analysis. Labov's innovations, consequently, have turned 'generative grammar' into an enterprise that makes no substantive ontological claims at all.

To return to our guiding question: How successful has Labov been in his attempt at rescuing the idea that *langue* is 'a common property of the speech community'. 'Not spectacularly', the answer seems to be. On one analysis of his attempt, Labov, like Saussure, has to locate *langue* in an ontologically nebulous entity, namely a 'group mind'. On another analysis, Labov has to say that *langue* is a 'theoretical fiction'.[18] If the claim that *langue* is something social does in fact reduce to either of these two positions, then 'social' is ontologically empty.[19]

No need to ask for it, Dear Buyer. Here is your third false assumption, freshly formulated as:

> The Figures Fallacy
> *Statistics can be sewn on to the seams of language.*

Also known as Bill's Blunder, the idea that language – as opposed to the use of language – has a quantitative dimension makes about as much sense ontologically as the notion of a natty nude. (This Bill, it is rumoured, is a distant cousin of the French Physicalist Vitalstatistix whose friends we met towards the end of chapter 1.)

5.4 Slipping into something Sapirean

Language is primarily a cultural and social product. This view has been taken by some to represent the core of Edward Sapir's (1949a: 160) linguistic ontology.[20] the question, of course, is: What has Sapir meant by saying that language is something 'cultural' or 'social'? Two things, in terms of relatively recent analyses by Katz (1981: 7–8) and Kaldewaij (1986: 52–3).

On the one hand, by saying that language is something cultural, Sapir (1921: 4) means that, like other cultural entities, language is learned. That is, Sapir contends that, unlike biological functions, language does not develop 'organically' in the individual. Thus, Sapir (1921: 4) states that 'Walking is an organic, and instinctive, function . . . speech is a non-instinctive, acquired, "cultural" function.'[21] Katz (1981: 8) observes that Sapir advanced this view of language acquisition in the first part of the century when the social sciences were in the ascendant. Within this context, the view that language is learned non-instinctively might have seemed obviously correct to many. But, Katz maintains, this view of language acquisition has become highly controversial since Chomsky's revival of nativism. Chomsky, Katz (1981: 8) notes, 'calls attention to factors that are completely overlooked in arguments like Sapir's: the possibility of ethological models of instinctive behavior which contain hypotheses about releasing mechanisms. . . .' That is, it will be recalled, Chomsky has presented evidence indicating that language acquisition is essentially a matter of biological 'growth'. On Chomsky's view, the environment – social, cultural etc. – plays the restricted role of triggering and shaping 'language growth'.[22] In support of his theory of language acquisition, Chomsky observes that for many of the linguistic principles acquired by children there is no evidence in the environment in which (first-)language acquisition takes place. Chomsky's observations – known as 'the argument from the poverty of the stimulus' – discredit Sapir's view that humans are not biologically predestined to talk. As a consequence, these observations undermine the first sense in which Sapir considers language to be something cultural.

Recall that Saussure, too, considered *langue* to be 'social' in the sense of 'learned through social interaction'. And as we have seen in section 4.2.1 above, Popper (1972: 49) has likewise contended that 'language learning' is not 'natural but cultural and social', a process that is not 'gene-regulated'. In fact, however, Chomsky's argument from the poverty of the stimulus empirically undermines any conception of language on which language is something cultural or social in the sense of 'developmentally noninnate'.[23] In connection with this generalization, it should be borne in mind that our interest in any particular conception of language is not primarily of a historical sort. We are concerned, rather, with the general ontological lessons which may be learned from influential conceptions of language, past and present.

On the other hand, by saying that language is something 'cultural', Sapir seems to mean that, like other cultural entities, language is subject to a striking measure of variation. The following remarks by Sapir (1921: 4) evidence this, second, sense of 'cultural':

> Speech is a human activity that varies without assignable limit as we pass from social group to social group, because it is a purely historical heritage of the group, the product of long-continued social usage. It varies as all creative effort varies – not as consciously, perhaps, but nonetheless as truly as do the religions, the beliefs, the customs, and the arts of different peoples.

Sapir, however, significantly qualifies this strong view of the 'limitless' variability of language. As shown by Hymes and Fought (1975: 993), Sapir does not believe that languages are completely unique.

For example, Sapir (1921: 200) observes that 'It would be easy to relieve ourselves of the burden of constructive thinking and to take the standpoint that each language has its unique history and therefore its unique structure.' Not only does Sapir reject this 'easy' standpoint or 'unconstructive' way of thinking; he also, positively, believes in the existence of linguistic universals.[24] This belief, Hymes and Fought (1975: 993–4) show, is manifested in Sapir's 'typology', in his 'universalizing investigations in semantics' and in his insistence that a (relativistic and distributional) classification of sound units should be done 'in terms which are drawn from the prevailing "universal" articulatory classification of sounds'.

Something not mentioned by Hymes and Fought (1975) is that Sapir appears to have believed that the variability of language in the *individual* is subject to innate constraints. Thus, comparing language to art, he (1921: 220) contends that, as a form of expression, language may be 'endlessly varied in the individual without thereby losing its distinctive contours; and it is constantly reshaping itself as is all art.' The constraints imposed by the 'distinctive contours' appear to be intended by Sapir in the sense of 'innate constraints', as witness his (1921: 218) following remark: 'If it can be shown that culture has an *innate form*, a series of contours, quite apart from subject matter of any description whatsoever, we have something in culture that may serve as a term of comparison with and possibly a means of relating it to language' (emphasis added).

Sapir's view that language has an 'innate form' – or that language has 'distinctive contours' of a fixed sort – that constrains its variability in the individual has, of course, to be reconciled in some way with his view that an innate form plays no role in language acquisition. How this is to be done is not clear to me. Equally unclear is the ontological category status of an entity that has an 'innate form' but that is of a 'cultural' rather than a biological sort. What is clear though is that, in regard to variability, language in Sapir's own view is 'cultural' to a lower degree than are religions, beliefs, customs and so on. Unfortunately, of course, all of this means that the second sense in which Sapir considers language to be cultural is less than transparent. And there are other important ways in which language (or linguistic patterns) differs from culture (or cultural patterns) in Sapir's view.[25]

First, cultural and linguistic entities differ in regard to the ways in which they change. Thus, Sapir (1921: 100, 102) believes cultural entities to change faster than linguistic forms. This is so because, on his view, people are more conscious of cultural entities than of linguistic forms. In this connection, Sapir (1949c: 100) concludes that 'changes in culture are the result to at least a considerable extent, of conscious processes or of processes more easily made conscious, whereas those of language are to be explained, if explained at all, as due to the more minute action of psychological factors beyond the control of will or reflection.' And, significantly, unlike the 'drift of culture', the 'drift of language' in Sapir's (1921: 219) view is 'not properly concerned with changes of content at all, merely with changes in formal expression'. Sapir (1921: 219) accordingly concludes that 'we shall do well to hold the drifts of language and of culture to be non-comparable and unrelated processes.'

Secondly, Sapir (1949c: 549) takes language to differ from many other 'cultural patterns' in regard to the 'functional significance' of its forms. He (1949c: 547) contends that, 'ordinarily', a cultural pattern is to be defined in terms of both 'function' and 'form', 'the two concepts being inseparably intertwined in practice, however convenient it may be to dissociate them in theory.' Sapir moreover provides for the possibility that, in the case of some cultural patterns, form has 'functional significance': their form can be explained in terms of its function(s), even though such an explanation may be possible 'after the event' only. But, Sapir (1949c: 549) notes,

> Language has the somewhat exceptional property that its forms are, for the most part, indirect rather than direct in their functional significance. The sounds, words, grammatical forms, syntactic constructions, and other linguistic forms that we assimilate in childhood have only value in so far as society has tacitly agreed to see them as symbols of reference.

In regard to 'functional significance', linguistic forms are more closely related to 'aesthetic products' or 'artistic productions' than to patterns of cultural behaviour. As Sapir (1949c: 550) puts it: 'Whatever may be true of other types of cultural behaviour, we can safely say that the forms of speech developed in the different parts of the world are at once free and necessary, in the sense in which all artistic productions are free and necessary.' Linguistic forms, he believes, 'bear only the loosest relation to the cultural needs of a given society'. So, even within Sapir's own conceptual framework, linguistic forms differ in important ways from (other) cultural products or patterns. This means, then, that even in a Sapirean sense language is not a typical 'cultural product'.

But, even just within the context of Sapir's own thought, more problems beset his (1949a: 166) view that language is a 'cultural product'. A first such internal problem concerns the alternative ways in which Sapir characterizes the relationship between (what he calls) 'language' and 'culture'. Thus in addition to claiming that language is a 'cultural product', he also states that language is one of the 'aspects of culture' (1949b: 7), that language is 'a phase of human culture' (1921: 11) and, later, that language is 'the symbolic guide to culture' (1949a: 162). But it is only in terms of the loosest of formulations, surely, that a thing A can be coherently conceived of as being at once a product of, an aspect of, a phase of and a guide to a second thing B! Nor is it immediately obvious how what seem to be four ontologically disparate characterizations of the relationship between 'language' and 'culture' are to be reconciled with one another.

A second internal problem concerns Sapir's use of the notion of a 'product' in his portrayal of language as a 'cultural product'. 'Culture', on an early definition of Sapir's (1921: 218), is '*what* a society does or thinks'. 'Language', by contrast, he (1921: 218) defines as 'a particular *how* of thought'. As for the relation between the two, Sapir (1921: 218) states that he cannot 'believe that culture and language are in any true sense causally related'. Yet, later, he is able to conceive of language as a '(cultural) product'. But, if B is the product of A, then conventionally one would conceive of A as having been involved in some sense in the causation of B. Again, this indicates how complex and opaque the relationship between 'language' and 'culture' is in Sapir's thinking.[26] Conceivably, it might be contended that all these 'complexities' and 'opacities' would disappear if one were to 'parcel out' seemingly conflicting views into different phases of Sapir's thinking, distinguishing, for example, between an 'earlier Sapir', a 'later Sapir', and so on.

Within each of these phases, so the contention might go, Sapir's linguistic ontology is free of internal conflicts, such conflicts being due to an unwarranted 'telescoping' of different views held by him at different times. But, however readily conceivable this line of thought may be, as of now it is mere speculation; all of it has yet to be shown.

Notice that if Sapir's early definition of 'language' as 'a particular *how* of thought' were taken literally, language would be something mental or psychological. This brings us to the second dimension of Sapir's conception of language: the dimension in terms of which language has certain psychological characteristics or properties. Sapir, indeed, has been considered by some to be an (embryonic) conceptualist: someone (embryonically) portraying language as a mental entity or phenomenon. This construal of Sapir's linguistic ontology has been standardly motivated with reference to his (1949c,d) contention that phonemes, as units within linguistic patterns or configurations, are 'psychologically real'.[27] In calling phonemes – e.g. *t* and *d* in English – 'psychologically real', Sapir appears to say essentially three things:

1 Phonemes are not physical entities in the sense of 'physical entities' defined in terms of objective articulatory and acoustic properties (1949d: 46).
2 Phonemes are not abstractions in the sense of 'fictions' created for descriptive purposes by linguists (1949d: 46–7).
3 Phonemes are entities which naive speakers and hearers 'feel' themselves to be pronouncing and hearing (1949d: 47).[28]

It is not clear whether the psychologism expressed in 3 could be extended in a coherent and systematic way so as to yield a conception in terms of which (a) language is something that naive speakers and hearers 'feel' themselves to be using. For example, whether there is an analogous way of assigning psychological reality to syntactic units or structures which of course are even more abstract than phonemes, is a question not discussed explicitly by Sapir. Nor does he attempt to relate his position on psychological reality to his earlier psychologistic definition of language as 'a particular *how* of thought'. What the ontological category of a 'how' would be in a psychological context is likewise left unclear.

Nor is either Sapir's position on psychological reality or his psychologistic definition of language explicitly linked by him with his attribution of a set of four 'psychological qualities/characteristics/peculiarities' to language. To these psychological qualities, which are of a functional sort, Sapir (1949b: 13) assigns the status of 'universally valid psychological facts'. In Sapir's own words, these properties are the following:

1. 'language is a perfect symbolism for experience' (1949b: 12): language is 'a medium for the handling of all references and meanings that a given culture is capable of . . .' (1949b: 10).
2. 'in the actual context of behavior [language] cannot be divorced from action' (1949b: 12–13); language does not only 'refer to', 'mould', 'interpret' and 'discover experience', but it also 'substitutes' for experience (1949b: 11).
3. 'language . . . is rarely a purely referential organization' (1949b: 11): 'it is the carrier of an infinitely varied expressiveness' (1949b: 13).
4. 'the referential form systems which are actualized in language behavior do not need speech in its literal sense in order to preserve their substantial integrity' (1949b: 13): as a symbolic means language has, in more contemporary terms, the property of medium-transferability.

Returning to the general point: what I have called the 'psychological dimension' of Sapir's linguistic ontology is difficult to fathom. Sapir's characterization of language as something psychological appears to consist of unconnected fragments, many of whose ontological import is less than clear.[29] This is perhaps unsurprising given Sapir's (1921: 11) view that:

> We can profitably discuss the intention, the form, and the history of speech, precisely as we discuss the nature of any other phase of human culture – say art or religion – as an institutional or cultural entity, leaving the organic and psychological mechanisms back of it as something to be taken for granted.

The remarks just quoted reflect a further aspect of Sapir's linguistic ontology that is insufficiently well articulated: the way in which language, as a 'phase of human culture', is related to the 'psychological mechanisms back of it'. Concretely: What has one to make of something that is at once a 'phase/product of culture' and 'a particular *how* of thought'? How is one to conceive of the ontological category of a 'cultural product' or 'a phase of culture' that has certain 'psychological qualities'? Questions such as these are not addressed directly by Sapir.

Sapir does, however, seem to regard the 'psychological mechanisms back of [language]' as belonging to individual psychology. This may be inferred from the way in which he (1949a) draws the distinction between 'individual' and 'social behavior'. Sapir (1949a: 544) takes it for granted that all human behaviour involves 'essentially the same types of mental functioning, as well conscious as unconscious.' He takes it for granted, moreover, that the term 'social' is no more exclusive of the concept 'unconscious' than is the term 'individual'. And accordingly he assumes that 'any kind of psychology that explains the behavior of the individual also explains the behavior of society.' This means that Sapir does not find the essential difference between individual and social behaviour to be in the psychology of the behaviour itself. He (1949a: 545) considers social behaviour to be 'merely the sum or, better, arrangement of such aspects of individual behavior as are referred to culture patterns that have their proper context, not in the spatial and temporal continuities of biological behavior, but in historical sequences that are imputed to actual behavior by a principle of selection.' He thus defines the difference between individual and social behaviour 'not in terms of kind or essence, but in terms of organization'. In regard to essence, therefore, social or cultural behaviour, on Sapir's view, is 'objectively no more and no less individual' than individual behaviour.

Sapir (1949a: 544, 548) accordingly rejects the idea of postulating a 'social unconsciousness', 'social mind' or 'racial mind' to account for the unconscious patterning of social and cultural behaviour. He believes that 'It [i.e. the concept of a "social" or "racial mind"] introduces more difficulties than it solves, while we have all we need for the psychological understanding of social behavior in the facts of individual psychology.'[30] This means that in so far as language is something psychological to Sapir, it is part of individual psychology. Within Sapir's (1949a: 545, 555) conceptual framework, therefore, 'social' contrasts not with 'individual' but rather with 'biological'. But these inferences are too general to contribute much to elucidating the specific way in which language, as 'a phase of human culture', is related to 'the psychological mechanisms back of it'.

To conclude: Sapir's linguistic ontology clearly does not provide sufficient support for the claim that language can be credibly construed as something cultural. Certainly his work is rich in content in various ways; certainly his work deserves the 'systematic, full scale study' called for by Hymes and Fought (1975: 994). But study of an exegetic sort is unlikely to produce satisfactory answers to questions about Sapir's linguistic ontology such as those raised above. That is, chances are slim, it appears to me, that exegesis would yield a well-articulated Sapirean 'cultural' conception of language.

Hymes (1970: 258), interestingly, argues that the 'thrust of Sapir's first writing on language in relation to culture . . . is to separate the two'. And, in positive terms, Hymes (1970: 260), contends that 'Sapir's work in this period can be seen as a hymn to the autonomy of linguistic form.' As regards the autonomy of linguistic form, Hymes (1970: 261) considers the 'parallel to the views of de Saussure in the same period [to be] striking'. This means that any systematic study of Sapir's linguistic ontology would have to explore also the way in which a third dimension, an 'autonomist' one, is intertwined with the other two.

Which brings us to a fourth false assumption:

> The Four-In-One-fallacy
> *Language is at once social, cultural, psychological and autonomous in essence.*

No, Dear Buyer, I don't recall ever hearing even just one good reason for the belief that language in essence *is a Metaphysical Mixture, a veritable Conceptual Dream Coat. Known also as Ed's Error, this fallacy is a product of practising metaphysics in a misconceived Mix-and-Match Mode. (To a related way of getting fit out ontologically we will return in section 6.1.3 below.)*

5.5 Getting dressed down like Dummett

That (a) language is a social phenomenon is a belief which philosophers too have commonly held. Many have done so under the influence of Wittgenstein, who on Michael Dummett's (1986: 471) reading 'is well known to have taken language primarily as a social activity'. Dummett's articulation of this belief gives one a good idea of what these philosophers have had in mind when portraying language as something social. Moreover, the shortcomings of Dummett's linguistic ontology, as these have been laid bare by Chomsky, illustrate some of the most fundamental flaws of this 'social' conception of language.

A language, Dummett (1986: 473) contends, 'is a practice in which people engage'.[31] This practice is 'social' in a dual sense: 'it is learned from others and [it] is constituted by rules which it is part of social custom to follow.' Dummett (1986: 474) stresses 'the role of convention [or rule] in language': 'Conventions, whether they be expressly taught or picked up piecemeal, are what constitute a social practice; to repudiate the role of convention is to deny that language is in this sense a social practice.' Dummett (1986: 468, 475) moreover takes as 'fundamental' the 'notion' or 'sense of a language' in terms of which a language 'exists independently of any particular speakers'. This notion, Dummett (1986: 468) observes, provides for 'a common language as spoken at a given time – either a language properly so called, such as English or Russian, or a dialect of such a language.' In terms of this 'fundamental sense' of a language, every individual speaker 'has' a language. But, Dummett 'acknowledges', any individual speaker has only a 'partial, and partly erroneous grasp of the language'.[32]

To Dummett (1986: 475), to say that a speaker 'grasps a language' is tantamount to saying that he 'has mastered a practice'. As for the notion of 'a practice', Dummett (1986: 475) considers it to require 'rather careful philosophical characterization': 'To the question whether mastery of a practice is theoretical or practical knowledge we can only reply that the characterization is too crude: it falls between.' Mastery of a language is not 'practical knowledge', for one cannot try to speak a language, say Spanish, or tell whether someone else is speaking it, if one does not know the language. This, in Dummett's (1986: 475) view, makes mastery of a language 'a genuine case of knowledge'. It does not however, in his view, make mastery of a language a case of 'theoretical knowledge'. This is because the content of 'theoretical knowledge' of a practice would be, for him, 'a fully explicit description' of the practice. And in the case of a language, Dummett (1986: 476) maintains, 'such a description would be a theory of meaning for that language. . .'. And such a description he considers 'exceedingly difficult' to give.

Dummett's conception of language instantiates what Chomsky (1989: 8) holds to be 'a picture . . . [that] is very widely accepted, and in fact, is implicit in most of the general discussions about language and thought among philosophers, linguists, psychologists, and others, and of course in common sense discourse'. And, Chomsky argues, this 'everyday' or 'common-sense' conception of language exhibits various serious flaws, to which we now turn.[33]

A first cluster of criticisms of Chomsky's is aimed at the well-foundedness, internal coherence and logic of the notions 'shared language', 'superlanguage', 'common language' and 'community language'. For example, Chomsky (1989: 9) observes that it is striking that despite the constant reliance on some notion of 'community language', 'there is virtually no attempt to explain what it might be'.[34] And even if some notion of 'shared language' could be developed, it is unclear to Chomsky (1989: 9) 'what is the point of the exercise'. As he puts it: 'For the inquiry into the nature of language, or language acquisition and change, or any of the topics of linguistic inquiry, the notion would appear to have no use . . . [not] even for sociolinguistics, if we treat it seriously.' Chomsky (1980a: 118), moreover, has argued that it is not clear that the notion of a 'superlanguage' is 'even coherent'. On his view, speakers of what is loosely called 'English' do not have partial knowledge of some English superlanguage, 'but rather have knowledge of systems that are similar but in part conflict'. Chomsky accepts Putnam's observation that in a 'sufficiently complex society' speakers will defer to 'experts' to explain the meaning of terms that they do not fully understand. But from this observation it does not follow, as Dummett seems to believe, that there exists 'a shared language', a kind of 'superlanguage'. Rather, Chomsky (1980a: 118) maintains, 'From this observation [of Putnam's] we may conclude merely that each person has an internalized grammar that leaves certain questions open, and is willing to turn to others to answer the open questions.'

The flawed nature of the logic involved in Dummett's postulation of the notion of 'shared language' is further illustrated by Chomsky (1989: 10) with reference to the pronunciation of words. Having invited his readers to consider the fact that Jones understands Smith when the latter uses the word 'tree' to refer to trees, Chomsky (1989: 10) argues:

> Does it follow that Jones and Smith grasp the same meaning, an object of the common or abstract language? If so, then we should draw the analogous conclusion about pronunciation, given that Jones understands Smith to be saying 'tree'; since Jones understands Smith, it must be that there is some object of the common language, the real or common pronunciation of 'tree,' that Jones and Smith both grasp. No one is inclined to make that move. Rather, we say that Jones and Smith have managed a mutual accommodation that allows Jones, sometimes at least, to select an expression of his own language that, for the purposes at hand, matches well enough the one that Smith has produced.

Chomsky sees no need to proceed to the 'absurd conclusion' that there is a common pronunciation that Smith and Jones share (in part), with a 'partially erroneous grasp' in Dummett's sense.

A second set of criticisms is directed by Chomsky at the rudimentary empirical import of Dummett's 'fundamental sense' of a language. To begin with, Chomsky (1980a: 118) queries the extension of this notion by asking: 'How broadly should the "super-language" German extend? To Dutch? If not, why not, since it will presumably cover dialects that differ from one another more or less in the way some of them differ from Dutch.' Chomsky (1988d: 3) further observes that people who live near the Dutch border can communicate quite well with those living on the German side. But, according to the sense of the term 'language' that Dummett takes to be 'fundamental', these people speak two different languages. And, Chomsky proceeds, the people on the German side of the border, with their 'partial knowledge' of German as a language in Dummett's sense, may understand nothing spoken by people who live in some other region and who 'have' a different 'partial knowledge' of German as a language in Dummett's sense. It is for reasons such as these, Chomsky concludes, that no concept of '(a) language' such as Dummett's plays any role in empirical inquiry into language and psychology.

Continuing this line of criticism, Chomsky (1988d: 3) argues that Dummett's concept of 'a language' is 'useless' in actual inquiry into language acquisition. Chomsky (1988d: 3) illustrates this claim with reference to a state of affairs that he sketches as follows:

> In ordinary usage, we say that a child of five and a foreign adult are on their way towards acquiring English, but we have no way to designate whatever it is that they 'have.' The child, in the normal course of events, will come to 'have' English (at least partially and erroneously), though the foreigner probably will not. But if all adults were suddenly to die and children were somehow to survive, then whatever it is they are speaking would be a human language, though one that does not now exist.

Dummett's 'ordinary usage' provides 'no useful way to describe any of this', Chomsky concludes. The reason for this is that this usage involves too many 'obscure concerns and interest'. As embodied in Dummett's 'fundamental sense of a language', these concerns and interests include, as Chomsky (1988c: 5) puts it, 'complex and obscure sociopolitial, historical, cultural and normative-teleological elements'. Chomsky allows for the possibility that these 'elements' may be of some interest for 'the sociology of identification within various social and political communities and the study of authority structure'. These 'elements' however, in Chomsky's opinion, lie 'far beyond any useful inquiry into the nature of language or the study of meaning or the psychology of users of language'.

A third set of criticisms is directed by Chomsky at the notions of 'social custom' and 'social practice' that form the conceptual core of Dummett's linguistic ontology. Chomsky (1988d: 4) expounds these criticisms with reference to the sentences (1) *Mary expects to feed herself* and (2) *I wonder who Mary expects to feed herself.* He notes that, whereas in (1) *feed herself* is to be taken to be predicated of Mary, in (2) *feed herself* is predicated of some (female) person distinct from Mary. From (2), accordingly, it follows for Chomsky that I wonder which female person Mary expects to feed that same person, but not that I wonder which person Mary expects to feed Mary herself. Chomsky considers 'pertinent' the question how we know these facts. The answer seems to him to be that the initial state of the shared language faculty incorporates certain principles concerning referential dependence. And, he contends, once certain options left undetermined in the initial state are fixed by elementary experience, we have no more choice in interpreting (1) or (2) than we have in perceiving something as, say, a red triangle or a person. Arguing along these lines, Chomsky (1988d: 4) arrives at the general point that 'Social custom appears to have nothing to do with the matter in such cases, though in all of them, early experience helps to set certain details of the invariant, biologically-determined mechanisms of the mind/brain.' This appears to Chomsky to be 'true rather generally' about the acquisition of knowledge of language. And he judges the proposals of Dummett and others concerning 'social practice' to be false as an empirical fact, if these proposals are taken literally. 'At the very least', Chomsky (1988d: 4) observes, 'some argument would be required to show why they should be considered seriously'.

Construing language as a social practice leads, Chomsky (1988d: 4) contends, to the belief that knowledge of language is the ability to engage in such practice, as Dummett in fact suggests. This belief, according to Chomsky, is consonant with the 'common construal of knowledge more generally as a kind of ability', a construal defended, for example, by Kenny (1984: 138ff.). In terms of the former belief and latter construal, there is no (sharp) distinction between having knowledge of a language and the ability to use one's language or, alternatively, to put one's knowledge to use. The failure to draw this distinction, Chomsky (1988d: 4–5) finds, is a substantial flaw in the conception of language as a social practice: 'the approach in terms of practical ability has proven entirely unproductive and can be sustained only by understanding "ability" in a way that departs radically from ordinary usage.' In fleshing out this criticism, Chomsky (1988d: 5) invites his readers to suppose that Jones, a speaker of some variety of English, improves his ability to speak his language by taking a public speaking course, or loses this ability because of injury or disease, later recovering that ability with the aid of a drug. In all such cases, Chomsky contends, something remains constant – what he calls a 'property K' – whereas ability to speak, understand etc. varies. This property K is said, in ordinary language, to be knowledge of language. Drawing a distinction between knowledge of language and the ability to use this knowledge makes it possible to say that Jones's knowledge of (a variety of) English remained constant, while his ability to use this knowledge improved, declined, recovered etc.

Because of their failure to draw a distinction between knowledge of language and the ability to use this knowledge, Dummett and others have to construct 'artificial concepts divorced from ordinary usage' to account for instances such as the Jones case. This point Chomsky (1988d: 5) unpacks as follows:

> If knowledge is ability, then the property K must be a kind of ability, though plainly not ability in the quite useful normal sense of the word, since ability varied while K remained constant. We must therefore contrive a new technical sense of the term 'ability,' call it *K-ability*. Then K-ability remained constant while ability varied. K-ability is completely divorced from ability, and has the properties of the old concept of knowledge, and might as well be called 'knowledge', doctrinal matters aside.

Chomsky considers it rather 'ironic' that these 'moves' by Dummett and others should be presented in the spirit of the later Wittgenstein. It was Wittgenstein, Chomsky notes, who constantly argued against the practice of constructing artificial concepts, divorced from ordinary usage, in defence of philosophical doctrines. The Wittgensteinian construal of knowledge as a species of ability seems to Chomsky (1988d: 5) to be 'a paradigm example of the practice that Wittgenstein held to be a fundamental source of philosophical error'.[35]

In response to Chomsky, Dummett and others could point out that they deliberately refrained from equating 'mastery of language' with 'practical knowledge'. But they would have to do more than this before they would have an effective counter to Chomsky's criticisms. That is, in clarifying their notions of 'social practice' and 'mastery of language', they would have to give in addition a detailed account of the 'Jones cases', an account which would have to be free of the questionable consequences brought to light by Chomsky.

As things stand at present, Chomsky has shown that the Dummettian or 'common-sense' conception of language is incapable of allowing an adequate factual account of various phenomena. Among these phenomena, the following are particularly embarrassing: the phenomenon of children and foreigners 'on their way towards acquiring a language'; the phenomenon of speakers acquiring and having knowledge of (differences in) the interpretation of sentences such as *Mary expects to feed herself* and *I wonder who Mary expects to feed herself*; and the phenomenon of variation in a mature speaker's ability to speak and understand his language.[36] The inability of the common-sense conception of language to provide a basis for understanding such factual phenomena goes to show, on Chomsky's (1988d: 3) analysis, that the view of rational inquiry held by Dummett and others is unfruitful. Rational inquiry, Chomsky observes, is not 'the study of everything'. Rather, he (1988d: 3–4) maintains,

> in rational inquiry we idealize to selected domains in such a way (we hope) as to permit us to discover crucial features of the world. Data and observations, in the sciences, have an instrumental character; they are of no particular interest in themselves, but only insofar as they constitute evidence that permits one to determine fundamental features of the real world. . . .

The study of 'language' in Dummett's sense verges, in Chomsky's opinion, on 'the study of everything'.[37] And this, ultimately, is why Dummett has failed to give, as Chomsky (1989: 11) puts it, 'useful sense' to the notion that language is a social phenomenon. Nor has the usefulness of this notion been enhanced by the careless use of concepts such as 'misuse of language', 'norms' and 'communities'. Chomsky (1988d: 20–1) considers these concepts 'obscure' and cautions in particular against the use of the notion of 'community': 'Communities are formed in all sorts of overlapping ways, and the study of communities and their norms quickly degenerates into the study of everything.' This point of Chomsky's, clearly, is damaging to all linguistic ontologies – including the Saussurian one – which provide for a notion of '(a) language' that is defined in terms of a nontechnical concept of '(a) community'.[38]

Fallacy Number Five concerns the factual focus of common-sense conceptions of language. It may be formulated, Dear Buyer, as

> The Focus Fallacy
> *A conception of language can do even if factually unfocused.*

Founded on this fallacy, known informally as Mike's Misser, 'social' conceptions of language such as the Dummettian one are indeed curious conceptual creations. Intended to enwrap everything, they were conceptually cut to serve as Metaphysical Maxis. Failing, however, to cover even the most familiar of factual phenomena, these conceptions, as a matter of fact, turn out to be less useful than Linguistic Loincloths. Ah yes, you do have my sympathy, Blushing Blue. As an Oxford (Wo)man dressed down in conceptions of the Common-sense Cu(l)t, you will of necessity find that these conclusions make you feel distinctly naked.

5.6 Poring over Pateman's pattern

This brings us to the attempt, mentioned by Chomsky (1989: 9), to explain what a 'community language' might be: Trevor Pateman's (1987: 73ff.) account of languages as 'sociopolitical facts'. The 'basic idea' of this account is that a language is an (intentional) object of (mutual) belief.[39] Given this basic idea, Pateman (1987: 75) contends, the reality of (the) English (language) is constituted as a sociopolitical fact through its appearance as the intentional object of speakers' mutual beliefs. The reply given by a (male) informant S to the question 'What language do you speak?' may be recorded by an anthropologist, Pateman (1987: 73) suggests, in the following form: 'S believes, of the language he speaks, that it is English.' 'English' appears here as the intentional object of S's belief. And the intentional occurrence of English is referentially opaque. This is so because, Pateman (1987: 74) observes, from the fact that some S believes he speaks *English*, it does not follow that he believes he speaks *Engelska*, since he may not know that '*Engelska*' is the Swedish for 'English'. This referential opacity of the name of the language makes it possible, on Pateman's view, for the language

S speaks and for S's beliefs about the language he speaks to vary independently of each other.

How are speakers supposed to acquire the beliefs attributed to them by Pateman? It is 'obvious', he (1987: 74) considers, that the beliefs speakers have as to which language they are native speakers of are not beliefs they acquired by inspecting the language they speak. Nor, Pateman holds, do speakers acquire such beliefs by matching the language they speak with some language previously named. Rather, Pateman (1987: 74) suggests, speakers are *told* which language they speak. For example, overhearing speakers of a foreign language for the first time, a speaker may be told 'They are speaking French. We speak English.' As Pateman (1987: 75) sees it: 'The belief [that we speak English] is acquired on authority and, consequently, is a mutual belief: I believe I am a speaker of English because you believe I am, and I believe you believe you are a speaker of English, and so on.' Pateman (1987: 77–9) believes there to be five 'advantages' to approaching languages as intentional objects of mutual belief. To illustrate the general *nature* of these 'advantages', I indicate below no more than the gist of each:

(A1) The approach allows for the possibility that speakers who agree that they are all speakers of English can genuinely disagree about what English is.
(A2) The approach allows for people to acquire, add to and change their beliefs about what English is.
(A3) The approach provides for a solution to the problem of the limits of the operation of prescriptivism in space and time.
(A4) The approach is able to 'handle' the phenomenon of hyper-correction 'with ease'.
(A5) The approach allows an 'approach' to questions about linguistic standardization and hegemony without abolishing the distinction between the 'external history' of language(s) and its/their 'internal history'.

In a nutshell, Pateman (1987: 79) considers his intentionalist approach to 'capture the hermeneutic moment of languages as non-linguistic, social facts: the moment in which actors define their world'.

What, then, are the 'disadvantages' of Pateman's conception of languages as 'social facts'? Chomsky's (1989: 9) diagnosis of these disadvantages is rather negative: 'It is very doubtful that this [intentionalist] account [of languages] – or any like it – captures a real object of the real world, psychological or social.' This is so, Chomsky argues, because people establish 'bonds of community' in all sorts of intersecting ways. They have, he suggests, all sorts of connections with others and also all sorts of beliefs about others and about themselves. Given the transient and fluctuating beliefs and associations of people, it is far from clear to Chomsky that there is a coherent notion of a 'common' or 'community language' here.[40] It is doubtful to Chomsky, moreover, that 'suitable idealization' would be of any help. To clarify this, he (1989: 9) compares the character of communities and the practices of their members to the height and weight of people:

> If we range people by height and weight, we will find some closer to others, but there are no objective categories of 'tall', 'short', 'heavy', and 'light', or any reasonable idealizations to be constructed. Communities and the linguistic practices of their members have much the same character, as far as is known. . . .

Chomsky accordingly concludes that there is no reason to believe that the notions forming the core of Pateman's intentionalist conception of language are 'coherent notions, at least for the purpose of theoretical understanding'. In similar vein, Carr (1990: 109) has found no reason to assume that the belief that one speaks a language should be taken to be a belief about an 'object of theoretical linguistic inquiry'.

Significantly, Pateman himself seems to believe that his intentionalist conception of languages as social facts is useless as a tool for arriving at some theoretical understanding of what languages are. This is clear from the fact that he (1987) adopts a 'dualist' linguistic ontology that provides for two conceptions of language. The first of these is the intentionalist conception on which a language is a 'social fact' that is not simultaneously a 'linguistic fact'.[41] The second conception of language adopted by Pateman (1987: 45ff.) is one that portrays a language as a 'natural kind'. On Pateman's (1987: 46) view, languages are 'natural kinds' in the sense that they are distinguishable from other human or animal semiotic systems by essential, natural and replicable properties. For Pateman, Chomsky's nativist conception of language instantiates a linguistic ontology which portrays languages as natural kinds.

Which brings us to a sixth false assumption:

> The Frills Fallacy
> *Philosophical frills can be used to create a function for social conceptions of language.*

A conception of language that fails to capture 'a real object in the real world' makes one think, Dear Buyer, of a garishly self-defeating garment: a garment such that there is no part of the body to wear it on! Trevor's Trap is the belief that such nonfunctionality is sufficiently fixed if the idea that languages are socio-political facts is prettified with a handful of Philosophical Frills.

5.7 Being in with Itkonen

Let us consider one more articulation of the idea that language is essentially something social, namely Esa Itkonen's (1978, 1983b) articulation. A philosopher of linguistics, Itkonen (1978: 95) has attempted to use 'the Wittgensteinian approach to prove the primarily social nature of knowledge and language'. The product of this attempt of his (1978: 136) is a 'social notion' of language in terms of which 'Language is a set of rules existing at the level of common knowledge, and grammar is a (theoretical) description of these rules, or of this knowledge.' Itkonen's (1978: 122) stock example of a rule of language is the 'rule of English that the definite article precedes (and does not follow) the noun'. This rule, in his terminology, is 'described by the rule-sentence "In English the definite article precedes the noun."'

Rules, Itkonen (1978: 122) contends, are 'norms which govern intentional social behaviour'. And rules, on his view, are 'in turn manifested by this same (rule-following) behaviour'. In virtue of the normative nature of rules of language, Itkonen (1978: 124) takes any speech act to be either correct (if it follows the rules) or incorrect (if it fails to follow the rules). The normativity of rules of language, in his (1978: 124) view, is not construed out of 'something more elementary'. That is, this normativity is not reducible to something that is ontologically more basic.

The behaviour governed by rules of language is intentional since, Itkonen (1978: 122) believes, intentions are necessary constituents of actions. He takes intentions, moreover, to be 'at least potentially conscious: to *do* something, one must be able to *know*, at least under some description, what one is doing.' Consequently, Itkonen considers knowledge to be inseparable from action. And, for Itkonen (1978: 123), this makes knowledge 'necessarily social'. From the belief that knowledge is necessarily social, Itkonen (1978: 123) judges, at least a trio of consequences 'follows':

> First, that to be able to do an action *x*, a person A must know the action-concept 'X', that is, he must be able to identify instances of 'X' done by himself or by others. Second, A must know that *others* know 'X' and, third, A must know that others know that *he* knows 'X'. When this is the case, we say that 'X' is an object of *common knowledge*.

To Itkonen (1978: 125), common knowledge is, 'in a nutshell', about 'what everybody knows that everybody knows, or ought to know'.

The common knowledge of language embodied in rules of language is considered by Itkonen (1978: 151) to be both 'general' and 'certain'. In addition, he provides for various types of linguistic knowledge that are not 'general' or 'certain', including 'uncertain atheoretical knowledge of language'. Itkonen (1978: 151) does this in order to account for such phenomena as linguistic change, linguistic variation and, what he calls, 'extraordinary use of language'. Rules involved in linguistic change are not 'certain': they 'hold only approximately', 'social control' having been 'decreased' in their case. And rules involved in linguistic variation, including idiolectal variation, are not 'general' in the sense of being common knowledge in a speech community. As for 'extraordinary use of language', Itkonen (1978: 152) claims it to be 'a self-evident truth that where something exceptional is being done, rules must prove insufficient.'

In what way, then, has Itkonen used 'the Wittgensteinian approach' to arrive at the ontological position that linguistic rules have a common knowledge character? What Itkonen (1978: 110–13) has done is, in essence, to invoke the Wittgensteinian argument against the existence of private languages. The core of this argument, as reconstructed by Pateman (1987: 65), is as quoted below:

> that an inner process stands in need of outward criteria (logical, but non-reductive, behaviourism); that for someone to be said to follow a rule, it must be possible for them to make a mistake and be corrected; and that this can only occur in interaction or possible interaction, since one's own memory cannot serve as the criterion for determining whether one has, on some occasion, followed a rule correctly. So if no one disputes that language involves rules, linguistic rules must be public rather than private objects, and the character of these public objects is elucidated in the common knowledge – i.e. social object – analysis.

The two fundamental theses of this Wittgensteinian argument, in Itkonen's (1978: 112) own formulation, are 'first of all, that such psychological concepts as knowledge [and language] are inseparable from outward criteria, and secondly, that rules must be intersubjective or social.' When these two theses are brought to bear on the question of the 'nature of language', Itkonen (1978: 112) claims, then it 'follows' 'that language, as well as knowledge of it, is inseparable from the use of language which conforms to social rules.' This conclusion has led Itkonen (1978: 133) to reject the Chomskyan conception of language since, in Itkonen's view, this conception is 'demonstrably equivalent to the private-language conception'. The same conclusion, moreover, has led Itkonen to reject the Chomskyan distinction between linguistic competence and linguistic performance.

Itkonen conceives of language as a set of rules existing at the level of common knowledge. This conception has rather serious shortcomings. A first one is its reliance on the Wittgensteinian argument against the possibility of private languages. Fundamental to this argument is the belief that behaviour is criterial for the ascription of mental states to people. This belief, Chomsky (1980a: 48, 52–3; 1986: 259) has convincingly argued, represents a piece of dogma that places a crippling constraint on normal scientific work. Rather than assigning to behaviour the status of a criterion for mental states, it should in Chomsky's view be considered a potential source of evidence for the existence of such states. And it is important, Chomsky (1980a: 48) has argued, that behaviour represents only one of the potential sources from which such evidence may in principle be derived: 'if such knowledge [of language] is characterized in terms of mental state and structure, behavior simply provides evidence for possession of knowledge, as might facts of an entirely different order – electrical activity of the brain, for example.' And to Dummett's (1981) unargued claim that we identify knowledge 'solely by its [behavioural] manifestations', Chomsky (1986: 259) has responded in similar vein:

> To say that we identify knowledge (or the structure of knowledge, or the internal state of knowledge, or the system of rules constituting knowledge, etc.) 'solely by its manifestations' is true only in the sense that the nineteenth-century chemist identified the structure of benzene 'solely by its manifestations'. In fact, we identify the system of knowledge of language that accounts for facts concerning (2) (= who was persuaded to like him), (3) (= John is too stubborn to talk to), and so forth by such manifestations of this knowledge as the judgments concerning referential dependence, by judgments concerning other expressions, by behavior of speakers of other languages, and in principle in many other ways as discussed earlier.

If behaviour is merely one of the potential sources of evidence for mental states, the Wittgensteinian argument against the possibility of private languages lacks the power attributed to it by Itkonen and others: from the absence of behavioural evidence for a mental state such as a private language it does not follow that this mental state does not exist. Itkonen, consequently, has failed to discredit the Chomskyan view that language and languages exist as mental states of individuals or, alternatively, as mentally represented bodies of 'individual' knowledge.[42]

Chomsky (1986: 225ff.) has also offered grounds of a more general kind for rejecting Wittgensteinian scepticism – as articulated by Kripke (1982) – about the ascription of the following of a private rule to a person (Jones). Such ascription, when done by a scientist, cannot be objectionable – Chomsky argues – if it is done within the framework of an explanatory theory satisfying the usual empirical criteria of adequacy. Chomsky (1986: 236–7) holds, that is, that scientists should adopt the following general approach:

> We amass evidence about Jones [the person to whom rule following is ascribed], his behavior, his judgements, his history, his physiology, or whatever else may bear on the matter. We also consider comparable evidence about others, which is relevant on the plausible empirical assumption that their genetic endowment is in relevant respects the same as his, just as we regard a particular sample of water as water, and a particular fruit fly as a fruit fly. We then try (in principle) to construct a complete theory, the best one we can, of relevant aspects of how Jones is constructed – of the kind of 'machine' he is, if one likes.

Provided that this 'complete theory' meets the required empirical constraints, it may legitimately be concluded that the person (Jones) is following the rules of the particular language.

A second shortcoming of Itkonen's conception of language concerns the ontological status of what he calls 'common'. Itkonen seems to believe that, since (knowledge of) language cannot be 'private', it has to be 'common'. But given the flawed basis of the private-language argument, this does not follow at all. What Itkonen has to do is to present arguments of the proper kind to the effect that whatever it is that is 'common', does not represent something that is ontologically derivative. That is, Itkonen has to show that what he portrays as 'common' knowledge of language is not ontologically a secondary (epi-)phenomenon: the ill-defined product of the overlapping of bodies of individual knowledge of language. In this connection, he (1978: 127) claims that 'since a rule exists at the level of *common* knowledge, it cannot be analysed as a set of particular beliefs held by individual persons.' But Itkonen fails to present considerations which are clearly pertinent to establishing whether what he portrays as 'common' represents an entity that is indeed ontologically fundamental. In this regard, note that accounting for the fact that what one person says is understood by another does not make it a necessary step to postulate 'a common knowledge of language' as ontologically fundamental. Note, too, that to take such a step would be, of course, to use the same flawed logic which on Chomsky's (1989: 10) analysis, is central to Dummett's construction of 'common languages' (see section 5.5 above).

A third shortcoming of Itkonen's ontological view that rules of language have a common knowledge character is of an empirical sort. Specifically, this view does not receive the necessary support from phenomena of language acquisition and linguistic inventiveness. As for language acquisition, Pateman (1987: 66) has shown that it is not necessary to invoke Itkonen's notion of 'common knowledge' in order to understand how a child can begin to speak and communicate successfully:

> To do that [i.e. to 'enter' a language community] the child must begin (on any but the strongest nativist view of language acquisition) by making falsifiable abductions about the linguistic conventions (rules) which obtain in its community, and which generate the speech output the child receives as input. On this basis, the child can begin to speak and communicate successfully. But that is to say that falsifiable knowledge is sufficient for the child to communicate, and that being a party to conventions is unnecessary to its doing so. No doubt the child insensibly becomes a party to conventions, if conventions define the language of its community, but that it does so appears on this view a contingent matter.

Moreover, Pateman (1987: 67) observes, the child 'abduces' its rules not from the rules held in common by its 'interlocutors', but rather from the output of those rules. According to Pateman, this indicates that the child makes no use of the common knowledge character of those rules.

As for linguistic inventiveness, Itkonen's 'common knowledge' conception of language obviously restricts language acquisition to the acquisition of already existing 'common languages'. But, as Pateman (1987: 67–72) argues in some detail, various acquisitional phenomena discussed in the literature indicate that children invent new rules, rules whose 'collectively shared character is missing'. Three phenomena, in particular, evidence this kind of linguistic inventiveness in language learning children. First, as has been argued by Bickerton (1981: 5–6), the children of each first creole generation 'outstrip' the knowledge of their parents; expanding the pidgin spoken by their parents, they acquire rules for which there is no evidence in this pidgin. Secondly, work by Corder (1981) and others indicates that learners of a second language, too, acquire a system, a so-called interlanguage, that exhibits what Pateman (1987: 86) calls 'spontaneously generated features'. These features are 'derivable' neither from the learners' first language nor from the language targeted by the learners for acquisition. Thirdly, evidence presented by Feldman et al. (1978), and more recently by Goldin-Meadow and Mylander (1990), highlights the linguistic creativity of deaf children. This evidence concerns isolated deaf children of hearing parents who do not use sign language. Such children, Pateman (1987: 69) emphasizes, spontaneously develop signing systems as a means of communicating with their 'hearing interactants'. Pateman (1987: 70) considers in detail the bearing which these three kinds of 'material' about linguistic inventiveness have on Itkonen's claim that rules of language have a common knowledge character. He concludes that there is no obvious way in which Itkonen can counter the 'falsifying character' of 'the operation of private rules' evidenced by this material. The facts involved, Pateman also argues, are linguistic facts that are not 'social facts' as well.

Since they relate to creolization, to second language acquisition and to (first) language acquisition by deaf children, the three phenomena considered above are in a sense 'special'. Data about ordinary first language acquisition by normal children, however, are equally, if not more, embarrassing to the contention that language exists as Itkonian common knowledge. These data indicate, as has been repeatedly pointed out by Chomsky (e.g. 1986: 7–8), that in the case of normal language acquisition too the stimulus is strikingly impoverished. For important aspects of the (I-) language acquired by normal children, that is, there is no evidence at all in their linguistic environment. In short: within the framework of poverty of the stimulus arguments, Chomsky (1980a: 134–5) has made a strong case for the conception of language as something biological, something that 'grows' or 'matures' in the individual.

Itkonen has yet to show that the conception of language as something social can be squared with such poverty of the stimulus data. To show this at all convincingly, he would have to proceed from a more adequate grammatical description of what it is that is acquired. Specifically, it will not do to proceed on the basis of a single, a-typically simple and relatively concrete rule such as 'In English the definite article precedes the noun.' Rather, to mount even a minimally convincing demonstration, Itkonen would have to account for the acquisition of the rules or principles which have standardly figured in Chomsky's poverty of the stimulus arguments.

In sum: in order to present a credible case for his 'social' conception of language, Itkonen would have to show that criticisms such as those outlined above do not really harm his contention that rules of language have a common knowledge character.[43]

Our seventh example of the fallacies weaved into the fabric of many 'social' conceptions of language is formulated in what may strike you at first as a funny form, Dear Buyer.

The Fatal Fallacy
Perish the thought that there are private languages.

Based as it is on two bits of dogma, this fallacy is in the modality of a Metaphysical Malediction. Bit One being the all too easy empiricist equation 'No behaviour, no private language.' Bit Two being the antiscientific stance 'Mind cannot be investigated by the normal means of theory construction.' Small wonder, then, that this fallacy has occasionally been labelled Ludwig's Lament.

5.8 Veiling it verbally

To say that something – for example an entity, structure, practice or whole realm of reality – is 'social' is not to characterize it ontologically in a fundamental way. This has been the position adopted by many leading social (meta-)theorists who have given serious thought to the question 'What is the nature of social reality?' 'Social' has not been found by them to be a basic ontological category. Rather, as is clear from studies such as Johnson et al.'s *The Structure of Social Theory* (1984: 13ff.), these scholars have attempted to characterize the nature of social reality as ultimately being in some sense material or ideal. Both the materialist and the idealist characterizations of the nature of social reality have come in two basic versions.

Materialism

1 *Empiricism*: Social reality is fundamentally material. It is made up, that is, of material events which are particular, individual, unique. It may be construed, moreover, as an infinite complex of causal relations between events. (Johnson et al. 1984: 35, 115).

2 *Substantialism*: Social reality is fundamentally material. It is made up, that is, of general configurational wholes, not of purely unique things. The real 'social' structures underlie and give rise to individual manifestations (Johnson et al. 1984: 115).

Idealism

1 *Subjectivism*: Social reality is fundamentally ideal. It is made up, that is, of meanings which are socially constructed. These meanings are ideas and interpretations which human actors hold about society (Johnson et al. 1984: 76).

2 *Rationalism*: Social reality is fundamentally ideal. It is made up, that is, of ideas. Yet it is a real and general 'thing-in-itself' which is independent of is elements (Johnson et al. 1984: 149, 150).

Johnson et al. (1984) show in some detail that much of sociological (meta-)theorizing – within what they call the 'projects' of Weber, Durkheim, Marx, Parsons and (more recently) Giddens and Bhaskar – has been concerned to develop specific ontologies which articulate, synthesize or transcend these four fundamental 'resolutions to the problem of the nature of social reality'. On Johnson et al.'s analysis each and every one of these 'resolutions' is, however, characterized by serious internal 'tensions'.[44] This means that the major attempts to infuse 'social' in a principled way with deeper ontological content have produced 'dilemmas' rather than the required 'resolution' to the problem of the nature of social reality. Thus, Johnson et al. (1984: 225–6) observe:

> We cannot, however, present as a conclusion to our argument such a dialectical resolution of the dilemmas of social theory. There is

> no such resolution available to be presented. We are here merely presenting a goal. Such a resolution has still to be thought; to be worked toward. It is a task that must be the work of generations of social scientists who are forced by the failure of one strategy or another to seek a resolution.

In a nutshell: the nature of social reality has still to be captured in more fundamental ontological terms.

What may be concluded, then, about the attempts made to date to characterize language(s) ontologically as 'social' in essence? On the one hand: the characterizations which have been given within what may be considered more principled 'resolutions' of the problem of the nature of social reality are still remarkably tentative and relatively shallow. On the other hand: the characterizations given outside such 'resolutions' are quite arbitrary and virtually empty.

Proponents of the idea that (a) language is something 'social' seem not to have fully grasped the ontological problems involved in portraying an entity or realm of reality as 'social'. Only more exotic characterizations of the nature of social (linguistic) reality, for example, the one involving recourse to a Durkheimian group mind, seem to have been appraised with the required measure of critical detachment by these scholars.[45] On the whole, conceptions portraying language(s) as 'social' do not make sufficient contact with the substance of more perceptive ontological discussions such as the one by Johnson et al.

Here is a last false assumption which you may wish to ponder in tandem with the Freestyle Fallacy, Bull-headed Blue:

> The Follow-up Fallacy
> *The nature of linguistic reality can be revealingly characterized by using 'social' in one of its better established technical senses.*

On the contrary, to characterize linguistic reality thus is to veil the essence of language with a word. I do know, Now-slightly-green-looking Blue, that the Veiled Look has for ages been considered by some the last word in Philosophical Fashionability. But why should practising linguistic ontology for ever remain an exercise in Conceptual Concealment?

5.9 Reviewing the rage

The desperate look in your eyes, Dear Shaken Shopper, says it all: the idea that language is something social has done nothing for the Ontological Angst induced by the question 'What is language in essence?' So, 'What good has come from our staking out the Social Sector of The Market?', you may wonder. Sherlock Holmes, himself no mean metaphysicist, once spoke a Burgessian word that may offer you some consolation: 'To write a thing down, Watson, is to control it and sometimes to exorcise it.' And, of course we have learned a general lesson or two from our excursions into this sector of The Market:

1 *On the essence of language: it is not social in any established sense.*
2 *On constructing a conception of language: make sure it has a factual focus.*
3 *On justifying a conception of language: ordinary (language) ontologizing is out.*
4 *On the pedigree of a conception of language: beware of Founding Father Folklore.*
5 *On appraising a linguistic ontology: inspect the seams.*
6 *On the function of an ontological predicate: don't use it as a Fig Leaf.*

As for the first three lessons, I have nothing much to add. Except perhaps to say that the third has an alternative, though equivalent, formulation: Common-sensers have lost their clout. But let us dwell a little longer on some peculiarities of Founding Fathers, Suspect Seams and Fig Leaves.

Figures hailed as Founding Fathers have the nasty habit of turning out to have been philosophically fickle. This, Dear Buyer, is clear from the history of amongst others Saussure and Sapir, who, on careful accounts, could not really make up their mind about what they liked best: language being something social, something psychological, something autonomous or something else. This philosophical 'fluidity' has been exploited in a mercenary manner, I am ashamed to say, by conceptioneers pushing their particular conception of language as prestigiously pedigreed by 'pointing out': by pointing out, for instance, that 'The social conception of language has its roots in the linguistic thinking of Saussure', or that 'Sapir, too, took language to be a social product', or that 'In the final analysis, both Saussure and Sapir were conceptualists', and so on. Founding Fathers' metaphysics, alas too often murky, has been rummaged through for some means of elevating a conception of language above competitors. The point has been well put by John Joseph (1990: 53) with reference to Saussure:

> *Certainly no linguist in the twentieth century has undergone as many ideologically-driven readings as Saussure – a combined result of the revolutionary nature of his thought, the way in which it was preserved, and the fact that he was not on the scene as an academic-political force to protest the egregiously ideological misreadings.*

So much for lesson number four.

Seaming, Dear Buyer, is all important: a point, so it seems, which has not been at all well understood by manufacturers of 'social' conceptions of language. Would I care to be a bit less 'abstruse'? Sure, Bilious Blue, let me see if I can manage in a monosyllabic metaphysical mode. Suppose you (still) believe that language is something 'social'. Suppose, moreover, that you cannot fashionably deny (any longer) the existence of individual minds. To arrive at a coherent overall ontology, you then have a seaming job on your hands: sewing the social panel and the individual mental panel harmoniously together. For doing this Social Seamsters sadly, however, seem not to have anything else to fall back on but the Slipped Stitch. Or do you, Bowed-but-not-Beaten Blue, happen to have up your sleeve a linguistic ontology on which languages as social entities are neatly patched on to individual minds? Only, for an answer here, please don't haul me into the House of Halliday (1978). Looking at its fashions, I see only my own lack of imagination, not knowing what to make of frocks with flies, lapelled Levi's and other comparably confusing creations. As I have had to confess before, I am conceptually incapable of getting the hang of this studio's ways of styling: telescoping terminology, conflating concepts, unstitching distinctions, collapsing categories, and so on. So I have to leave unexplored the ontological implications of the Hallidayan Hunch that language is a 'social semiotic'.[46] *This brings us to the end of lesson number five.*

Fig leaves, of course, were used to create the first Foundation Fashions. Which goes some way towards explaining their popularity with conceptioneers concentrating on the creation of 'social' conceptions of language. But, and this is what lesson number six is all about, the function of an ontological predicate such as 'social' is to reveal, to lay bare, to unveil. The essence of language, of course. Regrettably, however, both in its ordinary and technical senses, 'social' has instead been used as a Foundational Fig Leaf for scantily covering up ignorance about what language really is.

What to do now that Fig Leaf Philosophy, too, has not furnished an adequate answer to the tormenting question 'What is language in essence?'? Where do we go from here? Well, Despairing Buyer, it seems to me that we cannot any longer put off the final exercise – indeed, the Exercise Eschatological: balancing the Book of Good and Bad Buys.

6

Balancing the Book(s)

6.0 Philosophizing faunally

How would I like to be labelled a Metaphysical Mule? Well, not all that much, Unwontedly Abrasive Blue. But why ask? Ah, I see, mulishness might at least begin to account(!) for my bloody-minded insistence on books being balanced – on conceptions of language being apocalyptically appraised. A winding up which at its most benign is bound to be bruising.

But then, oh Forthright Fellow, in winding up our business on The Market, what line would you *prefer to take? What's that? So: unless I'm misled by these long ears of mine, what you're suggesting is this. That, given all the conceptions of language which we've inspected, there is no need at all to cull the best from the rest. That, indeed, there are tried and trustworthy techniques of muddling through metaphysically – techniques of which I seem ignominiously ignorant. That the three most popular of these you have boiled down, for Asinine Academics like me, to the following bare bones:*

(B1) *The ordinary linguist really needs no technical conception of language (or more comprehensive linguistic ontology).*

(B2) *The ordinary linguist is free to adopt any one of the better-known conceptions of language.*

(B3) *The ordinary linguist is free to adopt two or more conceptions of language at one and the same time.*

And, you submit, not a single one of these self-evidently sensible methods of minding one's metaphysics requires the kind of conceptual confrontation that my mulish mind seems bent upon.

But, my Dear Boorish Blue, I do distinctly recall hearing people discuss these ways of conducting oneself on The Metaphysics Market: ducking, dodging or dithering as one 'does' its various axes. So, by way of warming up for our final act – The Appraisal or Balancing of The Book(s) – let me try to explain why these are not, and what is worse cannot be, the right means of making it metaphysically. To give more kick to my account – mules, you may remember, are frankly physical items of fauna – I will throw in the occasional quote from a starkly unconventional compendium that I once discovered while rummaging around on The Market. Entitled Figments of Faunal Philosophy, *this compact little work combines two delightful features. One: it treats ontology as a fusion of fable and fairy tale. Two: it consists entirely of footnotes, all in the same formulaic format.*

6.1 Muddling through metaphysically

6.1.1 Having no need for niceties

Ordinary linguists – also called 'practically minded linguists', 'working grammarians', 'people doing descriptive work', 'scholars engaged in linguistic analysis', and so on – get on quite well with their job without worrying unduly about the niceties of linguistic ontology. Their stuff, it is pointed out in support of this widely held belief, gets published regularly in respected journals, prestigious volumes and internationally sold series. All of this, the argument goes, is clear proof that there is no need to fuss about the relative merits of alternative conceptions of language. Consequently, too, adopting either the best or even the worst of these conceptions will not make the slightest significant difference to the quality of the work done by such no-nonsense linguists. So why tie oneself in knots over the question of whether language is something physical, behavioural, mental, biological, abstract or social? Or, perhaps, something ontologically mixed?

This attitude to ontological 'niceties' is not confined to linguists; it is shared by the vast majority of sane scientists. Or so it is believed. Yet within the nub of this hard-nosed dismissal of ontology as otiose nestles a quite specific assumption:

(A1) The fact that ordinary scientists profess to have no need for ontologies shows that their work is free of ontological suppositions.

And this assumption is false, not only as it applies to scientists in general but also as it applies to linguists in particular.

As for science in general: as we saw in section 1.4.2 above, science is shot through with metaphysical assumptions, many of which are ontological in their import. Not only philosophers of science but eminent scientists too have furnished strong evidence for this position, as Bunge (1977) notes.[1] He identifies five 'areas' or 'regions' in which science and ontology 'overlap', 'mingle' or 'merge':

(R1) *Heuristics*: assumptions of an ontological sort guide scientific research.[2]

(R2) *Scientific problems*: some of the most interesting scientific problems are at the same time ontological.[3]

(R3) *Fundamental concepts*: fundamental and generic concepts making up the axiomatic foundations of scientific theories are explicated and systematized by ontology – not by specific sciences, which 'borrow [. . .] them leaving them in an intuitive or presystematic state'.[4]

(R4) *General theories*: certain 'extremely general theories' do not represent 'narrow species of things' but rather describe 'the basic traits of whole genera of things'.[5]

(R5) *Contemporary technology*: certain technological theories are so general – their application not being restricted to the nature of specific materials or mechanisms – that 'they qualify as theories in scientific metaphysics.'[6]

Bunge (1977: 24), in fact, sees no gap between 'good metaphysics' and 'deep science'. Rather, he regards every deep – that is, general – scientific theory as metaphysical. And every ontological theory that 'brings together and generalizes scientific results', or else 'occurs in the background' of a scientific theory, qualifies for Bunge as 'scientific'. In a nutshell: 'every scientific theory, if extremely general, *is* ontological; and every ontological theory, if exact and in tune with science, *is* scientific.'[7] Appraised against this background, assumption (A1), clearly, is false of science in general.

As for linguistics in particular: the work done by ordinary linguists is in many ways ontologically laden. Two concrete examples – the first furnished by Katz (1984), the second by Fodor (1985a) – should suffice to show that assumption (A1) is false of linguistics too.

The example provided by Katz (1984: 24ff.) is derived from the controversy that raged in the late sixties and early seventies between interpretive and generative semanticists about whose (formal) linguistic theory should be judged the best. Generative semanticists such as Postal (1972) considered the conceptually most homogeneous theory to be the best. Within the framework of such a theory grammatical rules are formulated as derivational constraints.[8] On the basis of conceptual parsimony, generative semanticists disallowed the postulation of an additional type of rule, namely semantic interpretation rules and of an additional, intermediate level of linguistic representation, namely deep structure.[9] Interpretive semanticists such as Chomsky (1972c), however, rejected this position. They took the best linguistic theory to be the one that most narrowly restricts the set of possible grammars from which the child has to 'select' the grammar of its language. And, they argued, one of the things that linguists have to be able to do in order to restrict this set sufficiently is to allow the postulation of semantic interpretation rules and a level of deep structure.[10] On account of (among other things) its failure to allow for the postulation of such restrictive formal devices as semantic interpretation rules and deep structure representations, generative semanticists' linguistic theory was unable to provide a solution for the logical problem of language acquisition. Therefore, on the view of Chomskyans, it was not the 'best' theory.

At first glance, this controversy seems to be about the possible types of rules and levels of linguistic representation that languages have. On closer inspection, however, it seems to be about the criteria by which to appraise alternative linguistic theories. Generative semanticists, that is, take (C1) to be the fundamental criterion, whereas interpretive semanticists assign this status to (C2).

(C1) That linguistic theory is best which is conceptually the most homogeneous.

(C2) That linguistic theory is best which is the most restrictive.

At bottom, however, the controversy we are looking at turns out to be about alternative conceptions of language. Why? Because the criterion (C2) is arbitrary, unless it is grounded in the ontological assumptions (O1) and (O2).

(O1) Language is a mental faculty.
(O2) Linguistic theory is a theory about the initial state of this mental faculty.

Conversely, the adoption of the criterion (C1) requires, among other things, that these two assumptions be rejected. What looks like a technical linguistic controversy about types of rules and representations is in essence, therefore, a conflict about alternative linguistic ontologies. And whether ordinary linguists do or do not realize this does not alter the matter. Similarly, assumption (A1) derives no support from working grammarians' failure to realize that in preferring generative semanticist formal devices to interpretive semanticist ones, or vice versa, they reflect their effective commitment to the ontological assumptions in question.

The second example illustrating that ontological 'niceties' are crucial to the work of ordinary linguists takes us back to section 4.1.4 above. There we considered various cases in which Platonists have resorted to stipulation in order to justify or defend aspects of their approach to linguistic inquiry. One, discussed at some length by Fodor (1985a: 151), involves Katz's (1981: 71) assigning linguistic intuitions the status of 'direct evidence' for the justification of linguistic theories. Fodor, we have seen, makes the point that any science is under an obligation to explain why *what it takes to be* data relevant to the justification of its theories *are* indeed data relevant to the justification of its theories. Typically, a scientist fulfils this obligation by exhibiting a causal chain that runs from the entities posited by his theories to the psychological states of the observers. Should the scientist be unable to establish such a chain, he has no warrant to appeal to those observations as evidence for (or against) his theories.

In the case of linguistic intuitions or intuitive evidence, the required causal chain cannot lead to anything other than psychological entities, as Fodor (1985a: 152) notes: 'We can use intuitions to confirm grammars because grammars are internally represented and actually contribute to the etiology of the speaker/hearer's intuitive judgements.' This view of Fodor's – a sound one, in my opinion – embodies various specific ontological assumptions or 'niceties', including (O1), (O2) and, in addition:

(O3) A grammar is a theory about the final state of the mental faculty in question.

Fodor, it will be recalled, notes that, in the absence of a chain linking linguistic intuitions or intuitive judgements causally to something psychological, Platonists' only possible defence for their use of such intuitions as evidence for (or against) linguistic theories is to say: '"We do it because we have always done it", or "We do it by stipulation".'

Mentalists and Platonists, of course, are by no means the only linguists to use linguistic intuitions as data in appraising linguistic theories. The vast majority of ordinary linguists or working grammarians do so too. Given this fact, those of them who subscribe to the 'hard-nosed dismissal of ontology' have the following two options. On the one hand, they can agree with Fodor that the use of intuitive evidence reduces ultimately to the ontological assumptions (O1)–(O3). On the other hand, they can argue that the use of such evidence can be justified in terms of alternative assumptions about the source and/or import of linguistic intuitions. And either of these options turns of course on their making certain ontological assumptions and, thereby, undoing assumption (A1). As for the conceivable alternatives of abandoning linguistic intuition as a source of evidence, or of simply ignoring Fodor's challenge – these are moves that do not seem to belong to ordinary linguists' options.

Of the Faunal Footnotes I referred to above, my Dear Fun-loving Fellow, the twenty-first one at the time took my fancy as being quite perceptive. And, indeed, to this day it seems to have retained its relevance.

Fn. 21 Once upon a time there was an order of Ordinary Ontological Ostriches. They lived for ever after,

> *but not happily. Blinded by the sand in which they had opted to hide their heads, they were unable to make out what it was that they had been pecking away at for so long.*

6.1.2 Doing one's own thing

A linguist should consciously hold a respectable ontology. But he/she should at the same time have the freedom to choose the ontology with which he/she 'feels most comfortable'. Subscribing to an ontology, after all, is very much like having a religion or some such body of beliefs. Like religious beliefs, ontological assumptions cannot be appraised in a straightforward way. So, the ecumenical stance of 'Believe and let believe' is very much applicable to ontological preferences too. Eliminative appraisal, accordingly, is to be shunned in this context.

The ontological ecumenicism just outlined seems so facile a position as not to deserve further discussion. Some of those who believe in (a version of) it, however, may take it to be based on assumption (A2), an assumption apparently in line with certain meta-theoretical views held by Katz (1981) and certain analytical practices engaged in by Chomsky (1981b).

(A2) A formal linguistic theory and the analyses done within its framework have only the loosest of links with a conception of language (or a more comprehensive linguistic ontology).

Given the looseness of these links, it may be argued, a formal linguistic theory and the associated analytical work may be compatible with (two or more) ontologies construed as alternatives. Hence, it does not really matter in what ontology a linguist believes, as long as it is reasonably clear and not obviously 'crazy'. So let us consider the beliefs of Katz's and the practices of Chomsky's that may appear to lend some support to assumption (A2).

Katz (1981: 24, 34, 38, 39, 47, 53, 57) holds a view in terms of which an 'ontological interpretation' can be assigned to the 'ontologically neutral core' of a formal linguistic theory.[11] Conversely, Katz provides for the possibility that the 'ontological interpretation' of a linguistic theory can be 'stripped away and replaced by a new one'. For example, on his (1981: 24) view,

> Chomsky's real innovation was to provide a new way of interpreting the formal apparatus of transformational grammar, which both recast the form of transformational grammar from the taxonomic to the generative and the subject-matter of transformational grammar from the external acoustic effects of speech to its internal psychological causes.

In similar vein, Katz and others have argued that Chomsky's 'conceptualist interpretation' of grammars and linguistic theory should be 'replaced' by another 'ontological interpretation', namely Platonism.

It is this distinction between a formal linguistic theory and an 'ontological interpretation' of such a theory that could be invoked in an attempt to justify assumption (A2). Suppose that it were indeed possible to 'separate' a 'formal linguistic theory' from its 'ontological interpretation' and to 'replace' such an 'interpretation' by a new one. This could then be taken as indicating that the links between the theory and its 'interpretation' were of an insubstantial sort. And this, in turn, could be interpreted to mean that what a linguist did or did not believe about the nature or essence of language had few or no consequences for the content of his or her formal linguistic theory. In sum: anyone doing formal linguistics would enjoy a considerable measure of freedom in choosing a linguistic ontology.

The idea that a linguist's ontology has no significant consequences for the content of his/her formal linguistic theory and associated grammars cannot, however, be correct. This is clear from various episodes in the history of Chomskyan linguistics. First, that is, Chomsky over the years has radically revised the concept of 'transformational rule' which initially he took over from Harris. And he was forced to do this by an ontological commitment: his belief that a general linguistic theory should provide a certain kind of characterization of the language faculty so as to be able to provide a solution to the logical problem of language acquisition, also known as Plato's problem. More specifically, in order to account for the fact that children are able to acquire their language in a relatively short period on the basis of an impoverished stimulus, Chomsky has had to claim that the child 'selects' the grammar of its language from a restricted set of possible grammars. But transformational rules of the type formulated in the sixties had so much formal power that they made it possible to construct too large a set of grammars for any specific language. Chomsky's mentalist commitment consequently forced him, and others who shared it, to place strong constraints on the formal power of transformational rules.

As mental entities, languages have to be learnable. Accordingly, if a formal linguistic theory embodied assumptions – specifically assumptions bearing on (non)permissible types of rules – in terms of which languages could not be acquired in a relatively short time on the basis of an impoverished stimulus, those assumptions would have to be abandoned or suitably modified. Linguists not sharing Chomsky's mentalistic commitments were under no obligation to adopt the constraints in question on the power of transformations. Some, in fact, modified their formal linguistic theories so as to incorporate even more powerful rule types, including so-called global rules. If they had the same ontological commitments as Chomsky, then clearly this would have been a bizarre thing for them to do.[12]

Secondly, as we saw in section 3.5.2 above, it has been a consequence of the Second Conceptual Shift in Chomskyan linguistics that languages are now seen as made up of principles and fixed parameters rather than of rules. This fundamental change in formal linguistic theory has also been motivated by Chomsky's ontological commitments. Specifically, this shift too has been motivated by Chomsky's concern with characterizing the human language faculty in a way which makes it possible to solve Plato's problem. Chomsky (1986: 83) fleshes out this point with reference to phrase structure rules and transformations:

> Both types of rules allow a wide range of options that are never realized and are presumably unrealizable, and the availability of these options makes it extremely difficult to account for the fact that a specific language is fixed by the available evidence. The device for phrase structure rules is particularly suspect, because these rules so closely reflect lexical properties. Statement of the

> lexical properties is ineliminable from the grammar: For example, the grammar cannot avoid stating that *claim* takes a propositional complement as part of its lexical entry. Therefore, it is to be expected that the phrase structure rules should be eliminable insofar as they merely restate, in another form, the essential content of lexical entries. In fact, it seems that such rules are eliminable more generally, that there are no rules of this type in language. In the case of transformational rules, we have no comparable reason for skepticism concerning their existence, but it seems that the variety of these rules can be significantly reduced, perhaps to Move-α or Affect-α, with some parametric variation. These steps sharply restrict the class of possible languages [available to the child]. . . .

Again, linguists not sharing Chomsky's mentalist/biologist ontology have no good grounds to change their formal linguistic theories in the respects identified by him as above. And should Chomsky's principles-and-parameters theory be 'separated from' or 'stripped of' its mentalistic 'ontological interpretation', these changes to his formal linguistic theory would become arbitrary. But this means that assumption (A2) – that a conception of language (or linguistic ontology) and a formal linguistic theory have only quite loose links – cannot be sustained.

Let us consider next an example of the analytical practices of Chomsky's that might be considered to furnish support for assumption (A2). These, in general terms, are practices that yield linguistic analyses not reflecting overtly Chomsky's mentalist/biologist ontology. In his book *Lectures on Government and Binding*, Chomsky (1981b: 13) takes 'the objective of reducing the class of grammars compatible with primary linguistic data' to be 'a guiding principle in the study of grammar'. Moreover, he considers 'accounting for the attainment of knowledge of grammar' to be 'the fundamental empirical problem to be faced'. In motivating specific principles of linguistic theory, however, Chomsky does not use arguments from the poverty of the stimulus, as one would have expected in view of the ontological commitments quoted above.[13] Central to his argumentation, rather, are considerations relating to predictive success, to the elimination of conceptual redundancy and to depth or unifiedness of explanatory principles. And these considerations do not reflect Chomsky's mentalistic ontology in any overt way. This means that various of the individual formal linguistic analyses proposed in the book in question have no direct links with Chomsky's ontology.

John Lyons (1991: 191) has recently generalized the latter point in the following way:

> just as Bloomfield's behaviouristic psychologism had very little effect on the description of languages that linguists who subscribed to it actually produced, so it is also with Chomskys [sic] very different psychologism (or cognitivism). Chomsky's linguistics, and most Chomskyan linguistics, as it is actually practiced, is (like Bloomfieldian linguistics and most other kinds of descriptive linguistics) 'autonomous'; and, I would say, very properly so.

Lyons's diagnosis of the lack of overt psychological import of Chomsky's/Chomskyan descriptive work represents an overstatement. In particular, it is not true of those descriptions that are modular, that use transformations of greatly restricted power, that are couched in terms of a principles-and-parameters format, and so on. But Lyons's judgement does represent independent support for the claim that, when practising formal linguistics, Chomsky and Chomskyans do not systematically live up to their ontological commitments.

But the fact that certain linguists occasionally – or even often – do not live up to their ontological commitments does not bear positively on assumption (A2). Rather, it bears negatively on the *modus operandi* of these linguists, indicating that their work is characterized by internal inconsistencies or 'disconnections'. Obviously, it makes little sense to argue strongly at a general level that a particular realm of reality has a certain kind of essence or make-up but at the same time to describe it at a level of specifics as if it did not have this kind of essence or make-up.

To conclude: if formal linguistic theories are to make nonvacuous claims about an independently existing realm of reality, assumption (A2) cannot be invoked in an attempt to avoid making a choice between alternative conceptions of language or linguistic ontologies. There is no obvious defence for investigating linguistic reality in terms of an approach on which formal linguistic theory is disconnected from linguistic ontology.[14]

Fn. 72 Once upon a time there was a division of Disciplinary Dodos. They may well have lived happily, but – as we know – certainly not for ever after. Handicapped by disconnections in their Conceptual Circuitry, they failed to get off the ground, and so never gained a bird's eye view of the reality they pedestrianly roamed.

6.1.3 Pursuing a pluralist policy

A third way of avoiding an eliminative appraisal of competing conceptions of language is to adopt what John Lyons (1991: 191) calls a 'position of ontological pluralism'. In terms of this position, a linguist is free – or even obliged – to hold two or more different conceptions of language at one and the same time. These may, presumably, include conceptions that have been portrayed in preceding chapters as distinct alternatives. At the heart of this pluralist position is an assumption – or, in fact, a cluster of assumptions – which Lyons (1991: 192–3) formulates as follows:

(A3) '[It is a] false assumption that there is only one kind of "reality": that languages must be either psychological or social entities, or, in terms of an alternative dichotomy that they must be either physical or non-physical.'

Lyons (1991: 193) believes that the several branches of linguistics, as it is structured at present

> each have their own legitimately different initial ('pre-theoretical' and more or less well-defined) notion of what a language is. Then, according to their own viewpoint, either 'autonomously' (in the case of microlinguistics) or 'non-autonomously' (in alliance with neighbouring disciplines), they each practice a particular kind of abstraction and idealization in the construction of their own ontologically (and methodologically) appropriate model of the underlying language-system.

And he (1991: 193) considers 'premature reductionism of whatever kind, generativist or physicalist, psycholinguistic or sociolinguistic [to be] detrimental to progress in linguistics. ' In this regard, Lyons (1991: 191, 193) is critical of Chomsky's lumping together and dismissing all noncognitivist 'parts of linguistics' by 'invoking an ill-defined and confusing concept of "E-language".'[15]

Lyons's (negative) assumption (A3) and the position of ontological pluralism based on it seem, however, to lack the right kind of justification. Before I give grounds for this judgement, it is necessary to note that Lyons (1991: 91) does not attempt 'to recite in full [his] own ontological *Credo*'. And it is not clear in what technical sense he uses expressions such as 'notion of what a language is' and 'ontological model'. It may be, consequently, that my problems with Lyons's ontological pluralism arise simply because the account he has given of it is less than full. With these provisos, then, let us return to assumption (A3), noting that it breaks down into at least the following two claims:

(C1) There is more than one kind of reality.
(C2) Languages are entities that exist simultaneously in various kinds of realities.

These claims cannot be considered 'evident', 'axiomatic' or the like. Nor can they be justified by inspecting reality in any simple or direct way. Lyons (1991: 191) is mistaken, moreover, in assuming that the claims (C1) and (C2) can be justified by dividing the field of linguistics into 'subfields' with the aid of the traditional dichotomies 'general *v.* descriptive', 'synchronic *v.* diachronic', 'macro- *v.* micro-', 'theoretical *v.* applied'. And by subsequently stipulating that each subfield or branch of linguistics has its own kind of reality, its own notion of what language is or its own ontological model. To proceed in this way is to do things in the wrong order.

Properly to justify the claims (C1) and (C2), it would be better to begin by proposing a conception of language focused on (a cluster of) what appear to be important linguistic phenomena. Proposing any conception of language includes, of course, justifying it with reference to standards of adequacy such as those used for appraising the various conceptions of language that we looked at in preceding chapters. These standards, stated in the form of questions, include the following:

(S1) Is the conception sufficiently focused?
(S2) Is the conception grounded systematically in nontrivial linguistic facts?
(S3) Does the conception provide a good basis for interlinking language with other linguistic entities, processes etc.?
(S4) Does the conception allow for the interlinking of linguistic reality with other, nonlinguistic, realities?
(S5) Are the ontological predicates used by the conception non-obscure?
(S6) Does the conception give a relatively deep ontological characterization of language?
(S7) Is the conception internally free of contradictions, tensions, spurious distinctions etc.?
(S8) Does the conception have sound philosophical foundations?
(S9) Is the conception free of undesirable epistemological presuppositions and/or consequences?
(S10) Has the conception shown itself to be heuristically fruitful?

Suppose now that, appraised on the basis of (S1)–(S10), the proposed conception of language has various merits and no fatal flaws. Suppose too, however, that certain linguistic phenomena remain outside the focus or scope of the conception. Given these circumstances, it would be proper to propose a second, complementary, conception (of something) in order to systematize the latter phenomena. And under these conditions it would be permissible to say that linguistic reality has a 'further realm'. It goes without saying, however, that the latter conception must itself satisfy criteria such as (S1)–(S10).

Only by proceeding in a non-aprioristic way, such as the one outlined above, would it be possible to provide proper justification for claims (C1)–(C2). And, only by proceeding in this way, would one have a non-arbitrary ontological basis on which to divide the field of linguistics into subfields or branches. To start out, as Lyons seems to do, by cutting up the field of linguistics with the aid of traditional dichotomies that do not demonstrably reflect the ontological considerations captured in (S1)–(S10) is not to proceed in a principled way. It does not help to point out, as Lyons (1991: 191–2) does, that the dichotomies in question are 'more or less generally accepted', that they are 'logically independent' or that they 'serve to structure the multidimensional field of linguistics'. To be ontologically pertinent, these dichotomies must emerge as consequences of the kind of ontological argumentation outlined above, not be assumed aprioristically as premises.[16]

What is being rejected here is not the idea of ontological pluralism as such, but an aprioristic form of pluralism based on traditional dichotomies not substantiated with recourse to the pertinent ontological considerations. It is of some importance to note in addition that, within a principled pluralist ontology, complementary conceptions of linguistic objects would all have to satisfy standards of adequacy such as (S1)–(S10). Ontological pluralism, clearly, does not and cannot license arbitrariness, apriorism or the like. Moreover, it would be wise to make a pluralist ontology subject to an appropriate version of an age-old ontological consideration against unnecessarily multiplying entities, levels, worlds, realities and so on.

Setting up a pluralist linguistic ontology in a principled way is, indeed, no simple matter. Various kinds of choices would have to be made in a motivated way. For instance, a pluralist ontology can be constructed by using one or more of various means, among them the following:

(M1) Postulate different ('kinds of') realities.
(M2) Provide for different ontological systems within one and the same ('kind of') reality.
(M3) Characterize each single ('kind of') reality at various levels.

Adopting one or more of such means as (M1)–(M3), again, cannot be a matter of arbitrary stipulation.[17]

Setting up a pluralist linguistic ontology, it should also be noted, is not to be equated with studying language(s) or other linguistic entities from a variety of viewpoints or perspectives. Nor with studying different aspects of language(s) or of other linguistic entities. A concrete example may help to clarify the point. Chomsky (1980a: 227, 229, 241) has noted that a biological entity or organ such as the heart can be studied from the point of view of function, internal structure, physical basis, development in the individual (i.e. ontogeny) and evolutionary development (i.e. phylogeny). Chomsky's list may be extended to include such further viewpoints as variation across members of a species, interaction with other organs, and (kinds of) pathology. Now, obviously, moving from one perspective to another in the study of the heart does not cause the heart to change into a different entity or a different kind of entity. In other words, the heart remains in essence a biological organ, regardless of the perspective from which it is studied. Nor does each change in perspective require the biologist to construct a new conception, concept or notion of what the heart is. And these, rather evident, considerations carry over to the study of language.

Language and languages are likewise studied from various perspectives: function, internal structure, physical basis, development in the individual, development in the species, variation in space, change over time, and so on. It would be bizarre indeed if the linguist's switching from one perspective to another in the study of language or a language caused language or the language – as an entity existing independently of his or her cognizing – to change into an essentially different *kind* of entity. And it would be strange for linguists or practitioners of linguistic ontology to propose a different conception of language to accompany each switch of perspective.

Fn. 129 *Once upon a time there was a colony of Conceptual Chameleons. They did live for ever after. But less happily than everybody thought. Completely occupied by changing their colours to match those of the fields they frequented, they failed to notice the nature of the things on which they sat.*

(The inert figure over there on the floor? That, Bemused Buyer, is our dear Beastly Blue, laid out cold, conceptually of course, by the kick of Mule Mataphysics.)

6.2 Exercising eschatologically

The question, then, is this: Which of the conceptions of language discussed in the preceding chapters is to be preferred? Judged by the relevant standards of adequacy, as we have seen, all these conceptions have shortcomings. The question, accordingly, has to be rephrased in less absolute terms: Which of the conceptions discussed in the preceding chapters offers the best basis for further work both in linguistic theory and in linguistic ontology?

To arrive at an answer to this more specific question, we have to compare the various conceptions of language with reference to two 'holistic' properties: heuristic fruitfulness and improvability/revisability. These are 'holistic' properties in the sense that they are determined by some of the more specific properties of conceptions of language, properties such as those on which the standards of adequacy (S1)–(S9) focus. The two questions that we will consider below, accordingly, are:

(Q1) Which of the various conceptions seems to be superior in regard to heuristc fruitfulness?

(Q2) Which of the various conceptions seems to have the biggest potential for revision or improvement?

To take these questions to be crucial in appraising conceptions of language is to proceed, as indeed one should proceed, from an assumption which has already been argued above:

(A4) Conceptions of language (or more comprehensive linguistic ontologies) are symbiotically interlinked with certain, more specific, linguistic theories.

This assumption means the following, amongst other things: work on a conception of language has consequences for work on a linguistic theory, and vice versa. In other words, the enterprise of (doing) theoretical work on language structure, use, acquisition, variation, change and so on and the enterprise of (practising) linguistic ontology do not represent disjunct disciplines. The differences between a linguistic ontology, on the one hand, and a more specific linguistic theory, on the other hand, are essentially differences in generality, in scope and in depth.

6.2.1 Focusing on their fertility

In preceding chapters we have seen that the mentalistic/biologistic focus of the Chomskyan conception has made it possible to gain a better understanding of the creativity of language use and of the freedom of language use from stimulus control. In addition, the Chomskyan portrayal of language as something mental/biological has provided a framework within which deeper insight has been gained into how language can be acquired despite the poverty of the stimulus. The Chomskyan conception of language, indeed, has been heuristically extremely fruitful, giving rise to a vast amount of new work, both in linguistics itself and in adjacent fields.

Within linguistics, the two conceptual shifts associated with this conception of language have led to a better understanding not only of linguistic structure but also of phenomena relating to language acquisition, linguistic change, speech perception, creolization, and so on.[18] And Lyons (1991: 208) goes so far as to suggest that Chomsky's work has even made a significant contribution to:

> the relatively non-theoretical day-to-day description of languages. Anyone who doubts that this is so has only to look at recently produced reference grammars, especially of English, but also of other major languages, and to compare them with what counted as authoritative a generation ago. Whole areas of grammar are now dealt with which were not mentioned before; and the rules that are given, whilst they may not be precise, are considerably more precise than they used to be. Much, if not all, of this increased coverage and increased precision can be attributed, directly or indirectly, to the Chomskyan revolution in theoretical linguistics.

As argued in section 6.1 above, it would be a mistake to believe that such 'day-to-day description of languages', because it is not couched in overtly mentalistic terms, can be divorced from the ontological assumptions embodied in the Chomskyan conception of language.

Outside linguistics, the Chomskyan conception of language has profoundly influenced work in areas central to which are questions of knowledge, language and mind.[19] To quote Lyons (1991: 209) once more: 'What can be safely said is that his work has inspired, and continues to inspire, an immense amount of research and discussion in any and every discipline that bears at all on the nature of language and mind. And there are few disciplines which do not!' The Chomskyan conception of language, in sum, has been remarkably fruitful in stimulating new work, both inside and outside linguistics.

None of the other conceptions of language considered in the preceding chapters (has) had an impressive track record in regard to heuristic fruitfulness. The sterility of the Bloomfieldian and behaviourist conceptions has been discussed in some detail above. And the Platonist and Popperian conceptions hold little promise of becoming more fertile in the future. Heuristic fruitfulness, we have noted, is a holistic property that arises from more specific other properties. And if a conception of language is incurably flawed in regard to the latter, more specific, properties, then it lacks the capacity to acquire the former, holistic, property. So it is question (Q2) that we next have to consider.

> *Fn. 173* *Once upon a time there was an assembly of Academic Apians. They stood a more than even chance of inheriting a life hereafter. Capable of filling their hive with honey in a way which made the fields around it flower, they were too useful altogether to be despatched without further ado to The Outer Darkness.*

Appended to this footnote, however, there is an ominous-sounding observation, Dear Buyer:

> *Some of these busy little beasts used to dispense stinging stuff to members of other species, a waspish trait that may well make for turmoil and even – who can tell? – for takeovers in the hereafter . . .*

6.2.2 *Probing their 'perfectability'*

Let us, then, consider the various conceptions of language with regard to their capacity for being improved. The most important shortcomings of both (Bloomfieldian) physicalist and behaviourist conceptions of language, we have seen, spring from their positivistic foundations. For those shortcomings to be remedied or removed, these foundations would have to be either revised radically or replaced completely. But positivism has been written off by the vast majority of philosophers and scientists as beyond redemption. Accordingly, neither physicalist nor behaviourist conceptions of language qualify as having the potential to be transformed into viable linguistic ontologies. Accordingly, too, it is simply not possible for language to be credibly portrayed as made up of such physical entities as sounds or scratches. And the emptiness of core behaviourist notions, when applied to language, forms an additional reason for not attempting to retain the idea that language is something behavioural or behaviourist.

Conceptions of language portraying language as something social are not all equally badly flawed. As a class, however, the ones with Wittgensteinian roots have to be completely rethought. These conceptions are in need of, amongst other things, a clear factual focus, proper justification not turning on anti-private language arguments, and ontological predicates that are neither shallow nor obscure. Moreover, these conceptions have to be squared with certain facts about language acquisition. And they have to be modified so as to be capable of interlinking language as something social with the capacities of individual psychology. To say these things, in fact, is to say that nearly everything that needs to be done in constructing a conception of language still remains to be done in the case of such 'social' conceptions of language. A variety of talented scholars in advocating this conception have, over many decades, been doing the wrong kind of things. Further work in the same vein is unlikely to contribute much to establishing the idea that language in essence is something social.

The Popperian conception of language as something autonomous is, likewise, little more than a skeleton of underdeveloped beliefs. To transform it into a reasonably well-articulated conception of language would be a daunting task: showing that Popper's notions of 'World 3', 'causation' and 'interaction' do not deserve dismissal, proposing respectable epistemological means for exploring languages as 'third world' entities, reconciling the idea of language as something 'third worldly' with a variety of facts about language structure, language acquisition, linguistic variation, linguistic change, language pathology, and so on. At present there is little reason, if any, to expect that all of this can be done satisfactorily.

The Platonist conception of language, to its credit, is based on a clear distinction between language and knowledge of language.

But portraying language as abstract in a Platonic sense has yielded a host of unwelcome consequences. Getting rid of these would include: showing that Platonic linguistic entities can be investigated by non-exotic epistemological means, giving up the idea that the scope of linguistics can be fixed by means of arbitrary stipulation, showing why linguistic intuitions constitute evidence which is relevant to the investigation of Platonic linguistic entities, explaining how Platonic linguistic objects can be related in a non-arbitrary way to linguistic processes and phenomena – for example, language acquisition, linguistic change, language variation, and so on – that are not inhabitants of Platonic reality. Not one of these is a trivial task. And the past ten years have not seen much done that gives one any reason to hope that these tasks can be carried out reasonably successfully. Unless these tasks can be carried out reasonably successfully, the Platonist conception of language will not acquire the desired measure of heuristic fruitfulness.

Before turning to the Chomskyan mentalist conception of language, let us dwell for a moment on a problem faced by Platonists and Popperians alike: to find an adequate epistemology for making their special worlds or realities amenable to systematic inquiry. In a related context, Moravscik (1990: 8) has adopted a position which would not 'rule out from the start any ontology that seems to cause trouble for one's epistemology'. Specifically, he would not wish to 'deduce' 'limitations on the realm of what exists' from 'constraints on the realm of human knowledge'. To engage in such deduction would, on Moravscik's view, amount to the same as 'fitting the glass slipper to the lady's foot by chopping off her toes'. And he (1900: 8) contends that we might have reasons to believe in the reality of a certain entity even if it can be shown that the nature of this entity cannot be known by us: 'For example, we might be able to prove that it is reasonable to admit the existence of certain very large numbers, or of God, or of faraway galaxies.' Even, however, if Moravscik were to be granted every one of his points, his position would not offer much in the way of solace to those who subscribe to a Platonist or Popperian linguistic ontology. Theirs is not 'merely' the problem of getting other scholars to 'admit' the existence of abstract or autonomous linguistic objects. Rather, it is to come up with a means to investigate these objects in detail and in depth. Unless hooked on to such a means of investigation, a conception of language is unable to fulfil one of its major functions: that of guiding fruitful inquiry.

The shortcomings of the Chomskyan conception of language require further work mainly of a conceptual sort. On the one hand, the problematic status of the distinction between 'language' and 'knowledge of language' has to be resolved. To this end, it will be necessary either to abandon the distinction as spurious or to provide it with the ontological content it lacks. Unless this can be done, 'language' will remain an opaque predicate within Chomskyan ontology. On the other hand, the internal conceptual 'tensions' or 'contraditions' claimed to plague this conception of language either must be shown not to exist or must be resolved.[20]

The task of rethinking Chomsky's distinction between 'language' and 'knowledge of language' cannot be a simple one, nor can that of dealing with the alleged internal 'tensions'. But these two tasks, taken together, do not amount to more than a small fraction of what has to be done to cure the ills of the other conceptions of language considered above. Let us assume, as a worst case scenario, that the alleged 'tensions' or 'contradictions' do exist. Then, even on the highly critical view of Katz and Postal (1989: 55), there are ways of 'eliminating' them. Over the years Chomsky has shown himself highly resourceful in radically revising his conception of language. The two conceptual shifts we considered in preceding chapters bear witness to this. So it is hardly realistic to expect that the problem of resolving the so-called tensions or contradictions will be tackled by Chomsky in a way that will leave him with no more than the 'pyrrhic victory' envisaged by Katz and Postal (1989: 57).

The Chomskyan conception of language – embodying what has been variously called '(scientific) mentalism', 'psychologism', 'cognitivism', 'biologism' or 'sophisticated/open-ended materialism' – seems to outscore the others heavily in regard to 'improvability'. In addition, it is of some importance to note what does *not* need to be done, either for the first time or all over again, in order to shore up this conception of language. Thus, it need not be furnished afresh with a proper focus, with the right kind of justification, with links relating it systematically to linguistic reality, with a basis for insightfully interlinking the various kinds of entities and processes making up linguistic reality, with a non-exotic epistemology for exploring this reality, or with (more) respectable philosophical roots. Obviously, further work could contribute to the solidity of the Chomskyan conception of language in the respects just listed. But at least this conception has something, in these respects, on which to build further.

> *Fn. 216 Once upon a time there was a family of Ontologizing Ophidians. They, too, stood some chance of inheriting a life hereafter. Being cold-blooded creatures, they proved themselves capable of shedding their Conceptual S(k)ins.*

Added to this note, too, there is a rather disturbing observation, Unsuspecting Shopper:

> *Feared for their fangs, these beasts were not a breed of Conceptual Companions with whom weaker species would like to share the same hereafter.*

Shutting up Shop

From the -ix Trix of about six chapters ago, down to the lately raised spectre of a Celestial Coup, my Ontic Antics have left the pair of you with a gnawing sense of unease? If that is so, Newly Fraternizing Fellows, there's one last stop you musn't miss before you leave The Market. At The Complaints Counter. This is where Conceptions Customers' complaints are countered – in particular, any gripes about the quality of the conceptual counselling received from consultants like me. So do feel free to relate your reservations to 'The Counterer', as The Market's School-tied Masters, in their whimsical way, call the worthy in question.

Counterer: *So then, what have we here? Not a Suicidal-seeming Linguist?*

Buyer: *Well, I thought I'd been promised a conceptual cure for my Angst – I mean, this Angst arising from over-exposure to the question 'What is language in essence?' And, all right, admittedly our Ontological Outing to The Market did afford me some moments of light relief. But deep down I'm still, let's face it, desperately distressed. And so, in short, I feel more than a little let down by The Conceptions Counsellor. And then the thought of all those poor, poor Producers not making it into The Hereafter. . . .*

Counterer: *There, there. Yes, yours is truly a tale that brings tears to the eyes. But, frankly, for your Noetic Neurosis the Compleate Cure is yet to be discovered. Meanwhile, nevertheless, small doses of Mass.-marketed Biological*

Balm, if taken in tandem with moderate shots of Mentalistic Morphia, are lucratively likely to alleviate the symptoms of this chronic condition.

Buyer: *But what about side-effects?*

Counterer: *To tell you the truth (again), there is a small problem. Mixing, as they do, intellectual ingredients that are less than entirely compatible, these Conceptual Compounds have been known to spark off seizures of Scholarly Schizophrenia. Fortunately, though, this condition can be fixed by Psychiatrix, a partner of The Market's 'venerable' Druid Doctor. (The mentalist medications are counterindicated, I may as well emphasize, only in cases with a clear history of Mind Closure.)*

Buyer: *Isn't there anything in the line of Alternative Antidotes?*

Counterer: *Not all that much. Indeed, I must caution you expressly against the use of a particular family of Philosophical Pharmaceuticals. Dispensed under the generic name of Davidsonian Dope, they are deservedly notorious for their hallucinogenic effects. They're based, you see, on the belief that 'there is no such thing as a language' And on, what is its corollary, the belief that 'there is no use for any concept of language.'[1] So all that these drugs will really do is to loosen your grip, tenuous as it already is, on linguistic reality.*

But time's up, I'm afraid, sir. I simply have to attend now to the complainer elbowing his way to the front of the queue.

Blue: *I was set up right at the start, only to be done down in the end. This character who goes around calling himself The Conceptions Counsellor is really a rather sharp Ontological Operator, putting Philosophical Foolery up as a front while in fact he's a partner in the Conceptualist Cartel. His so-called Mocking of Moses is the merest smoke screen, cynically contrived to conceal his real game: promoting the conceptionery of this much overrated Old Testamentical Ontologizer.*

Counterer: *Complaints about motives I have found very hard to handle. So, instead, let me remind you of some of the reasons why, for more than a quarter of century now, The Market has been dominated by this man Chomsky.*

One: isn't this the man who put physicalists and behaviourists finally out of business, and who, by so doing, halted the deepest slump ever experienced by The Market? Two: isn't this the man who has sent conception prices through the ceiling by creating the Biology Boom? Three: isn't this the man who has set the standards that have to be met by every Manufacturing Metaphysicist aspiring to be notable, and noted, on The Market?

Blue: *But . . .*

Counterer: *I ask you, if it were not for this man Chomsky, then where, conceptions-wise, would we all have been? Bored, bankrupt, beating our breasts . . .! So, please make way for my next complainer, a Bedraggled Businessman.*

B/man: *Over the years, I have grown used to the bumps and bruises picked up in the process of pushing a linguistic ontology. But getting busted and bankrupted by a premeditated Apocalyptical Act should not, I tell you, be part of the game. And no Conceptual Clowning, in whatever quantities, could ease the hurt or undo the damage inflicted by the italicized incisions on my ontological innards.*

Counterer: *This is going to strike you as funny. But, you know, having been at the receiving end of some apocalyptical action may yet prove a boon to your business. Think, for example, of all the free epistemic exposure that your product is receiving because the Counsellor has singled it out for special attention. I mean, so many more Conceptions Customers than before now know what you believe language to be in essence. And this may even translate into a boost for you in both readership and royalties. So go home, get yourself cleaned up conceptually and, tomorrow, come back for another day's dealing and wheeling on The Market.*

B/man: *But, surely,* apocalypse *means 'the end'. . . .*

Counterer: *Not in Marketese. The Counsellor did his job in strict accordance with the relevant Market Maxim, age-old yet ever-fresh, which says: 'An apocalypse a day keeps buyer boredom at bay.' But now, please note, your complaining time's run out.*

Before we say our philosophical farewells, there's one last feature you feel you must check out? The Counterer's rhetoric has such a familiar ring, and you couldn't help wondering if . . .? Forgive me, Unbluffable Buyer, for neglecting to inform you, before, of the professional name he practises under. But you've guessed it, of course. Yes, spot on, it's Al Ego.

And so we come to the end of what I hope you will have reason to remember as a profitable exploration of The Metaphysics Market. What this shared experience has taught us about various conceptions of language is indubitably nothing to be sneezed at. Even more important, though, are the inescapable and therefore indispensable general lessons which this experience has led us to learn. On sound (and unsound) ways of going about the business of conceptualizing the essence of language. And on the means of making it on metaphysics markets. After all, in the words of Arthur Clough, himself a one-time Oxford man:

Grace is given of God,
but knowledge is bought in the market.
(From The Bothie of Tober-na-Voulich*)*

Notes

1 Merchandizing Language as Matter

1 For this distinction between a conception and a dictionary definition see further Katz 1981: 46.
2 *Longman Dictionary of Contemporary English* (1984 reprint), p. 617.
3 I have found Katz's (1981, 1985: introduction) ontological characterization of the Bloomfieldian conception of language most instructive and will refer frequently to it below.
4 As observed by Bunge (1980: 3, 9), animism represents a specific view of the mind–body problem, the view that the mind 'affects', 'causes', 'animates', 'controls' or 'pilots' the body. Of the influential proponents that animism has had over the centuries, Bunge mentions Plato, Augustine, Aquinas, Freud, Popper and Toulmin.
5 As noted by Esper (1968: 27ff.), Wundt regarded language as originating in 'expressive movements' which were the physical components of 'psychophysical' processes. The primary function of speech is the expression of ideas, a sentence being the expression of an apperceptive, volitional process. Complete sentences express an aggregate idea partitioned into individual ideas. Cf. also Esper 1968: 42ff. for a discussion of Wundt's mentalistic view of syntax.
6 See Esper (1968) for an instructive account of the influence which the psychology of Weiss, Meyer and their German forerunners had on Bloomfield's thought.
7 See Esper (1968: 180) for a more detailed account of Weiss's view of psychology.
8 Chapter 2 will provide ample sustenance for this point.
9 For the different claims covered by these two tenets, see Campbell 1967: 179.
10 Bunge (1980: 3, 9) calls this form of materialism 'emergent materialism'. It characterizes the mind or mental as a set of emergent brain functions or bioactivities. A property of a thing or a function of a

system is considered emergent by Bunge (1977: 97) if (a) it is not possessed by every component of the thing or system, but (b) it can be explained in terms of the properties of the components without (c) being reducible to these properties. For example, being stable, being alive, having a certain structure and undergoing a social revolution are instances, on Bunge's view, of emergent properties of entities 'because they are not possessed by every component of the whole'. Emergentist materialism has a tradition whose contributors include Diderot, Darwin, Schneirla, Hebb and Brindera, among others.

11 Cf. Goodman and Quine 1947: 105. For a recent restatement of his nominalist position, see Goodman 1984a: 50–53.

12 For more recent but rather peripheral nominalist conceptions of a language see Pateman's (1987: 54ff.) and Wunderlich's (1979: 339ff.) discussion of views held by Hudson (1980) and Kanngiesser (1972), respectively.

13 Cf. Woozeley 1967: 203. As shown by Johnson et al. (1984: 15ff.), however, nominalism has figured prominently in sociological discussions of how social reality may be known.

14 For this and other problems with moderate forms of nominalism, cf. Woozeley 1967: 204–5 and Moravscik 1990: 9ff. Moravscik goes in some detail into a number of serious 'worries' about the nature and properties of the kind of particulars provided for by modern nominalists such as Goodman.

15 Cf. Katz 1964: 125ff. and Newmeyer 1980: 4. For some of the many senses in which the term 'positivist' has been used, see Phillips 1987: 37ff. For Bloomfield's 'logical positivism' see also Hiż and Swiggers 1989.

16 For a synoptic characterization of the concerns of the logical positivists, see Phillips 1987: 39. For a fuller account, see Passmore (1967), Feigl (1969) and other contributions to Achinstein and Barker (1969).

17 Cf. Phillips (1987: 39) for this formulation.

18 For a discussion of the basic ideas of empiricism and their history, see Hamlyn (1967a).

19 Cf. Ashby (1967) and Passmore (1967) for some discussion of its historical antecedents (in the work of Hume, Mill, Mach, Wittgenstein etc.), of its affinities with other philosophical positions (such as the pragmatism of Peirce, James and Dewey, and the operationism of Bridgman), of the different formulations that it received in the Vienna Circle itself, and of less stringent versions of it formulated in terms of concepts such as 'disconfirmability', 'falsifiability' and so on.

20 For Carnap's various formulations of the Verifiability Principle, cf. Carnap (1936, 1937). Dummett (1978: 443) portrays the principle of

'verification' as 'a sword with which they [members of the Vienna Circle] could slay numberless metaphysical dragons'.

21 Cf. Ashby (1967: 240ff.) for the following examples of these questions and some discussion of their implications: '(1) What is it to be applied to – propositions, statements or sentences? (2) Is it a criterion for determining what the meaning of any particular sentence is, or is it simply a criterion of whether a sentence is meaningful? (3) What is meant by saying that a statement is verifiable, or falsifiable, even if in practice it has not been, and perhaps cannot be, verified, or falsified? (4) What type of statement directly reports an empirical observation, and how do we ascertain the truth-value of such a statement? (5) Is the principle itself either analytic or empirically verifiable, and if not, in what sense is it meaningful? (6) Is the question that the principle is intended to answer (that is, the question "By what general criterion can the meaning or the meaningfulness of a sentence be determined?") a logically legitimate question?'

22 Cf. Bunge (1977: 16–18) for these and other metaphysical hypotheses of science and for a list of eminent scientists and philosophers who have stressed the metaphysical character of many scientific hypotheses.

23 For a characterization of these phenomena, see, for example, Chomsky 1964, 1972a and Lyons 1981: 228ff.

24 A more recent formulation of these questions by Chomsky (1986: 3) reads as follows:

1 What constitutes knowledge of language?
2 How is knowledge of language put to use?
3 How is knowledge of language acquired?

25 For example Twaddell 1935: 33ff.; Harris 1951: 18; Hockett 1961: 36. For further discussion see Swadesh 1935: 245; Anrade 1936: 11; Joos 1957a: 80, preface; Bar-Hillel 1966: 39, and Botha 1968: 84ff.

26 Feyerabend (1987: 192ff.) presents an interesting reconstruction of Mach's thinking on which his epistemology 'turns out to be no epistemology at all'. It is, Feyerabend contends, 'a general scientific theory (or theory-sketch) comparable in form (though not in content) to atomism, and different from any positivistic ontology'. On Feyerabend's analysis, the conventional reading of Mach's 'sensationalism' in general and his recourse to 'fictions' in particular presents a simple-minded picture of Mach's thinking.

27 This view Popper (1969: 114) characterizes as the 'Galilean doctrine that the scientist aims at a true description of the world, or of some of its aspects, and a true explanation of observable facts'.

28 From the account given by Hymes and Fought (1975: 1029ff.) of neo-Bloomfieldian linguistics, it is clear that some followers of Bloomfield's had a less rigorous logic, one allowing them to maintain the idea that linguistics aims at giving 'correct' descriptions of linguistic phenomena.

29 There are two other major views that are alternatives to instrumentalism, namely descriptivism and realism. To these we will come later below.

30 For some discussion of the various versions of instrumentalism see, for example, Nagel 1961: 129ff.; Kaplan 1964: 306–10; Hesse 1967: 407; Popper 1969: 107ff.; Rescher 1984: 153–9.

31 Nagel, incidentally, presents a quite sympathetic reconstruction of instrumentalism. For a recent discussion of 'instrumentalism in linguistics', see Carr 1990: ch. 3.

32 Cf. Newmeyer (1980: 6) for further elucidation of this point.

33 See Hymes and Fought (1975: 1050–1) for an explication of this position.

34 See Allan 1988 for an instructive discussion of the relevance of Einstein's views of science to an understanding of the metascientific foundations of linguistic theory. I am indebted to Allan for this and other references to the work of Einstein.

35 See, e.g. Popper 1965, 1969; Lakatos 1968a: 315–417; Watkins 1968. For a review of the various views of the roles of induction in scientific inquiry see Botha 1973: 57–70.

36 For attempts to characterize what is common to the various forms of (neo-)Bloomfieldian linguistics see, for example, Fries 1961, Bierwisch 1971, Stark 1972, Hymes and Fought 1975, Kaldewaij 1986, and Salverda 1985. The account by Hymes and Fought is exemplary in its attention to detail. It reveals in a striking way just how heterogeneous this approach to the study of language was.

37 For illuminating discussion bearing on this point see, for example, Bach 1965 and Allan 1988.

2 Billing Language as Behavioural

1 By, for example, Chomsky (1964: 25), who speaks explicitly of 'a taxonomic-behaviorist point of view concerning the nature of language'.

2 By, for example, Hockett (1987: 1) and Davis (1973: 173).

3 Pike (1967: 25) illustrates this position with reference to a party game in which a 'gesture song' is sung. The song is repeated various times. On each repetition a certain word is replaced by a gesture. In the end, only a few connecting words like *the* remain, 'a sequence of

gestures [being] performed in unison to the original timing of the song'.

4 For a detailed discussion of this approach, called 'tagmemics', see Pike 1967. For a more synoptic account see, for example, Davis 1973: 173ff.

5 The kind of behaviour that Bolinger (1980: 11) has in mind is 'communicative': 'Language is the most intensified part, but still only the inner part, of an enveloping scheme of communicative behavior.'

6 A second factor seems to be internal to Pike's (1967: 536) tagmemic approach: 'In behavioremics . . . the structural units always retain substance as relevant to their manifestation mode. . . .' For what this statement may mean see Pike 1967: par. 6.91, 7.85 and 8.82.

7 For the physicalist or materialist terms in which Bloomfield characterized the essence of language see section 1.2 above.

8 Cf. Hymes and Fought (1975: 1005) for references documenting this point.

9 Bloomfield, in fact, takes the stimulus to include more than the immediate cause of the action (*r*). It includes the whole of the situation of the speaker, both the external situation in which he finds himself and the condition of his body, including genetic properties, as is noted by Kaldewaij (1986: 72–3).

10 Cf. Kaldewaij 1986: 74 for a similar point. For Bloomfield's views on the nature of science, cf. section 1.4 above.

11 To say that Bloomfield's conception of language was materialist and not behaviourist is not to deny the existence of a principled link between materialism and behaviourism. To the nature of this link we will turn in section 2.4 below.

12 We will consider the conception of language as something cultural in section 5.4 below.

13 This study of Whitney's was first published in 1867.

14 This point will be fleshed out in section 2.2 below.

15 In section 2.2. we will consider specific examples of such conceptions of language held by behaviourist psychologists.

16 This ties in with Bloomfield's claim (noted above) that his views on language were not influenced by any psychological position. And it is also in line with Hall's (1964: 404) observation that 'In recent decades, linguistics has become somewhat estranged from both philosophy and psychology. . . .'

17 The view of science associated with behaviourism will be discussed in detail in section 2.4 below.

18 As observed by Fodor et al. (1974: 24ff.), structural linguists and more moderate behaviourist psychologists (of the Hullian school)

started in the fifties to cooperate in establishing the field of psycholinguistics. As is clear from, for example, Rosenberg's (1968: 63) work, psycholinguists commonly operated with the assumption that language is a system of habits, habits being uninformatively characterized as 'input-output constraints'. Incidentally, as noted by Dennett (1979: 61), there was a lack of interaction between leading behaviourist psychologists and philosophers too. Thus, on his reading, Skinner was 'oblivious' to Quine's arguments against intentional psychology, a remarkable state of affairs because, like his Harvard colleague, Skinner was opposed to intentional idioms in psychology too. We turn to Skinner's conception of language in section 2.2.1 and to Quine's in section 2.3.3.

19 For an analogous point about the status of the view that language is a 'social art' see section 5.3 below and the references cited there.

20 Cf. section 2.4 below for a reconstruction of the philosophical roots of the idea that language equals behaviour.

21 Earlier, J. B. Watson defended the extreme view that language – and thought in general – could be reduced to laryngeal movement, a view seriously criticized by Lovejoy (1922).

22 Lachman et al. (1979: 78) provide the following illustration of these notions: 'In the laboratory, a pigeon can be trained to peck a circle, by giving him food whenever he pecks it. It is further possible to get him to peck the circle when it is red, but not when it is green. This is done by feeding the pigeon only if the circle is red when he pecks it. His pecking gets no food when the circle is green. This common laboratory situation is a prototype of Skinner's explanations of language. The colour of the circle is the *stimulus*; it elicits the *response* of pecking. In Skinner's terms, pecking is *under the control of* the stimulus, "red circle". The appearance of the food is a *reinforcer*. Because it comes right after the pigeon pecks, it causes the pecking response to persist, and even increases its frequency.'

23 See Taylor (1967: 516) for this characterization of (psychological) behaviourism.

24 This view is not shared by all, a point to which we will return below.

25 Thus Chomsky (1972a: 12) observes that 'much of what we say in the course of normal language use is entirely new, not a repetition of anything that we have heard before and not even similar in pattern – in any useful sense of the terms "similar" and "pattern" – to sentences or discourse that we have heard in the past.'

26 Nor, in Chomsky's view, could this system be described in terms of the taxonomic methods of structural linguistics, or the notions of either

the mathematical theory of communication or the theory of simple automata.

27 See also Chomsky 1964: 17ff. for an elaboration of this claim. Here the expression 'creative aspect of language' denotes the innovative and productive aspect of language use as well as its freedom from stimulus control. The expression excludes here appropriateness to the situation as being a phenomenon that, in Chomsky's (1972a: 12) view, exceeds the bounds of mechanical explanation, whether behaviourist or other.

28 As noted in Botha (1989a: 19–20, 181–2), in later work Chomsky (e.g. 1980a) stresses an additional fact as crucial to the understanding of language acquisition: the so-called poverty of the stimulus.

29 Chomsky's theory of language acquisition will be discussed in some detail in chapter 3.

30 See Zuriff (1985: 1–3) for a discussion of each of the four points mentioned in this quotation.

31 Cf. Mace 1948–9: 2; Whiteley 1961: 165; Kaufman 1967: 268, 270; Zuriff 1985; 7–8, 204–5, 207–9.

32 For further discussion, see also Scriven 1969.

33 *Eliminative behaviourism* denies the legitimacy of mental(ist) language and asserts that, contrary to what has always been believed, people do not act on their ideas, they do not have beliefs, and they are not swayed by emotions (Zuriff 1985: 202).

Methodological behaviourism rules private events out of bounds because there could be no public agreement about their validity (Zuriff 1985: 27).

Radical behaviourism, as opposed to methodological behaviourism, does consider (nonmental) events taking place in the private world within the skin. It does not call such events unobservable and it does not dismiss them as subjective (Zuriff 1985: 27). Such events, however, must be characterized behaviourally in functional terms (Kaufman 1967: 272).

Molar behaviourism is the position that an autonomous science of behaviour independent of physiology is not only possible but also desirable. Lawfulness, it holds, can be found at the behavioural level without appeal to physiological events inside the body. (Zuriff 1985: 31; cf. also Taylor 1967: 517).

Molecular behaviourism holds that functional relations at the molar level could in all likelihood be accounted for in terms of physiological connections (Taylor 1967: 517).

The *reflexological model* or *S-R psychology*, in a strong form, claims that all behaviour can be analysed into discrete, stereotyped movements, each of which is elicited by an immediately preceding discrete impinging of energy on a sensory receptor. In a weaker form, it claims that behaviour consists of responses, each caused by antecedent stimuli (Zuriff 1985: 99).

Mediation theory, in contrast to the basic reflexological model, partially liberates behaviour from its total dependence on the environment by locating some causes of behaviour within the organism. These causes, however, are themselves instigated by external stimuli and mediate between the latter stimuli and responses (Zuriff 1985: 104).

Interbehaviourism studies so-called interbehaviour: the interactions of the stimulus and response functions forming the psychological situation. It contrasts with radical behaviourism in using the formula $S \leftrightarrow R$ rather than the formula $S \rightarrow R$ (Zuriff 1985: 108).

Purposive behaviourism takes the position that behaviour has descriptive properties beyond those of movements and achievements because behaviour has purpose (Zuriff 1985: 45).

34 For this tripartite distinction, see Koch 1964: 7–20.

35 Cf. Taylor 1967: 516; Zuriff 1986: 696–7; Moravscik 1990: 60. On Moravscik's (1990: 58–9) analysis, the various forms of behaviourism are characterized by six 'overlapping themes':

1. The vocabulary of that part of psychology which describes cognition should consist only of behavioural terms.
2. The intelligent mental operations of humans are definable in terms of actual and potential behaviour.
3. That part of the vocabulary of psychology which introduces the observables in connection with cognition should consist of behavioural terms.
4. The fundamental facts that psychology needs to explain can be described on the level of behaviour.
5. Psychological explanations of thinking should be in terms of behaviour.
6. Psychological explanations at their best link environment to behaviour, and show how the former can change the latter.

36 For typical examples of such defences, see Salzinger 1967, Wiest 1967 and MacCorquodale 1970. The major points of these and other similar defences have been summarized by Zuriff (1985: 130–49). For a typical rejoinder by Chomsky cf., for example, Chomsky 1972a: 92. As explained in some detail by Lachman et al. (1979: 61ff.), many cognitive psychologists (also referred to as 'information-processing psycholinguists') came to share Chomsky's criticisms of the behaviourist conception of language (behaviour): '[They] found the arguments against behaviorism compelling, and they focused on

language as a rule-governed, abstract system. They considered it important to develop theories of competence and imported such concepts as competence, grammar and generative grammar' (1979: 61). And: 'As a result of their contact with linguistics . . . many psychologists came to believe that satisfactory theories of language would never emerge from studying what people *do* unless we also attempt to explain what they *know* about language that enables to do it' (1979: 81).

37 Marshall refers to Zuriff 1985.

38 Cf., for example, Salzinger 1967: 34–5 and Zuriff 1986: 137ff.

39 Behaviourists have rejected introspective judgements and intuitions as useless, downright misleading and unscientific. (See, for example, Lachman et al. 1979: 85 for some discussion of this point.) But part of the initial motivation for adopting the concepts of 'competence' and 'generative grammar' was the concern of Chomskyan linguistics with explaining introspective judgements of linguists and intuitive judgements of native speakers about properties of utterances. How the former concepts could be retained, substantially unchanged, if the latter judgements were rejected, behaviourists have failed to explain. This further illustrates behaviourists' willingness to rely on empty terms, e.g. 'competence' and 'generative grammar', for defending their most basic beliefs.

40 Koch (in Wann 1964: 162) sees in this strategy 'an absolute contempt . . . for subject matter'. He, for example, considers the way in which behaviourists have constantly referred to experience as a 'field of private stimulation' to manifest 'an absolutely Philistine and almost malicious attitude toward the universe'. It exemplifies, to Koch, the 'constant, ubiquitous importation of . . . vaguely disguised experiential meaning into a quasi-objective vocabulary'. And he considers 'field of private stimulation' to represent the 'thinnest of metaphors'. Johnson-Laird (1988a: 19) has also commented on the way in which some behaviourists invented theoretical devices that enabled them to talk about internal processes without seeming to give up objectivity. This manoeuvre allowed mentalistic theories to be accommodated within behaviourism. On Johnson-Laird's view, this caused '[w]hat began as an objective science [to become] an ideology'.

41 There are more reasons than the three considered above. An additional one is that behaviourists and neobehaviourists have restricted their study of language behaviour to the use of individual words or untypically simple sentences, thereby evading the need to come to grips with the full complexity of normal language behaviour. As observed by Lachman et al. (1979: 81): 'Before Chomsky,

psychologists seldom studied sentences, preferring instead to deal with words. On those rare occasions when they did try to explain how sentences are understood, it was always by reference to the understanding of individual words. No neobehavioristic psychologist ever seriously tried to develop a theory of grammar. That would have required the recognition that rules, as well as words, were an internal part of language, and the neobehaviorist paradigm did not cope well with rules.'

42 Apologies to Walter Winckler for the wrinkles that I have put into his witticism. Incidentally, Skinner (1964: 84) does provide for events that take place within the skin, but these do not differ essentially from events taking place outside the skin: 'An adequate science of behavior must consider events taking place within the skin of the organism, not as physiological mediators of behavior, but as part of the behavior itself. It can deal with these events without assuming that they have any special nature or must be known in any special way. The skin is not that important as a boundary.' These comments do not indicate that Skinner concedes that invoking the mental is legitimate. Thus, he says: 'I am a radical behaviorist simply in the sense that I find no place in the formulation for anything which is mental'. Cf. Wann (ed.) 1964: 106 for the latter statement. The discussion in Zuriff (1985: 200ff.) makes clear, perhaps unintentionally, just how ambiguous behaviourist stances on 'mental concepts' and 'mentalistic language' have been.

43 For an outline of core ideas of Wittgenstein and the ordinary language philosophers, see Katz 1966: 68ff; Alston 1967: 387; Quinton 1967: 394–5.

44 There are nontrivial differences between Wittgenstein's later philosophy and the (Oxford) ordinary language philosophy. Here these differences do not matter that much. They will be referred to again in n. 49 below. A point of terminology: where these differences are not relevant to the discussion, I will use the simplifying expression *Wittgensteinians* to refer collectively to Wittgenstein and the ordinary language philosophers inspired by his work.

45 Cf. Quinton 1967: 395. This view contrasts with that in Wittgenstein's earlier work, represented by his *Tractatus Logico-Philosophicus*, that language is 'something whose essence can be displayed as a formal, logical calculus' (Quinton 1967: 395). In his *Tractatus*, Wittgenstein argued specifically for 'the acceptance of an ideal, artificial language in which concepts are precisely defined and propositions unambiguously express the real form of facts' (Katz 1966: 69). Wittgenstein in his later work operated with a notion of 'grammar' as well:

'Grammar is a free-floating array of rules for the use of language. It determines what is a correct use of language, but is not itself correct or incorrect' (Baker and Hacker 1985: 40). On the basis of this formulation one could argue that Wittgenstein drew a distinction between 'language' and 'use' and, moreover, that 'language' is not identical to 'activity'. This illustrates just how difficult it is to determine what Wittgenstein's views on the nature of language really were. The elusive nature of these views has caused Wittgenstein scholars to propose radically diverging exegeses of these views. This point is substantiated by, for example, the disagreement between Kripke (1982) and McGinn (1984) and that between Pateman (1987: ch. 6) and Baker and Hacker (1984). For comments on the former disagreement, see also Malcolm (1986: 154ff.).

46 Cf. Baker and Hacker 1980: 70ff. The idea that training is important in language learning is suggested by Wittgenstein's famous game analogy. He drew a number of analogies between the idea of language and that of a game (chess specifically), one of which concerns training. In the words of Baker and Hacker (1980: 93): 'The foundation of the ability to play a game lies in training. . . .' Baker and Hacker (1984: 256), strangely, attribute their behaviourist view of language learning to Chomsky too.

47 For an exegesis of Wittgenstein's notion of 'family resemblance' and an illustration of how he applies this notion to elucidate the meaning of the word 'game', see Baker and Hacker 1980: 325ff.

48 See Baker and Hacker 1980: 495. There is a way, though, in which Wittgenstein thought that philosophy could go about laying bare the essence of language: by giving an *Übersicht* of it. An *Übersicht* is a perspicuous survey that makes something 'transparent in a homely sense', 'capable of being seen all at a glance'. For this point, see Baker and Hacker 1980: 495.

49 For a discussion of a variety of cases of the misuse of words or expressions which on Wittgenstein's view caused philosophical confusions, see Baker and Hacker 1980: 468ff. Oxford ordinary language philosophers had a number of concerns that went much further than the Wittgensteinian concern of dispelling philosophical confusions and paradoxes caused by the misuse of language. Thus Quinton (1967: 394) notes: 'For the philosophers of ordinary language, however, metaphysical paradox is not simply a conceptual disorder to be cured: it is, rather, a convenient point of entry into the task of setting out the complex and informal logic of the philosophically crucial terms of ordinary speech, a task Ryle has called "logical geography" and Austin "rational grammar".' For an

insightful discussion of three specific points of difference between Wittgenstein and ordinary language philosophers see Katz 1966: 80–7. Dummett (1978: 445ff.), too, discusses some of the differences between Wittgenstein and ordinary language philosophers, contending that 'The doctrines of "ordinary language" philosophy was a caricature, but not a gross caricature of the views of the later Wittgenstein. . . .'

50 Quoted by Baker and Hacker (1980: 637). See also Baker and Hacker 1980: 339–40 and Kaufman 1967: 271 for further indications that Wittgenstein's views should not be interpreted behaviouristically in a psychological sense. In this respect Wittgenstein and certain Oxford philosophers differ from Quine (1960: 82), who explicitly couches his account of, for example, language learning in Skinnerian notions, as will be shown in section 2.3.3 below.

51 Cf. for example, Kaufman 1967: 271; Quinton 1967: 395, Zuriff 1984: 207–9. The term 'analytical behaviourism' is credited to Mace (1948–9: 1–2), who distinguishes analytical behaviourism from metaphysical and methodological behaviourism. Metaphysical behaviourists admit, in Mace's terminology, that it is conceivable that the world contains two sorts of stuff: the stuff of which material things are made and the stuff of mind. But they deny that mind, as so conceived, is realized in fact. They deny that mind or consciousness exists. Methodological behaviourists concede more. They admit not only that mind or consciousness is conceivable as irreducibly different from matter, but also that mind and consciousness, so conceived, are realized in fact. But they deny that mind or consciousness is amenable to systematic treatment by scientific method. To analytical behaviourists, by contrast, the existence of mind or consciousness, defined as irreducibly distinct from matter, is not conceivable in any positive terms. They contend that statements about mind or consciousness turn out to be, on analysis, statements about the behaviour of material things. Hanfling (1989: 78–9) has argued that Wittgenstein was *not* trying, like thinkers of a behaviourist persuasion, to deny or question the reality of mental processes. On Hanfling's analysis, Wittgenstein merely attacked 'the mental theory' that words express ideas or meanings which exist in the mind.

52 Cf. Urmson 1967: 270. Cf. also Katz 1966: 84–5 for further explication of this point. Wittgenstein's analysis of the mentalistic concept of 'understanding' is considered a prototypical instance of this kind of analysis. See Baker and Hacker 1980: 605 for a detailed discussion of this analysis.

53 The views under consideration have for decades been the subject

of vigorous debate. Thus 1989 saw the Fourteenth International Wittgensteinian Symposium, with nearly 70 participants. The literature on Wittgenstein's two philosophies forms a vast, ever-expanding corpus. See n. 45 above for a few sample contributions by philosophers to the discussion of Wittgenstein's later views on language. For one of the more substantive recent contributions by a linguist cf. Chomsky 1986: 221ff.

54 See Katz (1966: 87–8), who singles out Austin's analysis of performative uses of language, Ryle's and Vendler's discussions of achievement verbs, and Urmson's work on grading adjectives and parenthetical verbs as examples of 'careful and insightful linguistic description[s]' in the tradition of ordinary language philosophy. On the whole, however, the linguistic analysis of ordinary language philosophers is superficial. For a discussion of the 'superficiality' to which the rejection of generality by ordinary language philosophers led, see also Dummett 1978: 444–5.

55 A theory of linguistic structure is the basic link between a conception of language and linguistic reality, but not the only one. A conception of language should also be linked to other aspects of linguistic reality, including language change, language variation, language pathology and so on. The links required for this take on the form of theories of language change, language variation, language pathology, and so on. Such theories, however, presuppose a theory of linguistic structure, hence the latter is basic. It also follows that a conception of language is less directly linked to language change, language variation, and so on, than to linguistic structure.

56 See also Baker and Hacker (1980: 69ff.) for a discussion of Wittgenstein's views that are consonant with this characterization.

57 Assuming that Wittgensteinians are not concerned with defining the essence of language, with learning anything new or with practising (linguistic) science, why should one take the trouble to consider their kind of conception of language at all? In addition to the inherent interest of this conception, there are three strategic reasons for doing so. First, the way Wittgensteinians have construed the nature of language has influenced the linguistic ontology of many philosophers and linguists. Secondly, certain Wittgensteinians – e.g. Baker and Hacker (1984) – have been sharply critical of other conceptions of language, believing the Wittgensteinian one to be superior. For some discussion of this second point, cf. Pateman 1987: 120ff. Thirdly, with reference to the Wittgensteinian conception of language, it is possible to illustrate features which a conception of language cannot afford to have, e.g. insufficient coupling with structural aspects of linguistic reality.

58 Chomsky (1968: 58–9) argues, among other things, that Quine vacillates between two things which are not the same: a person's total 'disposition to verbal response under arbitrary stimulus conditions' and his 'dispositions to be prompted to assent or to dissent from the sentence' under the particular conditions of a *Gedanken-experiment* outlined by Quine. In addition to finding it difficult to determine the precise content of Quine's notion 'speech dispositions', Chomsky (1968: 57–8) has serious difficulties with assigning probabilities to sentences, as Quine's conception of a language as a 'complex of dispositions to verbal behavior' seems to require. Chomsky argues, for example, that the probability of his producing English sentences such as 'Tuesday follows Monday' and 'Birds fly' is indistinguishable from the probability of his producing a given Japanese sentence: 'Hence if a language is a totality of speech dispositions . . . then my language either does not include the sentences just cited as examples, or it includes all of Japanese.'

59 'The ghost in the machine' is Ryle's (1949: 15–16) expression for denoting the Cartesian 'dogma' or 'doctrine' that every human being has both a body and a mind, and that body and mind have different kinds of existence or status. Bodies exist in space and are subject to mechanical laws; minds, however, are not in space and their operations are not subject to mechanical laws. For a fuller characterization of what is also known as 'Cartesian dualism', see Ryle 1949: 11–13. We return to the above-mentioned Cartesian 'doctrine' in section 3.1.5 below.

60 Kitcher's (1978: 8) more recent portrayal of a speaker's linguistic ability as a set of psychological dispositions (to pass from one type of psychological state to another type of psychological state) is not, according to Chomsky (1980a: 262–3), any more meritorious than the original Quinian dispositional account.

61 Zuriff's discussion of these characteristics, on the whole, represents a consensus view. It reconstructs the positivist underpinnings of behaviourism as these have been identified earlier by a variety of other scholars. And it is in accord with such independent characterizations of these underpinnings as those by Koch (1964), Kaufman (1967), Taylor (1967) and Bunge (1980).

62 It has been suggested – see, for example, Zuriff (1985: 251; 1986: 698) – that behaviourist epistemology may be considered as a theory about the behaviour of scientists. Historically, however, this is false. Behaviourists have taken over their ontology and epistemology from logical positivist philosophers of science. For a discussion of this point, cf. Koch 1964: 10.

63 For a discussion of this point see sections 1.3 and 1.4 above. The technical philosophical literature dealing with the flaws under consideration is vast and cannot be surveyed here.

64 I base these questions on Kaufman's (1967: 269) discussion of problems involved in defining 'behaviour'.

65 Is the heart's pulsation a form of behaviour (cf. Kaufman 1967: 269)?

66 Should the sounds produced by movements of the vocal tract be considered part of verbal behaviour (cf. Kaufman 1967: 269)?

67 Should the motion of someone's arm by a hurricane be considered behaviour (cf. Kaufman 1967: 269)?

68 Though dreaming, reflecting, observing and inferring represent things that people do, should they be considered behaviour (cf. Kaufman 1967: 269)?

69 The difficulty which behaviourists have in defining 'behaviour' is compounded by their inability to agree on what observability is. Thus, commenting on Zuriff's 'pragmatic' definition of observability – namely, the test for observability is consensus – Hocutt (1986: 707), a fellow behaviourist, finds that he has to be 'a stick in the mud' and point out that the metaphysical question cannot be evaded by adopting Zuriff's pragmatist approach. It is remarkable that, though Zuriff and other behaviourists agree that 'behaviorism is the insistence that psychologists limit themselves to what is publicly observable' (Hocutt 1986: 706), they still disagree after 50 years on what they call 'the test for observability'. This, evidently, does not lend much credibility to their quest for 'objectivity'.

70 Moravscik (1990: 61), too, has drawn attention to 'a problem' with the 'very core' of behaviourism: its failure to give an adequate answer to the question 'What is behavior'. This question breaks down on Moravscik's analysis to a series of more specific questions: 'Does it [i.e. behavior] include all of the observable motions of the human body and its parts? Does the notion include only what could be described as physical behavior? In everyday discourse we would be allowed to say that we observed the grieving widow. Is this a behavioral description? Watson allowed notions like fear, rage, and love. Would a psychologist today describe these as behavioral notions? Can we rely on a commonsense conception of behavior, or is this notion theory-laden?'

71 For a discussion of how Chomsky has gone about drawing distinctions between notions such as these, see Botha 1989a: 47ff.

72 The ontological opacity of Halliday's (non)distinction between what he calls 'behaviour' and 'knowledge' is not cleared up in his *Language as Social Semiotic* (1978: 13) where he provides for the

possibility 'to treat language behaviour as if it were an aspect of knowledge of language (and hence to see it in terms of the capacity of the human brain), and also, though in a rather different sense, to treat the individual's knowledge of language as a form of behaviour'. We will return briefly to Halliday's conception of language in section 5.9 below.

3 Selling Language as Soul

1 See Katz and Postal 1989: 5. Chomsky, of course, is not the first leading twentieth-century linguist to have portrayed language as something mental. Recall that in chapter 1 we saw that in his early period Bloomfield (1914) took language to be something psychological in a Wundtian sense. And in chapter 5 we will see that both Saussure (1916) and Sapir (1921, 1949d) have been understood by some to be exponents of a mentalistic conception of language. There are other present-day linguists (e.g. Bickerton 1981, 1990) who have arrived relatively independently at a position on which language is something mental/biological. (Note again that as it is used in the expression 'a/the conception of language', the term 'language' standardly means both 'a language' or 'languages' and 'language in general.')

2 Cf. also Chomsky 1987a: 29ff.; 1987b: 37–8; 1987c: 1; 1989: 10 for this distinction. Chomsky does not distinguish explicitly between 'a notion of language', 'a concept of language' and 'a conception of language'. When referring to the Chomskyan conception of language, I will occasionally use the terms 'concept' and 'notion' as loose synonyms for 'conception'. Nothing of substance hinges on this terminological variation. A further point of terminology: I use the expression '*Chomskyan* conception' rather than '*Chomsky's* conception' in order to indicate that this conception of language does not represent an idiosyncratic set of beliefs held by Chomsky alone. For further discussion of the distinction *Chomskyan v. Chomsky's*, see Botha 1989a: 5–6.

3 Chomsky notes that this formulation has been attributed to Max Weinreich.

4 See chapter 1 for a discussion of the Bloomfieldian conception of language.

5 See, for example, Chomsky 1982: 18–19; 1986: 25ff.; 1987a: 33–7; 1987b: 38–47; 1987c: 2–4; 1988b: 5–7; 1990: 143.

6 Chomsky (1986: 28) has in mind here a common-sense notion of language in terms of which language is not construed in terms of the

sociopolitical and normative factors considered in section 3.1.1 above.

7 Chomsky (1987a: 35) has problems with the formal properties of sets too. He appears, however, to assign less weight to these problems than to those that underlie his two major criticisms of concepts of E-language.

8 Thus, Chomsky notes, the physicists' concepts of 'energy' and 'mass' are not those of 'ordinary usage'.

9 Chomsky (1987a: 36; 1987b: 48ff.; 1987c: 5–6; 1988d: 21; 1989: 12) standardly characterizes 'I-language' in such 'epistemological' terms. Note that he alternates between the expressions 'mind' and 'mind/brain'. We will return to this point in section 3.1.5 below.

10 Chomsky (1981a: 34–5) also provides for 'intermediate states', about which he does not say much.

11 See also Chomsky 1980a: 65, 187; 1987a: 34–5; 1986: 25–6 for a characterization of the initial state of the language faculty.

12 Chomsky (1981a: 34–5) has also called the initial state of the language faculty 'universal grammar (UG)' or 'the language acquisition device'. For further discussion of this state, cf. Botha 1989a: 25ff.

13 The principle of 'subjacency' is an example of a linguistic universal that attempts to capture a biologically necessary property of human language. This principle may be roughly formulated as follows: Nothing can be removed from more than a single binding category.

14 The statement 'A language must have sentences and words' expresses what might, according to Chomsky, be a logically or conceptually necessary property of language. Chomskyan linguistic universals are not so-called cross-linguistic generalizations either. The latter express statistical tendencies of a typological sort. Thus, Greenbergian cross-linguistic generalizations such as the following do not constitute linguistic universals in the Chomskyan sense: 'In declarative sentences with nominal subject and object, the dominant order is almost always one in which the subject precedes the object; In languages with prepositions, the genitive almost always follows the governor noun, while in languages with postpositions it almost always precedes.' For a more detailed discussion of the nature of Chomskyan linguistic universals, see Botha 1989a: 130ff.

15 For Chomsky's general characterization of this state see, for example, Chomsky 1986: 24–6. See Botha 1989a: 25–7, 57ff. for a discussion of important distinctions that have to be drawn in regard to this stable (or steady) state of the language faculty.

16 For a discussion of the nature of such 'triggering' and 'shaping', see Chomsky 1980a: 33, 34, 45, 142; and Botha 1989a: 16–17.

17 Chomsky (1980a) has variously referred to this state as 'knowledge of grammar', 'grammatical competence', 'mental grammar' and 'internalized grammar'. Cf. Botha 1989a: 74–5 for this point of terminology.
18 Cf. Botha 1989a: 55–7 for Chomsky's explication of this point.
19 Cf. Botha 1989a: 58–61 for this tripartite distinction of Chomsky's.
20 Cf. Botha 1989a: 47–9 for this distinction and see Chomsky 1988a: 9–12 for a more detailed discussion of it.
21 For some specifics about Chomsky's second conceptual shift, cf. Botha 1989a: 88–91. Strangely, both critics (e.g. Carr 1990: 33, 49) and supporters (e.g. Pylyshyn 1991: 235ff.) of Chomsky's ontological position discuss it as if Chomsky still took rules to be essential components of linguistic reality. Some of the consequences of this point will be considered in section 4.2.2. below.
22 Chomsky (1986: 23) further clarifies the nature of the statements of a grammar by saying that they are similar to the statements of a physical theory 'that characterize certain entities and their properties in abstraction from whatever may turn out to be the mechanisms that account for these properties'. As an illustrative example, he mentions a nineteenth-century theory of valence about properties expressed in the periodic table.
23 By, for example, Steinberg (1975: 220–1) and, more recently, Katz and Postal (1989).
24 See Langendoen and Postal 1985: 113 for an exegesis of these remarks.
25 The claim that knowledge of language constitutes a cognitive system forms a standard part of Chomsky's characterization of such knowledge. Thus, consider the following remarks of his: 'I will assume further that human language is one of these cognitive systems, one identifiable component of the human mind/brain with its specific properties and principles' (Chomsky 1987a: 6). 'Keeping to the concept of language as a cognitive system, a particular manifestation of the human language faculty . . .' (Chomsky 1987a: 7).
26 There are also earlier formulations suggesting that Chomsky draws the distinction in question: 'The aim of this series of studies, of which the present work is the first, is to deepen our understanding of *the nature of language and the mental processes and structures* that underlie its use and acquisition' (preface by Chomsky and Halle to Chomsky 1966: ix, emphasis added).
27 Cf. Katz and Postal 1989: 5–6 for this characterization.
28 See chapter 4. The Platonist conception of language in question has been defended by Katz, Postal, Bever, Langendoen and others.

29 For this view see also Chomsky 1980a: 5; 1982: 34; 1986: 23, 38; 1988a: 7; 1988b: 2–3; and Botha 1989a: 105–6.

30 For Chomsky's distinction between the cognitive sciences, including linguistics, and the brain sciences, see Botha 1989a: 200–11.

31 For a concise characterization of various forms of dualism (and monism), see Bunge 1980: 2–9.

32 Cf. Chomsky 1988b: 3 for some elaboration of this point.

33 See Botha 1989a: 146 for Chomsky's distinction between mysteries and problems.

34 Chomsky (1988c: 13), accordingly, is unwilling to predict that the natural sciences will someday 'annex', in Nagel's (1980: 211) sense, (all) mental phenomena.

35 This means that, within Chomsky's framework, known forms of dualism are rejected on *a priori* grounds. For a survey of the most influential forms of dualism and their flaws, see Bunge 1980: 2–9, 16–21. See also Jackendoff 1987: 7ff. for a neat summary of what he takes to be the major objections to the main 'dualist theories'.

36 For the nine other reasons, see Bunge 1980: 16–21. Bunge (1980: 10–16), in addition, demolishes ten of the main arguments offered in support of dualism. We return to Popper's version of interactionism in section 4.2 below.

37 Chomsky (1972a: 12) has stressed it, though, that the third phenomenon mentioned above, namely the coherence and appropriateness of language to situations, has remained a mystery, a phenomenon exceeding the bounds of mechanical explanation, whether behaviourist or otherwise.

38 This is the shift called by Chomsky (1986: 6, 24) the 'first conceptual shift' (associated with the birth of generative grammar). Recall that what he (1986: 146, 150–1) dubs 'the second conceptual shift' entails the portrayal of a language as a system of principles and parameters rather than a system of rules. These two conceptual shifts have been considered briefly in section 3.1.3 above.

39 For these formulations see, for example, Chomsky 1987c: 14; 1988b: 3. We have seen above that Chomsky does not consistently distinguish between 'language' and 'knowledge of language'. This is reflected by the fact that he (1987a: 64; 1987b: 20) formulates questions 2 and 3 in terms of 'language' as well:

2′ How is language acquired?
3′ How is language used?

40 For a discussion of typical examples of such discoveries and explanations, see Chomsky 1987a: 64–7; 1987b: 20–3. Also the second

conceptual shift has led in Chomsky's view to 'A great increase in the range of empirical materials discovered and subjected to serious inquiry within generative grammar'. For examples furnished in support of this claim, see Chomsky 1987a: 70–3; 1987b: 28–31.

41 There are different variants of these 'limits' of behaviourism and operationism. For a detailed discussion of these, see Zuriff 1985: 55ff.

42 In documenting these views, Chomsky (1989: 5, 24) refers to Nelson Goodman (1984b) too.

43 For further discussion of the similarities (and differences) between the ideas of Chomsky and those of Descartes, see e.g. Chomsky 1966; Fodor 1983: 3–10; and Gardner 1985: 49ff.

44 In Chomsky's (1987b: 4) view the major 'scientific' contribution by Descartes is his rejection of the neoscholastic idea that perception is a process in which the form of an object imprints itself somehow on the brain. In place of this conception, Descartes proposed that the mind uses its own resources and structural principles to construct a mental representation of an object.

45 Chomsky (1987b: 5) notes that both the Cartesian idea of how the mind works and the Cartesian concept of innate ideas have been 'revived' in the context of the cognitive revolution mentioned above. For an explication and defence of the four views of Descartes that are claimed to make up 'Cartesian linguistics', see Leiber 1991.

46 This problem, Chomsky (1986: xxv) notes, was also raised by Russell in the form of the question: How comes it that human beings, whose contacts with the world are brief and personal and limited, are nevertheless able to know as much as they do know?

47 Cf. also Botha 1989a: 3–4, 13–14, 18–19 for a discussion of this issue.

48 For a discussion of the respects in which Chomsky considers this evidence or experience to be impoverished, see Botha 1989a: 19–20.

49 For some discussion of the doctrine of anamnesis, see Hamlyn 1967b: 10; and Ryle 1967a: 325.

50 For an early discussion by Chomsky of Humboldt's conception of language, see Chomsky 1964: 17ff.

51 As far as Chomsky is aware, there is only one other known behavioural phenomenon that shares the properties of discrete infinity exhibited by language: the human number faculty. The language faculty and the number faculty, moreover, involve in Chomsky's view 'similar principles of digital computation'.

52 For particulars of the nature of the formal system in question see, e.g. Chomsky 1957; 1975a: ch. 4; and Bach 1974: chs. 2 and 8.

53 For instance, one looks in vain in Patricia Churchland's (1986) *Neurophilosophy* – a work of more than 500 pages whose aim is to

present 'the outlines of a very general framework suited to the development of a unified theory of the mind-brain' (p. 3) – for an explicitly articulated conception of language. Anderson (1989), in similar vein, observes that, as a cognitive scientist, Johnson-Laird (1988b) seems not to be particularly concerned with the less superficial properties of language(s).

54 Cf. Woozley 1967: 194–5. In addition to conceptualism there are two other leading theories of universals. Nominalism – which was considered in section 1.3.3 above – claims in its extreme form that only names or words are universal, the world being composed solely of particulars. Realism – to which we will return in section 4.1 below – holds that 'universals exist in themselves and would exist even if there were no minds to be aware of them' (Woozley 1967: 194).

55 Langendoen and Postal (1985: 125ff.) have argued that Chomsky's conceptualism has changed 'over the last few years'. On their analysis, Chomsky's newer view of linguistic reality represents 'radical conceptualism', which 'differs sharply from his earlier, standard conceptualist position'. On the latter position, Langendoen and Postal contend, sentences continue to be 'real things'; on the former position, sentences have lost this status. That is: in terms of standard conceptualism, grammars as mental entities still generate sentences but, in terms of radical conceptualism, grammars generate mental representations of sentences.

56 For further discussion of the function and properties of transducers, see Marshall 1984: 217; Pylyshyn 1984: ch. 6; Carston 1988: 41–2; Cam 1989: 167.

57 As noted by Fodor (1983: 14ff.; 1985b: 4), Marshall (1984: 216), Gross (1985: 16–17) and others, the existence of modular systems or 'vertical faculties' was anticipated in the 'mental organs' provided for by Franz Joseph Gall, the founding father of phrenology. Gall maintained that attention, perception, memory and imagination are not primitive faculties of mind, but only modes of activity of all or any intellectual faculties. The so-called 'horizontal mental faculties' he accordingly considered largely a fiction. Rather, individuating them in terms of specific content domains, Gall postulated a variety of specific propensities, dispositions, qualities, aptitudes and so on. Each of the fundamental faculties – for instance, the aptitude for music – would engage in 'horizontal modes of activity' or would partake in 'horizontal attributes' such as imagination, reason, memory, attention and so on.

58 Cf. also Bresnan and Kaplan 1982: xx–xxiv; and Pinker 1982: 665–6.

59 In Peacocke's (1989: 114) own phraseology: 'The proposal I wish to advance is, intuitively, that for a rule of grammar to be psychologically real for a given subject is for it to specify the information drawn upon by the relevant mechanisms or algorithms in that subject.' For some discussion of the respects in which this criterion is alleged to be superior to its 'rivals', see Peacocke 1989: 120–2. For a recent defence of what is claimed to be Chomsky's position on psychological reality – and for a critique of Bresnan's position – see Matthews 1991.

60 In regard both to its general assumptions and to its specific claims, Fodor's 'functional taxonomy of psychological processes' has provoked extensive criticism. For specimen criticisms see, e.g. Dennett 1984; Marshall 1984; Putnam 1984; Shallice 1984; Jackendoff 1987: 260ff.; Arbib 1989; Cam 1989; Ross 1990; and the various contributions to the Open Peer Commentary in *The Behavioral and Brain Sciences* (vol. 8, 1985: 6–33). See also Fodor's (1985b) reply to this commentary.

61 Katz (1981: 96) has objected along parallel lines to Fodor et al. (1975) singling out speech recognition as the touchstone of psychological reality.

62 Other scholars have noted this problem too. Thus, Carston (1988: 47) has asked: 'What is the relation between the grammar (competence) and the language input system (a performance system)?' And she has observed: 'Exactly how it [linguistic knowledge] is employed, what its relation is to the parsing procedures involved in language perception and whether either has any bearing on the development, ontogenetic or phylogenetic, of the other, are open questions.' Note, incidentally, that even within a Fodorian approach 'language' cannot be solely an input system; to be able to account for speech production, it has to be an output system as well. Which gives rise to the question how something could be both an input and an output system within Fodor's framework.

63 For numerous instances illustrating this point, see Botha 1989a.

64 Various other components of the Chomskyan approach to the study of language have been the subject of hostile criticism as well, including the various theories of linguistic structure, the methodological principles and practices associated with this approach and so on.

65 Expository considerations preclude the various alternative conceptions from being discussed in a section which is devoted to the alleged limitations of the Chomskyan conception of language.

66 As will be shown below, Piagetians such as Inhelder et al. (1974) criticized the Chomskyan language faculty on grounds essentially

similar to Piaget's. And Chomsky (1980a: 207–8) rejected their criticisms for essentially the same reasons as Piaget's.

67 'Motherese', alternatively referred to as 'caretaker speech' or 'baby talk', is defined by Richards et al. (1985: 34) as 'the simple speech used by mothers, fathers, babysitters, etc. when they talk to young children who are learning to talk. Caretaker speech usually has: (a) shorter utterances than speech to other adults, (b) grammatically simple utterances, (c) few abstract or difficult words, with a lot of repetition, (d) clearer pronunciation, sometimes with exaggerated INTONATION patterns.' For further discussion of the properties of motherese and its alleged role in language acquisition, see, for example, Ferguson and DeBose 1977; and Snow and Ferguson 1977. For critical appraisals of the role of such so-called simplified data in language acquisition, see, for example, Bickerton 1981: 139ff.; Gleitman and Wanner 1982: 39ff.; Newmeyer 1983: 22; and Romaine 1985: 261. For a discussion of other criticisms of the argument from the poverty of the stimulus, cf. Wexler 1991.

68 There are arguments against innate knowledge (of language) based on weaker versions of the empiricist condition of grounding in reasons. For a critical discussion of Goldman's (1975) weaker version of this condition, cf. Chomsky 1980a: 99–100. For other discussions of controversial aspects of the Chomskyan notion of 'innate knowledge of language', cf., for example, Chomsky 1969; Danto 1969; Hook 1969a; Quine 1969; Stern 1969; Wells 1969; Cooper 1972; 1975: 1–26, Stich 1978; D'Agostino 1986: 92ff.

69 Cf. also McGinn 1981: 290 for a version of this criticism.

70 For some discussion of these criticisms cf., for example, Cooper 1975; Chomsky 1980a; 1986; D'Agostino 1986; and Pateman 1987.

71 Cf., however, Chomsky 1986: 151 for a number of suggestive remarks on the matter.

72 For typical contributions to this debate see, for example Botha, 1968: 69ff.; 1973: 174ff.; 1981: 302ff.; Labov 1972; Dretske 1974; Cooper 1975: ch. 5; Ringen 1975; Itkonen 1976; Linell 1976; Sampson 1975: ch. 4; Newmeyer 1983: 48ff.; D'Agostino 1986: 74–7.

73 For some discussion of this argument, see Botha 1973: 155.

74 This supposition has been rejected out of hand by Chomsky (1980a: 197ff.; 1986: 36–7). See also Newmeyer 1983: ch. 2 for a detailed attempt to rebut certain versions of this argument.

75 The other two ways out of the 'paradox' seen by Katz and Postal are even more disastrous for mentalists. One entails defending a psychological view of logic, a position made impossible even to contemplate by Frege. The other entails giving up the belief that language

is psychological, adopting in its place a 'realist' conception of language.

76 As for the first assumption, Chomsky (1987c: 22–3; 1988c: 8; 1988d: 14) has indicated recently that he judges the question of the nature and basis of the distinction between truths of meaning and truths of empirical fact to be a matter that 'requires extensive rethinking, and that much of what has been generally assumed for the past several decades about these questions appears to be dubious at best' (1987c: 23). As for the second assumption by Katz and Postal: Suppose, as they claim, that language is not essentially something psychological. But whatever language is, it has to be acquired, known, produced, perceived, mentally stored and so on. This will be reflected in certain properties of language, properties that may be called 'psychological'. To account for the latter properties, they would have to be subsumed under certain 'psychological laws'. Being psychological, these laws would not, however, belong to the same ontological realm as the 'abstract' sentences of natural language. But the objects to which laws apply and those laws themselves can hardly belong to different ontological realms. . . . This is to say that the second assumption of Katz and Postal's could cause problems for their own conception of language as well.

77 Another example of such a 'logical fact' cited by Katz and Postal (1989: 4) is Chomsky's (1988a: 33–4) observation that the proposition expressed in *Whoever is persuaded to sing intends/decides to sing* is a truth independent of empirical fact.

78 As we have seen in section 3.4 above, Fodor – like Chomsky and the earlier Katz (of Chomsky and Katz 1974) – subscribes to what he calls 'the Right View'.

79 For some discussion of this point, see Newmeyer 1983: 75; Botha 1989a: 129–30.

80 Chomsky, as quoted by Katz and Postal (1989: 44), for example, says: 'mentally represented grammar and UG are real objects, part of the physical world, where we understand mental states and representations to be physically encoded in some manner. Statements about particular grammars or about UG are true or false statements about steady states attained or the initial state (assumed fixed for the species), *each of which is a definite real-world object, situated in space-time and entering into causal relations*' (emphasis added by Katz and Postal).

81 Chomsky (1988a: 33), for example, states: 'The statement that to persuade John to do something is to cause him to intend or decide to do that thing is necessarily true. It is true by virtue of the meaning

of its terms, independently of any facts; it is an "analytic truth" in technical jargon'.

82 See, for example, the quotation given in n. 80 above.

83 Katz and Postal (1989: 50) draw attention to the fact that George (1987) has pointed out a contradiction that is 'essentially the same' as the one construed by them. Thus George (1987) has observed: 'As such, an I-language is of course "an abstract entity", as Chomsky asserts (C 22). The confusion arises because Chomsky also declares that an I-language "is some element of the mind of the person who knows the language" (C 22) and consequently that statements about I-language are really "about actual states of the mind/brain and their components" (C 26/7). Now whatever they are, abstract objects are not constituents of the minds or brains of speakers and so I-languages are not states of human brains.' 'I-languages are not in the physical world, although the particular brain states that can be abstractly characterized as knowledge of them are.'

84 Chomsky (1988a: 169), for example, says that 'there is no limit in principle to how many words the sentence may contain' and 'Human language has the extremely unusual, possibly unique, property of discrete infinity. . . .'

85 Chomsky (1987a: 44), for example, says: 'But as distinct from sentences, which exist in mental representations and are realized in behavior. . . .'

86 Chomsky (1986: 26) states that: 'The system of knowledge attained – the I-language – assigns a status to every relevant physical event, say, every sound wave. Some are sentences with a definite meaning . . . Some are intelligible with, perhaps a definite meaning, but are ill-formed in one way or another. . . .'

87 Chomsky (1986: 28–9), for example, states that: 'The conceptual shift from E-language to I-language, from behavior and its products to the system of knowledge that enters into behavior, was in part obscured by accidents of publishing history, and expository passages taken out of context have given rise to occasional misunderstanding (n. 17). Some questionable terminological decisions also contributed to misunderstanding. In the literature of generative grammar, the term "language" has regularly been used for E-language in the sense of a set of well-formed sentences, more or less along the lines of Bloomfield's definition of "language" as a "totality of utterances". The term "grammar" was then used with systematic ambiguity, to refer to what we have here called "I-language" and also to the linguist's theory of the I-language; the same was true of the term UG, introduced later with the same systematic ambiguity, referring to S_o and the theory of S_o.'

88 Lyons (1991: 190) concurs, labelling Chomsky's current ontological position 'abstract . . . physicalism'.

89 Should/could one say that Chomsky or Fodor 'reduces' the mental to the physical? And should such 'reduction' be considered good or bad? Questions such as these are routinely raised in discussions of mentalist linguistic ontologies, recently, for example, by Carr (1990: 77ff.). The answers furnished to such questions are often less than instructive: it is not realized that 'to reduce to' and 'reduction' have a variety of technical senses and that little is to be gained by arbitrarily invoking a particular sense for the purpose of answering the above-mentioned questions. From the pertinent literature (e.g. Churchland 1986: Part II) it is clear just how easy it is to use the expressions 'to reduce to' and 'reduction' in ways that are uninformative, arbitrary or empty.

90 For an excellent discussion of this point, see Katz and Bever 1977.

91 For details of the often ferocious fighting alluded to in this statement, see Botha 1989a.

4 Pushing Language as Platonic (not to Mention Popperian)

1 In this connection, Katz mentions Lewis (1969, 1975), Montague (1974) and Partee (1979). Katz (1981: 92, n. 1) considers Hjelmslev a possible forerunner of Platonism. Hjelmslev (1936: 49) believed that extralinguistic criteria, i.e. physical, physiological or psychological criteria, cannot be relevant in defining linguistic elements such as phonemes. (For this belief cf. also Hjelmslev 1947.) Carr (1990: 116), however, does not consider Hjelmslev to have embraced realism.

2 Many scholars think of present-day Platonism primarily as a mathematical meta-theory. As such a theory, it consists of two distinct doctrines, called 'ontological platonism' and 'epistemological platonism' by Steiner (1973: 57). According to ontological Platonism, 'the truths of mathematics describe infinitely many real objects.' And in terms of epistemological Platonism 'we come to know facts about mathematical entities through a faculty akin to sense perception [i.e. a faculty of mathematical intuition], or at least some people do.'

3 For a discussion of three of these ontologies, namely physicalism, or materialism, behaviourism and mentalism, see respectively chapters 1, 2 and 3.

4 For a succinct characterization of the make-up of Platonist linguistic reality, see Katz 1981: 3, 6, 15, 48, 76–8, 231; 1984: 18, 24, 34; Bever 1982: 433, 436; Katz and Postal 1989: 1.

5 Cf. also Katz 1981: 55–6, 201, 230–1; Katz and Postal 1989: 5–6, 7–8, 37, 51–2.

6 We will see in section 4.2.2 below that Popperians who advocate an abstractist conception of language invoke a 'sentence-utterance' distinction too.

7 Cf. Katz 1981: 55–6; Katz and Postal 1989: 51–2.

8 For a discussion of some of the idealizations used by Chomsky see, for example, Botha 1989a: 152–3; and section 3.1.4 above.

9 Langendoen and Postal's (1985: vi) central claim is 'that the collection of sentences comprising each individual natural language (NL) is so vast that its magnitude is not given by any number, finite or transfinite.' This means to them 'that NLs cannot, as is currently almost universally assumed, be considered recursively enumerable, hence countable (denumerable) collections of sentences.' Rather, they maintain, these collections are 'mega-collections'.

10 This correlation is 'effable' in the sense that it is complete at both ends: 'there are sufficient sentences and senses so that, no matter what the performance capabilities of a speaker, there will never be a case where the non-existence of a sentence or a sense is the reason why a speaker is unable to express a thought' (Katz 1981: 225–6). 'Effability' denotes a property that more conventionally has been called 'unboundedness in scope' (Akmajian et al. 1970: 7).

11 Katz (1981: 229–30) refers to this characterization by means of '(LU)' and mentions recursiveness and compositionality as features that are linguistic universals in terms of (LU). With reference to recursiveness, Katz argues that if the rules of syntax were finite in number and not recursive, the language would be restricted to finitely many sentences. And since a sentence has only finitely many senses, the language would be unable on the expressive side to express all of the infinitely many propositions.

12 In this quotation, 'another conception' means 'a conception other than/distinct from the Chomskyan conception'. On the Chomskyan view, 'essential' is equated with 'innately specified or biologically necessary' (Botha 1989a: 130ff.; and section 3.1.3 above. Katz (1981: 224–5), however, contends that this equation cannot rule out all non-essential properties. Nor can it 'rule in' all essential properties: 'Some innately specified non-essential properties will count as part of the nature of language and some non-innately specified essential properties will not count as part of the nature of language' (p. 224).

13 For equivalent formulations, see e.g. Katz 1984: 18, 42–3.

14 **'The+ur+gy** (**'θiː,ɜːdʒɪ**) *n., pl.* **+gies**. 1. . . . 2. beneficient magic as taught and performed by Egyptian Neoplatonists and others [C16:

from Late Latin *theūrgia*, from Late Greek *theourgia* the practice of magic, from *theo-* THEO- + *-urgia*, from *ergon* work]' (*Collins Dictionary of the English Language*).

15 For a historical account of the way in which some of these beliefs originated, see Katz 1981: 4–6. For a technical discussion of the logico-semantic facts mentioned in (B2), see Katz 1972: 171ff.; 1981: 94ff., 179ff. Both Allan (1983: 678) and Carr (1990: 115) trace Katz's Platonism back to Katz 1972. Carr (1990: 114), however, considers Katz 1977 to constitute Katz's 'first public statement of an overtly Platonist line on linguistic representation'.

16 Katz and Postal (1980: 13) consider any property or relation determined on the basis of the structure of the sentences of an NL to be a feature of that NL.

17 For the earliest version of this theory, cf. Katz and Fodor 1963.

18 There are differences of opinion as to what level of grammatical structure it is that provides the semantic information necessary for the application of logical laws to sentences. In the words of Katz and Postal (1989: 9): 'Intensionalists take that level to be the sense structure of sentences; extensionalists take the logically relevant grammatical level to be that at which the referential apparatus of NLs is most transparently presented.'

19 Katz and Postal (1989) criticize conceptualism, in particular as it has been developed by Chomsky, for a wide range of other alleged flaws as well. Some of these have been considered in section 3.5.2 above.

20 According to Katz (1989: 76), this is the 'weaker' claim made by Platonism. The other, 'stronger', one is that sentences and languages are abstract objects (and that linguistics consequently is about abstract objects). Cf. also Katz 1981: 9; 1984: 25–6, 27–8 for equivalent formulations of the former, 'weaker', claim.

21 Recall that Katz and Postal (1989: 4) characterize these facts as 'covering every aspect of sentential structure, *viz.*, syntactic, morphological, phonological and semantic'. They furnish various typical examples of such facts, including those about analyticity and analytical entailment that were considered in section 4.1.2 above.

22 See in this connection the remarks by Katz and Postal (1989: 13) quoted above as well as similar comments in Katz 1981: 46.

23 Descartes, by contrast, believed in the infallibility of intuition. For a discussion of the various accounts of the nature of intuition within Platonism and for Katz's preference of a particular, Kantian, one, cf. Katz 1981: 200ff. We return to the Kantian account in section 4.1.4 below.

24 Other criticisms – which I do not propose to discuss here – include those indicated in the list below:

1 The advocates of Platonist linguistics have not 'demonstrated' that there are Platonic linguistic objects (see Chomsky 1987a: 34–5 and, for a reply, Katz and Postal 1989: 26).
2 Abstract (linguistic) objects are not to be found in the real world: they are 'constructed' by people (see Chomsky 1987a: 34–5 and, for a reply, Katz and Postal 1989: 26–7).
3 Katz 'is at least as mysterious as Plato on where these abstract objects exist . . .' (Allan 1983: 679).
4 Language is not 'ontologically homogeneous', i.e. it is 'one meeting place of the abstract object and the non-abstract' (MacQueen 1984: 417).
5 It would be more correct 'to let historical and social norms of language rather than "eternal" Platonic entities stand for the abstract objects analyzed by grammatical theory' (cf. Itkonen 1983a: 240–1; and Pateman 1983: 284; 1987: 51–2). To this criticism I will return in chapter 5.
6 There are 'obvious' differences between languages and other abstract objects such as mathematical entities: the former but not the latter are subject to diachronic change and social variation (see Itkonen 1983a: 241).
7 Platonist linguistics 'has no empirical relevance, no relevance to the real world' (see Chomsky 1987a: 35 and, for a reply, Katz and Postal 1989: 27).
8 Using Occam's Razor consistently, Katz has to dispose of abstract objects since, within his Kantian epistemology, they remain in themselves unknowable, our knowledge being confined to the phenomenal world of Katz's concepts of abstract objects (see Pateman 1983: 283; 1987: 50).
9 Katz's account of the analogy between formal logic and linguistic theory is too 'sketchy' to be convincing (Itkonen 1983a: 242).
10 Necessary truth is as amenable to a conceptualist as to a Platonist interpretation (see MacQueen 1984: 417).
11 Katz does not consider whether abstract theoretical constructs exist 'independently of theories of linguistic analysis' or 'independently of the minds of linguistic analysts' (Allan 1983: 679).
12 If linguistic Platonism rejects the psychologistic competence/performance distinction, then Katz has not yet 'disentangled him from the terms' (Allan 1983: 680).
13 It is mistaken to assume, as Katz does, that nominalism,

conceptualism and realism 'encompass the entire range of twentieth-century philosophies in linguistics' (Carr 1990: 115–16).

Note, incidentally, that one can argue that sentences and languages are abstract Platonic objects, without having to assume that numbers are such objects too. So, if it turned out that there are strong reasons for denying numbers the status of Platonic objects, the former case would not thereby collapse. But Katz, Postal and others have of course based their model of linguistics as a 'branch of mathematics' on the assumption that mathematics should be assigned a Platonistic ontological interpretation. And the latter assumption is still quite controversial as is clear from the continuing debate conducted in studies such as Steiner 1975 and Wright 1983 (esp. ch. 2).

25 For a discussion of the notion of 'E-language' see section 3.1.2 above. In terms of the alternative conception of I(nternalized) – language, the conception defended by Chomsky, a language is 'some element of the mind of the person who knows the language, acquired by the learner, and used by the speaker-hearer'. For an explication of Chomsky's notion of 'I-language' see section 3.1.3 above.

26 The distinction between the knowledge of a thing and the thing known that lies at the basis of Katz and Postal's use of the notion of 'relational' was considered in section 4.1.2 above.

27 Following Kant, Katz (1981: 204) takes a concept *in concreto* to be 'a particular concept of something, e.g. a cube, the number seventeen, or the sentence "They are flying planes", in the form of a concrete object of intuition'.

28 Katz (1981: 193) furnishes two general considerations as the basis for the claim that intuition exists: 'first hand experience with its operations, on the one hand, and the elimination of all other faculties as capable of supplying the knowledge in question, on the other'. His reference, via Hardy (1940), to the case of Ramanujan (see the quotation at the end of section 4.1.3 above) involves the first consideration.

29 For a more detailed discussion of this point, see Botha 1980: 77ff.; 1989a: 182–5; and Chomsky 1981b: 9; 1986: 34ff.

30 For just how difficult it is to say in Platonist terms something of substance about language acquisition, see Bever 1982.

31 Dillinger (1984a: 302) considers this interpretation of linguistic theories 'a regress for linguistics' since he takes progress in science 'to be showing new relations between things rather than assuming a head-in-the-sand position on old ones'.

32 The 'Right View' as instantiated, for example, by Chomskyan

conceptualism entails on Fodor's (1985a: 148–9) characterization the following: '(a) Linguistic theories are descriptions of grammars. (b) It is nomologically necessary that learning one's native language involves learning its grammar, so a theory of how grammars are learned is *de facto* a (partial [?]) theory of how languages are learned. (c) It is nomologically necessary that the grammar of a language is internally represented by speaker/hearers of that language; up to dialectical variants, the grammar of a language is what its speaker/hearers have in common by virtue of which they are speaker/hearers of the *same* language. (d) It is nomologically necessary that the internal representation of the grammar (or, equivalently for these purposes, the internally represented grammar) is causally implicated in communication exchange between speakers and hearers in so far as these exchanges are mediated by their use of the language that they share; talking and understanding the language normally involve exploiting the internally represented grammar.'

33 In section 4.2.2 below we will see that a condition with the general tenor of (C1) is pertinent to the appraisal of Popperian linguistic ontology as well.

34 Suppose that it turned out to be possible to present a well-argued case for including facts about analyticity and analytical entailment within the scope of linguistic theories. Then, would Katz and Postal's condition (10b) guarantee that the Platonist conception of language was more highly valued than the conceptualist one? Not necessarily, since – as we will see directly below – extensive coverage of data/facts is only one of several conditions pertinent to the appraisal of the linguistic theories constructed on the basis of a linguistic ontology.

35 Nor do they consider the well-known difficulties involved in assigning in a non-arbitrary way a clear content to the notion of 'simplicity'. For some of these difficulties, see e.g. Chomsky 1972b: 125, 129. See also Botha 1989a: 189ff. for the various notions of simplicity that play a role in Chomskyan linguistics.

36 Cf. Botha 1982: 6ff. and 1989a: 150–1 for the Chomskyan notions of 'deductive depth' and '(theoretical) unification'.

37 This account is based on Popper 1972 (chs 3 and 4) and 1977 (ch. P 2).

38 In Popper's earlier work 'first world', 'second world' and 'third world' denote what in his later work are called 'World 1', 'World 2' and 'World 3', respectively.

39 Popper (1972: 107, 154) maintains that his World 3 is not Hegelian either. Rather, his World 3 'has more in common . . . with Bolzano's theory of a universe of propositions in themselves, though it differs

from Bolzano's also. My third world resembles most closely the universe of Frege's objective contents of thought.'

40 Popper (1977: 48) does claim that language learning is 'a process in which genetically based dispositions, evolved by natural selection, somewhat overlap and interact with a conscious process of exploration and learning, based on cultural evolution'. What this is intended to mean in empirical terms, however, he does not spell out with reference to the acquisition of any specific linguistic forms, structures, rules etc. of any specific languages.

41 For these two conditions see section 1.5 above. Two sub-cases of the 'fruits' condition were considered in the discussion of the Platonist conception of language in section 4.1.4 above.

42 Similarly, Katz and Postal (1989: 5) take Chomskyan conceptualism to represent the 'current orthodoxy' in theoretical linguistics.

43 Interestingly, some of the most serious criticisms of (Chomskyan) SPE phonology were directed at the excessive 'abstractness' of its level of phonological representation (for references, see Goyvaerts and Pullum 1975: 2–4). And, of course, over the years Chomskyans have acquired the reputation of being the champions *par excellence* of an autonomous syntax. For some discussion and many references, see Newmeyer 1983: 5–27, 96ff.

44 For this form of argument see section 4.1.2 above.

45 For some discussion of this point, see sections 2.3.2 and 2.5 above.

46 Nor has Carr shown that his linguistic ontology would lead to a better understanding of 'external' or 'extra-grammatical' processes such as those considered above under point 5 of par. 4.1.4.

47 Mortensen (1978: 264), in similar vein, has argued that 'discussions [by Popper and Eccles] of recent physicalist strategies for dealing with mental phenomena are inadequate.'

48 For a detailed discussion of the late-eighties version of Chomskyan linguistic ontology, see chapter 3 above; and Katz and Postal 1989.

49 I have not discussed above – or in Botha in press – everything that I consider problematic in regard to Carr's linguistic ontology. Thus, I have not commented on the variety of hidden assumptions necessarily involved in Carr's argument for the 'public' nature of linguistic objects. Nor have I attempted to give an exhaustive survey of (philosophical) criticisms of Popper's ontological theory. For example, I have not gone into Platonist criticisms of the Popperian view that World 3 objects are man-made. Katz (1981: 201), for example, has observed that if objects of the third world are 'of our making' then 'Popper has to claim, inconsistent with realism, that numbers are contingent objects that didn't exist until humans came into

existence. Further, he has to claim that numbers can be destroyed just as honey and webs of spiders can.' And on Katz's (1981: 201) judgement, too, 'Popper seems not to appreciate the fact that objective entities with neither spatial nor temporal location cannot enter into causal relations.' For a variety of serious criticisms of Popperian interactionist dualism, see also Bunge and Ardila 1987: 10.

5 Stocking Language as Social Stuff

1 For references bearing out this claim see, for example, Spence 1957; Koerner 1973: 45ff.; Kaldewaij 1986: 16–20; and Pateman 1987: 57–9.

2 In the words of the *Cours* (1916: 30), *la langue* is '*un trésor déposé par la pratique de la parole dans les sujets appartenant à une même communauté, un système grammatical existant virtuellement dans chaque cerveau, ou plus exactement dans les cerveaux d'un ensemble d'individus; car la langue n'est complète dans aucun, elle n'existe parfaitement que dans la masse.*' Harris's recent translation (Saussure 1983: 13) of this formulation reads as follows: 'the/their language' is 'a fund accumulated by the members of the community through the practice of speech, a grammatical system existing potentially in every brain, or more exactly in the brains of a group of individuals; for the language is never complete in any single individual, but exists perfectly only in the collectivity.' Harris translates 'la langue' alternatively as 'linguistic structure' (p. 9, 76) and 'a language system' (p. 14).

3 In the words of the *Cours* (1916: 30–1), *la parole* is '*un acte individuel de volonté et d'intelligence, dans lequel il convient de distinguer: 1° les combinaisons par lesquelles le sujet parlant utilise le code de la langue en vue d'exprimer sa pensée personnelle; 2° le mécanisme psycho-physique qui lui permet d'extérioriser ces combinaisons.*' In Harris's translation (Saussure 1983: 14) this reads as follows: 'Speech . . . is an individual act of the will and the intelligence, in which one must distinguish: (1) the combinations through which the speaker uses the code provided by the language in order to express his own thought, and (2) the psycho-physical mechanism which enables him to externalise these combinations.'

4 In the words of the *Cours* (1916: 112): '*Évitant de stériles définitions de mots, nous avons d'abord distingué, au sein du phénomène total que représente le* langage, *deux facteurs: la* langue *et la* parole.' In Harris's translation (Saussure 1983: 76) here is how this reads:

'Avoiding the sterility of merely verbal definitions, we began by distinguishing, within the global phenomenon of *language*, between *linguistic structure* and *speech*.'

5 Over the years various scholars, emphasizing the influence of Durkheim's sociology on Saussure's linguistic thinking, have either explicitly or implicitly claimed this to be the case. Koerner mentions Vendryes (1952), Doroszewski (1962), Kukenheim (1966), Dinneen (1967) and Robins (1967) as cases in point. Koerner (1973: 52ff.) argues at some length against the contention that 'Saussure's linguistic theory is essentially Durkheimian in nature.'

6 Koerner (1973: 53) speculates that Saussure 'may have received his inspiration concerning the social character of language more probably from Whitney'. He bases this speculation on the fact that Saussure referred explicitly to the way in which Whitney 'had assimilated *langue* with [sic] a social institution'.

7 In the words of the *Cours* (1916: 143): '*Bref, la notion d'état de langue ne peut être qu'approximative. En linguistique statique, comme dans la plupart des sciences, aucune démonstration n'est possible sans une simplification conventionnelle des données.*'

8 In this quotation, 'CLG' refers to our Saussure 1916.

9 In the words of the *Cours* (1916: 112): '*Elle* [i.e. *la langue*] *est l'ensemble des habitudes linguistiques qui permettent à un sujet de comprendre et de se faire comprendre.*'

10 Koerner (1973: 52–3) continues: 'though it [i.e.'representation'] appears to imply what is meant by the German expression "Vorstellung"; in addition, there are no sources for either of the two occurrences of the term (cf. CLG(E), 44 and 149). The best example is perhaps Saussure's affirmation that a phoneme or an "image acoustique" is not identical with sound (which is purely physical), but [is] its "empreinte psychique". This observation, however, would not lead back to Durkheim's concept but to statements made by Baudouin de Courtenay during the 1890s. . . .'

11 Itkonen (1978: 59) comes to a similar conclusion in regard to the 'ontological and epistemological nature' of Saussure's 'language-game' (in terms of which, analogous to chess, language is a system of entities whose relations to each other were determined by conventions or rules): 'Nor did he inquire into its [the language's] psychological and sociological *substrata*, although he was fully aware of their existence. He clearly considered all these questions as lying outside of linguistics proper.'

12 In the words of the *Cours* (1916: 29): '*Entre tous les individus ainsi reliés par le langage, il s'établira une sorte de moyenne: tous*

reproduiront, – non exactement sans doute, mais approximativement – les mêmes signes unis aux mêmes concepts.'

13 In the words of the *Cours* (1916: 128): '*L'étude synchronique n'a pas pour objet tout ce qui est simultané, mais seulement l'ensemble des faits correspondant à chaque langue; dans la mesure où cela sera nécessaire, la séparation ira jusqu'aux dialectes et aux sous-dialectes. Au fond le terme de* synchronique *n'est pas assez précis; il devrait être remplacé par celui, un peu long il est vrai, de* idiosynchronique.'

14 In the words of the *Cours* (1916: 30): '*la langue n'est complète dans aucun, elle n'existe parfaitement que dans la masse.*'

15 Conventionally, the term *idiolect* is used to denote the linguistic system of an individual speaker, or – as Crystal (1985: 152) alternatively but equivalently defines it – the speaker's 'personal dialect'.

16 Black English Vernacular, in contrast to Standard English, 'shows the absence of *be* in a variety of syntactic environments', including the following (Labov 1977: 67–9):

1	_____ NP :	*She the first one started us off.*
2	_____ PA :	*He fast in everything he do.*
3	_____ Loc :	*You out the game.*
4	_____ Neg :	*But everybody not black.*
5	_____ Ving:	*He just feel like he gettin' cripple up from arthritis.*
6	_____ gon :	*He gon' try get up.*

17 For this point, cf. Bickerton 1971: 461; and Newmeyer 1983: 80. Other linguists (e.g. Wardhaugh 1986: 182) have argued that it is not clear what theoretical status variable rules have *vis-à-vis* any distinction that exists between linguistic competence and linguistic performance.

18 Pateman (1987: 60) thinks that Labov 'does seek to avoid the Platonism or vulgar Durkheimianism of making the variable rule a property of the community independent of the individuals collectively considered by attributing to individuals distributively a mentally represented grammar the rules of which are isomorphic with the community grammar'. On Pateman's judgement, however, 'there is no basis for this [attribution] claim' of Labov's.

19 For other problems with Labov's linguistic ontology, see Pateman 1987: 61–2. The use of variable rules has also been criticized from a non-ontological perspective. Wardhaugh (1986: 182), for example, has argued that in such cases as that of the variable (L) it is not possible to write 'even a single variable rule'. And various linguists (e.g. Kay and McDaniel 1979: 152; Newmeyer 1983: 79) have noted that as 'data-displaying devices' 'there is no sense in which such rules could be said to explain anything', to use a formulation of Newmeyer's.

20 See, e.g. Itkonen 1978: 62–3ff.; Katz 1981: 7–8; and Kaldewaij 1986: 52–3. Sapir is conventionally considered to have been one of the four 'great' or 'central' figures in the early development of structural linguistics in North America, the other three being Boas, Whorf and Bloomfield. For this appraisal see, e.g. Hymes and Fought 1975.
21 As noted by Katz (1981: 15), this quotation represents a typical case in which Sapir uses the terms 'language' and 'speech' interchangeably. More instances of this variable usage will be encountered below.
22 For a discussion of Chomsky's theory of language acquisition see, e.g. Chomsky 1986: 51ff.; and Botha 1989a: 12–47.
23 We will see below that, in a different context, Sapir does seem to provide for an innate aspect of language.
24 Some linguists (e.g. Teeter 1964: 200; McCawley 1967: 110; Katz 1981: 8) seem to have understood Sapir as having denied that there are linguistic universals.
25 This is clear from Hymes 1970: 258ff.; and Kaldewaij 1986: 53–4.
26 Hymes (1970: 258–66), in fact, has provided some historical perspective on the dynamics of Sapir's thinking on the relation between language and culture. But, though perceptive from a historical point of view, Hymes's discussion does not resolve or 'dissolve' the ontological questions raised above.
27 For references to the mentalistic dimension of Sapir's linguistic ontology see, e.g. Chomsky 1964: 97, 108; McCawley 1967; and, of a more recent date, Kaldewaij 1986: 55–6.
28 Kaldewaij (1986: 56) notes that Sapir's view of the psychological reality of phonemes is strikingly parallel to Saussure's view of phonological units: Saussure did not consider speech sounds as such to be significant from the point of view of the language system. What matters from the latter angle, rather, is the '*image acoustique*': the psychological representation of sounds in the form of signs.
29 Scattered through Sapir's works, there are many more such fragments: e.g. Sapir's (1921: 46, n. 2) view that, as the object of grammatical description, the 'idea' of speech has priority over actual speech. For some discussion of this view, see Itkonen 1978: 63.
30 Note, incidentally, that Sapir seems to differ from Saussure in regard to the existence of a 'social mind' or 'social unconsciousness'. To interlink the social and psychological 'sides' of *langue*, Saussure appears to have needed a 'social psychology' that provided for some kind of '*ésprit collectif*'.
31 This discussion of Dummett's linguistic ontology is based mainly on Dummett 1986. The basic claims of this ontology have however been

expressed in earlier studies as well, including Dummett 1975, 1976, and 1978: ch. 23.

32 In earlier work, Dummett (1975: 134–5) used the expressions 'a shared language' and '(a kind of) superlanguage' to denote what he now calls 'a common language'.

33 Some of these flaws have been outlined in section 3.1.1 above.

34 Chomsky knows of only one attempt 'to face the problem', Trevor Pateman's (1987). But he finds this attempt flawed for reasons to which we will return in section 5.6 below.

35 For Chomsky's criticisms of the identification of knowledge of language with the ability to use language see also his rejection of Kenny's (1984: 138ff.) contention that he, i.e. Chomsky, is seriously confused in drawing a distinction between knowledge of language and the ability (or capacity) to use language.

36 Chomsky (1988d: 3ff.) argues that his mentalistic/biologistic conception of language, by contrast, is capable of providing a satisfactory account of these phenomena since it incorporates the necessary conceptual distinctions. Central amongst these are, first, the distinction between knowledge of a language and the ability to use that knowledge and, secondly, the distinction between a 'generative procedure' and the 'internal representation of such a procedure'.

37 Recall that, on Chomsky's (1988c: 5) analysis, what Dummett believes to be the 'fundamental sense of language' involves 'complex and obscure sociopolitical, historical, cultural and normative-teleological elements'.

38 Dummett (1986: 474–5) has shown an awareness of some of the problems involved in the use of the notion of a 'language community': 'What, then, is a language community? It obviously cannot be defined geographically: it cannot be defined without using the concept of a language.'

39 Pateman (1987: 75, n. 17) adopts two conditions for '(intentional) objects of belief': that '(1) an object of belief may not exist as anything other than an object of belief (so that though people believe in witches or English, it does not follow that witches or English *exist*) and (2) that the objects in the *that*-clauses of beliefs are referentially opaque.'

40 Chomsky (1988d: 22, n. 4) observes that the fluctuating and transient nature of such beliefs of a person means, in terms of Pateman's conception of languages, that he or she may 'speak a great many languages, changing from moment to moment, depending on how he or she chooses to identify with one or another community. . .'.

41 Pateman (1987: 57) takes a linguistic fact to be 'the kind of fact

for which a grammar or a rule of grammar can be written'. A social fact he characterizes as 'a fact that pre-exists any individual considered *distributively* but does not pre-exist every individual considered collectively'.

42 For a more general discussion of the limitations of Wittgensteinian arguments against the possibility of private languages, cf. Pateman 1987: 122ff. And for a critique of (idiosyncratic) details of Itkonen's use of 'the Wittgensteinian approach', cf. Carr 1990: 101–2.

43 As has been argued by Carr (1990: 102–4), there are other problems with Itkonen's linguistic ontology. Thus Carr contends that Itkonen's portrayal of linguistic objects as 'fundamentally normative' is quite problematic. On Carr's analysis a 'fairly major defect' in Itkonen's proposals is that 'he *excludes* the objects of grammatical inquiry (sentences and their properties) in his philosophy of linguistics by claiming that the objects of inquiry are normative rules describable by means of rule sentences.' Carr, moreover, fails to see how notions such as 'function', 'constituency', 'hierarchicality', 'modification', 'complementation' and so on – notions that Itkonen would have to adopt in Carr's view to 'improve' his oversimplified rule-sentences – could be said to be normative. This brings us to a final example of a questionable aspect of Itkonen's conception of 'linguistic knowledge' not discussed above: his (1978: 127) contention that 'There is no language without consciousness, and no consciousness without social control of it.' It is unclear how this contention is to be reconciled with the fact that a speaker has only tacit knowledge of the vast majority of the rules postulated by a descriptively adequate grammar of his/her language.

44 Johnson et al. (1984) contend for example that:

(a) 'In empiricism . . . science and metaphysics are both connected and *dis*connected . . . metaphysics are allowed into science in accordance with the rules of empiricism . . . yet once allowed in, such imaginative insights open up empiricism to questions that undermine a strategy based entirely on experience as the sole source of knowledge' (p. 31).

(b) 'In a particular version of the 'subjectivist strategy', 'the inherent weakness and tension . . . is that it is finally forced into the sterility of the claim that all knowledge is locked for ever in the head of each individual – we can know nothing outside ourselves (i.e. solipsism)' (pp. 76–7).

(c) 'The core tension of substantialism manifests itself as a problem of validation. How is it possible to determine the truth or certainty of a statement about social reality when observation as a means of validation is rejected?' (p. 118).

(d) The 'tensions' in Durkheimian rationalism spring from its epistemology. Specifically, they spring from the rationalist belief that, 'although the empirical world is the object of explanation, rational analysis 'must purge individual thought of those elements that are acquired by virtue of lived experiences . . .' (p. 162).

45 Thus we have seen in section 5.4 above that Sapir rejected the idea of postulating such an entity.

46 Halliday's linguistic ontology includes 'language as behaviour', 'language as knowledge', 'language as system' and 'language as art', as he (1978: 11) indicates by means of the four boxes in the following diagram:

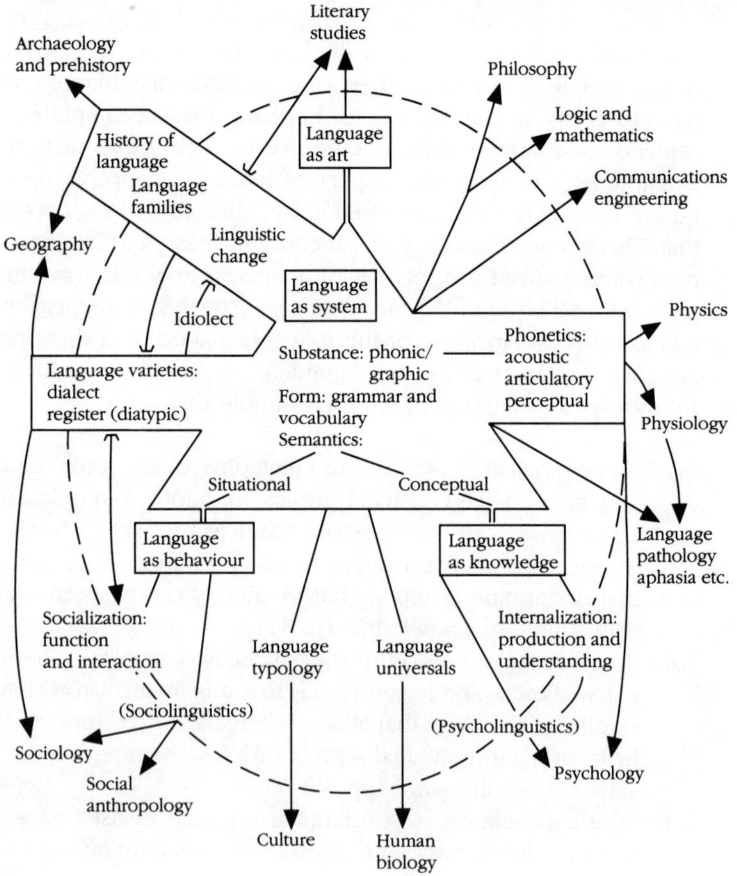

Halliday (1978: 13), moreover, contends that it is possible 'to embed one perspective inside the other: to treat language behaviour as if it were an aspect of our knowledge of language (and hence to see it in terms of the capacity of the human brain), and also, though in a rather different sense, to treat the individual's knowledge of language as a form of behaviour. In other words we can look at social facts from a biological point of view, or at biological facts from a social point of view.' How these views translate into more conventional ontological categories and distinctions is unclear to me. Even scholars who are sympathetic towards Halliday seem to find it quite hard to fathom concepts central to his thinking and to follow his reasoning, as is clear from Berry's (1982) and Butler's (1985: ch. 5) discussion of his work.

6 Balancing the Book(s)

1 The former philosophers of science include on Bunge's (1977: 16) account, in addition to himself, Woodger, Collingwood, Russell, Margenau, Harré, Körner, Agassi, Harvey, Rosenblueth and Lakatos. As examples of the latter scientists, Bunge (1977: 18) mentions Galilei, Descartes, Leibniz, Newton, Euler, d'Alembert, Priestly, Faraday, Darwin, Maxwell, Einstein, Born, Heisenberg, Schrödinger, Haldane, Bernal and Dobzhansky.

2 Bunge (1977: 16–17) gives the following examples of such assumptions: (1) There is a world external to the cognitive subject. (2) The world is composed of things. (3) Forms are properties of things. (4) Things are grouped into systems. (5) Every system, except the universe, interacts with other systems in certain respects and is isolated from other systems in other respects. (6) Everything changes. (7) Nothing comes out of nothing and no thing reduces to nothingness. (8) Every thing abides by laws. (9) There are several kinds of law (nomological pluralism). (10) There are several levels of organization: physical, chemical, biological, social, technological, etc. Bunge and Ardila (1987: 20) add ten more examples to this list.

3 Bunge's (1977: 19) examples include: (1) Is there an ultimate matter (*ápeiron* or *Urmaterie*)? (2) Is life characterized by an immaterial principle (spirit, entelechy, *élan vital* or any other substitute for ignorance), or has it emerged in a strictly natural evolutionary process? (3) Are biological species embodiments of Platonic archetypes, or just concrete populations, or something else? (4) Is the mental anything disjoint from and beyond the neural? (5) Is a society anything beyond and above the individuals that compose it or are

there societal laws in addition to the laws concerning individual behaviour?

4 As examples of such fundamental concepts, Bunge (1977: 20) lists 'part', 'juxtaposition', 'property', 'possibility', 'composition', 'state function', 'state', 'event', 'process', 'space', 'time', 'life', 'mind' and 'society'. Bunge goes on to observe that 'physics asks not "What is time?", biology "What is life?", psychology "What is the mental?", and sociology "What is sociality?". It is the task of ontology, jointly with the foundations of science, to try and supply answers to such questions and, in general, to clarify whatever idea science takes for granted or leaves in the twilight. That is, the metaphysician must fill some of the gaps in science.'

5 Bunge's (1977: 20–1) example is Lagrangian dynamics, which initially was proposed as a reformulation of classical particle mechanics but which was eventually generalized to cover mechanical, electrical, biological and social systems.

6 For example, Bunge (1977: 21) claims, a general control (or cybernetic) theory will not apply to machines with feedback loops only, but also to such goal-seeking systems as members of higher animal species.

7 Cf. Bunge 1977: 21. Like extremely general scientific theories, ontological theories cannot be tested empirically. Bunge (1977: 22) believes that 'like the generic theories of science, those of ontology are *vicariously testable*, i.e. through the checking of more special theories gotten from the general ones by conjoining them with subsidiary assumptions.'

8 For a fuller discussion of the dispute in question, see Botha 1973: 289–91, 318–19.

9 For a discussion of the nature of various kinds of derivational constraints and semantic interpretation rules, see Newmeyer 1980: 134–6, 144–8, 203, 230–1.

10 See also Jackendoff 1972: 10–14 for the general format of this argument.

11 'An ontological interpretation of a formal theory', in Katz's (1981: 53) view, 'is a set of statements that fix the highest category for the objects assigned to referring terms in the theory'. On his view, 'statements of an ontological interpretation can be as succinct as Harris's remark that the objective study of a natural language is about "sound waves or ink marks" or as lengthy as a full theory of the nature of the particular reality in question.'

12 For an account of the developmental history of transformational rules, see Newmeyer 1980: 175ff.

13 Lightfoot (1982: 51) claims that such arguments do represent 'the basic line of reasoning' adopted by Chomsky. For a critical discussion of this claim by Lightfoot, see Botha 1985: 112–13.

14 It is not clear how a theory expressly constructed to characterize a particular (realm of) reality, e.g. biological reality, could have an 'ontologically neutral core' that may be assigned distinct 'ontological interpretations'. In what sense could, for example, a theoretical principle such as subjacency be considered 'ontologically neutral'? The idea of an 'ontologically neutral core' to which various different 'ontologically interpretations' can be assigned may make more sense in the case of theories proposed initially merely as devices for 'systematizing observations' or 'computing predictions' about phenomena at the surface of an ontologically underspecified (realm of) reality. The notions of 'ontologically neutral core' and 'ontological interpretation' seem to reflect ideas forming part of positivist accounts of the structure of scientific theories such as those found in Nagel 1961 and Suppe 1974.

15 Lyons seems not to have taken into account the fact that Chomsky draws a distinction between linguistic theory and the field of linguistics. Chomsky has been understood (see, e.g. Botha 1989a: 129–30) to have placed restrictions on the scope of the former, not that of the latter.

16 Fields, as a matter of fact, are subdivided on the basis of a variety of considerations – pertaining, for example, to aims, methods and instruments of inquiry, epistemology etc. – that have no direct ontological import.

17 Cf. Bunge 1979 for an attempt at setting up a pluralist ontology in a principled way.

18 For accounts bearing out this judgement see, e.g. Lightfoot 1982: chs 8 and 9; Newmeyer 1983: chs 3 and 5; Chomsky 1986: 40ff.; Salkie 1990: 89ff.; as well as various contributions to Kasher 1991.

19 This has been overtly manifested in extended debates and controversies involving scholars from a variety of fields bordering on linguistics. For typical examples of such, often confrontational, discussions of fundamental issues concerning the nature and properties of knowledge (of language), language and mind, see, e.g. the discussion in *The Behavioral and Brain Sciences*, vol. 3, 1980, of Chomsky's (1980) book *Rules and Representations*; the debate involving Chomsky, Piaget and others at Royaumont, published in Piattelli-Palmarini 1983; and the interchanges between Chomsky and various other scholars in *Mind and Language*, Vol. 3, 1986. These and several

more debates involving Chomsky and nonlinguists are dealt with in Botha 1989a.

20 A third, potential, problem concerns the way in which Chomsky's conception of language is interconnected with his epistemology. Recall that he is driven to his mentalism by, amongst other things, his faith in 'normal scientific practice' or 'the standard practice of the natural sciences'. Recall, moreover, that Bloomfield was driven to his physicalist conception of language by his belief in what scientific practice should entail in order to be respectable (i.e. metaphysics-free) as well. But, as we have also seen, it was Bloomfield's empiricist epistemology that caused his conception of language to be fundamentally flawed. This would seem to indicate that if, in the course of time, Chomsky's faith in what he calls 'normal scientific practice' turned out to be unfounded, his conception of language could suffer the same fate as Bloomfield's. Such a possibility is a risk to which all 'epistemology-based' conceptions of language are exposed. In view, however, of the enormous growth of the natural sciences, and the remarkable fertility of the Chomskyan conception of language, Chomsky's faith in 'the standard practice of the natural sciences' does not seem to represent an error of judgement of the kind made by Bloomfield.

Shutting up Shop

1 For a defence of (one version of) the position that 'there is no such thing as a language', see Davidson 1986. And for criticisms of Davidson's case, see Dummett 1986; Hacking 1986; and Chomsky 1989.

Bibliography

Achinstein, P. and Barker, F. (eds) 1969. *The Legacy of Logical Positivism.* Baltimore: The Johns Hopkins Press.

Akmajian, A., Demers, R. A., Farmer, A. K. and Harnish, R. M. 1990. *Linguistics. An Introduction to Language and Communication,* 3rd edn. Cambridge, Mass.: MIT Press.

Allan, K. 1983. Review of Katz, *Language and Other Abstract Objects* (1981). *Language* 59: 678–83.

Allan, K. 1988. Linguistic metatheory. Unpublished manuscript.

Alston, W. P. 1967. Philosophy of language. In Edwards (ed.) 1967, vol. 4: 386–90.

Anderson, S. R. 1989. Review of Johnson-Laird, *An Introduction to Cognitive Science* (1988). *Language* 65: 800–11.

Anrade, M. J. 1936. Some questions of fact and policy concerning phonemes. *Language* 12: 1–14.

Arbib, M. A. 1989. Modularity, schemas and neurons: a critique of Fodor. In Slezak (ed.) 1989: 193–219.

Ashby, R. W. 1967. Verifiability principle. In Edwards (ed.) 1967, vol. 8: 240–7.

Austerlitz, R. (ed.) 1975. *The Scope of American Linguistics. The First Golden Anniversary Symposium of the Linguistics Society of America.* Lisse: The Peter de Ridder Press.

Bach, E. 1965. Structural linguistics and the philosophy of science. *Diogenes* 51: 111–28.

Bach, E. 1974. *Syntactic Theory.* New York: Holt, Rinehart and Winston.

Bacon, F. 1620. *Novum Organum.* English translation in R. L. Ellis and J. Spedding (eds) *The philosophical Works of Francis Bacon,* 1905, pp. 241–387. London: Routledge.

Bailey, C.-J. and Shuy, R. (eds) 1973. *New Ways of Analyzing Variation in English.* Washington, DC: Georgetown University Press.

Baker, G. P. and Hacker, P. M. S. 1980. *Wittgenstein: Understanding and Meaning.* Oxford: Basil Blackwell.

Baker, G. P. and Hacker, P. M. S. 1984. *Language, Sense and Nonsense. A Critical Investigaton into Modern Theories of Language.* Oxford: Basil Blackwell.

Baker, G. P. and Hacker, P. M. S. 1986. *Wittgenstein: Rules, Grammar and Necessity.* Oxford: Basil Blackwell.

Bar-Hillel, Y. 1966. On a misapprehension of the status of theories in linguistics. *Foundations of Language* 2: 394–9.

Beloff, J. 1978. Is mind autonomous? *The British Journal for the Philosophy of Science* 29: 265–73.

Berry, M. 1982. Review of Halliday, *Language as Social Semiotic* (1978). *Nottingham Linguistic Circular* 11: 64–94.

Bever, T. G. 1982. Some implications of the nonspecific bases of language. In Wanner and Gleitman (eds) 1982: 429–86.

Bever, T. G., Carroll, J. M. and Miller, L. A. (eds) 1984. *Talking Minds: the Study of Language in Cognitive Science.* Cambridge, Mass.: MIT Press.

Bever, T. G. and Katz, J. J. (eds) 1977. *An Integrated Theory of Linguistic Ability.* Hassocks, Sussex: The Harvester Press.

Bhaskar, R. 1978. *A Realist Theory of Science.* Hassocks, Sussex: The Harvester Press.

Bickerton, D. 1971. Inherent variability and variable rules. *Foundations of Language* 7: 457–92.

Bickerton, D. 1973. Quantitative versus dynamic paradigms: the case of Montreal *que.* In Bailey and Shuy (eds) 1973: 22–43.

Bickerton, D. 1981. *Roots of Language.* Ann Arbor, Mich.: Karoma Publishers.

Bickerton, D. 1990. *Language and Species.* Chicago and London: University of Chicago Press.

Bierwisch, M. 1971. *Modern Linguistics. Its Development, Methods and Problems.* (*Janua Linguarum, Series Minor* 110.) The Hague: Mouton.

Bloomfield, L. 1914. *An Introduction to the Study of Language.* New York: Henry Holt.

Bloomfield, L. 1931. Albert Paul Weiss. *Language* 7: 219–21.

Bloomfield, L. 1933. *Language.* New York: Henry Holt.

Bloomfield, L. 1936. Language or ideas? *Language* 12: 89–95.

Bloomfield, L. 1939. *Linguistic Aspects of Science.* (*International Encyclopedia of Unified Science*, vol. 1, no. 4.)

Bolinger, D. L. 1968. *Aspects of Language*, 2nd edn. New York: Harcourt Brace Jovanovich.

Bolinger, D. L. 1980. *Language – the Loaded Weapon. The Use and Abuse of Language Today.* London and New York: Longman.

Botha, R. P. 1968. *The Function of the Lexicon in Transformational Generative Grammar.* (*Janua Linguarum, Series Maior* 38.) The Hague: Mouton.

Botha, R. P. 1973. *The Justification of Linguistic Hypotheses. A Study of Non-demonstrative Inference in Transformational Grammar.* (*Janua Linguarum, Series Maior* 84.) The Hague: Mouton.

Botha, R. P. 1979. *Methodological Bases of a Progressive Mentalism* (SPIL 3). Stellenbosch: Department of General Linguistics, Stellenbosch University.

Botha, R. P. 1980. Methodological bases of a progressive mentalism. *Synthese* 44: 1–112.

Botha, R. P. 1981. *The Conduct of Linguistic Inquiry. A Systematic Introduction to the Methodology of Generative Grammar.* (*Janua Linguarum, Series Practica* 157.) The Hague: Mouton.

Botha, R. P. 1982. On the 'Galilean style' of linguistic inquiry. *Lingua* 58: 1–50.

Botha, R. P. 1985. *The Language Lottery*: Promises, promises . . . *Studies in Language* 9: 109–21.

Botha, R. P. 1989a *Challenging Chomsky. The Generative Garden Game.* Oxford: Basil Blackwell.

Botha, R. P. 1989b. *The Metaphysics Market: 1 Merchandizing Language as Matter* (SPIL 20 and SPIL PLUS 14). Stellenbosch: Department of General Linguistics, Stellenbosch University.

Botha, R. P. 1990a. *The Metaphysics Market: 2 Billing Language as Behavioural* (SPIL 21 and SPIL PLUS 15). Stellenbosch: Department of General Linguistics, Stellenbosch University.

Botha, R. P. 1990b. *The Metaphysics Market: 3 Selling Language as Soul* (SPIL 22 and SPIL PLUS 17). Stellenbosch: Department of General Linguistics, Stellenbosch University.

Botha, R. P. 1991a. *The Metaphysics Market: 4 Pushing Language as Platonist (not to mention Popperian)* (SPIL 23 and SPIL PLUS 19). Stellenbosch: Department of General Linguistics, Stellenbosch University.

Botha, R. P. 1991b. *The Metaphysics Market: 5 Stocking Language as Social Stuff* (SPIL 24). Stellenbosch: Department of General Linguistics, Stellenbosch University.

Botha, R. P. in press. Review of Carr, *Linguistic Realities* (1990). *Journal of Linguistics.*

Bresnan, J. 1978. A realistic transformational grammar. In Halle et al. (eds) 1978: 1–59.

Bresnan, J. (ed.) 1982. *The Mental Representation of Grammatical Relations.* Cambridge, Mass.: MIT Press.

Bresnan, J. and Kaplan, R. M. 1982. Introduction: Grammars as mental representations of language. In Bresnan (ed.) 1982: xvii–lii.

Bruck, A., La Galy, B. and Fox, G. (eds) 1974. *Papers from the Parasession on Natural Phonology.* Chicago: Chicago Linguistics Society.

Bunge, M. 1977. *Treatise on Basic Philosophy,* vol. 3. *Ontology I: The Furniture of the World.* Dordrecht/Boston: Reidel.

Bunge, M. 1979. *Treatise on Basic Philosophy,* vol. 4. *Ontology II: A World of Systems.* Dordrecht/Boston: Reidel.

Bunge, M. 1980. *The Mind-Body Problem. A Psychobiological Approach.* Oxford: Pergamon Press.

Bunge, M. and Ardila, R. 1987. *Philosophy of Psychology.* New York: Springer-Verlag.

Burton-Roberts, N. C. 1985. Utterance, relevance, and problems with text grammar. *Australian Journal of Linguistics* 5: 285–96.

Butler, C. S. 1985. *Systemic Linguistics. Theory and Application.* London: Batsford.

Cam, P. 1989. Notes toward a faculty theory of consciousness. In Slezak (ed.) 1989: 167–91.

Campbell, K. 1967. Materialism. In Edwards (ed.) 1967, vol. 5: 179–88.

Carnap, R. 1936–7. Testability and meaning. *Philosophy of Science* 3: 419–71; 4: 1–40.

Carr, P. 1987. Psychologism in linguistics, and its alternatives. In Modgil and Modgil (eds) 1987: 212–21.

Carr, P. 1990. *Linguistic Realities. An Autonomist Metatheory for the Generative Enterprise. Cambridge Studies in Linguistics* 53. Cambridge: Cambridge University Press.

Carston, R. 1988. Language and cognition. In Newmeyer (ed.) 1988, vol. III: 38–68.

Chomsky, N. 1957. *Syntactic Structures.* (*Janua Linguarum* IV.) The Hague: Mouton.

Chomsky, N. 1959. Review of Skinner, *Verbal Behavior* (1957). *Language* 35: 26–58.

Chomsky, N. 1964. *Current Issues in Linguistic Theory. (Janua Linguarum, Series Minor* 38.) The Hague: Mouton.

Chomsky, N. 1965. *Aspects of the Theory of Syntax.* Cambridge, Mass.: MIT Press.

Chomsky, N. 1966. *Cartesian Linguistics.* New York: Harper and Row.

Chomsky, N. 1968. Quine's empirical assumptions. *Synthese* 19: 53–68.

Chomsky, N. 1969. Linguistics and philosophy. In Hook (ed.) 1969b: 51–94.

Chomsky, N. 1972a. *Language and Mind.*, enlarged edn. New York: Harcourt Brace Jovanovich.

Chomsky, N. 1972b. *Studies on Semantics in Generative Grammar.* (*Janua Linguarum, Series Minor* 107.) The Hague: Mouton.

Chomsky, N. 1972c. Some empirical issues in the theory of transformational grammar. In Peters (ed.) 1972: 63–130.

Chomsky, N. 1975a. *The Logical Structure of Linguistic Theory.* New York: Plenum Press.

Chomsky, N. 1975b. *Reflections on Language.* New York: Pantheon Books.

Chomsky, N. 1977. *Essays on Form and Interpretation.* Amsterdam: North-Holland Publishing Company.

Chomsky, N. 1980a. *Rules and Representations.* New York: Columbia University Press.

Chomsky, N. 1980b. Rules and representations. *The Behavioral and Brain Sciences* 3: 1–15, 42–61.

Chomsky, N. 1981a. Principles and parameters in syntactic theory. In Hornstein and Lightfoot (eds) 1981: 32–75.

Chomsky, N. 1981b. *Lectures on Government and Binding.* Dordrecht: Foris Publications.

Chomsky, N. 1982. Mental representation. *Syracuse Scholar.*

Chomsky, N. 1983. On cognitive structures and their development: A reply to Piaget. As well as other contributions to the Abbay de Royaumont debate (October 1975). In Piattelli-Palmarini (ed.) 1983.

Chomsky, N. 1986. *Knowledge of Language: Its Nature, Origin and Use.* New York: Praeger.

Chomsky, N. 1987a. *Language in a Psychological Setting.* (Sophia Linguistica 22). Tokyo: The Graduate School of Languages and Linguistics.

Chomsky, N. 1987b. Generative Grammar: Its Basis, Development and Prospects. *S.E.L.L.* (Special Issue of Bulletin of English Department). Japan: Kyoto University.

Chomsky, N. 1987c. Language and problems of knowledge. Revised version of paper delivered at a conference in Madrid, 28 April 1986.

Chomsky, N. 1987d. Interview. In Peck (ed.) 1987: 2–55.

Chomsky, N. 1988a. *Language and Problems of Knowledge.* Cambridge, Mass.: MIT Press.

Chomsky, N. 1988b. A personal view. Paper presented at conference session *Linguistics and Adjacent Fields: the State of the Art*, Israel, April 1988. Published in Kasher (ed.) 1991: 3–25.

Chomsky, N. 1988c. Prospects for the study of language and mind. Paper presented at conference session *Linguistics and Adjacent Fields: the*

State of the Art, Israel, April 1988. Published in Kasher (ed.) 1991: 26–53.

Chomsky, N. 1988d. Language and interpretation: philosophical reflections and empirical inquiry. Contribution to University of Pittsburgh Series of Philosophy of Science.

Chomsky, N. 1989. Mental constructions and social reality. Paper delivered at conference on Knowledge and Language held in Groningen, May 1989.

Chomsky, N. 1990. On formalization and formal linguistics. *Natural Language and Linguistic Theory* 8: 143–7.

Chomsky, N. and Halle, M. 1968. *The Sound Pattern of English*. New York: Harper and Row.

Chomsky, N. and Katz, J. J. 1974. What the linguist is talking about. *Journal of Philosophy* 71: 347–67.

Churchland, P. S. 1986. *Neurophilosophy. Toward a Unified Science of the Mind-brain*. Cambridge, Mass.: MIT Press.

Cohen, D. (ed.) 1974. *Explaining Linguistic Phenomena*. Washington, DC: Hemisphere.

Cohen, L. J. 1979 Review of Popper and Eccles, *The Self and its Brain* (1977). *Mind* 88: 301–4.

Cooper, D. E. 1972. Innateness: old and new. *Philosophical Review* 81: 465–83.

Cooper, D. E. 1975. *Knowledge of Language*. London: Prism Press.

Corder, S. 1981. *Error Analysis and Interlanguage*. Oxford: Oxford University Press.

Cromer, R. F. 1980. Empirical evidence in support of non-empiricist theories of mind. *The Behavioral and Brain Sciences* 3: 16–18.

Crystal, D. 1985. *A Dictionary of Linguistics and Phonetics*. Oxford: Basil Blackwell.

Cummins, R. and Harnish, R. 1980. The language faculty and the interpretation of linguistics. *The Behavioral and Brain Sciences* 3: 18–19.

D'Agostino, F. 1986. *Chomsky's System of Ideas*. Oxford: Clarendon Press.

Danto, A. 1969. Semantical vehicles, understanding and innate ideas. In Hook (ed.) 1969b: 122–37.

Davidson, D. 1986. A nice derangement of epitaphs. In LePore (ed.) 1986: 433–46.

Davis, P. W. 1973. *Modern Theories of Language*. Englewood Cliffs, NJ: Prentice-Hall.

Davis, S. 1976. *Philosophy and Language*. Indianapolis: Bobbs-Merrill.

Dennett, D. C. 1978. *Brainstorms. Philosophical Essays on Mind and Psychology*. Hassocks, Sussex: Harvester Press.

Dennett, D. C. 1979. Review of Popper and Eccles, *The Self and its Brain* (1977). *The Journal of Philosophy* 76: 91–7.

Dennett, D. C. 1984. Carving the mind at its joints. A review of Fodor, *The Modularity of Mind* (1983). *Contemporary Psychology* 29: 285–6.

Dik, S. C. 1983. *Progress in Linguistics* (Publikaties Instituut voor Algemene Taalwetenschap, No. 41). Amsterdam.

Dillinger, M. 1984a. Review of Katz, *Language and Other Abstract Objects* (1981). *The British Journal for the Philosophy of Science* 35: 301–3.

Dillinger, M. 1984b. Review of Katz, *Language and Other Abstract Objects* (1981). *Philosophy of Science* 51: 175–6.

Dinneen, F. P. 1967. *An Introduction to General Linguistics.* New York: Holt, Rinehart and Winston.

Dinnsen, P. (ed.) 1979. *Current Approaches to Phonological Theory.* Bloomington: Indiana University Press.

Donegan, P. J. and Stampe, D. 1979. The study of natural phonology. In Dinnsen (ed.) 1979: 126–73.

Doroszewski, W. 1962. *Studia i szkice językoznawcze*, vol. 1. Warsaw: PWN.

Dretske, F. 1974. Explanation in linguistics. In Cohen (ed.) 1974: 21–41.

Dummett, M. 1975. What is a theory of meaning? Part 1. In Guttenplan (ed.) 1975: 97–138.

Dummett, M. 1976. What is a theory of meaning? Part 2. In Evans and McDowell (eds) 1976: 67–137.

Dummett, M. 1978. *Truth and Other Enigmas.* London: Duckworth.

Dummett, M. 1981. Objections to Chomsky. *London Review of Books*, 3–16 September.

Dummett, M. 1986. 'A nice derangement of epitaphs': Some comments on Davidson and Hacking. In LePore (ed.) 1986: 459–76.

Eccles, J. C. 1977. Part 2 of *The Self and its Brain* by K. R. Popper and J. C. Eccles. Berlin: Springer-Verlag.

Edgley, R. 1970. Innate ideas. In Vesey (ed.) 1970: 119–131.

Edwards, P. (ed.) 1967. *The Encyclopedia of Philosophy.* New York and London: Macmillan.

Einstein, A. 1973. *Ideas and Opinions.* London: Souvenir Press.

Epstein, R. 1986. Behaviorism as the praxist views it. *Behavioral and Brain Sciences* 9: 702–3.

Erwin, E. 1978. *Behavior Therapy. Scientific, Philosophical, and Moral Foundations.* Cambridge: Cambridge University Press.

Esper, E. A. 1968. *Mentalism and Objectivism in Linguistics. The Sources of Bloomfield's Psychology of Language.* New York: American Elsevier Company.

Evans, G. and McDowell, J. (eds) 1976. *Truth and Meaning.* London: Oxford University Press.

Feigl, H. 1969. The origin and spirit of logical positivism. In Achinstein and Barker (eds) 1969: 3–24.

Feldman, H., Goldin-Meadow, S. and Gleitman, L. 1978. Beyond Herodotus: the creation of language by linguistically deprived deaf children. In Lock (ed.) 1978: 351–414.

Ferguson, C. A. and DeBose, C. E. 1977. Simplified registers, broken language, and pidginization. In Valdman (ed.) 1977: 99–125.

Feyerabend, Paul. 1987. *Farewell to Reason.* London and New York: Verso.

Fodor, J. A. 1981. *Representations. Philosophical Essays on the Foundations of Cognitive Science.* Brighton: Harvester Press.

Fodor, J. A. 1983. *The Modularity of Mind. An Essay on Faculty Psychology.* Cambridge, Mass.: MIT Press.

Fodor, J. A. 1985a. Some notes on what linguistics is about. In Katz (ed.) 1985: 146–60.

Fodor, J. A. 1985b. Précis of *The Modularity of Mind. The Behavioral and Brain Sciences* 8: 1–5, 33–42.

Fodor, J. A., Bever, T. G. and Garrett, M. F. 1974. *The Psychology of Language. An Introduction to Psycholinguistics and Generative Grammar.* New York: McGraw-Hill.

Fodor, J. D., Fodor, J. A. and Garrett, M. F. 1975. The psychological unreality of semantic representations. *Linguistic Inquiry* 6: 515–32.

Frege, G. 1967. *The Basic Laws of Arithmetic.* Berkeley, Calif: University of California Press.

French, P., Uehling, T. and Wettstein, H. K. (eds) 1979. *Contemporary Perspectives in the Philosophy of Language.* Minneapolis: University of Minnesota Press.

Fries, C. G. 1961. The Bloomfieldian school. In Mohrmann et al. (eds) 1961: 196–224.

Gardner, H. 1985. *The Mind's New Science. A History of the Cognitive Revolution.* New York: Basic Books.

Garvin, P. L. (ed.) 1970. *Method and Theory in Linguistics.* The Hague and Paris: Mouton.

George, A. 1987. Review discussion of Chomsky, *Knowledge of Language* (1986). *Mind and Language* 3: 155–64.

George, A. 1989a. How not to become confused about linguistics. In George (ed.) 1989b: 90–110.

George, A. (ed.) 1989b. *Reflections on Chomsky.* Oxford: Basil Blackwell.

Givón, T. 1984. *Syntax: A Functional-Typological Introduction.* Amsterdam: Benjamins.
Gleitman, L. and Wanner, E. 1982. Language acquisition: state of the art. In Wanner and Gleitman (eds) 1982.
Goldin-Meadow, S. and Mylander, C. 1990. Beyond the input given: the child's role in the acquisition of language. *Language* 66: 323–55.
Goldman, A. I. 1975. Innate knowledge. In Stich (ed.) 1975: 111–20.
Goodman, N. 1984a. *Of Minds and Other Matters.* Cambridge and London: Harvard University Press.
Goodman, N. 1984b. *Ways of Worldmaking.* Indianapolis: Hackett.
Goodman, N. and Quine, W. V. 1947. Steps toward a constructive nominalism. *The Journal of Symbolic Logic* 12: 105–22.
Goyvaerts, D. L. and Pullum, G. K. (eds) 1975. *Essays on the Sound Pattern of English.* Ghent: E. Story-Scientia.
Gross, C. G. 1985. On Gall's reputation and some recent 'new phrenology'. *The Behavioral and Brain Sciences* 8: 16–18.
Gunderson, K. (ed.) 1975. *Language, Mind and Knowledge. Minnesota Studies in the Philosophy of Science* 7. Minneapolis: University of Minnesota Press.
Guttenplan, S. (ed.) 1975. *Mind and Language.* London: Oxford University Press.
Hacking, I. 1986. The parody of conversation. In LePore (ed.) 1986: 447–58.
Hall, R. A. Jr. 1964. *Introductory Linguistics.* Philadelphia and New York: Chilton Books.
Halle, M., Bresnan, J. and Miller, G. A. (eds) 1978. *Linguistic Theory and Psychological Reality.* Cambridge, Mass.: MIT Press.
Halliday, M. A. K. 1973. *Explorations in the Functions of Language.* London: Edward Arnold.
Halliday, M. A. K. 1978. *Language as Social Semiotic. The Social Interpretation of Language and Meaning.* London: Edward Arnold.
Hamlyn, D. W. 1967a. Empiricism. In Edwards (ed.) 1967, vol. 2: 499–504.
Hamlyn, D. W. 1967b. History of epistemology. In Edwards (ed.) 1967, vol. 3: 8–33.
Hamlyn, D. W. 1985. 'Higher criticism' of behaviorism. *The Behavioral and Brain Sciences* 9: 705.
Hampshire, S. 1966. The interpretation of language: words and concepts. In Mace (ed.) 1966: 267–80.
Hanfling, O. 1989. *Wittgenstein's Later Philosophy.* London: Macmillan Press.
Hardy, G. H. 1940. *A Mathematician's Apology.* London: Cambridge University Press.

Harris, Z. S. 1951. *Methods in Structural Linguistics.* Chicago: University of Chicago Press.

Harris, Z. S. 1970. *Papers in Structural and Transformational Linguistics.* Dordrecht: D. Reidel.

Hempel, C. G. 1965a. *Aspects of Scientific Explanation.* New York: Free Press.

Hempel, C. G. 1965b. Empiricist criteria of cognitive significance: problems and changes. In Hempel 1965a: 101–22.

Hempel, C. G. 1969. Logical positivism and the social sciences. In Achinstein and Barker (eds) 1969: 163–94.

Hesse, M. 1967. Laws and theories. In Edwards (ed.) 1967, vol. 4: 404–10.

Hiż, H. and Swiggers, P. 1989. Bloomfield, the logical positivist. Preprint nr. 122. Departement Linguistiek, Katholieke Universiteit Leuven.

Hjelmslev, L. 1936. Contribution to Proceedings of the International Congress of Phonetic Sciences, Cambridge.

Hjelmslev, L. 1947. Structural analysis of language. *Studia Linguistica*, I, 2: 69–78.

Hockett, C. F. 1952. Review of Harris, *Methods in Structural Linguistics* (1951). *American Speech* 27: 117–21.

Hockett, C. F. 1958. *A Course in Modern Linguistics.* New York: Macmillan.

Hockett, C. F. 1961. Linguistic elements and their relations. *Language* 37: 29–53.

Hockett, C. F. 1987. *Refurbishing our Foundations. Elementary Linguistics from an Advanced Point of View.* Amsterdam/Philadelphia: Benjamins.

Hocutt, M. 1986. Zuriff on observability. *The Behavioral and Brain Sciences* 9: 706–7.

Hook, S. 1969a. Empiricism, rationalism, and innate ideas. In Hook (ed.) 1969b: 160–7.

Hook, S. (ed.) 1969b. *Language and Philosophy. A Symposium.* New York: New York University Press.

Hooper, J. B. 1976. *An Introduction to Natural Generative Phonology.* New York: Academic Press.

Hornstein, N. and Lightfoot, D. (eds) 1981. *Explanation in Linguistics. The Logical Problem of Language Acquisition.* London and New York: Longman.

Hudson, R. A. 1980. *Sociolinguistics.* Cambridge: Cambridge University Press.

Hymes, D. 1970. Linguistic method in ethnography: its development in the United States. In Garvin (ed.) 1970: 249–311.

Hymes, D. and Fought, J. 1975. American structuralism. In Sebeok (ed.) 1975: 903–1176.

Inhelder, B., Sinclair, H. and Bovet, M. (eds) 1974. *Learning and the Development of Cognition.* Cambridge, Mass.: Harvard University Press.

Itkonen, E. 1976. Linguistics and empiricalness: answers to criticisms. Publication no. 4 of Department of General Linguistics, University of Helsinki.

Itkonen, E. 1978. *Grammatical Theory and Metascience.* Amsterdam: Benjamins.

Itkonen, E. 1983a. Review of Katz, *Language and Other Abstract Objects* (1981). *Lingua* 60: 238–44.

Itkonen, E. 1983b. *Causality in Linguistic Theory. A Critical Investigation into the Philosophical and Methodological Foundations of 'Non-Autonomous' Linguistics.* London and Canberra: Croom Helm.

Jackendoff, R. 1972. *Semantic Interpretation in Generative Grammar.* Cambridge, Mass.: MIT Press.

Jackendoff, R. 1987. *Consciousness and the Computational Mind.* Cambridge, Mass.: MIT Press.

Johnson, T., Dandeker, C. and Ashworth, C. 1984. *The Structure of Social Theory. Dilemmas and Strategies.* Houndmills, Basingstoke: Macmillan.

Johnson-Laird, P. N. 1988a. *The Computer and the Mind. An Introduction to Cognitive Science.* London: Fontana Press.

Johnson-Laird, P. N. 1988b. *An Introduction to Cognitive Science.* Cambridge, Mass.: Harvard University Press.

Joos, M. (ed.) 1957. *Readings in Linguistics: The Development of Descriptive Linguistics in America Since 1925.* Washington DC: American Council of Learned Societies.

Joseph, J. E. 1990. Ideologizing Saussure: Bloomfield and Chomsky's readings of the *Cours de linguistique générale.* In Joseph and Taylor (eds) 1990: 51–78.

Joseph, J. E. and Taylor, T. J. (eds) 1990. *Ideologies of Language.* London and New York: Routledge.

Kaldewaij, J. 1986. *Structuralisme en Transformationeel Generatieve Grammatica.* Dordrecht/Riverton: Foris Publications.

Kanngiesser, S. 1972. *Aspekte der Synchronen und Diachronen Linguistik.* Tübingen: Niemeyer Verlag.

Kaplan, A. 1964. *The Conduct of Inquiry. Methodology for Behavioral Science.* San Francisco: Chandler Publishing Company.

Kasher, A. (ed.) 1991. *The Chomskyan Turn.* Oxford: Basil Blackwell.

Katz, J. J. 1964. Mentalism in linguistics. *Language* 40: 124–37.

Katz, J. J. 1966. *The Philosophy of Language*. New York: Harper and Row.

Katz, J. J. 1972. *Semantic Theory*. New York: Harper and Row.

Katz, J. J. 1977. The real status of semantic representations. *Linguistic Inquiry* 8: 559–84.

Katz, J. J. 1981. *Language and Other Abstract Objects*. Oxford: Basil Blackwell.

Katz, J. J. 1984. An outline of Platonist grammar. In Bever et al. (eds) 1984: 1–33.

Katz, J. J. (ed.) 1985. *The Philosophy of Linguistics*. Oxford: Oxford University Press.

Katz, J. J. and Bever, T. G. 1977. The fall and rise of empiricism. In Bever and Katz (eds) 1977: 11–64.

Katz, J. J. and Fodor, J. A. 1963. The structure of a semantic theory. *Language* 39: 170–210.

Katz, J. J. and Postal, P. M. 1989. Realism vs. conceptualism in linguistics. Published (1991) in *Linguistics and Philosophy* 14: 515–54.

Kaufman, A. S. 1967. Behaviorism. In Edwards (ed.) 1967, vol. 1: 268–72.

Kay, P. and McDaniel, C. 1979. On the logic of variable rules. *Language in Society* 8: 151–87.

Kenny, A. 1984. *The Legacy of Wittgenstein*. Oxford: Basil Blackwell.

Kintsch, W. 1974. *The Representation of Meaning in Memory*. London: Wiley.

Kitcher, P. 1978. The nativist's dilemma. *The Philosophical Quarterly* 28: 1–16.

Kluckhohn, C. 1949. *Mirror for Man*. New York and Toronto: McGraw-Hill.

Koch, S. 1964. Psychology and emerging conceptions of knowledge as unitary. In Wann (ed.) 1964: 1–41.

Koerner, E. F. K. 1973. *Ferdinand de Saussure. Origin and Development of his Linguistic Thought*. Braunschweig: Vieweg.

Koerner, E. F. K. 1975. European structuralism: early beginnings. In Sebeok (ed.) 1975: 717–827.

Kripke, S. 1982. *Wittgenstein on Rules and Private Language*. Oxford: Basil Blackwell.

Kukenheim, L. 1966. *Esquisse historique de la linguistique française et de ses rapports avec la linguistique générale*, 2nd edn. Leiden: University Press.

Labov, W. 1972. Some principles of linguistic methodology. *Language in Society* 1: 97–120.

Labov. W. 1975. Empirical foundations of linguistic theory. In Austerlitz (ed.) 1975: 77–133.

Labov, W. 1977. *Language in the Inner City: Studies in the Black English Vernacular.* Oxford: Basil Blackwell.

Labov, W. n.d. *What is a linguistic fact?* Lisse: Peter de Ridder Press.

Lachman, R., Lachman, J. L. and Butterfield, E. C. 1979. *Cognitive Psychology and Information Processing: An Introduction.* Hillsdale, NJ: Lawrence Erlbaum Associates.

Lakatos, I. 1968a. Changes in the problem of inductive logic. In Lakatos (ed.) 1968b: 315–417.

Lakatos, I. (ed.) 1968b. *The Problem of Inductive Logic.* Amsterdam: North-Holland Publishing Company.

Lakatos, I. and Musgrave, A. (eds) 1968. *Criticism and the Growth of Knowledge.* Cambridge: Cambridge University Press.

Langendoen, D. T. and Postal, P. M. 1985. *The Vastness of Natural Language.* Oxford: Basil Blackwell.

Leech, G. 1983. *Principles of Pragmatics.* London and New York: Longman.

Leiber, J. 1991. 'Cartesian' Linguistics. In Kasher (ed.) 1991: 150–81.

LePore, E. (ed.) 1986. *Truth and Interpretation. Perspectives on the Philosophy of Donald Davidson.* Oxford: Basil Blackwell.

Lewis, D. 1969. *Convention.* Cambridge: Harvard University Press.

Lewis, D. 1975. Languages and language. In Gunderson (ed.) 1975, 3–35.

Lightfoot, D. 1982. *The Language Lottery: Towards a Biology of Grammars.* Cambridge and London: MIT Press.

Linell, P. 1976. Is linguistics an empirical science? *Studia Linguistica* 30: 77–94.

Lock, A. (ed.) 1978. *Action, Gesture and Symbol: The Emergence of Language.* London: Academic Press.

Loewer, B. and Rey, G. (eds) 1991. *Meaning in Mind. Fodor and his Critics.* Oxford: Basil Blackwell.

Lovejoy, A. O. 1922. The paradox of the thinking behaviorist. *Philosophical Review*: 135–47.

Lyons, J. 1981. *Language and Linguistics. An Introduction.* Cambridge: Cambridge University Press.

Lyons, J. 1991. *Chomsky*, 3rd edn. London: Fontana.

MacCorquodale, K. 1970. On Chomsky's review of Skinner's *Verbal Behavior. Journal of the Experimental Analysis of Behavior* 13: 83–99.

Mace, C. A. 1948–9. Some implications of analytical behaviourism. *Proceedings of the Aristotelian Society* 49: 1–16.

Mace, C. A. (ed.) 1966. *British Philosophy in the Mid-Century. A Cambridge Symposium*, 2nd edn. London: George Allen and Unwin.

Mach, E. 1893. *History and Roots of the Principle of Conservation of Energy.* Chicago: Open Court Publishing Company.

MacQueen, K. 1984. Review of Katz, *Language and Other Abstract Objects* (1981). *Journal of Pragmatics* 8: 411–17.

Malcolm, N. 1986. *Nothing is Hidden. Wittgenstein's Criticism of his Early Thought.* Oxford: Basil Blackwell.

Mandelbaum, D. G. (ed.) 1949. *Selected Writings of Edward Sapir in Language, Culture and Personality.* Berkeley and Los Angeles: University of California Press.

Marshall, J. C. 1984. Multiple perspectives of modularity. *Cognition* 17: 209–42.

Marshall, J. C. 1986. Is behaviorism under stimulus control? *The Behavioral and Brain Sciences* 9: 710.

Matthews, R. J. 1991. Psychological reality of grammars. In Kasher (ed.) 1991: 182–99.

McCawley, J. D. 1967. Sapir's phonological representation. *International Journal of American Linguistics* 33: 106–11.

McGinn, C. 1981. Review of Chomsky, *Rules and Representations* (1980a). *The Journal of Philosophy* 78: 288–98.

McGinn, C. 1984. *Wittgenstein on Meaning. An Interpretation and Evaluation.* Oxford: Basil Blackwell.

Modgil, S. And Modgil, C. (eds) 1987. *Noam Chomsky. Consensus and Controversy.* New York: The Falmer Press.

Mohrmann, C., Sommerfelt, A. and Whatmough, J. (eds) 1961. *Trends in European and American Linguistics.* Utrecht: Spectrum.

Montague, R. 1974. *Formal Philosophy.* New Haven: Yale University Press.

Moravscik, J. M. 1990. *Thought and Language.* London and New York: Routledge.

Mortensen, C. 1978. Review of Popper and Eccles, *The Self and its Brain* (1977). *Australian Journal of Philosophy* 56: 264–6.

Nagel, E. 1961. *The Structure of Science. Problems in the Logic of Scientific Explanation.* London: Routledge and Kegan Paul.

Nagel, T. 1980. *Mortal Questions.* Cambridge: Cambridge University Press.

Newmeyer, F. J. 1980. *Linguistic Theory in America. The First Quarter-Century of Transformational Generative Grammar.* New York: Academic Press.

Newmeyer, F. J. 1983. *Grammatical Theory. Its Limits and its Possibilities.* Chicago and London: University of Chicago Press.

Newmeyer, F. J. 1986. Has there been a 'Chomskyan revolution' in linguistics? *Language* 62: 1–18.

Newmeyer, F. J. (ed.) 1988. *Linguistics: The Cambridge Survey,* vol. III. *Language: Psychological and Biological Aspects.* Cambridge: Cambridge University Press.

Ohala, J. J. 1974. Phonetic explanation in phonology. In Bruck et al. (eds) 1974: 251–74.

Parsons, T. 1968. *The Structure of Social Action*, 2 vols. Glencoe, Ill.: Free Press.

Partee, B. 1979. Montague grammar, mental representation, and reality. In French et al. (eds) 1979: 195–208.

Passmore, J. 1967. Logical positivism. In Edwards (ed.) 1967, vol. 8: 52–7.

Pateman, T. 1983. Review of Katz, *Language and Other Abstract Objects* (1981). *Journal of Linguistics* 19: 282–4.

Pateman, T. 1987. *Language in Mind and Language in Society. Studies in Linguistic Reproduction.* Oxford: Clarendon Press.

Peacocke, C. 1986. Explanation in computational psychology: language, perception and level 1.5. *Mind and Language* 1: 101–23.

Peacocke, C. 1989. When is a grammar psychologically real? In George (ed.) 1989b: 111–30.

Peck, J. (ed.) 1987. *The Chomsky Reader.* New York: Pantheon Books.

Peters, S. (ed.) 1972. *Goals of Linguistic Theory.* Englewood Cliffs, NJ: Prentice-Hall.

Phillips, D. C. 1987. *Philosophy, Science and Social Inquiry. Contemporary Methodological Controversies in Social Science and Related Applied Fields of Research.* Oxford: Pergamon Press.

Piaget, J. 1983. The psychogenesis of knowledge. In Piattelli-Palmarini (ed.) 1983: 23–34.

Piattelli-Palmarini, M. (ed.) 1983. *Language and Learning. The Debate between Jean Piaget and Noam Chomsky.* London: Routledge and Kegan Paul.

Pike, K. L. 1967. *Language in Relation to a Unified Theory of the Structure of Human Behavior.* (*Janua Linguarum, Series Maior* 24.) The Hague and Paris: Mouton.

Pinker, S. 1982. A theory of the acquisition of lexical interpretive grammars. In Bresnan (ed.) 1982: 655–726.

Popkin, R. 1979. *The History of Scepticism from Erasmus to Spinoza.* Berkeley, Calif.: University of California Press.

Popper, K. R. 1965. *The Logic of Scientific Discovery.* New York: Hutchinson.

Popper, K. R. 1969. *Conjectures and Refutations. The Growth of Scientific Knowledge.* London: Routledge and Kegan Paul.

Popper, K. R. 1972. *Objective Knowledge. An Evolutionary Approach.* Oxford: Clarendon Press.

Popper, K. R. 1976. *Unended Quest.* La Salle, Ill.: Open Court.

Popper, K. R. 1977. Part 1 of *The Self and its Brain* by K. R. Popper and J. C. Eccles. Berlin: Springer-Verlag.

Popper, K. R. and Eccles, J. C. 1977. *The Self and its Brain. An Argument for Interactionism.* Berlin: Springer-Verlag. [References to the edition published in 1983 by Routledge and Kegan Paul.]

Postal, P. M. 1972. The best theory. In Peters (ed.) 1972: 131–70.

Putnam, H. 1983. What is innate and why: comments on the debate. In Piattelli-Palmarini (ed.) 1983: 287–309.

Putnam, H. 1984. Models and modules. *Cognition* 17: 253–64.

Pylyshyn, Z. 1984. *Computation and Cognition.* Cambridge, Mass.: MIT Press.

Pylyshyn. Z. 1991. Rules and representations: Chomsky and representational realism. In Kasher (ed.) 1991: 231–51.

Quine, W. V. O. 1960. *Word and Object.* Cambridge, Mass.: MIT Press.

Quine, W. V. O. 1969. Linguistics and philosophy. In Hook (ed.) 1969b: 95–8.

Quine, W. V. O. 1990. *Pursuit of Truth.* Cambridge, Mass. and London: Harvard University Press.

Quinton, A. 1967. British philosophy. In Edwards (ed.) 1967, vol. 1: 369–96.

Rescher, N. 1984. *The Limits of Science.* Berkeley, Calif.: University of California Press.

Rex, J. 1961. *Key Problems of Sociological Theory.* London: Routledge and Kegan Paul.

Rey, G. 1991. Introduction to Loewer and Rey (eds) 1991: xi–xxxvii.

Richards, J., Platt, J. and Weber, H. 1985. *Longman Dictionary of Applied Linguistics.* Harlow: Longman.

Ringen, J. 1975. Linguistic intuition and introspective 'observation'. Paper presented at the LSA Winter Meeting, San Francisco, 28 December 1975.

Robins, R. H. 1967. *A Short History of Linguistics.* Bloomington: Indiana University Press.

Romaine, S. 1985. Why the problem of language acquisition should not be explained logically. *Studies in Language* 9: 255–70.

Rosenberg, S. 1968. Language habits and the recall of connected discourse. In Zale (ed.) 1968: 63–74.

Ross, D. 1990. Against positing central systems in the mind. *Philosophy of Science* 57: 297–312.

Rozeboom, W. W. 1986. Average behaviorism is unedifying. *The Behavioral and Brain Sciences* 9: 712–14.

Ryle, G. 1949. *The Concept of Mind.* London: Hutchinson.

Ryle, G. 1967a. Plato. In Edwards (ed.) 1967, vol. 6: 314–33.

Ryle, G. 1967b. Platonism and the Platonic tradition. In Edwards (ed.) 1967, vol. 6: 333–41.

Salkie, R. 1990. *The Chomsky Update. Linguistics and Politics.* London: Unwin Hyman.

Salverda, R. 1985. *Leading Conceptions in Linguistic Theory.* Dordrecht: Cinnaminson.

Salzinger, K. 1967. The problem of response class in verbal behavior. In Salzinger and Salzinger (eds) 1967: 35–54.

Salzinger, K. and Feldman, R. (eds) 1973. *Studies in Verbal Behavior: An Empirical Approach.* New York: Pergamon Press.

Salzinger, K. and Salzinger, S. (eds) 1967. *Research in Verbal Behavior and some Neurophysiological Implications.* New York: Academic Press.

Sampson, G. 1975. *The Form of Language.* London: Weidenfeld.

Sapir, E. 1921. *Language.* New York: Harcourt.

Sapir, E. 1949a. The status of linguistics as a science. In Mandelbaum (ed.) 1949: 160–6.

Sapir, E. 1949b. Language. In Mandelbaum (ed.) 1949: 7–32.

Sapir, E. 1949c. Sound patterns in language. In Mandelbaum (ed.) 1949: 33–45.

Sapir, E. 1949d. The psychological reality of phonemes. In Mandelbaum (ed.) 1949: 46–60.

Sapir, E. 1949e. Language and environment. In Mandelbaum (ed.) 1949: 89–103.

Saussure, F. de 1916. *Cours de Linguistique Générale.* Paris: Payot.

Saussure, F. de 1983. *Course in General Linguistics.* Translated and annotated by Roy Harris. London: Duckworth.

Schnaitter, R. 1986. The gentrification of behaviorism. *Behavioral and Brain Sciences* 9: 714–15.

Scriven, M. 1969. Logical positivism and the behavioral sciences. In Achinstein and Barker (eds) 1969: 195–209.

Searle, J. R. 1976. Discussion in *Times Literary Supplement,* 10 September 1976.

Sebeok, T. A. (ed.) 1975. *Current Trends in Linguistics,* vol. 13. *Historiography of Linguistics.* The Hague: Mouton.

Shallice, T. 1984. More functionally isolable subsystems but fewer modules. *Cognition* 17: 243–52.

Shaphere, D. 1969. Notes towards a postpositivistic interpretation of science. In Achinstein and Barker (eds) 1969: 115–60.

Shuy, R. and Bailey, C.-J. (eds) 1974. *Towards Tomorrow's Linguistics.* Washington, DC: Georgetown University Press.

Silverstein, M. (ed.) 1971. *Whitney on Language. Selected Writings of William Dwight Whitney.* Cambridge, Mass.: MIT Press.

Skinner, B. F. 1957. *Verbal Behavior.* New York: Appleton-Century-Crofts.

Skinner, B. F. 1964. Behaviorism at fifty. In Wann (ed.) 1964: 79–97.

Slezak, P. (ed.) 1989. *Computers, Brains and Minds. Essays in Cognitive Science.* Dordrecht: Kluwer.

Smith, N. 1989. *The Twitter Machine. Reflections on Language.* Oxford: Basil Blackwell.

Snow, C. E. and Ferguson, C. A. (eds) 1977. *Talking to Children: Language Input and Acquisition.* Cambridge: Cambridge University Press.

Soames, S. 1985. Semantics and psychology. In Katz (ed.) 1985: 204–26.

Spence, N. C. W. 1957. A hardy perennial: the problem of *la langue* and *la parole. Archivum Linguisticum* 9: 1–27.

Stark, B. R. 1972. The Bloomfieldian model. *Lingua* 30: 385–421.

Steinberg, D. D. 1975. Chomsky: from formalism to mentalism and psychological invalidity. *Glossa* 9: 218–52.

Steiner, M. 1973. Platonism and the causal theory of knowledge. *The Journal of Philosophy* 70: 57–66.

Steiner, M. 1975. *Mathematical Knowledge.* Ithaca and London: Cornell University Press.

Stern, K. 1969. Neorationalism and empiricism. In Hook (ed.) 1969b: 191–7.

Stich, S. P. (ed.) 1975. *Innate Ideas.* Berkeley and Los Angeles: University of California Press.

Stich, S. P. 1978. Empiricism, innateness, and linguistic universals. *Philosophical Studies* 33: 273–85.

Stich, S. P. 1985. Grammar, psychology and indeterminacy. In Katz (ed.) 1985: 126–45.

Suppe, F. (ed.) 1974. *The Structure of Scientific Theories.* Urbana: University of Illinois Press.

Swadesh, M. 1935. Twaddell on defining the phoneme. *Language* 11: 244–50.

Taylor, C. 1967. Psychological behaviorism. In Edwards (ed.) 1967, vol. 6: 516–20.

Teeter, K. V. 1964. Descriptive linguistics in America: triviality vs. irrelevance. *Word* 20: 197–206.

Twaddell, F. W. 1935. *On Defining the Phoneme.* Language Monograph 16. Baltimore: Linguistic Society of America.

Twaddell, F. W. 1949. Meanings, habits and rules. *Language Learning* 2: 4–11.

Urmson, J. O. 1967. Gilbert Ryle. In Edwards (ed.) 1967, vol. 7: 269–71.

Valdman, A. (ed.) 1977. *Pidgins and Creoles.* London and Boston: Routledge and Kegan Paul.

Vendryes, J. 1952. *Choix d'Etudes Linguistiques et Celtiques*. Paris: C. Klincksieck.

Vennemann, T. 1974. Phonetic concreteness in natural generative phonology. In Shuy and Bailey (eds) 1974: 202–19.

Vesey, G. N. A. (ed.) 1970. *Knowledge and Necessity*. London: Macmillan.

Wann, T. W. (ed.) 1964. *Behaviorism and Phenomenology. Contrasting Bases for Modern Psychology*. Chicago: University of Chicago Press.

Wanner, E. and Gleitman, L. (eds) 1982. *Language Acquisition: The State of the Art*. Cambridge: Cambridge University Press.

Wardhaugh, R. 1986. *An Introduction to Sociolinguistics*. Oxford: Basil Blackwell.

Watkins, J. W. N. 1968. Non-inductive corroboration. In Lakatos and Musgrave (eds) 1968: 61–6.

Wells, R. S. 1947. De Saussure's system of linguistics. *Word* 3: 1–31.

Wells, R. S. 1969. Innate knowledge. In Hook (ed.) 1969b: 99–119.

Wexler, K. 1991. On the argument from the poverty of the stimulus. In Kasher (ed.) 1991: 252–70.

Whiteley, C. H. 1961. II. Behaviourism. *Mind* 70: 164–74.

Whitney, W. D. 1971. Language and the study of language. In Silverstein (ed.) 1971: 7–110.

Wiest, W. A. 1967. Some recent criticisms of behaviorism and learning theory. *Psychological Bulletin* 67: 214–25.

Wittgenstein, L. 1922. *Tractatus Logico-philosophicus*. Translated by C. K. Ogden. London: Routledge and Kegan Paul.

Wittgenstein, L. 1967. *Philosophical Investigations*, 2nd edn. Translated by G. E. M. Anscombe. Oxford: Basil Blackwell.

Wolfram, W. and Fasold, R. W. 1974. *The Study of Social Dialects in American English*. Englewood Cliffs, NJ: Prentice-Hall.

Woozley, A. D. 1967. Universals. In Edwards (ed.) 1967, vol. 8: 194–206.

Wright, C. 1983. *Frege's Conception of Numbers as Objects*. Aberdeen: Aberdeen University Press.

Wunderlich, D. 1979. *Foundations of Linguistics*. Cambridge: Cambridge University Press.

Zale, E. M. (ed.) 1968. *Proceedings of the Conference on Language and Language Behavior*. New York: Appleton-Century-Crofts.

Zuriff, G. E. 1985. *Behaviorism: A Conceptual Reconstruction*. New York: Columbia University Press.

Zuriff, G. E. 1986. Précis of *Behaviorism: A Conceptual Reconstruction*. *Behavioral and Brain Sciences* 9: 687–724.

Index

ability, 77, 107, 131
  to use language, 88, 223, 225
abstract concept/notion, 104
abstract object, 21, 91, 93, 150–8, 161, 162, 166–7, 169–70, 172–5, 189, 294n, 298n
abstracted object, 92, 93, 152
abstraction(s), 92, 93
  see also idealization
Achinstein, P., 271n
actions/activities, 83
actual object, 153
aesthetic product, 214–15
Akmajian, A., 296n
Allan, K., 175, 273n, 297n, 298n
Alston, W. P., 279n
American structuralist conception of language, 141, 162–3
anamnesis, 109
analytic/logical entailment, 132–3, 138, 160, 161, 162, 178, 293n
analytical behaviourism, 53–4, 63, 70, 281n
analyticity, 160–1, 162, 178, 293n
Anderson, S. R., 290n
animism, 6–7, 15, 30, 270n
Anrade, M. J., 272n
anti-mentalism, 7, 15, 38, 40, 45, 71
anti-metaphysicalism, 71
Aquinas, T., 270n
Arbib, M. A., 291n
Ardila, R., 302n, 309n
Ashby, R. W., 16, 271n, 272n
Augustine, A., 270n
Austin, J. L., 59, 280n, 282n
autonomous/objective object, 184, 189
autonomy of existence, 183–5

baby talk, 125, 292n
Bach, E., 30, 273n, 289n
Bacon, F., 30
Baconian induction, 30–1
Baker, G. P., 60–1, 280n, 281n, 282n
Bar-Hillel, Y., 272n
Barker, F., 271n
behaviour, 36–7, 173–4, 284n
  as evidence, 233
  biological, 218
  communicative, 274n
  cultural, 40, 214–15, 218
  individual, 218
  intentional, 231
  as rule-following, 230
  social, 76, 218, 230
  symbolic, 43
  verbal, 37, 43ff., 68
  vocal, 44
  see also language behaviour
behaviour potential, 76
behavioural conception of language, 36–43
behaviourism
  bases and general characteristics, 53, 70–4, 277n, 284n
  analytical, 53–4, 63, 70, 281n
  classical, 54

eliminative, 54, 276n
inter-, 54, 277n
logical, 53–4, 232
mediation-theoretical, 54, 277n
meta-scientific, 40
metaphysical, 281n
methodological, 54, 277n, 281n
molar, 54, 276n
molecular, 54, 276n
neo-, 54, 279n
neo-neo-, 54
philosophical, 53–4, 63
psychological, 8–9, 51, 54, 70, 275n
purposive, 54, 277n
radical, 54, 276n, 277n, 279n
reconstructed, 54
reflexological, 54, 276n
scientific, 54
S-R, 50, 276n
substantive, 40
behaviourist
conception of language, 36, 43ff., 60, 100, 261, 262, 277n, 278n
epistemology, 72, 283n
psychology, 8, 9, 51, 70, 83, 94, 101–2
radical, 43
see also behaviourism
view of science, 18
belief, justified, 126
Beloff, J., 193, 194
Berry, M., 309n
Bever, T. G., 149, 287n, 295n, 299n
Bhaskar, R., xiii, 238
Bickerton, D., 208, 209, 235, 285n, 292n, 304n
Bierwisch, M., 273n
biological linguistic endowment, 87, 99
Bloomfield, L., 4, 5, 6, 7, 8, 9, 10, 12, 14, 15, 16, 18, 19, 21, 22, 28, 31, 39, 41, 42, 83, 270n, 273n, 274n, 285n, 294n, 305n, 312n
Bloomfield's mentalism, 6–7
Bloomfieldian
conception of language, 4ff., 83, 100, 180, 253, 261
linguistics, 32, 273n
body
Chomsky's view of, 95–6
Cartesian notion of, 95, 143
v. mind, 94, 143
as a physical entity, 95
Bohr, N., 27
Bolinger, D. L., 37, 274n
Bolzano, B., 300n–1n
Botha, R. P., 180, 196, 272n, 273n, 276n, 284n, 285n, 286n, 287n, 288n, 289n, 291n, 292n, 293n, 295n, 296n, 299n, 300n, 301n, 305n, 310n, 311n, 312n
brain, 94, 143
Bresnan, J., 116, 117, 290n, 291n
bridge law, 144
Bridgman, P. W., 271n
Bunge, M., xiii, 3, 11, 18, 75, 245, 270n, 271n, 272n, 283n, 288n, 302n, 309n, 310n, 311n
Burton-Roberts, N. C., 190
Butler, C. S., 309n

Cam, P., 290n, 291n
Campbell, K., 10, 270n
capacity, 69, 77
to use language, 88
caretaker speech, 125, 292n
Carnap, R., 15, 271n
Carr, P., 169, 172, 174, 188, 189, 190, 191, 192, 194, 195, 196, 273n, 287n, 295n, 297n, 299n, 301n, 307n
Carston, R., 114, 290n, 291n
Cartesian dualism, 53–4, 63, 95–6, 107–8, 112, 143, 283n
causal explanation, 7, 9
causal interaction, 152, 184–5, 193–4
see also interactionism
central processors/systems, 113, 114, 115, 118
Chomsky, N., 11, 19, 20, 31, 45–51, 54, 56, 57, 68, 69, 77, 81–113, 117, 118, 119, 121–47, 168, 170, 171, 172, 189, 195, 212, 220–7, 229, 230, 232–7, 246, 249, 250–3, 255, 257, 260, 264, 267, 268, 272n, 273n, 275n, 276n, 277n, 278n, 280n, 282n,

284n, 285n, 286n, 287n, 288n, 289n, 290n, 291n, 292n, 293n, 294n, 295n, 296n, 297n, 298n, 299n, 300n, 305n, 306n
Chomsky's view of (the)
body, 95–6, 143–4
dualism, 95–6, 98
innateness, 108–9
language: *see* Chomskyan conception of language
language acquisition, 50, 87–8, 108–9, 140–1, 211–12, 223–4
linguistic reality, 89, 143–4, 226, 290n
linguistic variation, 136
mind, 94–7, 107–8, 143–4
rules of language/grammar, 88, 129, 189, 190, 195
science, 69, 103–6, 143–4, 226
sentences, 138–9, 290n, 294n
world, 88, 226, 227
Chomsky's epistemology, 104–5
ontology, 113, 141
Chomskyan conception of language, 80ff., 143–4, 162–3, 195, 199, 230, 232, 251–3, 259–61, 264–5, 290n
mentalism, 94, 101–5, 143–4, 191–2, 195, 196, 199, 259–60, 264–5, 290n, 295n, 299n–300n, 301n, 311n, 312n
'Chomskyan' v. 'Chomsky's', 285n
Churchland, P. S., 289n, 295n
classical behaviourism, 54
classification(s), 24–5
cognitive revolution, 101, 103, 110
see also conceptual shifts: first
cognitive status of theories, 26–8
cognitive system, 89, 91, 94, 100, 287n
cognizing (v. knowing), 127
Cohen, L. J., 193, 194
common (v. private), 234
common sense conception of language, 81, 82–3, 145, 171–2, 221, 226–7, 285n
community
social, 223, 226
see also language community; speech community
competence: *see* linguistic competence
conception of language: characteristics
conditions/standards for, 33–4, 145–6, 160, 179–81, 191–3, 197, 240–2, 255–9, 282n
properties of, 2–4, 33, 65–7, 76–7, 145–6, 259
conception of language: distinctions
v. dictionary definition, 3, 270n
v. linguistic epistemology/ methodology, 3, 263–4, 312n
see also epistemology and ontology
v. linguistic ontology, 3, 263–4, 312n
see also ontology and epistemology
v. theory of linguistic structure, 3, 259, 282n
conception(s) of language: diversity
American structuralist, 141, 162–3
Bloomfieldian, 4ff., 83, 100, 180, 253, 261
behavioural, 36–43
behaviourist, 36, 43ff., 60, 100, 261, 262, 277n, 278n
Chomskyan, 80ff., 143–4, 162–3, 195, 199, 230, 232, 251–3, 259–61, 264–5, 290n
conceptualist, 289n
see also Chomskyan conception of language
cultural, 40
common-sense, 81, 82, 83, 145, 172–3, 221, 226–7, 285n
Davidson's, 267, 312n
Dummet's, 220ff., 281n
E-language, 83–5, 89, 139, 140, 145, 146, 170–1, 181, 286n
Firthian, 76–7
Fodor's, 111–19, 291n
Halliday's, 76–7, 241–2, 308n–9n
Hamboldt's, 110–11, 289n
I-language: *see* Chomskyan conception of language
Itkonen's, 230ff., 307n
Katz's: *see* Platonist/realist conception of language

materialist/physicalist, 4ff., 180, 261, 262
see also Bloomfieldian conception of language
mentalist: *see* Chomskyan conception of language; Fodor's conception of language; Sapir's conception of language, Saussure's conception of language; Wundt's conception of language
nominalist, 271n
see also Bloomfieldian conception of language
ordinary language philosophers', 61ff., 280n–1n
Pateman's, 227ff.
Platonist/realist, 148ff., 197–8, 261, 262, 263, 293n
Popperian, 183ff., 261, 262, 263
post-Bloomfieldian, 36ff., 261, 262
pre-theoretical, 254
principles-and-parameters, 88, 129, 140
private language, 232–3
Quine's (dispositional), 68–70, 283n
realist: *see* Platonist/realist conception of language
Sapir's, 211ff.
Saussurean, 83, 202ff., 226
Skinnerian, 163ff., 180
social, 59, 81, 199ff., 262
technical, 83, 86
Wittgensteinian, 59ff., 220, 262, 280n, 282n
Wundt's, 7
first, 86, 101, 102, 260, 288n, 294n
second, 88, 140, 260, 288n, 289n
conceptualism, 113, 141, 150, 162, 163, 216, 290n
see also mentalism
conceptualist conception of language, 289n
see also Chomskyan conception of language
conceptual shifts in Chomskyan linguistics
consentement collectif, 202, 203
convention, 220m 235
see also social conventions
constructivism, 123–5
Cooper, D., 292n
Corder, S., 236
Courtenay, B. de, 303n
creative aspect of language use, 19, 49–50, 99–100, 101, 260, 277n
creole (language), 235–6
criteria for linguistic theories
conceptual homogeneity/ parsimony, 246
deductive depth, 182, 252
factual coverage, 167, 181, 300n
parameter-fixing considerations, 195
poverty of the stimulus considerations, 195, 251
restrictiveness, 246, 250–2
simplicity, 167, 181, 182, 300n
truth: *see* truth
unifying power, 182, 252
Cromer, R. F., 125
cross-linguistic generalizations, 286n
see also linguistic universals
Crystal, D., 304n
cultural conception of language, 40
culture, 183, 211–13
innate form of, 213
custom, 223

D'Agostino, F., 292n
Danto, A., 292n
Darwin, C., 271n, 309n
Davidson, D., 312n
conception of language, 267, 312n
Davis, P. W., 39, 273n, 274n
Davis, S., 128
DeBose, C. E., 292n
deep structure, 246
Dennett, D. C., 48, 51, 52, 114, 119, 131, 132, 192, 193, 194, 196, 275n, 291n
Descartes, 63, 108, 112, 289n, 297n, 309n
descriptive linguistics, 83
Dewey, J., 271n
dialect (v. language), 81, 206

Diderot, D., 271n
Dik, S. C., 205
Dillinger, M., 168, 175, 177, 299n
Dinneen, F. P., 303n
discrete infinity of language, 110, 289n, 294n
dispositions (to verbal behaviour), 68–9, 77, 283n
Donegan, P. J., 191
Doroszewski, W., 205, 303n
Dretske, F., 292n
drift
  of culture, 214
  of language, 214
dualism, 288n
  Cartesian view of, 53–4, 63, 95
  Chomsky's view of, 95–6, 98
  Popper's view of, 192
Dummett, M., 220–6, 233, 235, 271n, 282n, 305n, 306n, 312n
  conception of language, 220ff., 281n
Durkheim, E., 205, 209, 238, 303n

Eccles, J. C., 192, 193, 301n
ecumenicism, ontological, 249
Edgley, R., 126
effability of language, 154, 296n
Einstein, A., 27, 31, 273n, 309n
E-language, 83, 88, 110, 130, 170, 255
  conception of language, 83–5, 89, 139, 140, 145, 146, 170–1, 181, 286n
  grammar of an, 83–4
eliminative behaviourism, 54, 267n
emergent(ist) materialism, 270n, 271n
empiricism, 30, 72, 238, 307n
  see also logical positivism
entailment, analytic/logical, 132–3, 138, 160, 161, 162, 178, 293n
epistemology
  behaviourist, 72, 283n
  Chomsky's, 104–5
    see also Chomsky's view of science
  empiricist, 72
  linguistic, 3, 76, 189
  and ontology, 263–4, 312n
  Platonist/realist, 150–7, 165–8, 172–5, 179, 181, 186, 197, 247, 248
  Popperian, 185–6, 189, 192–4
Epstein, R., 55
Erwin, E., 58
Esper, E., 8, 9, 14, 20, 270n
ésprit collectif, 202, 203, 305n
essence/essential properties of language, 2–3, 60–1, 64, 77, 154–7, 280n, 282n, 296n
evidence for linguistic theories, 129–31, 134, 135
  see also informant judgements; introspection; linguistic evidence
experience in language acquisition, 87, 109, 124–6, 212, 224
externalized language: *see* E-language

fact, a
  biological, 309n
  linguistic, 306n–7n
  social, 306n–7n, 309n
faculté linguistique, 204
Fasold, R. W., 208
Feigl, H., 271n
Feldman, H., 236
Ferguson, C. A., 292n
Feyerabend, P. K., 272n
fiction(s), 23, 24, 28
  convenient, 14, 25, 27
  descriptive, 22–3, 216
  theoretical, 210
Firth, J. R., 76
  conception of language, 76–7
fluency, 38
Fodor, Janet, 116
Fodor, Jerry A., 11, 41, 111–19, 121, 136, 142–5, 176, 178, 179, 189, 196, 246–8, 274n, 289n, 290n, 291n, 292n, 295n, 297n, 300n
  conception of language, 111–19, 291n
Fought, J., 30, 39, 212, 213, 219, 273n, 274n, 305n
freedom from stimulus control, 19, 47–8, 99, 100, 103, 260, 276n
  see also language behaviour

Frege, G., 161, 162, 292n
Freud, S., 270n
Fries, C. G., 273n

Gall, F. J., 290n
Gardner, H., 111, 112, 139, 147, 289n
Garret, M., 116
generalizations
  linguistically significant, 191–2
  Wittgensteinian view of, 66–7
generative enterprise, 189, 190, 195
generative grammar, 56, 101, 110, 210
generative semantics, 246–7
generative procedure, 91, 110, 306n
genetic language programme, 87, 109, 122
  see also innate linguistic endowment
genetic linguistic endowment: *see* innate linguistic endowment
George, A., 117, 294n
ghost in the machine, 69, 72, 283n
Giddens, A., 238
Givón, T., 191
Gleitman, L., 292n
Goldin-Meadow, S., 236
Goldman, A., 292n
Goodman, N., 271n, 289n
Goyvaerts, D. L., 301n
grammar, (a/an): kinds
  E-language, 83–4
  generative, 56, 101, 110, 210
  internalized, 49
  internally represented, 119, 300n
  lexical-functional, 116–17
  mental, 84, 290n
  particular, 88, 89, 93, 155–6
  structuralist, 84
  taxonomic, 29, 31
  traditional, 84
  transformational, 250
  universal, 84, 87, 89, 93, 286n, 294n
grammar
  ambiguity of Chomskyan term, 294n
  knowledge of, 88
  Wittgensteinian view of, 62, 279n–80n
grammatical theory, 155–8
  see also linguistic theory
grammatical universal: *see* linguistic universal
Gross, C. G., 290n

habit, 37–8, 77, 204, 275n
  formation, 9
  and language, 38
  oral-auditory, 38
  post-Bloomfieldian notion of, 42
  and speech, 38
Hacker, P. M. S., 60, 61, 280n, 281n
Hacking, I., 312n
Hall, R. A., 37, 38, 40, 274n
Halle, M., 288n
Halliday, M. A. K., 76, 77, 201, 241, 284n, 285n, 308n, 309n
  conception of language, 76–7, 241–2, 308n–9n
Hamlyn, D. W., 57, 59, 271n, 289n
Hampshire, S., 61
Hanfling, O., 281n
Hardy, G., 299n
Harnish, R., 113
Harris, R., 302n
Harris, Z. S., 5, 14, 24, 25, 30, 250, 272n, 310n
Heisenberg, W., 27
Hempel, C. G., 17, 54
Hesse, M., 273n
heuristic fruitfulness, 20, 34, 175–6, 180–1, 191–2, 256, 259–61
Hiz, H., 271n
Hjelmslev, L., 295n
Hobbes, T., 53
Hockett, C. F., 37, 38, 272n, 273n
Hocutt, C. F., 284n
Hook, S., 292n
Hooper, J. B., 191
Hudson, R. A., 271n
Humboldt, W. von, 107, 110, 289n
Hume, D., 271n
Hymes, D., 30, 39, 212, 213, 219, 273n, 274n, 305n
hypercorrection, 228

idealism, 237–8
idealization, 153, 226, 229, 254
 of a homogeneous speech community, 137
 of an ideal speaker-listener, 137, 153
 langue, 203–4
idiolect, 207, 304n
I-language, 84ff., 91, 105, 110, 129, 130, 131, 138, 139, 170, 195, 236, 294n
independent variable, 43
indifference, ontological, 244
inductivism, 29ff.
informant judgements, 131, 134, 135, 136, 140, 160, 178, 195, 233, 278n
 see also intuition; introspection
Inhelder, B., 132, 291n
innate linguistic endowment/innateness, 86, 87, 109, 122–7
 Cartesian notion of, 107, 109
 Chomskyan notion of, 108–9
 and language acquisition, 50, 109
 Platonist notion of, 173
 Sapir's view of, 213
 see also knowledge of language, innate; nativism
input systems/analysers, 113–14, 115, 116, 118
instrumentalism, 26–8, 72, 73, 273n
intention, 231
intentional behaviour, 231
interactionism, Popperian, 193–4, 197–8, 302n
interbehaviourism, 54, 277n
interlanguage, 236
internalized grammar, an, 49
internalized language: *see* I-language
interpretive semantics, 246–7
introspection, 127, 128, 165–6, 278
 v. intuition, 130, 165–6
 v. perception, 165–6
intuition
 Cartesian, 297n
 faculty of, 173–4
 intellectual, 150–1, 165–7, 169–70, 185
 v. introspection, 130
 Kantian, 166–7, 172–4, 197
 Katz's theory of, 173–4, 299n
 linguistic, 129–30, 178–9, 194, 195, 196, 247–8, 278n
 v. perception, 165–6
 Platonic, 166, 185
 see also informant judgements; introspection
Itkonen, E., 230–7, 292n, 298n, 303n, 305n, 307n
 conception of language, 230ff., 307n

Jackendoff, R., 288n, 291n, 310n
James, W., 271n
Jespersen, O., 92
Johnson, T., 237, 238, 239, 271n, 307n
Johnson-Laird, P. N., 278n, 290n
Joos, M., 84, 272n
Joseph, J. E., 241
Jung, C. G., 128

Kaldewaij, J., 202, 203, 204, 206, 211, 273n, 274n, 302n, 305n
Kanngiesser, S., 271n
Kant, I., 299n
Kantian intuition, 166–7, 172–4, 197
Kaplan, A., 273n
Kaplan, R. M., 290
Kasher, A., 311n
Katz, J., 2, 5, 6, 12, 14, 19, 20, 23, 24, 25, 29, 60, 63, 64–7, 112, 113, 116, 119, 132–42, 149, 151–83, 189, 192, 200, 211, 246, 247, 249, 250, 264, 270n, 271n, 279n, 281n, 282n, 285n, 287n, 291n, 292n, 293n, 295n, 296n, 297n, 298n, 299n, 301n, 302n, 305n, 310n
 conception of language: *see* Platonist/realist conception of language
Kaufman, A. S., 53, 54, 73, 276n, 281n, 283n, 284n
Kay, P., 206, 304n
Kenny, A., 131, 224, 306n
Kintsch, W., 117
Kitcher, P., 283n

Kluckhohn, C., 40
knowing (v. cognizing), 127
as action, 231
as evidence (v. criterion) for, 233
knowledge: forms
a posteriori, 165
a priori, 88, 150, 165
caused, 88
common, 231, 235
conscious, 127
individual, 233
innate, 108–9
justified, 126
linguistic: *see* knowledge of language
mutual, 90
objective, 183, 190
positive, 71
practical, 220–1, 225
propositional, 126
social, 231
theoretical, 220–1
unconscious, 127–8
knowledge
knowledge of language, 69, 77, 86–7, 88, 101, 102, 109, 122, 131, 140, 164, 222–3, 230, 284n–5n, 309n
v. ability to use language, 224–5, 306n
atheoretical, 231
common, 231, 234
individual, 233, 234
innate, 109, 126–7, 208, 292n
see also innate (linguistic) endowment
v. language, 90–3, 141, 162–3, 168–70, 176, 197
partial, 222–3, 232
social, 230
(un)certain, 231
(un)conscious/tacit, 88, 122, 126, 127, 128, 307n
Koch, S., 56, 57, 58, 73, 75, 277n, 278n, 283n
Koerner, E. F. K., 201, 202, 203, 205, 302n, 303n
Kripke, S., 233, 280n
Kukenheim, L., 303n
Labov, W., 207, 208, 209, 210, 292n, 304n
Lachman, R., 275n, 277n, 278n
Lakatos, I., 273n, 309n
langage, le, 202, 302n
Langendoen, D. T., 149, 154, 287n, 290n, 296n
language, (a): conceived
as abstract (Platonic) object, 91, 138, 148ff., 261, 262, 263, 298n
as abstracted entity, 92, 93, 97
as activity/behaviour, 35ff., 308n
see also language behaviour
as art, 308n
as autonomous object, 183ff., 219, 253, 261, 262
as activity/behaviour, 35ff., 280
as cognitive system, 89, 91, 100, 287n
as common-knowledge rules, 230
as contingent feature of mind/brains, 138
as conventions, 220
as cultural object/product, 186, 211ff., 215
as formal logical calculus, 279n
as generative procedure, 91, 110, 306n
as input system, 115–19, 291n
as intentional object of mutual belief, 227–8, 305n
as man-made product, 186
as mathematical object, 138
as mental state, 88, 233, 251, 259–61
as natural kind, 229–30
as parser, 117–18
as real-world physical object, 138, 293n
as rule system, 88, 127–29, 189, 195, 287n
as set of speech dispositions, 68–70, 283n
as set/system of habits, 38, 275n
as set of sentences, 139–40, 153–4, 170–1, 189, 195, 294n, 296n
as social art, 199, 200
as social fact, 200, 228
as social institution, 200

as social practice, 200, 220, 224
as social product, 211
as social semiotic, 76–7, 241–2, 308n–9n
as sociopolitical fact, 228
as something abstract, 148ff., 261, 262–3
as something autonomous, 183ff., 219, 261, 262
as something behavioural 35ff., 261, 262
as something behaviourist, 43ff., 261, 262
as something biological, 236
as something cultural, 211ff.
as something material/physical, 4ff., 261, 262
as something mental/ psychological, 6–7, 79ff., 204–5, 216–18, 259–60, 264–5
as something semiological, 205
as something social, 199ff., 262
as something terminological, 93

language: distinctions
v. dialect, 81, 206
v. knowledge of language, 90–3, 141, 162–3, 168–70, 176, 197
v. speech/use, 37, 141, 187, 211, 280n, 302n–3n

language, (a/an): forms/kinds
common, 220, 221, 222, 229, 235, 306n
community, 81, 221, 227, 229
creole, 235–6
E(xternalized), 83, 88, 110, 130, 170, 255
individual, 154, 153–6
I(nternalized), 84ff., 91, 105, 110, 129, 130, 131
inter-, 236
particular, 169
pidgin, 235–6
private, 232, 307n
second, 236
shared, 221, 222, 306n
sign, 236
super-, 221–2, 306n
see also language in general

language, (a): general characteristics
accidental properties of, 2–3
acquisition of: *see* language acquisition
biologically necessary properties of, 87, 296n
conceptions of: *see* conceptions of language
discrete infinity of, 110, 289n, 294n
domain of, 133–6
effability of, 154–5, 158, 296n
essence of, 2–3, 60–1, 64, 280n, 282n, 296n
essential properties of, 2–3, 77, 154–7, 296n
functions of, 217
(general) nature of, 2–3, 154, 155, 221–3
genetically determined properties of, 87
invariances of, 156–7
knowledge of: *see* knowledge of language
logical properties of, 133–4, 293n
logically/conceptually necessary properties of, 87, 286n
mastery of, 220–1, 225
medium-transferability of, 217
mental nature of: *see* mentalism; mental state; mental structure
normativity of, 230–1, 307n
parameters of, 88, 129, 140
physical mechanisms of, 88, 94
see also body; brain
principles of, 88, 129, 142
psychological properties of, 217, 293n
quantitative dimension of, 208–11
rule of: *see* rules, linguistic: nature of; rules, linguistic: views of; rules of grammar: types of
sociopolitical dimension of, 81, 82, 89, 144, 189, 223
structure of: *see* linguistic structure
theory of, 85
unboundedness in scope of, 196n
underlying system of, 254
universals of: *see* linguistic universals

use of: *see* language behaviour
variation of: *see* linguistic variation
language: related
to aesthetic products, 215
to culture, 215
language acquisition: factors
impoverished stimulus in, 124–6, 212, 236–7, 251, 252, 260
language faculty in: *see* language faculty
linguistic experience in, 87, 109, 124–6, 212, 224
logical problem of, 246, 250–1
motherese in, 125, 292n
training in, 280
see also innate linguistic endowment; linguistic inventiveness; nativism; Plato's problem
language acquisition: nature
as biological growth, 87, 107, 212
as a cultural process, 186
as learning by means of general mechanisms, 122, 123
as maturation, 50, 109
language acquisition: targets
of a creole, 235–6
of a second language, 236
of a sign language, 236
language acquisition: views
behaviourist view of, 51, 60, 102
Chomsky's earlier view of, 50
Chomsky's recent view of, 87–8, 108–9, 140–1, 211–12, 223, 224
Dummett's view of, 220
empiricist view of, 125
Labovian view of, 209–10
Piaget's view of, 123–5
Popper's view of, 186, 212, 301n
principles-and-parameters view of, 87–8, 108–9, 140–1
Putnam's view of, 125
Quine's view of, 68–70, 125
Sapir's view of, 211–12
Saussure's view of, 202–3, 212
Skinner's view of, 50, 125
Wittgensteinian view of, 60, 65, 125
language acquisition device, 102, 286n
language behaviour: properties
appropriateness/coherence of, 99, 100, 276n, 288n
creativity of, 49–50, 99, 102, 140–1, 203, 260, 276n
freedom from stimulus control of, 47–8, 100, 203, 260, 276n
nongeneralized nature of, 47
novelty of, 47, 48, 56, 276n
productiveness of, 48, 56, 276n
rule-governed nature of, 102
unboundedness in scope of, 99, 100, 110
unreinforced nature of, 47
language behaviour: views
behaviourist view of, 43–5
Chomskyan view of, 47–9, 102, 129, 140–1
Halliday's view of, 284n–5n, 309n
Skinner's view of, 43–50
see also linguistic performance
language community, 81, 226, 306n
see also masse parlante; speech community
language faculty, 87, 92, 102, 109, 119, 122, 126, 127, 140, 195, 224, 251, 289n
attained/stable state of, 87, 109, 122, 127–31
initial state of, 87, 102, 109, 122, 224
see also faculté linguistique; number faculty, human
language in general, 2, 151, 153–5, 158, 189
language perception, 140–1
language processing mechanisms, 115–16, 188
language production, 140–1
langue, (la), 37, 187, 202–7, 210, 302n, 304n, 305n
Leech, G., 198
Leiber, J., 289n
Leibniz, G., 109, 309n
Lewis, D., 88, 295n
lexical entry, 251–2
lexical-functional grammar, 116–17
lexicon, 190

Lightfoot, D., 311n
Linell, P., 292n
linguistic change, 214, 231
lingusitic competence, 37, 49, 56, 69, 76–7, 100, 110, 118, 119, 129, 141, 162, 163, 164, 177, 187, 232
  see also knowledge of language
linguistic epistemology, 3, 76, 189
  see also epistemology
linguistic evidence, 140, 175–7, 179, 247–8
  see also evidence; informant judgements; introspection; intuition; linguistic theories, justification of
linguistic experience, 87, 109, 124–6, 212, 224
  see also language acquisition
linguistic fact, a, 306n–7n
linguistic inquiry: *see* linguistics
linguistic inventiveness, 235–6
linguistic knowledge: *see* knowledge of language
linguistic methodology, 3, 67
linguistic ontology, 3
  and linguistic theories, 249ff.
  and linguistics, 249, 259ff.
linguistic performance, 20, 37, 69, 77, 110, 111, 118, 119, 141, 162, 163, 177, 189, 232
  see also language behaviour
linguistic philosophy, 59
linguistic reality, 65, 67, 84, 85, 189
  Chomsky's view of, 89, 143–4, 290n
  Fodor's view of, 144–5
  Platonist view of, 151, 158, 175–7, 185
  Popperian view of, 185–8
linguistic standardization, 228
linguistic structure, theory of, 3, 65, 76, 192
linguistic theory/theories, 24, 112, 154–8, 300n
  criteria for: *see* criteria for linguistic theories
  justification of, 181–2, 195, 246–9
  v. linguistics, 137, 249–53, 311n
  ontological interpretation of, 249ff.
  ontologically neutral core of, 249, 311n
linguistic universals, 84, 87, 154–8, 212–13, 286n, 296n
  see also cross-linguistic generalizations; innate linguistic endowment; language faculty; initial state
linguistic variation,
  Chomsky's view of, 136
  Itkonen's view of, 231
  Sapir's view of, 212–13
  Saussure's view, 206–7
linguistically significant generalizations, 191–2
linguistics: forms
  autonomous, 253, 254
  Chomskyan, 103–6, 134–5, 250–1
  descriptive, 253
  Katzian/Platonist, 134–5, 164–7
  micro-, 254
  ordinary/no-nonsense, 244–9
  proper, 159–60, 303n
  synchronic, 206
linguistics: limits
  data base of, 136, 178–9, 195, 196
  scope of, 133–5, 160, 177–8
  sources of evidence of, 175–7
  subject matter of, 134, 136, 137, 177
linguistics: links
  and logic, 164–5, 167
  and mathematics, 164–5, 167, 177, 182
  and ontology, 249, 259ff.
  v. linguistic theory, 137, 311n
  v. psycholinguistics/psychology, 164–5, 167
logic, 133, 141, 161, 163, 164
  laws of, 134, 141, 159, 161
logical behaviourism, 54, 277n
logical empiricism, 30, 54, 65, 72
logical positivism, 14ff., 55, 70ff.
Lovejoy, A., 275n
Lyons, J., 253, 254, 256, 260, 272n, 295n, 311n

McCrawley, J. D., 305n
MacCorquodale, K., 46, 58, 277n
McDaniel, C., 208, 304n
Mace, C. A., 276n, 281n
McGinn, C., 280n, 292n
Mach, E., 15, 22, 23, 271n, 272n
MacQueen, K., 298n
Malcolm, N., 280
Malinowski, B., 76
Marshall, J. C., 56, 278n, 290n
Marx, K., 238
masse parlante, 202, 203
  see also language community; speech community
materialism, 7ff., 30, 143–5, 191–2, 195, 196, 199
  Bloomfieldian, 11
  Chomsky's, 143–4
  eliminative, 71
  emergent(ist), 270n, 271n
  extreme, 10–11
  Fodor's, 144–5
  reductive, 53
  simplistic, 71
  see also physicalism
material object/thing, 10–11, 153, 183
mathematics, 163–4
  and linguistics, 164–5, 167, 177, 182, 299n
matter, 143–4
  see also body, Chomsky's view of
Matthews, R., 291n
maturation, 50
  see also language acquisition
meaning, 132–3, 161, 221, 222
  expressive, 217
  lexical, 190
  sentence, 190
  theory of, 221
meaning potential, 76–7
meaningfulness v. meaninglessness, 14–15, 272n
mechanism, 8ff., 18
mediation theory, 54, 277n
medium-transferability, 217
mental entity/object, 38, 94
mental module, 87, 114ff.
mental organ, 87
mental phenomenon, 11
mental state, 88, 93, 112, 183, 293n
mental structure, 88
mental representation, 88, 91, 114, 289n, 293n
mentalism
  animistic, 6–7, 15, 30
  anti-, 7
  Bloomfield's, 6–7
  Chomskyan, 79ff., 94, 101–5, 143–4, 191–2, 195–6, 199, 259–60, 264–5, 290n, 295n, 299n–300n
  Fodor's, 112, 144–5
  nineteenth-century, 6–8
  Sapir's, 216–18
  Saussure's, 204–5
  Wundt's, 6–7
mentalistic language, 63, 276n
metaphysical behaviourism, 281n
metaphysics
  Continental/traditional, 15, 65
  scientific, 245
  Wittgenstein's view of, 62
  see also epistemology
Meyer, M., 8, 9, 270n
Mill, J. S., 128, 271n
mind: characteristics
  module/modularity of, 87, 114ff.
  physical mechanisms of, 88, 94
  state of, 88, 93, 112, 183
  structure of, 88
mind: 'kinds'
  animistic, 7
  collective, 204–5
  group, 209–10, 239
  individual, 86ff., 94–8
  miracle-working, 52
  racial, 218
  self-conscious, 183, 193
  social, 218, 305n
  see also mentalism
mind: nature
  and brain, 83, 87, 88, 92, 101, 286n
  v. body/brain, 94, 143
mind: views
  analytical behaviourists' view of, 63, 281n
  Cartesian view of, 95, 107–8, 112

Chomskyan view of, 94–7, 107–8, 143–4
Fodor's view of, 112
metaphysical behaviourists' view of, 281n
methodological behaviourists' view of, 281n
Popper's view of, 183–4, 193
representational theory of, 107
theory of, 88
Wittgensteinian view of, 62
see also dualism; interactionism; monism
mind-body problem, 95–6, 143, 270n
module/modularity of mind, 87, 114ff., 290n
molar behaviourism, 54, 276n
molecular behaviourism, 54, 276n
monism, 71, 143, 144
Montaque, R., 295n
Moravscik, J. M., 263, 271n, 277n, 284n
Mortensen, C., 194, 301n
motherese (in language acquisition), 125, 292n
see also language acquisition
Mylander, C., 236
mysteries (v. problems), 97, 288n

Nagel, E., 23, 26, 27, 28, 273n, 311n
Nagel, T., 288n
nativism, 112, 132, 211–12
see also innate linguistic endowment
natural kind, 229–30
natural science, 103–4, 143
naturalism, objective, 8, 9
naturalistic psychology, 9
necessary truth, 138, 159–61, 167, 170, 298n
necessity, logical, 142
neobehaviourism, 54, 279n
neo-neobehaviourism, 54, 279n
Neurath, O., 15
Newmeyer, F. J., 41, 121, 137, 208, 271n, 273n, 292n, 293n, 301n, 304n, 310n, 311n
Newton, I., 95, 96
nominalism, 12–13, 22, 71, 113, 163, 290n
nominalist conception of language, 271n
see also Bloomfieldian conception of language
norm, social, 189, 226, 230
normative-teleological element of language, 82
normativity of language, 230–1, 307n
novelty of language behaviour, 47–8
number faculty, human, 289n
numbers, Platonist view of, 152, 163, 164–5, 301n–2n

object: kinds
abstract/Platonic, 150–8, 161, 162, 166, 167, 169, 170, 172–5, 189, 294n
abstracted, 152
actual, 153
autonomous/objective, 184, 189, 302n
biological, 257–8
cultural, 213–15, 217
dualistic, 189
fictitious, 23, 24, 28, 210
ideal(ized), 152, 153
intersubjective, 190
linguistic, 190, 214–15
logical, 133, 134
man-made, 184
material/physical, 10–11, 153, 183
mental, 38, 94
of belief, 227–8, 306n
psychological, 133, 153, 189, 204
public, 190
social, 189, 201
unembodied, 184
unobservable, 184–5
objectivity, ontological, 183–4
observability, 284n
Occam's Razor, 15, 298n
Ohala, J. J., 191
ontological ecumenicism, 249ff.
ontological indifference, 244ff.
ontological interpretation of a theory, 249–52, 311n

ontological pluralism, 254ff.
ontological scepticism, 244
ontological stance
  of ecumenicism, 249ff.
  of indifference, 244ff.
  of pluralism, 254ff.
  of scepticism, 244
ontological status of theories, 26–8
ontologically neutral core of a theory, 249, 311n
ontology: links
  and epistemology, 263–4, 312n
  and linguistics, 243ff.
  and science, 245, 309n–10n
ontology: views
  Chomsky's, 113, 141
  general, 3
  conceptualist, 113, 141, 150, 162, 163, 216
  linguistic, 3, 249ff., 259ff.
  nominalist, 12–13, 22, 71, 113, 163
  Platonist, 149–51
  Popperian, 183–6, 192–4
  realist, 113
operant, 43
operation(al)ism, 18, 104, 271n
ordinary language philosophy, 59, 64–7, 280n–1n
Oxford philosophers, 59, 280n–1n

parameters of language(s), 88, 129, 140
parole, (la), 37, 187, 202, 302n
parser, a, 117–18
parsimony, conceptual, 246
Parsons, T., 238
Partee, B., 295n
particular grammar, (a), 88, 89, 93, 155–6
particulars (v. universals) 12, 271n
Passmore, J., 17, 271n
Pateman, T., 130, 169, 200, 206, 208, 227–30, 232, 235, 236, 271n, 292n, 298n, 302n, 304n, 306n, 307n
  conception of language, 227ff.
Paul, H., 205
Peacocke, C., 117, 291n
Peck, J., 106
Peirce, C. S., 152, 271n
perception, 165–6
  v. intuition, 165–6
  v. introspection, 165–6
perception of language, 140–1
Phillips, D. C., 271n
philosophical behaviourism, 53–4, 63
philosophy
  of language, 67
  of mind, 53
phrenology, 290n
physical mechanisms, 88, 94
physicalism, 18–19, 144–5, 295n
physics (and matter), 96–7
phrase structure rules, 251–2
Piaget, J., 123, 125, 221, 311n
Piattelli-Palmarini, M., 311n
pidgin (language), 235–6
Pike, K. L., 36, 37, 39, 40, 273n, 274n
Pinker, S., 290n
Plato, 107–9, 148–51, 185, 270n
Platonic intuition, 166, 185
P(latonic) language, 93
Platonic object/entity, 93, 150–8, 161, 162, 166, 167, 169, 170, 172–5, 189
Platonic resemblance, 109
Platonism/realism, 149–51, 295n, 298n
  Katz's account of, 151ff., 297n
Platonist/realist conception of language, 148ff., 197–8, 261, 262, 263, 293n
Platonist/realist epistemology, 150–7, 165–8, 172–5, 179, 181, 186, 197, 247, 248
Plato's problem, 108–9, 250–2
pluralism ontological, 254ff.
Popkin, R., 105
Popper, K. R., 16, 17, 27, 31, 97, 150, 151, 183–8, 192, 193, 194, 196, 198, 212, 270n, 273n, 288n, 300n, 302n
  conception of language, 183ff., 261, 262, 263
  epistemology, 185–6, 189, 192–4
  ontology, 183–6, 192–4
  view of language acquisition, 182, 212

postivism: *see* logical positivism
Postal, P. M., 132–5, 137–42, 149, 152, 157, 159, 165, 167, 168, 170–2, 177–82, 246, 264, 285n, 287n, 290n, 292n, 293n, 295n, 296n, 297n, 298n, 299n, 300n, 302n
post-Bloomfieldian conception of language, 36ff., 261, 262
poverty of the stimulus, 124–6, 212, 236–7, 251, 252, 260, 292n
  see also language acquisition
practice, a, 60
  social, 223–5
pragmatism, 271n
preexistence, 109
prescriptivism, 228
pre-theoretical conception of language, 254
Priestly, J., 128, 309n
principles-and-parameters conception of language, 88, 129, 140
principles of language(s), 88, 129, 142
private (v. common), 234
private language argument, 232, 307n
private language conception of language, 232–3
problem-solving, 114
production of language, 140–1
propositions (v. sentences), 187
psychological behaviourism, 8–9, 51, 54, 70, 275n
psychological reality, 116, 117, 216, 291n
psychology: focuses
  individual, 89, 218
  social, 218–19, 305n
psychology: perspectives
  behaviourist approaches to, 8–9, 51
    see also behaviourism
  Katz's view of, 164–5, 167
  naturalistic, 9
  Wittgenstein's position on, 62
psychology v. linguistics, 164–5, 167
Pullum, G. K., 301n
purposive behaviourism, 54, 277n
Putnam, H., 123, 125, 221, 291n
Pylyshyn, Z., 287n, 290n

Quine, W. V. O., 68, 69, 70, 125, 200, 271n, 275n, 281n, 292n
  (dispositional) conception of language, 68–70, 283n
Quinton, A., 279n, 280n, 281n

radical behaviourism, 54, 276n, 277n, 279n
rational inquiry, 226
rationalism, 238, 308n
realism, (Platonic), 113, 149–51, 290n
reality: domains
  linguistic, 65, 67, 84, 85, 189
  objective, 105
  physical, 143–4
  pluralist, 254–8
  social, 237–9, 271n
  transcendental, 150
reality: views
  Chomsky's view of, 89, 143–4, 226
  Platonist view of, 149–51, 185–6
  Popperian view of, 150, 183–5, 192–4
  see also conceptualism; nominalism; realism, Platonic; world
reconstructed behaviourism, 54
reductionism, 192, 196, 254, 295n
reflexology, 54, 276n
reification, 71–2, 210
reinforcement, 45, 47, 48, 52, 275n
  in language acquisition, 50, 68
  in verbal behaviour, 48, 275n
Rescher, N., 273n
response, 39–40, 43, 45, 48, 88
  see also stimulus
response class, 56, 57
Rex, J., 209, 210
Rey, G., 144
Richards, J., 292n
Ringen, J., 292n
Robins, R. H., 303n
Romaine, S., 292n
Rorty, R., 71

Rosenberg, S., 275n
Ross, D., 291n
Rozeboom, W., 55
rules, linguistic: nature
  conventional, 220
  normative, 230–1
rules, linguistic: views
  Chomskyan, 88, 129, 189, 190, 195
  Itkonen's, 230–1
  Wittgensteinian, 60, 61, 65
rules of grammar: types
  derivational constraint type of, 246
  global, 231
  phrase structure, 251–2
  semantic interpretation, 246
  transformational, 250–2
  variable, 207–10
rules of language: kinds
  common knowledge, 232–7
  intersubjective, 232
  private, 236
  public, 232
  social, 232
Russell, B., 289n, 309n
Ryle, G., 59, 63, 66, 72, 150, 280n, 282n, 289n

Salkie, R., 143, 144, 311n
Salverda, R., 204, 205, 273n
Salzinger, K., 57, 277n, 278n
Sampson, G., 292n
Sapir, E., 4, 84, 211–19, 285n, 305n, 308n
  conception of language, 211ff.
Saussure, F. de, 37, 83, 202–7, 210, 219, 241, 285n, 302n, 303n, 305n
  conception of language, 83, 202ff., 226
Schlick, M., 15
Schnaitter, R., 55
Schneirla, L., 271n
science, aims of, 23–5
science: views
  Baconian, 30
  behaviourist, 69, 103–6, 143–4, 226
  Bloomfield's, 18, 19
  Chomsky's, 69, 103–6
  positivist, 15, 18
science and ontology, 245, 309n–10n
scope of linguistics, 133–5
Scriven, M., 15, 276n
Searle, J. R., 127, 128, 132
second language acquisition, 236
semantic interpretation rule, 246
semantic representations, 116
semantic theory, 133–4
semantics
  generative, 246–7
  interpretive, 246–7
sensori-motor intelligence, 123–4
sentences
  as elements of language(s), 83–4, 137–8, 139, 189, 190
  Chomsky's view of, 138–9, 290n, 294n
  comprehension of, 116
  meaning/sense of, 133–4, 161
  Platonist view of, 151–2
  v. propositions, 187
  semi-grammatical, 85, 171
  ungrammatical, 117–18
  v. utterances, 152, 187, 190
  see also language as a set of sentences; type (v. token)
Shallice, T., 291n
Shaphere, D., 194
sign language, 236
simple induction, 29
simplicity, 167, 181, 182, 300n
skepticism
  constructive, 105
  Wittgensteinian, 233
skill, 77, 102
Skinner, B. F., 41–9, 51, 52, 54, 58, 68, 71, 125, 275n, 279n
  conception of language, 163ff., 180
Smith, N., 120, 139
Snow, C. E., 292n
Soames, S., 117
social, 202, 203, 210, 237–9
  behaviour, 76, 218, 230
  conception of language, 59, 81, 199ff., 262
  conventions, 220

custom, 223, 224
fact, 202, 228
habits, 38
institution, 183, 202
knowledge of language, 231
linguistic reality, 210
mind, 218, 305n
norms, 189, 226, 230
object, 189, 201
practice, 220, 223–4
psychology, 218–19, 305n
reality, 237–9, 271n
semiotic, 242
theory, 238
unconsciousness, 218, 305n
sociopolitical dimension of language, 81, 82, 89, 144, 189, 222
Socrates, 108
soul, immortal, 109
speaker-listener
actual, 153
ideal, 137
naive, 216
speech
on Saussure's view, 302n–3n
on Skinner's view, 44
v. language, 37, 87
see also language behaviour
speech act, 230
speech community, 83, 137, 202, 207–10, 226
ideal(ized) v. real, 137
see also community; language community
speech dispositions, 283n
speech events, 39
as elements of language(s), 83
speech habits, 38
see also language production
Spence, N. C. W., 202, 302n
S-R psychology, 50, 276n
Stampe, D., 191
Stark, B., 273n
Steinberg, D., 139, 287n
Steiner, M., 295n, 299n
Stern, K., 292n
Stich, S. P., 136, 178, 292n
stimulus, 39–40, 43, 45, 48, 68, 274n, 275n
control, 47–8, 51, 275n
freedom from, 47–8, 100, 203, 260
generalization, 49
and response learning, 9, 50
structuralist grammar, (a), 84
subjacency, 286n
subjectivism, 238, 307n
substantialism, 238, 307n–8n
substantive behaviourism, 40
Suppe, F., 311n
Swadesh, M., 272n
Swiggers, P., 271n
symbolic behaviour, 40

tagmemics, 274n
taxonomic grammar, 29, 31
Taylor, C., 54, 275n, 276n, 277n, 283n
technical conception of language, 83, 86
Teeter, K. V., 305n
theory
of language, 85
linguistic, 24, 112, 154–8, 300n
of linguistic structure, 3, 65–6, 76, 282n
of mind, 88
semantic, 133–4
thinking, 114
Thorndike, L., 41
thought, 184
token (v. type), 152
Tolman, L., 41, 54
Toulmin, S., 270n
traditional grammar, 84
transducer, 113
transformational grammar, 250
transformational rule, 250–2
truth, 23–5, 72, 84, 93, 105, 181, 307n–8n
necessary, 138, 159–61, 167, 170
Twaddell, F. W., 40, 272n
type (v. token), 152

unconsciousness, social, 218
universal grammar/UG, 84, 87, 89, 93, 286n, 294n

universals, 12–13, 113, 149–51
see also conceptualism; linguistic universals; nominalism; Platonism; realism
Urmson, J. O., 281n, 282n
use (of language): *see* language behaviour; linguistic performance
utterances
as elements of language, 37, 83
as linguistic data, 178
as tokens, 152
v. sentences, 152, 187, 190

variable rules, 207–10
variation: *see* linguistic variation
Vendler, Z., 282n
Vendryes, J., 303n
Vennemann, T., 191
verbal behaviour, 37, 43ff., 68
verifiability (principle of meaning), 15, 16, 17, 271n
Vico, 128
Vienna Circle, 15, 271n
vocal behaviour, 44

Waissmann, F., 15
Wann, T. W., 58, 278n, 279n
Wardhaugh, R., 208, 304n
Watkins, J. W. N., 273n
Watson, J. B., 41, 54, 71, 275n
Weber, M., 238
Weinreich, M., 285n
Weiss, A. P., 8, 15, 39, 270n
Wells, R. S., 202, 292n
Wexler, K., 292n
Whiteley, C. H., 276n
Whitney, W. D., 40, 84, 200, 274n
Whorf, B. L., 305n
Wiest, W. A., 277n
Wittgenstein, L., 59, 60, 61, 64, 67, 125, 220, 225, 271n, 279n, 280n, 281n, 282n
conception of language, 59ff., 220, 262, 280n, 282n
Wittgensteinian view of
generalizations, 66–7
grammar, 62, 279n–80n
language acquisition, 65, 66, 125
metaphysics, 62
mind, 62
psychology, 62
rules of language, 60, 61, 65
Wolfram, W., 208
Woozeley, A. D., 12, 150, 271n, 290n
world, the material, 143–4
world, the,
Chomsky's view of, 88, 226, 229
Platonist view of, 149–51, 185–6
Popperian view of, 150, 183–5, 192–4
Wright, C., 299n
Wunderlich, D., 271n
Wundt, W., 7, 8, 9
conception of language, 7

Zuriff, G. E., 53–9, 70, 71, 72, 74, 276n, 277n, 278n, 279n, 283n, 284n, 289n